A Just Peace Ethic Primer

A Just Peace Ethic Primer

Building Sustainable Peace and Breaking Cycles of Violence

Eli S. McCarthy Editor

Georgetown University Press
Washington, DC

The publisher is not responsible for third-party websites or their content. URL links were active at time of publication.

Library of Congress Cataloging-in-Publication Data

Names: McCarthy, Eli Sasaran, editor.
Title: A Just Peace Ethic Primer : Building Sustainable Peace and
    Breaking Cycles of Violence / Eli S. McCarthy, editor.
Description: Washington, DC : Georgetown University Press, 2020. |
    Includes bibliographical references and index.
Identifiers: LCCN 2019018170 (print) | ISBN 9781626167551
    (hardcover : alk. paper) | ISBN 9781626167568 (pbk. : alk. paper) |
    ISBN 9781626167575 (ebook : alk. paper)
Subjects: LCSH: Peace—Religious aspects—Catholic Church. |
    Christianity and justice. | Peacebuilding.
Classification: LCC BX1795.P43 J87 2020 (print) | LCC BX1795.P43
    (ebook) | DDC 241/.6242—dc23
LC record available at https://lccn.loc.gov/2019018170
LC ebook record available at https://lccn.loc.gov/2019980231

♾ This book is printed on acid-free paper meeting the requirements of the American National Standard for Permanence in Paper for Printed Library Materials.

21 20   9 8 7 6 5 4 3 2   First printing

Printed in the United States of America.
Cover design by Jim Keller.

I dedicate this book to my five-year-old daughter, Rose.
May your dancing and singing give life to many!

CONTENTS

ACKNOWLEDGMENTS

There are moments in life when the sun rises and the abundant light reveals fresh horizons, inviting us into a transformation perhaps before unimagined. My experience particularly over the last few years with a close collaboration of friends and colleagues has been somewhat like this. I am deeply and forever grateful.

It began with a small conversation with Marie Dennis, co-president of Pax Christi International. We asked, "What can we do to draw the Catholic Church closer to Jesus's way of nonviolent love?" Then with José Henríquez Leiva, who was then the secretary general of Pax Christi International, we developed a concept note for an international conference in collaboration with the Vatican. This helped usher in the April 2016 conference in Rome, numerous subsequent university and regional dialogues, and local initiatives to scale-up the understanding and practice of active nonviolence. I am grateful to the international steering committee that developed the conference and stimulated much of the follow-up. I am also grateful to the many practitioners of nonviolence living in violent conflict zones who attended the conference and oriented the outcomes. These include people like Sr. Nazik Matty from Iraq; Fr. Francisco de Roux, SJ, from Colombia; Bishop Paride Taban from South Sudan; Archbishop John Baptist Odama from Uganda; and Mairead Maguire from Ireland; as well as many others. In 2017–2018 we organized five global roundtables that discussed key topics for nearly a year such as the Bible and nonviolence, theology of nonviolence, power of nonviolence, integrating nonviolence throughout the Catholic community, and a new moral framework.

This book arose out of these riveting experiences and discussions. I am so grateful for the contributors who were so generous and so wise in their offerings to this project, particularly Gerald Schlabach and Lisa Sowle Cahill for writing framework essays and being gentle mentors and companions on the way. I am also grateful to Ken Butigan; Rose Berger; Sr. Ann Scholz, SSND; Pat Gaffney; Loreta Castro; Sr. Sheila Kinsey, FCJM; Sr. Hirota Shizue, MMB; Felix Mushobozi, CPPS; Gerry Lee; Greet Vanaerschot; Kevin Carroll; Judy Coode; Terry Rynne; Sr. Anne McCarthy, OSB; John Dear; and many others who have helped to shepherd this larger process over the past few years. I also thank other interlocutors and thinkers shaping the trajectory of this project, such as Glen Stassen; Susan Thistlewaite; Maria Stephan; Drew Christiansen, SJ; David Kaulem; David Cochran; Maryann Cusimano Love; Bill O'Neill, SJ; and Jarem Sawatsky. I am grateful for publication support from the Leadership Conference of Women Religious, Columban Center for Advocacy and Outreach, Clinton Franciscans, George Washington University, and Russ Vandenbroucke of the University of Louisville.

To those doing the exhausting work of teaching me how to grow in everyday love so that I am less of a resounding gong or clanging cymbal (1 Cor. 13:1), I thank you for your everlasting patience and love: Rose, Lazarus, Joy, and the DC Peace Team.

With this chorus of witnesses, I give glory to the God of love who gives us life and draws us to everlasting, abundant, and intimate love.

A FERTILE MOMENT

Context and Scope

ELI S. McCARTHY

As long as corruption, poverty, and the scourge of rape plagues families and our society, there will be no lasting, nor meaningful peace. . . . Let us not be mistaken: the behavior of men during conflicts reflects their behavior during peace time, except that during wars . . . the violence that was sleeping in the family and the community, is set free and explodes.

Dr. Denis Mukwege from the Democratic Republic of Congo

War is the mother of ignorance, isolation, and poverty. . . . I say this as a daughter of war. We can't respond to violence with worse violence. In order to kill five violent men, we have to create 10 violent men to kill them. This encourages the spiral of violence up and up. And the people are so exhausted because they don't know what's happening. It's like a dragon with seven heads. You cut one and two others come up.

Sr. Nazik Matty from Iraq

How can we build a more sustainable peace? Why do we so often get stuck in vicious cycles of violence even with good intentions? How do we become better at constructively engaging conflict?

By reflecting on cases of contemporary issues and conflicts, this book enables us to address these pressing questions and see more clearly the value of a just peace ethic. This book informs people about an emerging just peace ethic and deepens the imagination about how it might provide fruitful moral guidance for various types of situations. Compared to other ethical frameworks, the just peace approach is still relatively underappreciated in addressing some of the world's most difficult questions. There are ecumenical, interfaith, and multicultural expressions of a just peace ethic. Arising from voices living in violent conflict zones, there is also movement in the Catholic community, including 2016 and 2019 conferences in Rome sponsored by the Vatican's Pontifical Council for Justice and Peace (2016) and then the Dicastery of Integral Human Development (2019), both times along with Pax Christi

1

International, that called for official development of a just peace approach.[1] The United Nations (UN) and some governments are starting to draw more on the basic elements of a just peace approach. Thus, we may be at a tipping point for norm change.

Social and Political Context

Today's social and political context offers a range of key trends to attend to as we read the signs of the times. Without intending to be exhaustive, here are some of these trends. Nonviolent action and civil resistance are becoming increasingly understood, valued, effective, researched, and invested in. This is particularly illuminated by Maria Stephan in chapter 8. Likewise, peace-building practices and institutions are gaining traction in a diverse set of social sectors. At the UN, a sustaining peace agenda is gathering steam. In the US, there are particular signs of hope such as youth organizing around gun violence as well as more women resisting a culture of sexual assault and running for and being elected to political office. There are also other minority communities engaging, especially with intersectional organizing taking place around issues of racism, poverty, mass incarceration, ecological damage, and militarism.

However, there are also dubious signs of the times. Civil wars, nonstate armed actors, and proxy military interventions are considerable issues and are even increasing in some regions as "negative peace" is on a ten-year decline.[2] In turn, we have seen historically high rates of refugees and internally displaced persons. The arms trade continues to multiply as corporations develop new technology that, even more quickly we are told, needs to be outdone to ensure military advantages.[3] Nuclear weapons continue to threaten our existence even as the vast majority of the world has called for their destruction and prohibition. Ecological damage and related disasters in terms of environmental and destructive conflict are increasing. The gap between people who are wealthy and poor is widening at a high rate, especially in the US. In various countries and in the US, there is a reflexive, narrow nationalism that has led to breakdowns in cooperation, a sense of one human family, and a sense of care for our common Earth. The US continues to struggle with racism and white privilege while also manifesting a spectrum of dominance across the world through a web of coordinated political, economic, and military maneuvers.

As a white male who lives in the US, particularly the Washington, DC, area, I am also affected by this social and political context. The impact is felt on my lens, perspectives, interpretations, priorities, categories, habits, and feelings. Such acknowledgment corresponds with a willingness to learn from others, to be challenged, to be corrected, and to grow. Yet this social and political context is also formed and challenged by an ecclesial context.

Ecclesial Context and Trends

The way of Jesus has been increasingly reappropriated in contemporary theology toward a way of just peace. For example, in the Catholic Church, most of the earlier documents of Catholic social teaching from *Rerum novarum* in 1891 through *Pacem in terris* in 1963 primarily drew on a natural law framework and used a deontological model of moral theology. However, at Vatican II there was a noticeable shift to draw more readily on the Bible, especially the Christian Scriptures, with its clearer resonance to virtue ethics, and to extend the call to holiness to all persons, not merely clergy or religious orders. This has contributed to positions in Catholic social teaching and thought that have increasingly integrated the concepts of justice and peace. Thus, the Catholic imagination is opening up to visions of the church as a "peaceable and nonviolent community," which also increasingly values the realistic potential of "peacebuilding," "reconciliation," or "nonviolent peacemaking" practices for public policy.[4] This trend has continued through Pope Paul IV, Pope John Paul II, Pope Benedict XVI, and now, in a more pronounced way, with Pope Francis. Lisa Sowle Cahill's framework chapter (chapter 2) describes this trend and ongoing dilemmas in more detail.

Notably, in the context of an ecumenical opening in the Catholic Church, the turning to elements of just peace in official Catholic Church teaching has also been coupled with some similar turnings to just peace by other Christian church organizations. For example, the United Church of Christ (UCC) formally declared itself a "Just Peace Church" in 1985 and numerous congregations followed, declaring themselves "Just Peace" congregations.[5] Susan Thistlethwaite developed an integrated "Just Peace Church" program for the UCC.[6] Glen Stassen coordinated with other Christian theologians to develop a "just peacemaking theory," which consists of a set of normative practices arising into view by both tracking effective practices and using the analogical imagination with the scriptural witness.[7] Stassen wanted to address the question of what practices have worked to prevent war and make us into peacemakers. A number of scholars have written about his work, and interfaith approaches to just peacemaking have developed.[8] Further, in 2011 the World Council of Churches produced a document titled "Ecumenical Call to Just Peace."[9] They defined just peace as "a collective and dynamic yet grounded process of freeing human beings from fear and want, of overcoming enmity, discrimination and oppression, and of establishing conditions for just relationships that privilege the experience of the most vulnerable and respect the integrity of creation."[10] In 2012 the United Methodist Church recognized that war is incompatible with the teachings and example of Christ and thus rejected war as an instrument of national foreign policy.[11] In November 2013 the World Council of Churches adopted the "Way of Just Peace" as part of its 10th Assembly.[12]

More recently, a key conference occurred in Rome on April 11–13, 2016, and the Vatican's Pontifical Council for Justice and Peace, members of the Justice and Peace Commission of the International Union of Superior Generals and Union of Superior Generals (Global Leaders of Women and Men Religious Institutes), US Conferences of Women and Men Religious Leaders, Pax Christi International, and more than eighty-five representatives (including six bishops) from around the world were all part of this conference focused on gospel nonviolence and just peace.[13] Many participants came from contexts of violence and war—for example, Democratic Republic of Congo, South Sudan, Iraq, Afghanistan, Palestine, Philippines, and Colombia.

The focus was on active nonviolence in order to help the Catholic community develop a deeper understanding and commitment to nonviolence: nonviolence is the positive reverence for inviolable dignity and life as well as the refusal to dehumanize, to kill, or to engage in any type of violence. Always contextualized, nonviolence is the *power* of love in action; a *spirituality*, way of life; and a *virtue*; the *path* to fuller truth; a *strategic method* and *constructive force* for social justice, transforming conflict, challenging all forms of violence (direct, structural, and cultural), protecting all people and creation, and building sustainable peace.[14]

The participants heard from Catholic leaders who negotiated with very violent armed actors and from others who experienced such violence. For example, Archbishop John Baptist Odama in Uganda successfully negotiated with the Lord's Resistance Army; Father Francisco de Roux, SJ, in Colombia successfully negotiated with Fuerzas Armadas Revolucionarias de Colombia (FARC; Revolutionary Armed Forces of Colombia) and the paramilitaries; and Sister Nazik Matty from Iraq called us to stop the militarization of her country, stop bombing, and rely on nonviolent strategies. Mairead Maguire, a Nobel Peace Prize winner from Ireland, and Father de Roux argued that despite some good intentions, the just war way of thinking is too often getting in the way of nonviolent practices.[15]

At the end, the participants crafted an appeal to the Catholic Church, which included asking the pope to write an encyclical on nonviolence, scale up key nonviolent practices and education, initiate a global conversation, and shift focus to a just peace approach.[16] This transformative event has developed into the Catholic Nonviolence Initiative, which has a rich website with many resources such as expert background papers, videos from the conference, educational resources, and a page to endorse the appeal as an individual or organization.[17] In addition to US leadership conferences of religious institutes, more than one hundred individual religious orders in the US have endorsed the appeal. The national bishops' conferences of Japan and Belgium also have endorsed the appeal.[18]

This conference was followed by numerous campaigns and dialogue events around the world, including at many universities in the US and at the UN. Five virtual global roundtables embarked on deeper dives into these issues, including one on a new moral framework. In turn, these broad dialogues led, in April 2019, to a second global gathering at the Vatican with the Dicastery of Integral Human Development.[19]

Scope

There are various articulations of just peace approaches and some limited reflections with aspects of earlier versions of these approaches on different topics, such as lethal drones, nuclear weapons, the conflict in Syria, and, more recently, the US–Iran conflict.[20] Although the formulations of a just peace ethic have advanced, we still lack a thorough, diverse collection illustrating how such an approach might function in particular cases, including both within the US and internationally. In chapters reflecting on, applying, and refining a virtue-based just peace ethic in the context of cases, this book takes a significant step toward addressing this gap.

The common framing of the book is solidified in three chapters that each author used in developing his or her own chapter. The three framing chapters are on (1) the gospels and just peace, with an accent on the Sermon on the Mount's practical guidance by Gerald Schlabach (chapter 1); (2) trends in the Christian tradition and the recent emergence of the just peace concept, particularly in Catholic social teaching, by Lisa Sowle Cahill (chapter 2); and (3) a virtue-based just peace ethic by Eli McCarthy (chapter 3).

The cases include both US domestic and international conflicts to demonstrate the range of applicability of a just peace ethic. The first US domestic case is the US immigration system and the practice of sanctuary (chapter 4). The increasing flow of immigrants here and around the world is often exacerbated by violent conflict. The case on environmental justice and racism in the US (chapter 5) focuses on the water crisis in Flint, Michigan, to illuminate how a just peace ethic and related virtues could transform the situation. The chapter on white violence and racism in the US (chapter 6) draws on the case of Michael Brown in Ferguson, Missouri. This issue is central to understanding the deeper habits and logics that turn into different forms of violence within some of our Christian communities and in US society and that are often projected onto our foreign policy. The case on the death penalty in the US (chapter 7) illuminates the need to transform a predominant understanding of justice for dealing with conflict.

The international cases include a chapter on some of the latest research to explain the importance of integrating nonviolent direct action and peace building (chapter 8). Two chapters engage overlapping issues of nonstate terrorism and mass atrocities, such as with Islamic State in Iraq and Syria (ISIS) operating in Iraq (chapter 11) and the conflict in South Sudan (chapter 9), in order to face the more difficult and complex questions about responding to violence. The case on South Sudan in particular illustrates the proven practice of unarmed civilian protection. Another chapter includes situations of intense gang violence in El Salvador (chapter 10) as a microcosm of some other larger conflicts. The Kenya case (chapter 12) draws on indigenous practices to illuminate how a just peace ethic addresses the issue of ethnic violence in the context of struggles over resources and political power. The Democratic Republic of Congo case (chapter 13) illuminates how to address gender-based violence, which is a common characteristic of most violent conflict zones. The Philippines case (chapter 14) illustrates the role of civil society and women in mitigating a conflict between the government and an armed resistance organization.

Each chapter author was asked to use the just peace ethic laid out in chapter 3. What does this just peace ethic reveal about the conflict? Does this particular conflict case illuminate something to enhance this just peace ethic? In light of this dialectic, what action steps would the author recommend for transforming this conflict via a just peace approach? In each chapter, after each case study and the conclusion, discussion questions are provided for teachers or groups.

In light of the cases, the final chapter summarizes what a virtue-based just peace ethic contributes and how it might be refined. Drawing on these insights, this book offers recommended next steps for Catholic and other Christian communities to mainstream this approach with an eye toward engaging with other religious actors and society at large.

Although this scope is comprehensive and robust, there are key questions and issues this book does not directly or thoroughly treat. For example, this book is not about the various types of pacifism. I would particularly ask the reader to bracket that lens as you read this book because there are too many negative connotations with that frame and it too often functions as a distraction from the arguments being posed. This book is also not an analysis of the just war ethic or tradition. However, there are some significant implications for both of these modes of moral reasoning in this book, and a few authors briefly allude to them for the sake of comparison.

I hope you enjoy this analysis of just peace and that the moral imagination is stirred about how we can better build sustainable peace, engage conflict constructively, and break vicious cycles of violence.

Notes

First *epigraph*: Regarding the conflict in the DRC, see Women for Women International, "Read Dr. Denis Mukwege's Speech Accepting the 2015 Champion of Peace Award," November 2015.

Second *epigraph*: Quoted in Rose Marie Berger, "Game Changer," *Sojourners*, December 2016, 17–23.

1. "An Appeal to the Catholic Church to Re-commit to the Centrality of Gospel Nonviolence," April 13, 2016, https://nonviolencejustpeace.net/final-statement-an-appeal-to-the-catholic-church-to-re-commit-to-the-centrality-of-gospel-nonviolence/.

2. Institute for Economics & Peace, "Global Peace Index 2018: Measuring Peace in a Complex World," June 2018.

3. "U.S. Military Risks Falling Victim to China's Effort to Gain Technology Edge, Report Warns," *Washington Post*, June 6, 2019.

4. Regarding visions of the church community, see Emmanuel Katongole, "The Church of the Future: Pressing Moral Issues from Ecclesia in Africa," in *The Church We Want: African Catholics Look to Vatican III,* ed. A. Orobator (Maryknoll, NY: Orbis, 2016), 166–67; and for practices for public policy, see Robert J. Schreiter, R. Scott Appleby, and Gerard F. Powers, eds., *Peacebuilding: Catholic Theology, Ethics, and Praxis* (Maryknoll, NY: Orbis, 2010); Dan Philpott, *Just and Unjust Peace: An Ethic of Political Reconciliation* (Oxford: Oxford University Press, 2012); Eli S. McCarthy, *Becoming Nonviolent Peacemakers: A Virtue Ethic for Catholic Social Teaching and U.S. Policy* (Eugene, OR: Wipf and Stock, 2012).

5. 15th General Synod of the UCC, "Pronouncement on Affirming the United Church of Christ a Just Peace Church," 1985, http://www.ucc.org/justice_just-peace.

6. Susan Brooks Thistlethwaite, *A Just Peace Church* (Cleveland, OH: United Church of Christ Press, 1986).

7. Glen H. Stassen, ed., *Just Peacemaking: New Paradigm for Ethics of Peace and War*, 3rd ed. (Cleveland, OH: Pilgrim Press, 2008).

8. Simeon O. Ilesanmi, "So That Peace May Reign: A Study of Just Peacemaking Experiments in Africa," *Journal of the Society of Christian Ethics* 23, no. 1 (Spring/Summer 2003): 213–26; Charles Kimball, "The Just Peacemaking Paradigm and Middle East Conflicts," *Journal of the Society of Christian Ethics* 23, no. 1 (Spring/Summer 2003): 227–40; Lisa Sowle Cahill, "Just Peacemaking: Theory, Practice, and Prospects," *Journal of the Society of Christian Ethics* 23, no. 1 (Spring/Summer 2003). For inter-religious examples, see Susan Thistlethwaite and Glen Stassen, "Abrahamic Alternatives to War: Jewish, Christian and Muslim Perspectives on Just Peacemaking," USIP Special Report, 2007; Susan Thistlethwaite, ed., *Interfaith Just Peacemaking: Jewish, Christian, and Muslim Perspectives on the New Paradigm of Peace and War* (New York: Palgrave, 2012).

9. World Council of Churches, "Ecumenical Call to Just Peace," 2011.

10. "Ecumenical Call to Just Peace," para. 11.

11. United Methodist Church, *The Book of Discipline* (Nashville, TN: United Methodist Publishing House, 2012), 140.

12. World Council of Churches, "Way of Just Peace," November 8, 2013. Also see Fernand Enns and Annette Mosher, eds., *Just Peace: Ecumenical, Intercultural, and Interdisciplinary Perspectives* (Eugene, OR: Pickwick, 2013).

13. Marie Dennis, ed., *Choosing Peace: The Catholic Church Returns to Gospel Nonviolence* (Maryknoll, NY: Orbis, 2018).

14. This description was developed through Catholic Nonviolence Initiative discussions before, during, and after the conference.

15. See "videos from the conference" at www.nonviolencejustpeace.net. In 2017, US Bishop Robert McElroy claimed that just war principles have "become only a

little bit less than a green light" for war and that the church must "recognize the increasing incapacity of the just war tradition to be an effective constraint on warfare in the modern age." Quoted in Joshua McElwee, "Pope Condemns Possession of Nuclear Weapons," *National Catholic Reporter*, November 10, 2017.

16. "Appeal to Catholic Church to Re-commit to Centrality of Gospel Nonviolence," April 13, 2016. The appeal also included a bold but controversial call to consider pivoting away from the idea of "just war" as a Catholic approach. Conversation and discernment continue in the Catholic Church about this element.

17. Catholic Nonviolence Initiative, www.nonviolencejustpeace.net.

18. Catholic Nonviolence Initiative, "Organizational and Individual Endorsements of the Appeal."

19. "Path of Nonviolence: Towards a Culture of Peace," April 4–5, 2019. https://nonviolencejustpeace.net/2019/04/03/path-of-nonviolence-toward-a -culture-of-peace/.

20. Regarding drones, see "CMSM Response to Armed Drones Policy," May 30, 2013, http://cmsm.org/wp-content/uploads/2015/10/05-30-13_MediaRel -CMSM_Armed_Drones.pdf; regarding nuclear weapons, see Maryann Cusimano Love, "Building a Better Peace: A Future Worthy of Our Faith," *America* 213, no. 3 (2015); for the conflict in Syria, see Eli McCarthy, "Religious Leaders Urge a Just-Peace Response to ISIS," *Huffington Post*, November 19, 2014; and for the US–Iran conflict, see Eli McCarthy, "Iran: Break Cycles of Violence with a Just Peace Framework," *The Hill*, July 11, 2019.

PART I

FRAMING ESSAYS

1

A "MANUAL" FOR ESCAPING OUR VICIOUS CYCLES

Practical Guidance from the Sermon on the Mount for a Just Peace Ethic

GERALD W. SCHLABACH

The fresh reappraisal of war in the modern world that the Second Vatican Council called for is well under way.[1] In his 2017 World Day of Peace message, Pope Francis continued that process of churchwide discernment as he built on the work of predecessors while responding to Catholic peacebuilders and activists.[2] He thus recognized the role of policymakers and diplomats even as he urged that "active and creative nonviolence" become our "style of politics for peace." Consistent with Pope John Paul II's insistence that peacemaking is essential to the vocations of all the faithful,[3] Francis not only identified "peacebuilding through active nonviolence" as "a programme and a challenge for political and religious leaders" but even included in that calling "the heads of international institutions, and business and media executives." The virtues in Jesus's Beatitudes of meekness, mercy, nonviolent peacemaking, purity of heart, and hunger and thirst for justice that open his Sermon on the Mount (Matt. 5:3) must in all cases characterize "the exercise of their respective responsibilities." After all—posited Francis in a theological move at once stunning and subtle—the "manual" that Jesus has given the church to guide its strategy of peace building at every level is the Sermon on the Mount itself.[4]

Francis's move was stunning because so much reflection by Christian thinkers through the centuries has taken as given that a nearly insuperable chasm separates Jesus's ethical teachings from the stubborn exigencies of modern politics (or indeed any worldly politics). The move was subtle because Francis's unobtrusive choice of the word "manual" planted a flag reclaiming the far side of the chasm—where Catholic moral approaches such as "manualism" have sought to do moral casuistry by drawing on "natural law" reasoning with minimal reliance on biblical resources.

Still, insofar as centuries and cultural gaps do require a bridge to connect our own historic situations with that first-century mount on which the gospel writer placed Jesus's sermon, Francis's World Day of Peace message cast a sturdy plotline but left the faithful to complete the structure. Fortunately, exegetical and conceptual resources are newly available for doing so, as the burden of this chapter is to explain. Textual analysis by Christian ethicist Glen Stassen argues strongly that the Sermon on the Mount offers far more practical guidance than theologians have assumed; meanwhile, emerging insights from social psychology into the mimetic processes that have formed human cultures suggest why. Although these may not be classic sources in the natural law tradition, they take us within range by elucidating the dynamics that make just peacemaking practices effective.

The Reappraisal: A Progress Report

Against the backdrop of what Francis called a "horrifying *world war fought piecemeal*" across the globe, the pope insisted that violence cannot be a "cure for our broken world."[5] After all, it inevitably perpetuates cycles of suffering and retaliation even when used "at best" to counter other violence. In contrast, "When victims of violence are able to resist the temptation to retaliate, they become the most credible promoters of nonviolent peacemaking." This is the courageous, life-giving, and creative nonviolence that Jesus lived and taught as the way to break free from chains of injustice. This active kind of nonviolence is not simply for some simpler first-century setting; after all, "Jesus himself lived in violent times." Nor should it be falsely confused with "surrender, lack of involvement and passivity"; instead, it is a "radically positive approach."[6] Indeed, as his predecessor Benedict XVI had said and Francis now underscored, Christlike love of one's enemies "constitutes the nucleus of the 'Christian revolution.'" As such, and on the world's stage, not just in Christian hearts, nonviolence is "more powerful than violence."[7]

Highlighting the power of gospel nonviolence in this way indicated how far the Catholic Church had come in its reappraisal of war, yet Francis also pointed toward a continuing area for discernment as he affirmed a complementarity in the church's work for peace: "Peacebuilding through active nonviolence is the natural and necessary complement to the church's continuing efforts to limit the use of force by the application of moral norms; she does so by her participation in the work of international institutions and through the competent contribution made by so many Christians to the drafting of legislation at all levels."[8]

Pope Francis was exercising the Vatican savvy that characterizes many church documents by alluding here to the possible use of "just war" criteria yet leaving the theory unnamed—for the moment, neither rejected outright nor defended. What Pope Francis did name instead is the space that the Vatican and Catholic moral traditions through the centuries have hoped the "just war" theory would fill. However, Francis was not done.

While affirming that the space for church engagement in international diplomacy and public policy work stands in a mutually supportive relationship with active nonviolence, what Pope Francis did next in his World Day of Peace message is breathtaking. For it is precisely here where he insisted that "Jesus himself offers a 'manual' for this [integrated] strategy of peacemaking in the Sermon on the Mount." The full weight of the message's title thus bears down: gospel nonviolence guided by the Sermon on the Mount is supposed to be a "style of politics for peace." It is not just for the personal lives of particularly saintly Christians. It applies to the public realm.

This is the nub of the challenge for any just peace ethic that would ground itself in the biblical message generally, or the gospels in particular, or the Sermon on the Mount specifically. Because the entire biblical narrative witnesses to God's yearning to heal relationships broken through domineering and fratricide (Gen. 3:11), Christian thinkers have been able to draw on numerous texts and themes in order to ground peacemaking and nonviolence according to varying approaches, which we can only begin to list: Leo Tolstoy's rule-based reading of the gospels, like that of some "historic peace churches" before him, may have been overly literalistic, but it still helped inspire Mahatma Gandhi's sophisticated development of active nonviolence.[9] For proponents of the "social gospel," liberation theologians, progressive evangelicals, and many others, Jesus's proclamation of the Kingdom or Reign of God has offered a vision of just and peaceable human thriving—"shalom" in Hebrew—that beckons and pulls God's people toward a new future. Recognizing the need for formation if this people is to respond well and faithfully to God's call, Protestant and Catholic theologians alike have recovered the theory and ethics of virtue and found in Jesus's Beatitudes the quintessential character traits that Christians need to become compassionate peacemakers living in solidarity, especially with the neediest.[10]

Nevertheless, any and all of these approaches will falter in the face of tough real-world situations if they seem only to offer aspirational ideals. Even the most virtuous of persons might have to look elsewhere for guidance after all, unless Jesus's teachings are demonstrably practicable. This, as I say, is the nub of the challenge that we must face for any reappraisal of war to give way to a just peace ethic and gain traction.

Can the Gospel Really Be Our "Manual"?

Francis's choice of the word "manual" is a most intriguing one. "Manualism" was the neo-scholastic mode of Catholic moral deliberation ascendant from the seventeenth century until the Second Vatican Council. Drawing on St. Thomas Aquinas's carefully reasoned reflection on the natural law, the manualist mode sought to rival Enlightenment rationalism. Whatever its virtues, it tended therefore to de-emphasize biblical sources and thus offered a comfortable home for "just war" casuistry.[11] To now instead call the Sermon on the Mount the church's manual for peacemaking cannot have been an accident.

One could trace centuries of ethical debate among Christian thinkers by following a thick central thread of contention over whether Jesus's Sermon on the Mount can be such a straightforward manual for *any* tough moral issue. Among all such issues, the justifiability of killing and the possibility of enemy love has often been paradigmatic. Christians appealing to alternative authorities in order to give reasons why they might legitimately override the words and example of Jesus have most often turned to some version of "natural law" or a theological account of what is "realistic." At its best the impulse for this move has been a desire to name shared moral norms that might be accessible to those in positions of public responsibility. In order to reappropriate Jesus's teachings and live out the virtues he held up in his Beatitudes—even while "thinking with the church" as it draws on centuries of experience facing difficult moral issues—we need to accept that challenge and explore how Jesus's radical call to a distinct way of being in the world might actually be realistic.

Historically, the Catholic Church may never have explicitly denied the applicability of Jesus's teachings to public affairs.[12] It has not officially endorsed a view like that of the leading twentieth-century Protestant thinker Reinhold Niebuhr. Niebuhr bluntly argued that while human beings might barely be able to practice Jesus's ethic or "law of love" in a small face-to-face community or *Gemeinde*, Jesus's teachings could never apply to complex, modern industrial societies—much less the international arena where the rough justice of a balance of power based on national self-interest is the best we can hope for.[13] Yet the working Catholic tradition has in effect taught exactly that for centuries by long drawing almost entirely on natural-law categories to address public affairs and by sometimes relegating Jesus's "hard sayings" to "evangelical counsels" for those with special vocations calling them to holiness.

By insisting on God's "universal call to holiness," the Second Vatican Council began to change this. That call came in the context of related developments. In the twentieth century, first among theologians, then with the endorsement of the council, and then among the faithful, Catholics have been rediscovering scripture. In moral theology, that has not only meant taking a fresh look at the relevance of biblical sources rather than natural law alone, it has meant supplementing abstract principles with a fuller account of how Christians grow in virtue as they let the narrative shape of Jesus's life and the lives of the saints shape the pattern of their own lives. Virtue ethics encourages us to act in ways that are analogous to what we see in Jesus's parables and teachings, or in the lives of those mentors we call saints, even if our modern circumstances inevitably differ in important details. The project of many leading moral theologians since the Second Vatican Council has thus been to bridge the biblical and modern worlds in just this way.[14] Still, if Jesus's teachings turn out to have been even more practical in the first place than we have been assuming, then that project—while certainly helpful and necessary for bridging centuries and cultures—will take on a different shape and may even prove less urgent.

With its universal call to holiness, then, the council implicitly abandoned long-standing Catholic tendencies to assume that different vocations for lay people and clergy or others in consecrated religious life implied that only some Christians are expected to follow Jesus as disciples through those "evangelical counsels." But then, one way or another, the church's teachings on war and peace would also have to begin changing. One could thus draw a direct line from the council's call to holiness in its 1964 dogmatic constitution, *Lumen gentium*, to the council's praise in *Gaudium et spes* a year later for those who renounce using violence to vindicate their own rights in an act of personal holiness, to the growing recognition of active nonviolence in public affairs since John Paul II's *Centesimus annus,* to Francis calling the Sermon on the Mount the church's manual for peacemaking.[15] The council's universal call to holiness was a massive tectonic shift, a slow-moving earthquake, and Catholic moral theology as well as pastoral practice are still trying to recover their footing.

The clue for recognizing Francis's move as more than mere idealism, and the mandate for drawing on a fresh way of interpreting and receiving Jesus's words, is the attention Francis gave in his World Day of Peace message to vicious cycles. In both the Sermon on the Mount and Francis's message, a diagnosis of vicious cycles and a path for escaping them is the link between the virtues of the Beatitudes and practical action in worldly affairs. What Francis calls the "horrifying world war [being] fought piecemeal" in the twenty-first century results from "countering violence with violence" over and over. The pope certainly did not deny that war may sometimes respond to injustice and attempt to counter it. Yet, he asked, "Where does this lead? Does violence achieve any goal of lasting value?" No, it leads "to retaliation and a cycle of deadly conflict" rather than to any "cure for our broken world." That is why "the force of arms is deceptive." Gospel nonviolence is the truly revolutionary alternative, therefore, because "responding to evil with good" rather than "succumbing to evil" by responding in kind means "thereby breaking the chain of injustice."[16]

Christians long locked into the standard impasse between pacifism and just war theory have begun to find common ground by acknowledging that even putatively just wars plant the seeds for new wars.[17] Meanwhile, groundbreaking literary analysis of the Sermon on the Mount demonstrates that Jesus was not simply giving his disciples idealistic "hard sayings" either to stretch them to do at least a little better morally or to convict them of sin that they might turn to God in forgiveness. Rather, in teaching after teaching, he provided realistic and practicable guidance for escaping vicious cycles. In this context, even the difficult challenge of loving our enemies turns out to be relevant—politically relevant.

This is the way to receive Francis's stunning claim that the Sermon on the Mount is the church's very "manual" for peacebuilding. By attending to vicious cycles of violence and what it takes to escape them, Christians may also be able to escape the standoff over war that has left them vacillating between "idealism" and "realism"—between the church's call to holiness and growth in virtue, and effective action in our complicated and often unforgiving world.

Learning to Think like Jesus

If the Sermon on the Mount has not served as our "manual" for peacemaking, that is arguably because of a widespread, long-standing, understandable, yet no less misleading approach to its interpretation. *We have read it in twos, not threes*—as a series of stark binaries, dyads, or antitheses rather than as triads. Admittedly, a drumbeat of contrasts does set the pace in Matthew 5: "You have heard it said . . . but I say unto you . . ." Six times. The ready impression is that Jesus's goal was to set a really high bar with a series of nearly impossible ideals: don't even be angry, don't even lust, don't take any oaths, don't even resist an evildoer, love even your enemies and persecutors without discrimination, thus be as perfect as your Father in heaven. Jesus must have thought that these high bars would at least make us jump a little higher, we conclude—before we despair. To be a manual for politics, business, and peacemaking at every level, the Sermon on the Mount must be practical, and all this sounds noble but it isn't very realistic, we say. Practical morality must look instead to common sense, or natural law, or the utilitarian necessity wherein "you do what you gotta do" and ask forgiveness later. So goes the standard interpretation as it vacillates between idealistic rigorism and a moral despair that calls itself realism.

In a widely accepted exegesis of the Sermon on the Mount, the late Christian ethicist Glen Stassen demonstrated otherwise.[18] It is no accident that Stassen was also the force of nature who led a group of Christian ethicists and political scientists from both historically pacifist and historically just war churches in developing and advocating for "just peacemaking theory."[19] The project reflected wider efforts to reframe Christian ethics in response to war and violence in some kind of "just peace" or "just peacemaking" framework, and it has become one of the most influential. Biblical exegesis and efforts to forge a new ecumenical consensus emerged side by side in Stassen's original

1992 book on just peacemaking.[20] In the wake of the Cold War, he then drew other scholars into a wider just peacemaking project that seized on the opportunity to identify how, realistically and empirically, an unexpected measure of peace had broken out. Key both to the practicability of the Sermon on the Mount and to contemporary just peacemaking practices is the power of *transforming initiatives* that break us out of *vicious cycles* of violence and sin in ways that the *traditional righteousness* "you have heard it said" cannot do.

Notice the triad I have just named. This threefold pattern of teaching is most identifiable in Matthew 5, but Stassen convincingly showed it to structure Matthew 6 and 7 as well in a series of fourteen triads. With only slight and explainable variations that are the exceptions that prove the rule, Jesus *first* named the traditional righteousness that his Jewish listeners had heard either from rabbis or popular morality, *then* diagnosed the vicious cycles from which traditional righteousness could not escape, *and then* offered realistic, practicable transforming initiatives to escape those vicious cycles at last. Sometimes the triads are more obvious than others; sometimes they come with anomalies that turn out to be revealing in themselves. Ultimately the pattern holds with remarkable consistency and an ability to resolve long-standing interpretive puzzles. Yes, they had heard it said, and yes, Jesus now said unto them. But what Jesus then said unto them in his own distinct teachings came in a second and then a third part. Also—how did we miss this for centuries?—in Greek his imperatives consistently came not in what we hear as hard sayings but in that third part, the transforming initiative. This is where the accent was to be for his disciples. This is where the accent should be for the church in all its teaching and programming.

The first of the fourteen triads that Stassen identified in the Sermon on the Mount illustrates well both the triadic literary pattern and its practical ethical import. The Matthew 5:21–26 passage is the first of the fourteen teachings that constitute the long central portion of the Sermon, and it demonstrates the issues and pattern most transparently. If we see in the 5:21–26 passage a two-part teaching that places Old Testament teachings against murder on one side of Jesus's "but I say to you" and then places a radically interiorized prohibition against anger on the other side, many standard difficulties interpreting and applying Jesus's teachings surface immediately. Is the passage about murder? That is what verse 21 seems to announce. However, then Jesus shifts our attention to anger and name-calling, and we hear Jesus saying never to be angry at all. So maybe it is about anger. But then we start to protest: *That's impossible. In fact, Jesus himself got angry.*[21] So what is the paragraph really about? Such difficulties are only the beginning.[22]

We are starting to dismiss Jesus's teaching before we have even gotten through half of the first triad! If we do continue reading, a dyadic interpretation will have to assume that the latter half of the passage about promptly seeking reconciliation is some kind of illustration rather than the point of the whole teaching. In fact, if we were not so hasty we would notice that Jesus never actually gave the imperative, "Don't ever get angry." Nor did he lower the threat of hell fire on those who fail. Rather, his phrase was, "if you are angry." *If* you are angry, judgmental, and insulting, certain things will logically follow. You are setting up a standard of judgment to which you yourself will be liable. By implication, so too will those who judge you. Unchecked, the ensuing cycle will spiral from an interpersonal "calling out," to a community council, to the ultimate judgment you are inviting from God. This is not a threat. It is simply a description of how things work, a diagnosis of a vicious cycle. There is certainly nothing wrong with the ancient injunction against murder. But in and of itself, that traditional righteousness "said to those of ancient times" does not come with guidance about how to avoid the conditions that lead to temptation, hypocrisy, and recrimination, much less an ultimate breakdown of human relations through fratricide.

If our habit were to expect a climactic third element in the outline of Jesus's teachings, we would anticipate Jesus's gracious guidance. Giving that practical guidance is Jesus's primary concern, and a triadic exegesis puts the accent back where Jesus's intention lay: *Take the initiative to seek out the one whom you have offended. Don't wait! Leave the altar itself if necessary! Get going, and don't drag your feet.* The imperatives, six of them, now come quickly, "staccato-like."[23] In other words, take the initiative—the initiative that will free you from vicious cycles of resentment, anger, counter-judgment, and potential violence—the initiative that will transform your relationship through reconciling practice. In teaching "as one having authority" (Matt. 7:29), Jesus has placed the accent here.

Practical Grace

Turning to the two triads at the end of Matthew 5 that also relate to violence and enmity, we find the Hebrews' functional precedent for Christian "just war" attempts to regulate and delimit warfare encapsulated in "an eye for an eye and a tooth for a tooth," the so-called *lex talionis*. This expression of traditional righteousness was certainly an improvement over the code of Lamech that promised a seventy-seven-fold retaliation against any threat, exponentially upping Cain's promise of a sevenfold retaliation (Gen. 4:15, 23–24). Likewise, in "Love your neighbor, hate your enemy," we have traditional background assumptions at work when any tribe or nation prioritizes self-defense over everyone else's good. As crassly tribalistic as that formula sounds, we can recognize that it too is an obvious improvement over Cain's fratricide of his own brother, Abel (Gen. 4:1–16). But an eye for an eye for an eye or a tooth for a tooth for a tooth still perpetuates the cycle of violence.

The vicious cycle that Jesus diagnoses is implicit not only in the eyes and teeth but in Jesus's alternative response: *mē antistēnai tō ponērō*. The famous phrase in Matthew 5:39 about how to respond in the face of evil has often been translated in a way that is easily dismissible as totally passive nonresistance: "Do not resist evil," or a little better, "Do not resist the evil one." But a far better translation recognizes the dative Greek word behind our English word "evil" not as substantive but as instrumental, and renders the phrase "Do not resist *in an evil way*."[24] In other words, do not respond *in kind*. Cycles of reciprocal retaliation were also implicit in Paul's take on Jesus's teaching in Romans 12: "Do not repay anyone evil for evil. . . . Do not be overcome by evil but overcome evil with good." Older than the Gospel of Matthew, Paul's letter to the Romans is probably citing the oral tradition that initially conveyed Jesus's teaching, and in any case it fits the context of the Sermon on the Mount perfectly: Jesus diagnoses the vicious cycles from which traditional righteousness will not extricate us. An eye for an eye, after all, can easily issue in an endless cycle of retaliation, or more likely escalate, despite the best efforts of those who apply the *lex talionis* in hope of checking violence with mathematical equity.

So how to escape? After naming the traditional righteousness of the *lex talionis* and underscoring its limits, Matthew 5:38–42 concludes with Jesus's three famous teachings to turn the other cheek, go the second mile, and give freely. Stassen has hardly been alone among recent interpreters who see those three practices not as passive nonresistance but as prototypical examples of active nonviolence that transform conflict by humanizing oppressor and oppressed alike.[25] Examined closely in their first-century social context, offering the left cheek specifically in order to stand as an equal, giving up one's cloak in order to shame a loan shark in what was probably a debtor's court, or going a second mile when a Roman soldier pressed a subject under occupation into service were all ways to transform the power dynamics of oppression through social creativity. Jesus was actually giving the oppressed ways to resist but not in kind, not violently, not hatefully.[26] For Jesus's immediate audience, these were potent, recognizable examples of the trickster smarts that the folktales of oppressed peoples of many cultures celebrate: Anansi the spider in West Africa, Br'er Rabbit in Afro-Caribbean and African American cultures, Loki in Scandinavia, and Jacob for the ancient Hebrews. Like those of classic tricksters, Jesus's tactics evened the power without giving the oppressor excuses to smash them. For us they are prototypes for the creative strategies of nonviolent action we have to invent for our own historical junctures.[27]

In Matthew 5:43–48 on love of enemy, one anomaly is that the order of the last two elements of the triad is reversed. Stassen speculated that Matthew placed the transforming initiative of love for enemy ahead of the vicious cycle in this triad in order to signal the climax of the subsection of the Sermon that contains its first six triadic teachings. This makes sense. Emphasizing Jesus's call to transcend the vicious cycle by which we tend merely to love those who love us in return highlights precisely the way in which Jesus has fulfilled, and would have his disciples fulfill, the law and the prophets (Matt. 5:17–20). Traditional righteousness as passed down and developed since Moses is wise and good and affirmed so far as it goes, but Jesus has prompted us to empathize more widely and imagine more creatively.[28]

If Stassen's exegesis required him to account for a few anomalies and do some reading between the lines, commending it is a capacity to solve far more irregularities and long-standing interpretive puzzles.[29] Thanks to its explanatory power, Stassen's exegesis of the Sermon on the Mount has been quite well received among biblical scholars. Although not a New Testament scholar per se, his detailed exegesis was published in the highly selective *Journal of Biblical Literature* in 2003,[30] and he received an enthusiastic response when he presented his exegesis to the Matthew section of the Society of Biblical Literature in 2006.[31] Dale C. Allison, a leading scholar of the Gospel of Matthew, has explicitly accepted Stassen's correction of his own interpretation.[32] This wide reception of Stassen's exegesis includes historic peace church scholars. For example, the longtime dean of Mennonite New Testament scholars, Willard M. Swartley, has offered a full-throated endorsement of Stassen's interpretation. In his major book on New Testament peace theology, *Covenant of Peace*, Swartley called Stassen's "structural analysis . . . impressive and persuasive" and went on to explain: "Stassen's tightly argued contribution . . . is most helpful, for his emphasis on the transforming initiatives puts the Sermon directly into the service of peacemaking."[33]

Stassen's exegesis also points toward ways of solving some of the most abiding puzzles in the field of Christian ethics. His exegesis rescues Jesus's teaching from the idealism that so often gets it dismissed as impracticable, unrealistic, or simply a series of hard sayings that serve to set up some other theological point. As we will see, it offers a way to reintegrate the Catholic Church's call to grow in holiness through the practice of biblically inspired virtues with its tradition of reflection on natural law. Stassen's triadic exegesis may initially have looked like a technical matter of literary analysis, but by showing that Jesus was placing the accent of his teachings on transforming initiatives, Stassen has done nothing less than point us back to the seamless unity in Jesus's teachings. The gracious deliverance without which there can be no proclamation of good news must be God's initiative and ultimate doing alone; this is not about "works-righteousness." Yet Jesus's ethical teachings, in fulfillment of Torah, are no less integral to God's deliverance, and so too are the practices of discipleship by which Christians participate in God's salvation.

The Political Relevance of Enemy Love

"Love your enemies" (Matt. 5:44) is not simply a high-minded principle, then. Jesus has fleshed it out with practical guidance that offers us trans-forming initiatives and the promise of real-world deliverance from cycles of retribution. The overarching pattern helps explain what is going on when *any* just peacemaking practice takes risks, but thus takes the initiative, in ways that break out of vicious cycles. To recognize the power and priority of trans-formative initiatives, we need to recognize the power of all kinds of cycles of social reciprocity both to capture us through *vicious* cycles and to liberate us through *virtuous* cycles—which is precisely what transforming initiatives aim to initiate.

Mimesis Has Made Us Human (for Better and Worse)

Catholic social thought works from a core assumption about what makes us human: the human person is constituted through relationship.[34] Reciprocity, in other words, is formative; virtuous and vicious cycles together have made us who we are. But one hardly needs to rely on theological assertion alone to affirm this. A foundational school of thought within classical social psycholo-gy, lately receiving fresh confirmation through the emerging field of neuro-anthropology, helps explain why. If the social theorist George Herbert Mead was on to something roughly a century ago, that is, or the neuroscientist Merlin Donald and the sociologist Robert Bellah have accurately been filling out details in the last few decades,[35] then the reciprocal processes of social mirroring known as mimesis generated not only language and culture among early human ancestors but also mind and self-consciousness themselves.[36]

According to these theorists, self-consciousness began in a "conversation of gestures."[37] Although only instinctively at first, our hominin ancestors recognized danger in some other creatures, and comfort or collaboration in others. It was not that the dog or the chimp or the early human *decided* on flight or fight, much less determined to glare or snarl in response. Yet at some point, as brains evolved in size and complexity, our ancestors surely noticed that the gesture might substitute for the act. Threatening gestures had always been more efficient than actual aggression. Coos might reassure an infant from a distance. To notice that one's own growl was similar to the other's growl opened the possibility of self-consciousness. To then anticipate and choose such gestures deliberately rather than instinctively was to be-gin to signify—to project intended meaning through kinetic action and raw vocalization. Such signification was a long way from language, to be sure, and whether language emerged early or late in the process remains a matter of dispute.[38] But to deliberately signify at all, even if purely through gestures, required one to see oneself being seen, or hear oneself being heard. As we began to become objects to ourselves, self-consciousness and indeed self were emerging.[39]

Sociality and culture were thus constitutively prior to self or self-consciousness. Cognitive reflexivity, after all, required a social matrix within which the self could recognize itself. As Mead explained, while the subject "I" is certainly more than the object "me," nonetheless the "I" can emerge through the "me" only by becoming aware of itself as perceived by others.[40] Notice, though, that every time we speak of a conversation of gestures, or reflexive self-recognition, or mimetic action, or even simply "meaning," we are naming or at least alluding to a cycle of human interaction, whether vicious or virtuous.

Although vicious cycles can ultimately prove destructive, they nonetheless played a powerful role in the building of civilization and the deepening of culture. To be sure, not all formative mimetic action would have been aggressive. If our hominin ancestors were like modern primates, they spent far more time in reciprocal grooming and interactive childcare than they did fending off predators or fighting with rivals. Toolmaking was undoubtedly a group project; passing on the sophisticated art of chipping the proper stones at the best angle for producing sharp edges required mimetic pedagogy over many millennia.[41] Still, it is striking how often scholars find in the aggressive mimesis of predators and rivals their paradigm case for explaining human origins.[42]

Indeed, the ancients did so themselves, in their own more mythological way. Coming from the very era when nomadic culture was giving way to settled civilization through agriculture and hierarchical divisions of labor in Mesopotamia four millennia ago, the Sumerian *Epic of Gilgamesh* may well be the world's oldest surviving work of literature.[43] In its first story cycle, Gilgamesh the semi-divine king of Uruk does battle with his opposite, Enkidu the wild animal-man. Nearly fighting to a draw, Gilgamesh wins but knows he has met his equal. Having come to respect one another, he and Enkidu become fast friends. In the process, both, in differing ways, are humanized. Through friendship with an equal, Gilgamesh finds relief from his solitude and becomes less tyrannical, while Enkidu learns to shave, wash, and eat cooked food. Once the two are exhausted as competitors, each is able to see himself in the other.[44]

Yet now that they are equals and friends, Gilgamesh and Enkidu seem to need some new enemy in order to cement their friendship. They determine to do battle against Humbaba, whom they describe as evil but whom the gods have favored as protector of sacred groves of trees. When the elders of Uruk counsel that it is imprudent to transgress sacred boundaries, Gilgamesh insists that he must prove his strength and win an enduring name for himself. Later he explains that he must make the servants of the divine serve humanity instead, in order to build towns from the sacred.[45] So he does, and yet the tragic poignancy of the trade-off is evident as the elders' warning is eventually fulfilled. When Gilgamesh continues to defy the gods, they send the Bull of Heaven against Gilgamesh. In the ensuing battle, his comrade Enkidu is killed. The remaining story cycles play out the sense of tragedy as a grieving Gilgamesh quests in vain for secret life-giving means to restore his friend to life.

In other words, the identification or even the outright creation of enemies offers a certain reprieve from in-group violence, which often passes for peace, as mimetic rivalry within one community vents itself and seals camaraderie through fear of some outsider—then another—always another.[46] Whatever actual or manufactured threat that enemies pose, they have consistently provided the occasion for human beings to build up civilization through vicious cycles of oppositional bonding. Yet vicious cycles vitiate even otherwise virtuous cycles of friendship, as Gilgamesh's grief for Enkidu attests. Such a peace is always fragile at best, and this is not simply the inevitable fragility of vulnerable mortality. It is a fragility we build into our cultures and social systems, at some level knowingly.

The Possibility of Social Creativity

Still, and more hopefully, mimetic theory also demonstrates why social creativity is also possible. Mimesis is not simple imitation; it does not leave us locked into endless replication of inherited patterns. Against more deterministic schools of thought, the theorists I am citing not only allow for but expect that mimesis will issue in innovation. Even among pre-linguistic early humans, Donald has noted, "A purely mimetic culture can evolve. Mimetic acts are expressive and thus inherently inventive and creative."[47] Paradoxically, doing the expected more self-consciously underdetermines the expected.[48]

This process is especially obvious in the great change agents of history—Mead named Jesus, the Buddha, and Socrates as examples.[49] These are "geniuses" of mind and character not simply in terms of brainpower, for they take in the attitudes of their society so deeply that they are able both to embody the whole of the community and to envision, then demonstrate, how it could transform. *All* conscious minds live "at the cognitive cutting edge of culture," Donald has clarified; "this is true of everyone, not only of geniuses." However, those who most clearly represent "the strange phenomenon we call 'genius'" demonstrate both what makes them notable and why they must always be part of a larger social movement in order to have their effect: "Under the right circumstances, the cognitive resources of an entire culture can become concentrated inside a single mind, and this can bring about an awesome concatenation of forces."[50]

Recognizing the dynamics of mimetic processes, then, allows us to recognize why the Niebuhrian commonplace—that those who would seek to follow Jesus's teachings by loving their enemies must thereby render themselves politically irrelevant—seems both so obvious *and yet is so misleading*. To love a community's enemy will never enjoy broad political support; this is nearly a truism. Yet in times of crisis, creative initiatives that embody enemy love may be precisely what the social order needs in order to become more fully itself according to its best emerging values, to discover win-win solutions, or even to survive. Loving sentiments toward enemies may be quite optional here. What matters is to break out of vicious cycles of regard merely for one's own kind, through precisely the salvation–historical transforming initiative that Jesus introduced when he taught "love your enemies" in Matthew 5:43–48, doing so according to practical strategies drawn from the paradigmatic transforming initiatives of Matthew 5:38–42.

Love of enemies may seem like the most unattainable of the virtues to which Jesus pointed in Matthew 5—even more difficult than the Beatitudes. Yet it is also the most powerful and fundamental because it breaks the deep and ancient vicious cycle that the *Epic of Gilgamesh* so poignantly represents, by which rivals within one community forge camaraderie and a measure of social peace only by uniting against outsiders whom they join in fearing. Lest "love your enemies" simply come to us as a "hard saying," Jesus has bent the arc of history and civilization by stretching our imaginations with four simple rhetorical, yet revolutionary, questions: "For if you love those who love you, what reward do you have? Do not even the tax collectors do the same? And if you greet only your brothers and sisters, what more are you doing than others? Do not even the Gentiles do the same?" (Matt. 5:46–47).[51]

To practice love for aggressive, hateful, life-threatening enemies is obviously harder indeed, yet if anything all the more politically creative. The Israeli martyr for peace Prime Minister Yitzhak Rabin once stated what should be obvious: "You don't make peace with friends; you make it with very unsavory enemies." On the really tough issues where one's society most needs to escape its vicious cycles, *only* those who practice unsentimental love of enemies may be the relevant, socially responsible ones. And by offering us concrete, prototypical, transforming initiatives, Jesus has freed us from sentimentality. As Martin Luther King Jr. said of his nemesis "Bull" Connor—the infamous police commissioner in Birmingham, Alabama, who turned police dogs and fire hoses on civil rights protesters, including children—one didn't have to like him to love him as a misguided child of God.

Nor is the power of transforming initiatives only evident in heroes of Christian nonviolence such as King, or in local, face-to-face settings. Although the prototypes we find in the Sermon on the Mount inevitably come from first-century Palestine, once we begin to discern their dynamic, we will recognize their power at work even at the highest level of international affairs. Whether Richard Nixon subjectively loved Mao Zedong is immaterial; the phrase "Nixon-to-China" and the dynamic it represents have found a place even in popular culture.[52] Egyptian President Anwar Sadat likewise launched the Egyptian-Israeli peace process by unexpectedly announcing he would visit Jerusalem. Nelson Mandela won the grudging respect of white South Africans and averted the bloodbath that most expected would come in the wake of apartheid by mastering the art of the unexpected gesture; among the most vivid was his appearance at the 1995 Rugby World Cup finals, during a critical phase of political transition, wearing the jersey of the white South African team despite its long association with apartheid.[53]

The manual for peacemaking that is the Sermon on the Mount is therefore accessible and translatable even in geopolitics. For when a movement or figure we least expect does the unexpected, the mimesis that sets up vicious cycles starts to spiral over into a virtuous cycle instead.[54] More often the unexpected comes not from leaders on the world stage but from the apparently powerless, who, as Pope Francis noted, "resist the temptation to retaliate, [and thus] become the most credible promoters of nonviolent peacemaking."[55] Yet this power is not inaccessible anywhere on the sociopolitical map. A Christian may narrate it as the power of the gospel at work in a world that at best only dimly acknowledges the gospel. Whatever domestic and geopolitical reasons a Nixon might have had for tapping unwittingly into that power, the church has more and better reasons for nurturing the creativity and imagination needed to recognize openings for transforming initiatives sooner and more consistently. That nurturing—that stepping into the breach—is where the church should be investing its resources and taking its own risks.

Just Peacemaking Practices

A Christian theology of peace is always first about ecclesiology and the formation of Christians as a people of peace. Often it is less urgent to identify actions, tactics, strategies, and policies to counter injustice, defuse violence, or nurture peace than it is to find peacemakers who have been formed in the virtues that prepare them to practice peacemaking. Yet the question of *what to be* can never ignore the question of *what to do*.

If we survey the ten "normative practices" that Glen Stassen and his colleagues have commended in their "just peacemaking theory" for their empirically demonstrable, realistic track records, we may discern the role of modern transforming initiatives in all of them. Although their project has been a translation into practices and policies that are accessible in the public square without constant reference to biblical sources, Stassen's exegesis of the Sermon on the Mount is always visible just under the surface as the conceptual foundation for that project of translation, and on at least one occasion, he made the cross-references explicit.[56]

1. *Support nonviolent direct action* (cf. Matt. 5:38–43).[57] Strategic nonviolence appears first on the list of just peacemaking practices for good reason. Done well, boycotts, strikes, marches, civil disobedience, public disclosure of wrongs, accompaniment of the politically vulnerable, and the creation of safe spaces are not simply pressure tactics.[58] Echoing Jesus, they are ways to resist evil but not in kind. They are fresh and creative ways to redirect the social forces at work in one's historical moment (what nonviolence strategist Gene Sharp called "political jiu-jitsu") in order to expose injustice for what it is and turn the violence of the opponent into reasons for more and more erstwhile bystanders to withdraw their consent and shift their support.

2. *Take independent initiatives to reduce threat* (cf. Matt. 5:38–43).[59] This just peacemaking practice demonstrates the power of Jesus's transformative initiatives even for those with no particular commitment to principled nonviolence, even in the sphere of geopolitics. Nixon going to China is but one example. Trust-building gestures to suspend nuclear testing or the production of certain classes of weapons were the key to unlocking arms reduction talks between the United States and the Soviet Union at various junctures. Prisoner releases and partial withdrawals from occupied territory have likewise brought adversaries to the table in regional conflicts.[60]

3. *Use cooperative conflict resolution* (cf. Matt. 5:21–26).[61] When parties are locked in conflict, their relationship may not be particularly "cooperative," much less enemy-loving. The art of back-channel negotiators who get them to the table, and the skill of mediators who lead them toward win–win solutions, is to initiate a transformation from limited self-interest to mutual recognition of shared interests. With or without sentiment, this is love of enemy at work in a way that we may not immediately recognize, but only because it is so concrete, so nuts-and-bolts.

4. *Acknowledge responsibility for conflict and injustice and seek repentance and forgiveness* (cf. Matt. 7:1–5).[62] Nothing sustains complex historical conflicts so much as mutual recrimination. After decades if not centuries of violent self-defense, all parties to a conflict are likely to have committed injustices or crimes, and thus have reasons to blame the other. As hard as it is for individuals to confess sins and ask forgiveness, it is harder still for groups and nations. Yet doing so, whether publicly or in behind-the-scenes negotiations, has sometimes been the key move that has led to historic peace accords, as when Germany's chancellor Willy Brandt knelt silently at the Warsaw Ghetto Memorial in 1970 in repentance for Nazi crimes against the Polish people, or Guatemalan insurgents and military representatives rescued failing talks in Norway in 1990 by beginning to admit their mistakes.[63]

These first four just peacemaking practices demonstrate especially clearly the character of Christian peacemaking by means of transforming initiatives. The dynamics are proactive, as practitioners do their part without letting other parties' blame excuse them from taking the initiative. They recognize the dignity and legitimate interests of enemies without approval for dysfunctional positions and wrongful acts. They confront in a way that is invitational rather than destructive, thus strengthening relationships and drawing into community. As a full reading of *Just Peacemaking: The New Paradigm for the Ethics of Peace and War* would confirm, these practices are all historically based and empirically validated. Although the role of transforming initiatives may be subtler in the remaining just peacemaking practices, similar dynamics are crucial nonetheless.

To commit to resolving conflicts through democratic politics rather than warfare requires a prior commitment to recognizing others as legitimate claimants whose good is interdependent with those of oneself and one's own kind. Hence, normative practice number 5: *Advance democracy, human rights, and interdependence* (cf. Matt. 6:19–34).[64] A transforming initiative is at work in practice number 6, too, insofar as economic development necessarily encourages virtuous cycles of win–win exchange: *Foster just and sustainable economic development* (cf. Matt. 6:19–34).[65] Any effort to reinforce the positive dimensions of globalization over negative ones is an opportunity to extend our circles of moral regard beyond our own kind. Hence, number 7: *Work with emerging cooperative forces in the international system*. After all, if work for just and peaceful social change is to be sustainable, practitioners must welcome rather than begrudge the need to institutionalize the changes they have been calling for. Number 8 does so on the world stage: *Strengthen the United Nations and international efforts for cooperation and human rights*.[66]

To be sure, much national and international institutionalization has emerged through vicious cycles like that of Gilgamesh and Enkidu, who formed their bonds of civilization through battles that required the identification of enemies and the manufacture of scapegoats. When the risks inherent in such vicious cycles threaten to spin out of control, risking the transforming initiative of arms reduction instead may not bring the peace of the heavenly city—to use Augustine's terminology—but will nonetheless be a service that helps the earthly city at least to save itself from itself. Hence, normative practice number 9: *Reduce offensive weapons and weapons trade* (Matt. 26:51–52).[67]

Finally, number 10: *Encourage grassroots peacemaking groups and voluntary associations*. For any of the other just peacemaking practices to take shape in history, we need the most basic transforming initiative of all—the formation of people who will "be the change they seek in the world." This foundational work of formation is essential to fulfilling the mandate of recent popes for all the Catholic faithful to confirm their vocation as peacemakers and builders of justice, in collaboration with other Christians and all people of good will.[68] Grassroots peacemaking-as-*people*building is always more than "community organizing" alone. Done in faith, hope, and love, it participates in God's own great transforming initiative, launched through Abraham and Sarah, as God blesses one particular people but always with a view toward how they are to become a blessing to all nations. As Archbishop Hélder Câmara of Brazil used to preach so energetically, beyond any mere coalition is the "greater and no less indispensable alliance being forged between those minorities that I call 'Abrahamic.' They already exist; it is not necessary to create them. The Spirit of God raises them up deep within every race, in every religion, every nation, every human group. Who belongs to these Abrahamic minorities? All those who, like Abraham, hope against hope and decide to work to the point of sacrifice for a more just and humane world."[69]

Even Augustine of Hippo, who did so much to bring Roman just war theory into the Christian tradition, had to acknowledge the power of nonviolence done in faithfulness to Jesus's teachings. Writing to his friend the Roman tribune Marcellinus of Carthage, no less, and having just discussed Matthew 5:38–48, Augustine concluded, "Every righteous and pious person, then, ought to be ready to endure with patience evils from those whom he wants to become good in order that the number of the good may rather increase and that he may not add himself by an equal sinfulness to the number of the evil."[70] The power of gospel nonviolence lay precisely in its capacity to change the social dynamic between adversaries through virtues that were more valuable than anything the enemy might seize. So too with every transforming initiative to escape our vicious cycles.

Notes

A longer version of this chapter was produced for the journal *Modern Theology* and is available in Early View on its website in advance of its appearance in a 2020 special issue on "Love of Enemies" (Wiley Online Library, DOI:10.1111/moth.12470, available at https://rdcu.be/bfWNE).

1. See the Second Vatican Council, *Gaudium et spes* [Pastoral constitution on the Church in the modern world] (1965), §80.
2. The most immediate prompt for Pope Francis's 2017 World Day of Peace message was a conference organized by the Catholic peace organization Pax Christi International, which was held in Rome, April 11–13, 2016, and its well-publicized final document.
3. Pope John Paul II, "Peace on Earth to Those Whom God Loves," Message of His Holiness Pope John Paul II for the celebration of the World Day of Peace (2000), §20.
4. Pope Francis, "Nonviolence: A Style of Politics for Peace," Message of His Holiness Pope Francis for the celebration of the fiftieth World Day of Peace (2017), §6.

5. Francis, "Nonviolence: A Style of Politics for Peace," §2; emphasis *sic.*

6. To illustrate, Francis cited examples of how the "decisive and consistent practice of nonviolence has produced effective results" in campaigns by the Hindu Mahatma Gandhi, the Muslim Khan Abdul Ghaffar Khan, the Christian Dr. Martin Luther King Jr., Liberian women led by Leymah Gbowee, and in the fall of Communist regimes in 1989 Europe, where Pope John Paul II himself played a role. Citing his predecessor Pope Benedict XVI, Francis especially reminded Christian readers that for them, "nonviolence is not merely tactical behaviour." After all, it responds with a person's entire "way of being" to God's love as it reciprocates by extending such love even to enemies.

7. Francis, "Nonviolence: A Style of Politics for Peace," §1–4. Quotations from Benedict XVI are from his "Angelus" message of February 18, 2007, in St. Peter's Square.

8. Francis, "Nonviolence: A Style of Politics for Peace," §6.

9. In his autobiography, Gandhi especially credited Tolstoy's *The Kingdom of God Is Within You* and *The Gospels in Brief: What to Do?* for the impression that they made on him.

10. See chapter 3 (this volume) by Eli McCarthy. Yiu Sing Lúcás Chan, SJ, summarized why virtue ethics commends itself for bridging biblical interpretation and Christian ethics this way: "Several dimensions of virtue ethics make it effective for interpreting scripture: The first is its turn to dispositions and character formation. Scripture orients believers around certain values and virtues that reflect God's self-revelation in Christ, shaping character and identity in a distinctly Christian way. The second is the role of the exemplar. The Bible contains many '"characters"' who model for us distinct moral characters and virtues. The third is the shaping of the community and communal identity." See "Biblical Ethics: 3D," *Theological Studies* 76, no. 1 (March 2015): 118–19. Chan offered his own study and application of the Beatitudes as part of his book *The Ten Commandments and the Beatitudes: Biblical Studies and Ethics for Real Life*, foreword by Daniel J. Harrington, SJ, and James F. Keenan, SJ (Lanham, MD: Rowman & Littlefield, 2012).

11. For example, other than organizing his work according to the Decalogue and placing his discussion of self-defense, dueling, and warfare under the heading of the fifth commandment against killing, Henry Davis, SJ, made no reference whatsoever to biblical sources. See Henry Davis, *Moral and Pastoral Theology: A Summary*, Heythrop Series (New York: Sheed & Ward, 1952), 54–58; and Henry Davis, SJ, *Moral and Pastoral Theology in Four Volumes*, ed. L. W. Geddes, SJ, Heythrop Series, no. 2, 7th ed. (London: Sheed & Ward, 1958), 148–51.

12. Less than a decade before the Second Vatican Council began to rehabilitate conscientious objection to war by recognizing the moral integrity of those who forgo violent self-defense in favor of other means (*Gaudium et spes* §78), Pope Pius XII in his 1956 Christmas address was saying otherwise. After recapitulating the broad requirements for war to be justifiable, he noted, "Therefore a Catholic citizen cannot invoke his own conscience in order to refuse to serve and fulfill those duties the law imposes." Pope Pius XII, *The Major Addresses of Pope Pius XII*, vol. 2, ed. Vincent A. Yzermans (St. Paul, MN: North Central Publishing Company, 1961), 225.

13. Reinhold Niebuhr, *Moral Man and Immoral Society*, reprint ed., The Scribner Lyceum Editions Library (New York: Scribner's, 1960); Reinhold Niebuhr, "Why the Christian Church Is Not Pacifist," in *Christianity and Power Politics* (New York: Charles Scribner's Sons, 1940), 1–32.

14. See Lúcás Chan, *Biblical Ethics in the 21st Century: Developments, Emerging Consensus, and Future Directions* (New York: Paulist Press, 2013).

15. Regarding the council's call to holiness, see Second Vatican Council, *Lumen gentium* [Dogmatic constitution on the Church] (1964), §39–42; for renouncing violence as an act of personal holiness, see Second Vatican Council, *Gaudium et spes*, §78; and for active nonviolence in public affairs, see Pope John Paul II, *Centesimus annus* [On the hundredth anniversary of *Rerum novarum*], encyclical letter (1991), §23.

16. Francis, "Nonviolence: A Style of Politics for Peace," §2–4.

17. See Duane Friesen, "Peacemaking as an Ethical Category: The Convergence of Pacifism and Just War," in *Ethics in the Nuclear Age: Strategy, Religious Studies, and the Churches*, ed. Todd Whitmore (Dallas, TX: Southern Methodist University Press, 1989).

18. Stassen laid out his exegetical evidence in greatest detail for biblical scholars in "The Fourteen Triads of the Sermon on the Mount (Matt. 5:21–7:12)," *Journal of Biblical Literature* 122, no. 2 (Summer 2003): 267–308. His most accessible elaboration for a general audience is *Living the Sermon on the Mount: A Practical Hope for Grace and Deliverance* (San Francisco: Jossey-Bass, 2006).

19. Glen H. Stassen, ed., *Just Peacemaking: The New Paradigm for the Ethics of Peace and War*, 3rd ed. (Cleveland, OH: Pilgrim Press, 2008); Glen H. Stassen, "The Unity, Realism, and Obligatoriness of Just Peacemaking Theory," *Journal of the Society of Christian Ethics* 23, no. 1 (2003): 171–94; Glen H. Stassen, "Just Peacemaking as Hermeneutical Key: The Need for International Cooperation in Preventing Terrorism," *Journal of the Society of Christian Ethics* 24, no. 2 (Fall/Winter 2004): 171–91.

20. Glen H. Stassen, *Just Peacemaking: Transforming Initiatives for Justice and Peace* (Louisville, KY: Westminster John Knox, 1992), 42–51.

21. See Matt. 23 and Mark 3:5.

22. See Stassen, "Fourteen Triads," 271–72 and 268–69.

23. Stassen, "Fourteen Triads," 273, quoting Robert A. Guelich, *The Sermon on the Mount: A Foundation for Understanding* (Waco, TX: Word Books, 1982), 190.

24. That neglected but legitimate translation of *tō ponērō* solves nagging interpretive problems in its own right, by the way. Stassen credits Clarence Jordan for noticing that the dative can be instrumental rather than substantive, and that this better accords with parallel passages in Rom. 12:17–21; Luke 6:27–36; 1 Thess. 5:15; and the *Didache* 1:4–5. See Stassen, "Fourteen Triads," 281–82; and Stassen, *Living the Sermon on the Mount*, 89–91.

25. Stassen, "Fourteen Triads," 279–81; Stassen, *Living the Sermon on the Mount*, 89–98. See also Walter Wink, *Engaging the Powers: Discernment and Resistance in a World of Domination* (Minneapolis, MN: Fortress Press, 1992), 175–94; and Walter Wink, "Breaking the Spiral of Violence," in *The Powers That Be: Theology for a New Millennium* (New York: Doubleday, 1998), 98–111.

26. Wink, *Powers That Be*, 98–111; Stassen, *Living the Sermon on the Mount*, 91–95.

27. Cf. Glen H. Stassen, "Transforming Initiatives of Just Peacemaking Based on the Triadic Structure of the Sermon on the Mount," Matthew section, Society of Biblical Literature (2006), 1 and 5, https://www.sbl-site.org/assets/pdfs/Stassen_Transforming.pdf.

28. Another *possible* anomaly is that when Jesus names the relevant item of traditional righteousness—"You shall love your neighbor and hate your enemy"—the latter half of this saying seems not to come from Hebrew Scriptures at all but from the Essene community of Qumran, and perhaps from popular Judaism as well. Although the phrase "hate your enemies" does not appear in the Hebrew Scriptures per se, the sentiment surely does. It is not just that the imprecatory psalms, for example, serve a cathartic function by letting the faithful get out of their system a desire to cast their captors' babies against the rocks (Ps. 137:8–9). It is that hatred of enemies is held up as a positive sign of pious identification with God's justice and God's cause, as for example in Psalm 139:19–22.

29. Most strikingly, Stassen offers a cogent explanation of the dogs, swine, and pearls verse, Matthew 7:6, which has long befuddled interpreters to the point of despair. See Stassen, "Fourteen Triads," 289, citing Ulrich Luz, *Matthew 1–7: A Commentary*, trans. Wilhelm C. Linss (Minneapolis, MN: Augsburg, 1989), 419.

30. Stassen, "Fourteen Triads."

31. Stassen, "Transforming Initiatives of Just Peacemaking." In an October 16, 2012, email to me, Stassen commented, "At the conclusion of the [2006] panel, the moderator declared: 'Well we have reached one consensus: The Sermon on the Mount is transforming initiatives.' Many NT scholars have spoken to me agreeing. No NT scholar that I know of has either written or spoken against it."

32. Dale C. Allison, "The Configuration of the Sermon on the Mount and Its Meaning," in *Studies in Matthew: Interpretation Past and Present* (Grand Rapids, MI: Baker Academic, 2005), 183n23. See also Frederick Dale Bruner, *Matthew: A Commentary Vol. 1, The Christbook, Matthew 1–12* (Grand Rapids, MI: Eerdmans, 2004), 207.

33. Willard M. Swartley, *Covenant of Peace: The Missing Piece in New Testament Theology and Ethics* (Grand Rapids, MI: Eerdmans, 2006), 65–66. See also 426–27.

34. An "individual" can never really be simply *individual*, for—as Pope John Paul II constantly quoted Vatican II—a human being "can fully discover his true self only in a sincere gifting of himself" (see *Gaudium et spes*, §19 and 24).

35. George Herbert Mead, *Mind, Self, and Society: From the Standpoint of a Social Behaviorist*, in *Works of George Herbert Mead*, vol. 1, ed. Charles W. Morris (Chicago: University of Chicago Press, 1962 [1934]); Merlin Donald, *A Mind So Rare: The Evolution of Human Consciousness* (New York: Norton, 2001). See also Merlin Donald, "Mimetic Theory Re-examined, Twenty Years after the Fact," in *Evolution of Mind, Brain, and Culture*, ed. Gary Hatfield and Holly Pittman (Philadelphia: University of Pennsylvania Museum of Archaeology and Anthropology, 2013), 169–92; and see Robert N. Bellah, *Religion in Human Evolution: From the Paleolithic to the Axial Age* (Cambridge, MA: Belknap Press of Harvard University Press, 2011).

36. Along with Mead, Donald, and Bellah, corresponding analysis could also come from René Girard and the "Girardians" he has influenced.

37. Mead, *Mind, Self, and Society*, 42.

38. See Mead on early development of language (*Mind, Self, and Society*, 51–59) compared to Donald (*Mind So Rare*, 274, 279–80, 291–94).

39. On becoming "objects to ourselves," see Mead, *Mind, Self, and Society*, 136, 138, 140–41; and Donald, "Mimetic Theory Re-examined," 183.

40. Mead, *Mind, Self, and Society*, 178–79. See also 171–77, 197–98, and 214.

41. See Donald, "Mimetic Theory Re-examined," 179–83; Bellah, *Religion in Human Evolution*, 123–25. Donald summarizes the ways that archaeological evidence from stone cutting confirms mimetic theory on pp. 179–80.

42. Note the recurrence of mimetic scenarios involving aggression, bullying, violence, dogfights, etc. in Mead, *Mind, Self, and Society*, 14–15, 20, 42–49, 53–56, 63, 66, 147, 181. Also note Donald, *Mind So Rare*, 180–81; and Bellah, *Religion in Human Evolution*, 119, 130.

43. John Gardner and John R. Maier, trans., *Gilgamesh: Translated from the Sîn-Leqi-Unninnī Version* (New York: Alfred A. Knopf, 1984). For an accessible, interpretive rendering of the story, a modern English speaker might wish to consult Herbert Mason, *Gilgamesh: A Verse Narrative* (New York: New American Library, 1972).

44. This is the summary comment in the modern rendering. See Mason, Gilgamesh, 24.

45. Mason, *Gilgamesh*, 40–41. See Gardner and Maier, *Gilgamesh*, 145–47.

46. René Girard's further insight was that often these outsiders are actually insiders made into scapegoats, and likely they are innocent scapegoats besides. For a summary of the scapegoating mechanism according to Girard, see Pierpaolo Antonello and Paul Gifford, eds., *Can We Survive Our Origins? Readings in René Girard's Theory of Violence and the Sacred, Studies in Violence, Mimesis, and Culture* (East Lansing, MI: Michigan State University Press, 2015), xxix–xxxii.

47. Donald, "Mimetic Theory Re-examined," 189.

48. Mead, *Mind, Self, and Society*, 173, 176–78.

49. Mead, *Mind, Self, and Society*, 217.

50. Donald, *Mind So Rare*, 299–300.

51. Meanwhile, Jesus has also flustered the casuist by upending the very definition of neighbor and making an outcast Samaritan the model for imitation if one wants to claim to be following the God-given moral code of any people that believes itself chosen.

52. Witness a version of the phrase in the iconic science fiction series *Star Trek*, specifically in the 1991 movie *Star Trek VI: The Undiscovered Country*.

53. Leon Marincowitz, "South Africa: Positive Mimesis and the Turn toward Peace," in Antonello and Gifford, *Can We Survive Our Origins?*, 223–31.

54. Girardians sometimes speak of "bad mimesis" and "good mimesis," or moving "from negative to positive mimesis." See Antonello and Gifford, *Can We Survive Our Origins?*, 191–92, 198–99, 228.

55. Francis, "Nonviolence: A Style of Politics for Peace," §1.

56. See Stassen, *Just Peacemaking*, 20–22, "Transforming Initiatives of Just Peacemaking," for a collation of nine of the ten just peacemaking practices with transforming initiatives in the Sermon on the Mount and elsewhere in the Gospel of Matthew.

57. Stassen, "Transforming Initiatives of Just Peacemaking," 5–6.

58. The list here is hardly exclusive but simply reflects the tactics used as examples on pp. 44–56 of Stassen, *Just Peacemaking.*

59. Stassen, "Transforming Initiatives of Just Peacemaking," 6–7.

60. Stassen, *Just Peacemaking,* 59–64.

61. Stassen, "Transforming Initiatives of Just Peacemaking," 3–5.

62. Stassen, "Transforming Initiatives of Just Peacemaking," 9–10.

63. Regarding Brandt's repentance for Nazi crimes in Poland, see Stassen, *Just Peacemaking,* 102; and for Guatemalan peacemaking efforts in Norway, see Rudolph Nelson et al., *Precarious Peace: God & Guatemala,* video recording (Worcester, PA: Gateway Films, 2003).

64. Stassen, "Transforming Initiatives of Just Peacemaking," 8–9.

65. Stassen, "Transforming Initiatives of Just Peacemaking," 8.

66. See Stassen, "Transforming Initiatives of Just Peacemaking," 7–8, for Stassen's discussion of how these last two just peacemaking practices respond in a more general way to Jesus's teachings in the Sermon on the Mount by seeking to "include your enemies in the community of neighbors."

67. Stassen, "Transforming Initiatives of Just Peacemaking," 10.

68. See, for example, John Paul II, "World Day of Peace Message 2000," §20.

69. Benedicto Tapia de Renedo, ed., *Helder Camara: Proclamas a la Juventud,* Serie PEDAL, no. 64 (Salamanca: Ediciones Sigueme, 1976), 189. I have made translations of the speech from which this quote is taken—"Un pacto digno"—along with two others at http://courseweb.stthomas.edu/gwschlabach/docs/manitese.htm.

70. Augustine, "Letter 138," To Marcellinus [412] in *Letters 100–155* (Epistulae), vol. II/2 of *The Works of Saint Augustine: A Translation for the 21st Century,* ed. Boniface Ramsey, trans. Roland Teske, SJ (Hyde Park, NY: New City Press, 2003), 2, 11–12.

2

CATHOLIC TRADITION ON PEACE, WAR, AND JUST PEACE

LISA SOWLE CAHILL

Following a long tradition from Augustine and Aquinas through the modern social encyclicals, contemporary Catholic social teaching (CST) celebrates the ideal of peaceful and just political life, accomplished through human solidarity, commitment to the common good, respect for the dignity of all persons, and inclusion in participatory and equitable social, legal, and political institutions. This ideal vision of political life may be captured by the phrase "just peace." Justice and peace are interdependent and mutually necessary goals that can and should be achieved together. The twofold inspiration of this tradition as a tradition of Christian politics is the narrative of creation, upholding the image of God in humanity and the "one flesh" unity of all human beings, and the gospel, with its messages of love of neighbor, inclusion, and reconciliation.[1]

The political vision of CST, however, also incorporates recognition of human sin and brokenness, and the reality that inequality, strife, and violence afflict and even destroy human societies with appalling regularity. Wars between or among nation-states declined rapidly after World War II. Although a nuclear exchange between the United States and North Korea has recently threatened, and states continue to confront one another with the potential use of military force, the globe reached a point with no interstate wars in 2015. However, levels of violence worldwide continue, with intrastate conflicts or "societal violence" now being the most common (e.g., civil wars, insurgencies, cross-border conflicts, terrorist movements). Societal warfare has been on the increase since the early 2000s, predominantly in North Africa and the Middle East. Whereas gradually fewer numbers of combatants are killed in war, civilians have become the primary victims of today's conflicts, accounting for 87 percent of those killed in war since 2000. Moreover, war causes huge devastations of societal systems, bringing additional deaths as middle-term and long-range effects of war.[2] As Pope Francis poignantly notes,

While the last century knew the devastation of two deadly World Wars, the threat of nuclear war and a great number of other conflicts, today, sadly, we find ourselves engaged in a horrifying *world war fought piecemeal*.

It is not easy to know if our world is presently more or less violent than in the past, or to know whether modern means of communications and greater mobility have made us more aware of violence, or, on the other hand, increasingly inured to it.[3]

Over centuries, CST has struggled with the problem of how to respond to violence and other injustices, given the gospel commands to love God, neighbor, and even enemy. If God's reign is already breaking into history through the ministry of Jesus, that empowers human beings to follow his example by avoiding and transforming conflict through peaceful means. It is a tragic but undeniable fact, however, that such efforts are not always successful, leaving vulnerable neighbors exposed to grievous harm, including death. This presents Christians with the dilemma of how to respond to violent situations in a way that is responsible to God, to all neighbors, and to the common good.

Contemporary Catholic teaching puts the emphasis squarely on nonviolence as required by conformity to Jesus Christ and as also the most effective way to end cycles of violence and restore the conditions of just and peaceful social existence. According to Pope Francis's 2017 World Day of Peace message, nonviolence is not just an inner-ecclesial practice or a distant ideal; it is "a style of politics for peace." Francis challenges "political and religious leaders, the heads of international institutions, and business and media executives . . . to build up society, communities and businesses by acting as peacemakers."[4]

At the same time, the possibility of using armed force has not been entirely excluded, with Popes John Paul II, Benedict XVI, and Francis all leaving the door open to limited justifications of humanitarian intervention or self-defense. Resort to armed force has, however, been decisively minimized and marginalized in all papal teaching since the Second Vatican Council. This chapter provides background to the evolution of CST in this period by first reviewing the teaching and practice of the early church, the just war ethics of Augustine and Aquinas, and the peace movements that have remained strong in Christian churches despite the theoretical dominance of just war theory.

Since Christianity's inception, peace has been its guiding norm for political ethics. As Kenneth Himes explains, the ideal is a "positive peace," not simply and negatively the absence of war. Political peace is not as complete as the eschatological peace of the reign of God, but it does hold up the standard of "a political community that is rightly structured, meaning that people live in truth, charity, freedom, and justice directed toward the common good."[5] In other words, the political peace of CST is a just peace. In a rightly ordered political community to which all contribute with charity and justice, the use of lethal armed force is neither necessary nor tolerable. In fact, just war theory has been premised on a general presumption against the use of violence and war.[6] According to the US bishops, "Catholic teaching begins in every case with a presumption against war."[7]

Yet a reality of the Christian life as also a form of political existence in historical societies is that it can be very difficult at the practical level to embody universal forgiveness and nonviolence while at the same time ful-filling one's obligations of love and justice to vulnerable neighbors whom violence threatens and who rely on protection by stable and just social in-stitutions. The apparent conflict of love and justice in such situations pres-ents Christian ethics and CST with a moral dilemma. Christians face the question of how to participate both justly and charitably in the political or-der. The earliest Christians completely rejected killing as incompatible with Jesus's teaching. They were willing to accept that fidelity to the gospel might preclude important types of political participation, such as government and military roles.

Modern CST, originating with Leo XIII's *Rerum novarum* (*On the condi-tion of labor*) in 1931, works from the premise that social engagement for a just society is demanded by the gospel and by the common good. There-fore, responsible political participation (for individuals, groups, and the church itself) is a driving moral concern. When faced with the dilemma of war to protect human rights and the common good, the modern popes are mindful not only of the example of Jesus but also of the clear tendency of "justified" violence to result in more violence. Thus their solution has been to place an almost exclusive emphasis on discovering and implementing nonviolent means of resistance to injustice and of conflict transformation. CST has increasingly distanced itself from the elaboration of criteria for, and the institutionalization of, armed force as a solution to social problems. Meanwhile, the nonviolent commitment of the historic "peace churches" and of Catholic pacifism has devoted increasing energy to making non-violent solutions more effective and "mainstream," both ecclesially and politically.

Many major figures and groups in Christian tradition, whether pac-ifist or just war thinkers, have recognized at least tacitly that the effort to embody the reign of God in an unjust world involves ambiguities and paradoxes. Yet key just war thinkers Augustine and Aquinas fall short of confronting, much less resolving, this challenge. In the modern period, due to the injustices that always accompany use of lethal force, just war thinking has become much more stringent and restrictive, incorporating elements specifically designed to prioritize peace and nonviolence. This development, combined with the continuing scourge of both international and intrastate violence, opens the door to "just peace" as a more adequate way to respond to military and societal violence than the application of just war theory, both from a Christian and from a political or humanistic standpoint.

Early Christianity and Historic Peace Movements

Christians in the first three centuries after the death of Christ did not have much prospect of exercising political power, but they did benefit from the relatively peaceful conditions established by the Roman imperial government and known as the *Pax Romana*. It is clear that Christian teachers not only excluded the compatibility of killing with Christian identity under any circumstances but also warned that the soldier's lifestyle already presented considerable dangers. Foremost among these was idolatry, as soldiers were required to participate in formal ceremonies honoring the emperor as a god. Nevertheless, not all authorities forbade military service in every case (if killing could be avoided).[8] According to Irenaeus (c. 120/140–c. 200/203), the government can use the sword justly, and Origen of Alexandria (c. 185–254) distinguishes between just and unjust wars.[9] Some Christians did hold government office and some were even members of the military, as evidenced by tombstone inscriptions and by heroic tales of Christian soldiers, such as the "Thundering Legion," who reputedly won battles by miraculous intervention.[10]

However, authorities like Tertullian of Carthage (c. 155/160—died after 220) and Origen took for granted that to follow Jesus means to place oneself outside of and often against the prevailing societal ethos. Tertullian grounds his teaching against killing in a stringent reading of the Sermon on the Mount, both on swearing and on nonviolence.[11] He defines Jesus as a peacemaker whose power consists in the pursuit of peace (citing Isa. 2:3–4).[12] Christ is the "giver of the new law" and announces "the new kingdom which is not corruptible." Christians in their historical existence are called and enabled to follow his example.[13] In God's kingdom as already present, swords are beaten into plowshares (Isa. 2:4) and "fierce and cruel" dispositions become peaceable.[14]

Tertullian generally is regarded as a pacifist and definitely holds up nonviolence as a Christian ideal, yet he does not demand Christian withdrawal from all government roles. On the one hand, he regards most public roles as dangerous to Christian belief and practice. On the other hand, he appeals for tolerance of Christianity on the grounds that Christians pray for the emperor and for the stability of the Roman Empire. "We respect in the emperors the ordinance of God, who has set them over the nations. We know that there is that in them which God has willed."[15]

Origen believes that the kingdom is realized in one's life through a process of gradual sanctification by the Holy Spirit. The entire Christian life is a movement toward God, occurring within a cosmological drama of reunion with the divine, enabled by the Logos or Word and guided by the Spirit. In their present historical existence, Christians must avoid both violence and political roles, leading progressively better lives.[16] Those outside the faith will still carry on "necessary" wars, which should be kept as "just and ordered" as possible.[17] Origen agrees with Tertullian that Christians support the emperor through prayer, intercession, and asceticism, "composing a special army of piety."[18] Early Christian thinkers recognize that there is a tension between the duty toward government and the common good, and the duty not to kill; nevertheless, they insist that when the former collides with the latter, the duty not to kill takes priority.

In the fourth century the picture changes and just war theory rises to the surface. Yet the determination of Christians to forgo violence as a tool of politics survives and has been given practical, historical expression in a variety of figures, campaigns and movements, up to the present day.[19] For example, in the tenth and eleventh centuries, violence was spreading through Europe as familial properties were conserved intact by allotting them only to elder sons, leaving bands of young men roaming the countryside in search of conquest, wealth, and status. The Peace of God and the Truce of God sought limits on means used in intra-European fighting.[20] For example, fighting was off limits during holy days and seasons. There should be no attacks on women or clergy; nor on pilgrims, merchants, peasants, or visitors to church councils; nor on agricultural lands and implements; nor on farm animals.[21]

The sixteenth-century humanist Erasmus of Rotterdam accepts that the civil government has the responsibility to order the peace and security of society, by force when necessary. Yet he deplores killing as contrary to human nature and as especially offensive to the Christian calling, above all, when Christians are killing one another. Erasmus's most extensive discourses on war are *An Essay on War* (*Bellum*, published originally as a commentary on the adage "War is sweet to those who know it not") and *The Complaint of Peace* (*Querela Pacis*).[22] Although allowing some exceptions in the case of self-defense against non-Christians, Erasmus endeavors to persuade rulers that violence is not necessary as a tool of statecraft and that government can proceed on more peaceable terms. Indeed, like some twentieth-century politically engaged peace activists (of whom a significant number are Catholic), Erasmus seems to hope for an eventually peaceful world society, on the premise that nonviolence is generalizable as a mode of government.[23] Humanity was created for cooperation and to develop "the attachments of friendship and love."[24] Moreover, "Our Lord did not come to tell the world what enormity was permitted, how far we might deviate from the laws of rectitude, but to show us the point of perfection at which we were to aim with the utmost of our ability."[25] Erasmus seems close to the insights and commitments of recent

CST in that he not only urges the church and its members to embody the ideal of nonviolence but also presents it as a practicable "style of politics" that can and should have wide-ranging political effect. Like the popes, he recognizes armed force as possibly required in extreme situations but is convinced that at a basic level, such force always violates fellow humanity and results in more violence, even if and when exceptional circumstances demand it. Erasmus is not concerned with justifying force, but with promoting peace as a reachable goal.

Meanwhile, the "historic peace churches," such as the Anabaptists, Mennonites, and Quakers, have also been central to the Christian peace witness. Where they resemble the early church and differ from Roman Catholicism is that, at least historically, they expected their witness not only to be countercultural but to be rejected and ineffective in changing the political status quo, with its ready resort to coercive government and armed force. Central to their vision was the death of Christ on the cross, a fate they themselves often anticipated (although this was less true of the Quakers). In recent decades, however, many of these communions have responded to globalization with a mission to alleviate worldwide poverty and conflict, bringing them closer to Catholics in terms of their just peacemaking social agenda. A salient example is the Mennonite Central Committee, which works internationally for "relief, development and peace in the name of Christ."[26]

The Emergence of Just War Theory

In the first four centuries after Christ, his followers had little opportunity to become a powerful force for social change. In addition, there was little cultural or religious support (in Christianity or elsewhere) for a view of history as moving forward to embrace ideals such as inclusion of the poor, the reversal of status hierarchies, and reconciliation across cultures and traditions. The latter was virtually impossible until after the Enlightenment and twentieth-century movements for democracy, decolonization and human rights. But the former—political opportunity for Christians—came within reach during the reigns of Constantine (c. 272–337) and Theodosius (347–395). These Christian emperors set the scene for Augustine (354–430) and his epic view of history as a contest between "two cities," the heavenly city of God and the earthly city of temporal human existence and politics. According to Augustine, human life and politics can only be rightly ordered and virtuous if they place love of God at the center. If not, self-love takes over, and morality and politics are reduced to pride, the quest for worldly honor, and the drive to dominate others (*libido dominandi*).[27] This does not mean that Christians should abstain from politics, because it is important to secure "tranquility of order" and "well-ordered concord" as far as possible in the earthly city. Christians help stabilize and protect social institutions while realizing that the results will be far from true virtue.[28] The heavenly city is "a captive and a stranger in the earthly city" although it obeys the earthly city's laws in order to secure the common life of both cities in this world.[29]

When Constantine and Theodosius accepted Christianity, the situation of the church improved. Constantine granted Christianity full legal protection, and Theodosius went so far as to outlaw traditional Roman religious cults and practices. This fact, combined with the assaults on the empire from Germanic invaders going on during Augustine's lifetime, gave Christians powerful incentive to join in defense of the Roman regime.

Augustine does not have a systematic theory of war and discusses justice and injustice in war mainly in the context of other subjects, such as defending the consistency of the Old and New Testaments, or giving advice to Christians serving in political office or the military. Yet Augustine expresses three basic criteria for going to war that become formative for the later tradition on war, especially as elaborated in the thirteenth century by Thomas Aquinas. These are the goals of peace, lawful authority, and a right (loving) intention. Preserving the peace requires punishing crime and aggression, according to Augustine. As he writes to a Christian general, "Your primary aim should be peace; war should be fought only out of necessity in order to ensure that God will remove the cause and allow all to live in peace."[30] Civil authorities have the right to declare war because their authority comes from God; ordinary soldiers are called to obey. Yet the Christian combatant must always be guided by an intention of love, not retaliation or hatred.

Different from a more typical modern Christian rationale for war, Augustine does not direct the loving intention toward the vulnerable objects of unjust aggression. Instead, he focuses on the one killed, arguing problematically that killing in war should be seen as loving punishment. A favorite simile is a father punishing a child. Those with earthly authority to wage war can and should punish with the same fatherly "goodwill."[31] Needless to say, this is not only counterintuitive but offensive to modern conceptions of parental love. As if aware of the implausibility of portraying killing as a direct expression of charity, Augustine offers another justification, which is that, even while engaged in killing, one can still preserve an inward intention of love.[32] Jesus's love command is a "precept with regard to the preparation of the heart, and not with regard to the visible performance of the deed."[33]

Yet to posit such a disjunction between one's inner moral outlook and virtues and one's commanded outward action is to fragment the self and split qualities of Christian character from the Christian way of life. The dangerous consequences of this kind of argument are quickly seen in the reality of what today are known as "post-traumatic stress disorder" and "moral injury," often suffered by soldiers precisely because the conduct of war threatens their sense of personal and moral integrity.[34]

Augustine fails to confront the genuine difficulty entailed in arguing that love and war can be reconciled. If it is true that just peace requires both charity and justice, then justification of war will always involve moral ambiguity and even contradiction. Killing is patently incompatible with love of neighbor and the example of Jesus, even if Jesus's example and teaching also urge us to take risks to help those in mortal danger. For CST, if killing is defensible in some rare cases, it must also be recognized that it will involve a mixture of good and evil, justice and injustice, even if the choice seems a forced one and the least evil among unsatisfactory alternatives.

Thomas Aquinas (1225–1274) was born in Italy under the Holy Roman Empire of Frederick II. Although he joined the Dominicans, a mendicant order of preachers; taught at the University of Paris; and was an adviser to the pope, he came from a family of knights and military men. He lived and wrote at a time when the thinking of Aristotle was being introduced into European intellectual life. Bringing together the philosophy of Aristotle and the theology of Augustine, Aquinas accomplished a remarkably comprehensive systematization of Christian theology and ethics, the *Summa Theologiae*. His approach to war is more internally coherent than that of Augustine, but it also fails to reconcile killing in war with the Christian virtue of love in a successful and convincing way.

Aquinas raises several objections to the morality of war, including the teachings of Jesus. He then invokes Augustine and the New Testament to argue that war can be justified if and only if certain conditions are met. "In order for a war to be just three things are necessary": the authority of the sovereign,[35] a just cause, and a right intention aiming to advance the good.[36] The most important difference between Augustine and Aquinas is that Aquinas puts the emphasis on the common good ("common weal"), not on punishment in itself. Although he quotes Augustine's characterization of war as punishment, this is not a point Aquinas develops. Instead, elaborating both on right intention and on lawful authority, he compares public authorities who defend "the common weal against internal disturbances, when they punish evildoers" to those who declare war to defend "the common weal against external enemies." The necessary "rightful intention" for going to war is to "intend the advancement of good, or the avoidance of evil."[37]

Like Augustine, Aquinas has difficulty bringing the love command into a coherent relation to the justification of war. Rather than trying to argue that love is operative in killing itself, he adopts the strategy of saying love does not apply in the circumstances of war. Jesus's instruction "not to resist evil" (Matt. 5:39) does not apply in situations of injustice.[38] "Such like precepts, as Augustine observes (De Serm. Dom. in Monte i. 19), should always be borne in readiness of mind, so that we be ready to obey them, and, if necessary, to refrain from resistance or self-defense. Nevertheless it is necessary sometimes for a man to act otherwise for the common good, or for the good of those with whom he is fighting."[39]

In the case of war, it seems especially difficult to reconcile the requirements of the common good (measured by justice) with those of the gospel (inspired by charity). Aquinas distances love from killing by arguing that exceptionless embodiment of Christlike love is assigned to a special class of Christians, the clergy, who are not or should not be involved in war at all. Clerics and bishops must not fight, because "warlike pursuits . . . hinder the mind very much from the contemplation of Divine things." The clergy have a special vocation to imitate the nonviolence of Christ and must do so literally.[40]

Aquinas's approach to the morality of war is more systematic than that of Augustine and more coherent because it is easier to give a reasonable justice-based defense of killing than an evangelical charity-based one. Yet some ambivalence around the role of love in relation to war can be detected in the way Aquinas brackets the practical enactment of charity for warriors, and divides the church into two classes in order to accommodate in a Christian political perspective what seems both to be mandated by justice and prohibited by charity.

The Christian tradition of just war certainly expands beyond Augustine and Aquinas, and there is a significant time gap between Aquinas and modern CST.[41] Yet these two major figures provide the essential framework within which Christian just war thinking is structured today. Although Augustine admirably keeps love or charity close to the center of the Christian life no matter what the circumstances, he ends in justifying some dubious practices in the name of love, including killing. Aquinas commendably avoids portraying killing as in itself loving; however, he ends by exempting some Christians from the most basic requirement of the gospel. Both seek a straightforward justification of war (given certain limiting and constraining conditions) and fail to recognize that, considered in relation to the love command, war presents a moral dilemma that is difficult if not impossible to resolve.

John Courtney Murray, one of the foremost Catholic transmitters of just war tradition, writes in the wake of the two "World Wars," at a time when the focus of just war theory was on conflicts among nation-states and when such conflicts seemed like regrettable necessities from the standpoint of thinkers in the victorious Allied nations. Yet Murray is cognizant of the horrors of war, even if he thinks justice and peace require resort to arms "in the extremity."[42] He grants there is a "paradox" in fitting violence within the pursuit of justice, a paradox that "is heightened when this effort takes place at the interior of the Christian religion of love."[43]

Sometimes armed coercion appears the only way to secure the conditions of a just peace, but violence and killing are also contrary to the very meaning of a just peace. In fact, in Murray's view, "the whole Catholic doctrine of war is hardly more than a *Grenzmoral*, an effort to establish on a minimal basis of reason a form of human action, the making of war, that remains always fundamentally irrational."[44] If so, and Murray's verdict seems indisputable, then it is all the more important that all stakeholders in conflict situations strive passionately, practically, and politically to discover and implement nonviolent ways of transforming conflicts and building just peace.

In fact, just war theory itself has seen an evolution in this regard, with the emergence since the early 2000s (and in light of the US invasions of Iraq and Afghanistan) of a new category of just war thinking called *jus post bellum* (justice after war).[45] The essential contribution of this innovation is to make just war thinking more accountable to the certainty that armed force devastates the necessary conditions of social and political society, and it typically creates conditions that make reconstruction toward a just peace after war difficult if not impossible. If armed force is contemplated, justified by analysts, and undertaken, part of the moral responsibility of warriors is to plan in advance of war and during its prosecution for the most just outcome, with the least harm to noncombatants and to the social infrastructure, so that rebuilding will be possible and successful. *Jus post bellum* standards of war incorporate considerations of postwar justice, such as "acknowledgment of wrongdoing, apologies, punishments, forgiveness, and amnesty."[46] *Jus post bellum* extends into transitional justice after the war, and a restoration phase as reconciliation and reconstruction proceeds.

On the whole, as Gerard Powers argues, Catholic tradition on war has become extremely restrictive, "providing a moral rationale for opposing resort to military force" rather than for validating it, as well as limiting force when it does occur, and improving chances for "a sustainable peace."[47] The obvious practical and political question is whether the new, more stringent theory of just war has any real effect on political and military decision-makers. The evidence is mixed. In their 2017 posturing and threats regarding a nuclear exchange, US President Donald Trump and North Korean Supreme Leader Kim Jong-un did not in any apparent way refer to just war constraints. Yet since the mid-2000s, the US Army has implemented a policy of "counterinsurgency" that aims to spare civilian lives and build bridges with local communities, and the Department of Defense and Department of State have incorporated peacebuilding initiatives.[48]

Recent Catholic Social Teaching

Official Catholic teaching similarly has become highly critical of armed force and reluctant to validate it, especially after the Second Vatican Council. During World War I, Benedict XV, an Italian, was already leading the way to nonviolent conflict mediation and peace.[49] Elected in 1914 by a bare two-thirds majority in a contested vote, Benedict XV was from the start eager to overcome divisions. He had a background in ecclesial diplomacy and had served as the undersecretary to the papal secretary of state. He had also witnessed the corrosive effects of church politics, which resulted in the defeat of his mentor in the 1903 papal election. At the time of his own election, there was a breach between Modernists and anti-Modernists, leading Benedict to write his first encyclical on ecclesial hostility and name-calling. There he also addressed the devastation of war, around which there was additional division among Catholics internationally. The effort to bring peace among warring nations consumed the first four years of Benedict's papacy. In 1917, when the two alliances were at a standoff, he called for an end to the war by compromise, calling the conflict "useless carnage." His diplomatic efforts did not see success, but he overextended Vatican resources in the creation of relief programs. Among these were the Christmas truce of 1914, a Vatican-run project to reunite prisoners of war with their families, and relief efforts for war-torn areas.

During the World War II pontificate of Pius XII, Christians in general participated in and supported anti-Semitic attitudes and policies. Bishops were active participants or complicit, and Pius XII did not mount the direct rejection of anti-Jewish persecution for which justice and the gospel indubitably called.[50] He was overly concerned to maintain neutrality and pastoral openness toward all Catholic parties to the conflict and to remain at the level of generality seemingly required by "universal" teaching.[51] Nevertheless, Pius XII did teach that both charity and justice require dedication to the ideal of peace.

At the same time, Pius XII followed "mainstream" Christian tradition in proposing the application of just war to validate the right of nations to defend themselves from attack. Governments have the right to demand the participation of citizens. Thus, in the case of a just war, "a Catholic citizen cannot invoke his own conscience in order to refuse to serve and fulfill those duties the law imposes."[52] Pius XII does not support the independent right of individuals to make an evaluation of justice. Yet he goes further than past tradition by denying individual states the right to resort to arms in order to vindicate wrongs or redress violations of legal rights. He also calls for international conventions to condemn research on and use of nuclear weapons and to establish arms control.[53]

The first encyclical to be devoted entirely to the subject of war, *Pacem in terris* (1963), was written in the middle of the Cold War by Pius's successor, John XXIII.[54] This pope marks a decisive shift in the tradition toward nonviolence and peacemaking by diplomacy and social justice initiatives, if not entirely toward pacifism. John XXIII's outlook and style is pastoral,

ecumenical, and progressive. In the opening address of *Pacem in terris*, he famously calls on "all men of good will" to come together around historically
attainable ideals of peace with justice. Pope John repudiates the arms race for
perpetrating a climate of fear, international mistrust, and radical economic
injustices. No justice is possible when wealthy, militarized nations dedicate
disproportionate resources to the arms race while ignoring the needs of the
poor. Because of "the terrible destructive force of modern arms . . . it is hardly
possible to imagine that in the atomic era war could be used as an instrument
of justice."[55] "Justice, then, right reason and humanity urgently demand that
the arms race should cease," that nuclear stockpiles be progressively disman-
tled and nuclear weapons banned. The "true and solid peace of nations" must
rest "on mutual trust alone," not on equalization of destructive capacity and
the fear it intentionally engenders.[56] Drew Christiansen observes that the
approach to peace of *Pacem in terris* is distinctively Catholic in that it bases
peace on justice, an approach to be confirmed by Vatican II.[57] "The encyclical advances the view that peace consists in the promotion, safeguarding, and
defense of human rights at every level of social life, whether interpersonal,
social, political, international, or global. Peace consists in the realization of
the common good conceived as the realization of rights." This includes or
implies addressing issues such as income inequality, educational disparities,
gender and racial discrimination, and political participation. For a complete
Catholic approach to just peace today, however, further themes would need
to be added, such as the effectiveness of nonviolence and the role of political
forgiveness.[58]

The Second Vatican Council produced *Gaudium et spes* (*The Pastoral
Constitution on the Church in the Modern World*), which reiterates the Catholic
premise of the possibility of just use of force but continues to foreground and
strengthen the presumption against war, a trend that has only increased in subsequent decades. The Council still upholds the right of nations to "legitimate
defense once every means of peaceful settlement has been exhausted." But for
the first time, the right to conscientious objection is explicitly asserted. Laws
should make "humane provisions for the case of those who refuse to bear
arms, provided however that they accept some other form of service to the
human community."[59] Nuclear attacks, which inevitably and purposefully
target civilians, are unequivocally denounced. "Any act of war aimed indis-
criminately at the destruction of entire cities or of extensive areas along with
their population is a crime against God and man himself. It merits unequivocal and unhesitating condemnation."[60] The Council repeats John XXIII's
demand for progressive disarmament, to be carried out under the supervision
of an international authority with "effective power" to safeguard peace, because true peace "must be born of mutual trust among nations."[61] The heart
of *Gaudium et spes*, however, is not a condemnation of social injustice, but

the hope that positive peace and justice can result from human cooperation inspired by the gospel and humanity's highest values. The Council calls Christians "to 'practice the truth in love' (Eph. 4:15) and to join with all true peacemakers in pleading for peace and bringing it about."[62]

The integral connection of peace and justice was affirmed perhaps most radically and influentially by Paul VI, who declared, "If you want peace, work for justice."[63] And most famously, "The new name for peace is development."[64] When conflict has occurred or is occurring, then "reconciliation is the way to peace," remembering that peace and hence true and lasting reconciliation require social justice.[65]

In a line that was to be repeated by every successive pope up to and including Francis, Paul VI exhorts the United Nations early in his pontificate, "No more war, war never again! Peace, it is peace which must guide the destinies of people and of all mankind."[66] He dares to hope (with *Gaudium et spes* calling us to "strain every muscle") that war will eventually be prohibited by international law.[67] At the very least, and leading the way, "the Church cannot accept violence, especially the force of arms."[68] But nonviolence is not exclusive to the Catholic Church or Christianity. As Mahatma Gandhi envisioned, nonviolence can become a national and international way of action toward peace.[69]

Yet the legitimacy of armed force to resist grave offenses to human dignity and the common good is still neither excluded by Paul VI nor by the tradition as a whole.[70] That being said, John XXIII, *Gaudium et spes*, and Paul VI do not see violence as a means of resolving violence that is likely to be successful, much less just. They agree that the only true way to peace is to engage social partners constructively to realize economic, social, and political rights by means of the rule of law and participatory institutions. Benedict XV, Pius XII, John XXIII, and Paul VI all had personal experience of war and the suffering and lasting devastation that are not incidental to war but part of war's very means and purpose. They were therefore extremely critical of "the utility of widespread violence," even "at the service of defending or restoring an order of justice."[71] They may not go so far as to say that war is unequivocally wrong in principle, but they reject the de facto historical presumption that war is a normal way to deal with conflict. They renew and reinforce a presumption against war as a just and effective means of winning political objectives. They give the self-defeating nature of violence and the vocation of peace much more emphasis than any validation of armed force.

This trend not only continues but gains momentum with the pontificates of John Paul II, Benedict XVI, and Francis. John Paul II insists that "violence is evil," "a lie," and "the enemy of justice."[72] He follows predecessors in what has become a papal refrain: as a practical matter, whatever the theoretical justifications, violence leads to more injustice. When specific uses of violence are on the table, including military interventions in the Persian Gulf and a US invasion of Iraq, the pope rejects war as "a decline for humanity" and "a defeat for humanity."[73] Furthering the theme of just peace as involving economic participation, John Paul II titles his 1987 World Day of Peace message "Development and Solidarity: Two Keys to Peace."[74] Yet, like the popes of the two world wars, John Paul II is influenced by specific instances of widespread violence that blight his own era. The 1990s saw humanitarian disasters met with international apathy or ineffectiveness in Rwanda, Somalia, and the former Yugoslavia. Hence this pope validates the new concept of "humanitarian intervention," recognized by the United Nations in the form of a "Responsibility to Protect" in 2004.[75] As John Paul asserts regarding Bosnia, when "populations are succumbing to the attacks of an unjust aggressor, States no longer have a 'right to indifference.' It seems clear that their duty is to disarm this aggressor, if all other means have proved ineffective."[76] Again mindful of recent events, John Paul allows for a nation's right of defense against terrorism.[77] Yet how we are to disarm and defend remains an open and challenging question that Benedict deepens.

Following John Paul II, Benedict XVI endorses humanitarian intervention under the rubric "responsibility to protect."[78] A caveat is added in *Caritas in veritate* (2009), however, that the responsibility to protect must be implemented "in innovative ways."[79] Specifically refusing violence and embracing gospel nonviolence, Benedict calls "love your enemies" the gospel's "magna carta."[80] On a visit to Cameroon, he reaches across religious borders, stating that all genuine religion rejects violence in any form.[81] "Violence never comes from God."[82]

Like Paul VI and John Paul II, Benedict is clear that peace cannot exist without justice: respect for human rights, economic equity, and political participation. He repeatedly confirms this justice aspect of Catholic teaching on war in his World Day of Peace messages (2009, 2010) and makes justice the centerpiece of *Caritas in veritate*, an encyclical written to commemorate *Populorum progressio*.

Pope Francis carries forth this trajectory by summoning international parties in conflict to seek peace by dialogue, reconciliation, negotiation, and compromise. He does not see war as a "necessity."[83] Beyond a mere "defeat" or "decline," he calls war the "suicide of humanity."[84] Francis appeals repeatedly for nonproliferation and disarmament, especially of nuclear arms. Taking forward themes of *Pacem in terris*, he denounces not only the use of nuclear weapons but also the possession.[85] When Francis is confronted by the prospect of a 2013 military "humanitarian" intervention in Syria by US and French "superpowers," he is insistent that "War brings on war! Violence brings on violence."[86] Instead Francis leads a peace vigil for Syria at the Vatican that attracts over one hundred thousand people.

Although Francis does not explicitly reject armed humanitarian intervention or self-defense against terrorism, he is strong on the importance of putting all possible efforts into nonviolent conflict mediation, negotiation, and diplomacy. Even in the case of the so-called Islamic State, or ISIS, he calls for stopping aggression through some means less than lethal force. "The means by which he may be stopped should be evaluated. To stop the unjust aggressor is licit, but we nevertheless need to remember how many times, using this excuse of stopping an unjust aggressor, the powerful nations have dominated other peoples, made a real war of conquest."[87] Even with ISIS, he says to "never close the door" on dialogue.[88]

To date, this pope's most extended and important statement on peace is his 2017 World Day of Peace message promoting nonviolence as "a style of politics for peace." The point of departure for this message is the practical reality of pervasive political and societal violence, and the futility of violence—however justified in principle—in bringing lasting peace. The message itself is practical, political, and alliance building. Active nonviolence is not only faithful to the example of Jesus, it is also "a way of showing that unity is truly more powerful and more fruitful than conflict."[89] Compassionate and peacebuilding efforts against injustice and in favor of war's victims are "typical of many religious traditions . . . . Let us never tire of repeating: 'The name of God cannot be used to justify violence. Peace alone is holy. Peace alone is holy, not war!'"[90]

In summary, recent CST is a practical more than a theoretical response to the moral dilemma of killing. At the most fundamental level, the popes are committed to embodying the gospel of compassion, forgiveness, reconciliation, and peace with justice. The transformation of conflicts through practices that best represent these values or virtues is their most important commitment and the one they most embody, advocate, and promote through words and symbolic actions. Distinctive of the post–Vatican II popes is their outreach to all cultures and religions, aware not only that conflicts reach across boundaries of identity, culture, religion, and geography but that diverse people and faiths bring indispensable resources for a more just and peaceful world.

At the same time, and reflecting their practical experience and awareness, the popes know not only that violence feeds cycles of violence but that radical assaults on human life and dignity are a present and grave form of historical evil for which Christians bear moral and political responsibility. Although nonviolent alternatives are not only ideal but obligatory, a dilemma arises if these alternatives are unsuccessful immediate responses to concrete instances of rape, torture, killing, and massacres or genocide. It may be inferred from the paradoxical nature of papal teaching (as vehemently and repeatedly ruling out violence from a gospel perspective while secondarily and more briefly gesturing toward the limited justice of armed force) that these evils confront Christians with a moral dilemma. On the one hand, violence not only violates the dignity of life and the example of Jesus, it is a notoriously unsuccessful way to accomplish lasting peace. On the other hand, refusal to resort to armed force against extreme violations of human dignity threatens to turn those with power to intervene into "guilty bystanders" (in the phrase of Thomas Merton). The modern popes never endorse specific instances of armed force. Yet their refusal to rule out self-defense and humanitarian intervention entirely signals their awareness that even attempts to live out gospel nonviolence can be morally ambiguous. They clearly envision their role as Christian leaders and teachers, not as elaborating justifications of armed force but as maximizing the visibility, appeal, uniting power, and effectiveness of nonviolence and just peace.[91] This is the essential significance of the reign of God for a broken world, a world desperately in need of a new nonviolent politics of change and hope.

Notes

1. In Genesis 2:23, the first man recognizes the second human being God has made, a woman, by exclaiming, "This at last is bone of my bones and flesh of my flesh." Although later interpreters infer that this refers to the sexual union of woman and man in marriage, the text does not state this. The most significant fact about the woman is that Adam finds her a more suitable partner than the animals God has previously made. They are the two first human beings, and the creation of the woman establishes human society, based on the common nature of all human beings. This was recognized in fact by John Calvin (*Commentary on Genesis*, chap. 30).

2. See Center for Systemic Peace, "Global Conflicts Trends," 2017, especially figures 3 and 8, http://www.systemicpeace.org/conflicttrends.html.

3. Pope Francis, "Nonviolence: A Style of Politics for Peace," World Day of Peace Message, 2017, no. 2, https://w2.vatican.va/content/francesco/en/messages/peace/documents/papa-francesco_20161208_messaggio-l-giornata-mondiale-pace-2017.html.

4. Francis, "Nonviolence," no. 6.

5. Kenneth R. Himes, "Peacebuilding and Catholic Social Teaching," in *Peacebuilding: Catholic Theology, Ethics, and Praxis* (Maryknoll, NY: Orbis, 2010), 269.

6. See James F. Childress, "Just-War Theories: The Bases, Interrelations, Priorities and Functions of Their Criteria," *Theological Studies* 39, no. 3 (1978): 427–45.

7. United States Conference of Catholic Bishops, *The Challenge of Peace: God's Promise and Our Response* (1983), no. 3, www.usccb.org/upload/challenge-peace-gods-promise-our-response-1983.pdf.

8. For a critical overview of the complicated evidence for the views of early Christian writers, as well as of the practices of ordinary Christians, see Ronald J. Sider, *The Early Church on Killing: A Comprehensive Sourcebook on War, Abortion, and Capital Punishment* (Grand Rapids, MI: Baker Academic, 2012).

9. Sider, 181–84, 192.

10. See Sider, 190–91; and David G. Hunter, "A Decade of Research on Early Christians and Military Service," *Religious Studies Review* 18 (1992): 87–94.

11. For Tertullian on swearing, see *On Idolatry* 11, p. 67; on nonviolence, see *Apology* 37, p. 45.

12. Sider, *Early Church on Killing*, 174, citing *Against Marcion* 3.21.

13. *An Answer to the Jews* 6, p. 157.

14. *Against Marcion* 1, p. 346.

15. *Apology* 32, pp. 42–43.

16. *Against Celsus* 8.74, p. 510.

17. *Against Celsus* 4.82, p. 249.

18. *Against Celsus* 8.73, p. 509.

19. David Cortright, *Peace: A History of Movements and Ideas* (Cambridge: Cambridge University Press, 2008).

20. Frederick Russell, *War in the Middle Ages* (Cambridge: Cambridge University Press, 1975), 34. See also Thomas Massaro and Thomas A. Shannon, *Catholic Perspectives on Peace and War* (London: Sheed & Ward, 2003), 16.

21. Alexander Gillespie, *A History of the Laws of War: Volume 3: The Customs and Laws of War with Regards to Arms Control* (London: Bloomsbury, 2011), 59–60. According to Gillespie, these restraints did not have much practical effect on customary ways of defeating an enemy, such as starvation by siege and despoilation of property.

22. *An Essay on War* is included in *Bellum: Two Statements on the Nature of War* (Barre, MA: Imprint Society, 1972), 11–37. See also *The Complaint of Peace by Erasmus* (New York: Scholars' Facsimiles and Reprints, 1946).

23. On this point, see James T. Johnson, "Two Kinds of Pacifism: Opposition to the Political Use of Force in the Renaissance-Reformation Period," *Journal of Religious Ethics* 12 (1984): 39–60.

24. *Erasmus: Handbook of the Militant Christian*, trans. John P. Dolan (Notre Dame, IN: Fides Publishers, 1962), 13.

25. *Erasmus: Handbook of the Militant Christian*, 32. The gospel teaches "in decisive words" that "we must do good to them who use us ill." Further, not only the apostles, but "all Christian people," "the whole body," should be "entire and perfect" (33).

26. Mennonite Central Committee US website, https://mcc.org/.

27. Augustine, *City of God*, XIV.28, IV.4, XIX.17.

28. *City of God*, XIX.10, 12, 13.

29. *City of God*, XIX.17.

30. Augustine, "Letter 189, to Boniface," no. 6.

31. Augustine, *On the Sermon on the Mount*, I.1.20.63.

32. Augustine, *Letter to Faustus*, XXII.76; and "Letter 138: To Marcellinus."

33. Augustine, *Letter to Faustus*, XXII.76; "Letter 138: To Marcellinus;" and *On the Sermon on the Mount*, 1.19.59 and 58.

34. Cf. David Grossman, *On Killing*; Tobias Winright and E. Ann Jeschke, "Combat and Confession: Just War and Moral Injury," in *Can War Be Just in the 21st Century? Ethicists Engage the Tradition*, ed. Tobias Winright and Laurie Johnston (Maryknoll, NY: Orbis, 2015), 169–87; and Pristo R. Hernandez, US Army Command and General Staff College, "Killing in War as a Persisting Problem of Conscience," *Journal of Catholic Social Thought* 11, no. 1 (2013): 203–28.

35. In *Summa Theologiae* II–II.Q64.a2, Aquinas also justifies the killing of a criminal to safeguard the common good. (The same point is made in the *Summa Contra Gentiles,* bk. 3, pt. 2, 148.4.) In *Summa Theologiae* II–II.Q64.a3, he stipulates that this is the prerogative of a public authority only, not of a private individual.

36. Aquinas, *Summa* II–II.Q40.1.

37. Aquinas, *Summa* II–II.Q40.1.

38. See Schlabach's argument in chapter 1 of this volume on how this gospel passage has a better translation as "do not resist in an evil way" or "do not violently resist."

39. Aquinas, *Summa* II–II.Q40.a1.r.obj.2.

40. Aquinas, *Summa* II–II.Q40.a2; II–II.Q64.a4.

41. Just war theory was endorsed officially by the Roman Catholic Church in the *Catechism of the Catholic Church,* no. 2309 (1992, http://archeparchy.ca/wcm-docs/docs/catechism-of-the-catholic-church.pdf). For further background, see Massaro and Shannon, *Catholic Perspectives on War and Peace;* and Tobias Winright and Laurie Johnston, eds. *Can War Be Just in the Twenty-First Century? Ethicists Engage the Tradition* (Maryknoll, NY: Orbis, 2015).

42. John Courtney Murray, "Remarks on the Moral Problem of War," *Theological Studies* 20 (1949): 56.

43. Murray, 57.

44. Murray, 52.

45. See Mark J. Allman and Tobias L. Winright, *After the Smoke Clears: The Just War Tradition and Post War Justice* (Maryknoll, NY: Orbis, 2010); and "Growing Edges of Just War Theory: *Jus ante bellum, jus post bellum,* and Imperfect Justice," *Journal of the Society of Christian Ethics* 32, no. 2 (2012): 173–91.

46. Allman and Winright, *After the Smoke Clears,* 107–16.

47. Gerard F. Powers, "From an Ethics of War to an Ethics of Peacebuilding," in *From Just War to Modern Peace Ethics* (ed. Heinz-Gerhard Justenhoven and William A. Barbieri Jr. (Berlin: De Gruyter, 2012), 292.

48. See Joseph H. Felter and Jacob N. Shapiro, "Limiting Civilian Casualties as Part of a Winning Strategy: The Case of Courageous Restraint," *Daedalus* (Winter 2017): 44–58; and Maryann Cusimano Love, "What Kind of Peace Do We Seek?," in *Peacebuilding: Catholic Theology, Ethics, and Praxis,* ed. Robert J. Schreiter, R. Scott Appleby, and Gerard F. Powers (Maryknoll, NY: Orbis, 2010), 56–91.

49. John F. Pollard, *Benedict XV (1912–1922) and the Pursuit for Peace* (London: Bloomsbury, 2000).

50. For the context of Pius XII, his outlook, and his teachings on war, see John P. Langan, "The Christmas Messages of Pius XII (1939–1945: Catholic Social Teaching in a Time of Extreme Crisis)," in *Modern Catholic Social Teaching: Commentaries and Interpretations,* ed. Kenneth R. Himes (Washington, DC: Georgetown University Press, 2017), 183–98.

51. Langan, "Christmas Messages," 197.

52. Pius XII, Christmas Radio Message, December 23, 1956.

53. Pius XII, "Nuclear Weapons and Armament Control," Christmas Message, December 24, 1955.

54. This is the only war encyclical as of 2017. See Drew Christiansen, "Commentary on *Pacem in terris (Peace on Earth),*" in Himes, *Modern Catholic Social Teaching,* 226–52.

55. John XXIII, *Pacem in terris*, no. 127.

56. John XXIII, nos. 112, 113.

57. Christiansen, "*Commentary on Pacem in terris*," 232. The emphasis on justice and human rights may be distinctively Catholic, but it is not uniquely so. See especially Glen H. Stassen, *Just Peacemaking: Transforming Initiatives for Justice and Peace* (Louisville, KY: Westminster John Knox, 1992); and the Just Peace initiative of the World Council of Churches.

58. Christiansen, "*Commentary on Pacem in terris*," 232, 233.

59. *Gaudium et spes (Pastoral Constitution on the Church in the Modern World)*, 1965, no. 79.

60. *Gaudium et spes*, no. 80.

61. *Gaudium et spes*, no. 82. The expense and danger of weapons, and their corrosion of international relations, was reiterated by Paul VI (Paul VI, Address to the General Assembly of the United Nations, October 4, 1965, no. 23).

62. *Gaudium et spes*, no. 78.

63. Paul VI, 1972 World Day of Peace Message; citing the 1971 Synod of Bishops' *Justitio in mundi*, no. 6.

64. Paul VI, *Populorum progressio*, no. 87.

65. Paul VI, 1975 World Day of Peace Message.

66. Paul VI, 1965 Address to the United Nations General Assembly.

67. Paul VI, 1965 Address to the United Nations General Assembly.

68. Paul VI, *Evangelium nuntiani*, no. 37, 1975.

69. Paul VI, 1976 World Day of Peace Message.

70. Paul VI, *Populorum progressio*, no. 31.

71. Himes, "Peacebuilding," 279.

72. John Paul II, Homily at Drogheda, Ireland, 18–20, 1979; quoted in the 2006 *Compendium of the Social Doctrine of the Church*, no. 496. The pope further comments that "violence destroys what it claims to defend: the dignity, the life, the freedom of human beings."

73. John Paul II, Address to the Diplomatic Corps, no. 7, 1991, and Address to the Diplomatic Corps, no. 4, 2003, respectively.

74. John Paul II, 1987 World Day of Peace Message "Development and Solidarity: Two Keys to Peace." He titles his 2002 World Day of Peace message "No Peace without Justice, and No Justice without Forgiveness," which extends Paul VI's phrase "no peace without justice" in a way that clarifies justice as restorative and further illuminates the meaning of just peace.

75. John Paul II, 2002 World Day of Peace Message, no. 11.

76. John Paul II, Address to the Diplomatic Corps, January 16, 1993.

77. John Paul II, 2002 World Day of Peace Message, no. 5.

78. Benedict XVI, Address to the General Assembly of the United Nations, New York, 2008.

79. Benedict XVI, *Caritas in veritate*, no. 7, 2009.

80. Angelus Address, 2007; see also Good Friday Message, 2011.

81. Benedict XVI, "The Saving Message of the Gospel Needs to Be Proclaimed," 2009.

82. Benedict XVI, Good Friday Message, 2011.

83. Pope Francis, "Message to Sant' Egidio International Peace Meeting in Antwerp," *Zenit*, September 7–9, 2014.

84. "Pope Francis: War Is the Suicide of Humanity," Vatican Radio, June 6, 2013, http://www.news.va/en/news/pope-francis-war-is-the-suicide-of-humanity.

85. See Gerald O'Connell, "Nuclear Disarmament Now A 'Moral Imperative' As Pope Francis Rejects Deterrence," *America*, November 13, 2017, https://www.americamagazine.org/politics-society/2017/11/13/nuclear-disarmament-now-moral-imperative-pope-francis-rejects.

86. Pope Francis, Angelus Address, August 31, 2013.

87. Pope Francis, 2014 Press Conference, during return flight from South Korea, as quoted in Francis X. Rocca, "Pope Talks Airstrikes In Iraq, His Health, Possible US Visit," *Catholic News Service*, August 18, 2014, https://www.ncronline.org/news/world/pope-talks-airstrikes-iraq-his-health-possible-us-visit?_ga=2.180740327.1546312816.1511305791-2123628133.1507130389.

88. "Dialogue with Terrorists Is Almost Impossible, But The Door Must Always Remain Open" (La Stampa, Pubblicato il 25/11/2014).

89. Francis, "World Day of Peace," 2017, no. 6.

90. Francis, no. 4.

91. An important line of development here is the promotion of nonviolent political action as feasible and effective, not simply a utopian ideal. See Erica Chenoweth and Maria J. Stephan, *Why Civil Resistance Works: The Strategic Logic of Nonviolent Conflict* (New York: Columbia University Press, 2011); Maria J. Stephan, Sadaf Lakhani, and Nadia Naviwala, "Aid to Civil Society: A Movement Mindset," special report, US Institute of Peace, February 23, 2015; Maria J. Stephan, "Non-violent Strategies to Reduce Terrorism and Violent Extremism," *Concilium* (2017/4): 138–44; and Maria J. Stephan "Nonviolent Options and Just Peace," Keynote Address, University of San Diego, October 6, 2017.

3

JUST PEACE ETHIC
A Virtue-Based Approach

ELI S. McCARTHY

In this chapter, I offer a virtue-based approach to a just peace ethic, complementing the first two chapters on the gospels and just peace as well as the development of just peace in the Christian tradition, particularly Catholic social teaching (CST). First, I explain why virtue is an essential component of a just peace ethic. Second, I discuss some just peace virtues and suggest some ways to acquire these virtues for transformative praxis. Third, I draw on these virtues and describe the guiding norms of a virtue-based just peace ethic.

Context

As we saw elaborated in the earlier chapter on the gospels and just peace (chapter 1), it is God's promise that "justice and peace shall embrace."[1] This image is the embodiment of God's vision for our world—God's shalom. "Shalom" is often translated as "peace," but its Hebrew roots imply a deeper meaning of peace that goes beyond cessation of violence toward a holistic vision of well-being, healing, and restoration involving all areas of social and economic life. This active work of God calls people to likewise participate and reminds us both that peace requires justice-making *and* justice requires peacemaking.

Jesus Christ, the presence and manifestation of God's love on Earth, concretizes these themes in a set of formative and core practices. Jesus makes it clear that he was not in favor of a negative peace based on the sword but rather a positive peace based on human dignity and social justice.[2] Jesus models the way of just peace by becoming vulnerable; inviting participation in the reign of God; caring for the outcasts; prioritizing those in urgent need; loving and forgiving enemies; challenging the religious, political, economic, and military powers; healing persons and communities; praying and fasting, along with risking and offering his life on the cross to expose and transcend both injustice and violence.[3]

Jesus centers shalom on the embodiment of mercy and compassion in the Good Samaritan story. Jesus draws us to this "righteousness," which refers to living in accord with the will of God.[4] We know this will primarily through how Jesus lives; hence the "new commandment" from Jesus is to "love *as I have* loved you"—that is, the nonviolent love of neighbor, strangers, and enemies. With Jesus's focus on healing and reconciliation, even with enemies, we have been increasingly learning that the kind of justice Christ leans us toward is restorative justice—that is, a focus on the wounds to relationships and how to heal those wounds.[5]

In this context, most of the literature on just peace ethics focuses on practices or principles. For example, as discussed in chapter 1, Glen Stassen coordinated with other Christian theologians to develop a just peacemaking theory. This consists of a set of normative practices that are historically verifiable and that guide action in preventing war.[6]

Another example is Maryann Cusimano Love's just peace principles. She argues that these principles, based on effective practices, apply to *all* stages of conflict, including once violence has broken out. They include just cause (dignity, life, common good); right intention toward positive peace; participatory process for decision-making; right relationship: vertical (between high visibility leaders, middle range, and grassroots) and horizontal (across but within a social level) reconciliation; restoration (as material, psychological, spiritual); and sustainability.[7] She argues that unlike the practice approach, her principles always apply to all types of conflict, actors, and stages of conflict.

Jarem Sawatsky's *Justpeace Ethics* does initiate a virtue-based approach that goes beyond the prevention of war to the broader issues of conflict and harm. He argues for a just peace ethic that calls forth "means/ends consistency" or "reflexivity." The "how" must be consistent in character with the "what" we hope to accomplish if we are to in reality reach such an accomplishment.[8] That is, means and ends are reflective to the degree feelings, thoughts, and behaviors of the end sought are reflected in the means. We may not get these perfectly aligned in this world, but we should do our best in practice and expect the consequences for misalignment.[9] However, Sawatsky's approach has not yet been closely integrated with the valuable threads found in Stassen's normative practices and Cusimano Love's principles; nor does it go into detail of how we can acquire these virtues.

Need for Virtue

Stassen and Cusimano Love, as well as most of the just peace literature, besides Sawatsky, are missing adequate attention to the need for virtue. In general, virtue ethics is a teleological approach, which is based on the premise that all human action is directed toward an end. Virtue ethics also implies that the human person is oriented toward a human good, end, or *telos*. Most virtue ethicists offer a broad, complex, comprehensive, and inclusive understanding of the human good. Thus, not all but many forms of life, cultures, and ways of embodying the virtues seem compatible with the human *telos*.[10] Further, our understanding of the human good or *telos* will change and develop during our journey.[11]

In virtue ethics, the human good or end is often described as human flourishing or excellence. Human flourishing entails a life lived in accord with virtue and participation in virtuous relationships.[12] Being virtuous means having a set of related virtues that enable a person to live and act morally well, not simply to do a morally good action—that is, a proximate good.[13] Following Thomas Aquinas and William Spohn, I understand virtue as a disposition to act, desire, and feel that involves an exercise of judgment and leads to a recognizable human excellence, an instance of human flourishing.[14] Virtues are actualized and cultivated through paradigmatic or core practices.

Oriented by the gospels and overlapping with other traditions, a virtue-based approach can help us to focus on developing the character, healthy habits, virtue, and corresponding practices of a just peace ethic. Thus, we will be better motivated and prepared to creatively imagine nonviolent ways to transform conflict, to choose, and to sustain those ways through difficult situations. A virtue-based approach would amplify the development of character and the kind of imagination that engages and creatively applies, extends, and even corrects some of the practices of Stassen's just peacemaking theory as well as CST. Stassen's practices and much of CST may help prevent some wars, but a virtue-based approach would integrate and complement much of Stassen's approach to enhance the prevention and sustainable transformation of violence. Thus, it would ultimately strengthen the prevention of war as well as the capacity to defuse active wars. A virtue-based approach would also help prepare us better to orient, apply, and perhaps develop the just peace principles of Cusimano Love.

Further, a virtue-based approach will better equip us to transform not only direct violence but also structural and cultural violence.[15] By cultural violence, I mean those aspects of culture that can be used to justify or legitimate either direct or structural violence. Examples include language, conflict habits, symbols, ideology, moral frameworks, media and propaganda, racism, sexism, and generational trauma. Thus, a virtue-based approach would also cultivate persons who would better marginalize and delegitimize the use of violence or lethal force. Thus, by including just peace virtues we would act more consistently with the call from Vatican II "to strain every muscle as we work for the time when all war can be completely outlawed" and more likely get our society closer to the out-lawing of war.[16]

Examples of Virtues for a Just Peace Ethic

In the context of Vatican II's extension of the call to holiness to laity, and building on the Catholic trajectory of Franz Tillman, Bernard Haring, William Spohn, and Lisa Sowle Cahill, I want to highlight the need for a distinct and central virtue of nonviolent peacemaking, which I argued and explained in my book *Becoming Nonviolent Peacemakers*.[17] Identifying non-violence as a virtue is also consistent with non-Catholics such as Stanley Hauerwas, Mahatma Gandhi (Hindu), Abdul Ghaffar Khan (Muslim), and Martin Luther King Jr. This is not the same as pacifism understood as a rule against violence, in large part because it clearly challenges us to become bet-ter people and societies in engaging conflict. I define this virtue as a habit of realizing the goods of (1) a conciliatory love that draws enemies toward friendship and (2) the truth of our ultimate unity and equal dignity.[18]

Some corresponding practices to cultivate and actualize this virtue include prayer or meditation oriented to nonviolence, including for some creating and using an optional Eucharistic prayer with explicit references to Jesus's love of enemies; training and education in nonviolent peacemaking and re-sistance, including forming nonviolent peacemaking communities; intra/interreligious dialogue; constructive program or social uplift with particular focus on people in poverty and those who are marginalized; conflict trans-formation analysis and restorative justice approaches; engaging in nonviolent resistance and disruption movements; unarmed civilian protection; and non-violent civilian-based defense.[19]

Regarding the practice of forming nonviolent peacemaking communities, Emmanuel Katongole reflects from his experience in Africa and calls the church to recover its "identity and mission as sacrament of God's peaceable kingdom."[20] He argues that church communities must go beyond recommendations for rec-onciliation and peaceful coexistence. Instead, they must articulate and live an "explicit vision of the church as a peaceable and nonviolent community."[21]

In the context of such communities, we can better engage conflict trans-formation analysis, which is a type of meta-practice that includes attention to personal, relational, structural, and cultural dimensions of conflict.[22] Con-flict is not problematic and something merely to manage or resolve but rather is a creative opportunity for growth or transformation.[23] In contrast, conflict management or conflict resolution approaches too often legitimate violent responses or yield short-lived peace agreements between elites, as the roots of the conflict are left unaddressed. For example, the violent responses may take the form of police repression to a nonviolent social movement because they are "stirring up conflict" and the conflict needs to be "managed," or they may take the form of lethal military actions to "resolve" a conflict.

Instead, the approach to conflict as being potentially creative and constructive is important for understanding the power and strategic effectiveness of nonviolent resistance. Gene Sharp has identified key sources of power and pillars of support of oppressive regimes, on which nonviolent resistance movements should strategically focus.[24] In this approach, the resistance can achieve its political goals and shift power away from the oppressor even without a "change of heart" by the oppressor. Recent history has demonstrated that this has worked against very ruthless leaders.[25] In fact, recent research has discovered that contemporary nonviolent resistance movements have been twice as successful in achieving their political objectives as violent revolutions. Even more telling, successful nonviolent movements have led to "durable democracies" at least *ten times* (some argue thirty times) more often than so-called successful violent revolutions.[26] To the degree such nonviolent resistance movements become integrated with the virtue of nonviolent peacemaking, I suggest their success would be even higher, especially regarding durable democracy and, more significantly, a sustainable just peace.

Unarmed civilian protection entails an outside party intervening in a conflict as nonpartisan, with compassion for all parties, without violence, and with the aim of defusing violence and of creating a space for reconciliation and peacebuilding. This proven practice includes tactics such as protective presence and accompaniment, proactive engagement with armed actors, physical interposition, monitoring/documenting, modeling nonviolent behavior, connecting local persons to national and international resources, and providing safe places from violence or for restorative dialogue. For example, two unarmed Nonviolent Peaceforce officers directly saved fourteen women and children during an armed militia raid in South Sudan, when they courageously refused on three separate occasions to obey the militia's orders to leave the women and children.[27] In addition, when they accompanied women to get firewood or water because they were regularly getting sexually assaulted or raped by armed actors from all groups in the area, they reduced these incidents from regularity to zero in those areas.[28] Further, in the United States and abroad, Cure Violence has hired credible neighborhood messengers and interrupters who have lowered instances of shootings and homicides by 41–73 percent, and even down by 88 percent in the neighborhoods in which they work in Honduras.[29] Some of the forty-three organizations that offer unarmed civilian protection also include Peace Brigades International, Christian Peacemaker Teams, Meta Peace Team, the DC Peace Team, and Operation Dove, which is a Catholic version.

Civilian-based defense entails using nonviolent resistance to defend against military invasion, occupation, or coups d'état. For instance, the resisters do not necessarily physically prevent invading troops from entering their territory. Yet most people in some way participate in the resistance, taking responsibility for their defense rather than delegating it to an elite group.[30] This primarily entails noncooperation with key orders from the opponent and perhaps creation of parallel institutions or government, to the point of making it inconvenient to nearly impossible for the occupying force to benefit or even stay. Civilian-based defense has taken different forms and been developed a number of times in the past century, and some governments recently incorporated it into their defense planning. Past examples include the 1923 resistance to Wolfgang Kapp's attempted coup d'état in Germany, the Norwegian and Danish resistance against German occupation during World War II, the Czechoslovakian resistance against Soviet occupation in 1968, the Baltic countries in 1990–1991, and the Philippines in 1986.[31] Sweden, Austria, Switzerland, and Lithuania have incorporated civilian-based defense into their defense planning by providing research and development funds to create nonviolent methods to prevent military occupation.[32]

The virtue of nonviolent peacemaking or active nonviolence would also uplift other related virtues, such as mercy, humility, compassion, empathy, solidarity, and hospitality, as well as qualify key virtues such as courage and justice. For example, Thomas Aquinas understood the virtue of mercy as the greatest of the virtues that unites a person with a neighbor. Pope John Paul II describes mercy as "promoting and drawing the good from all the forms of evil existing in the world" and in persons.[33] Jim Keenan, SJ, describes mercy as the willingness to enter into the chaos of another so as to answer them in their need.[34] The virtue of mercy enables and is cultivated by the practices of listening, being present, and considering the human needs such as meaning, bonding, autonomy, and subsistence. Mercy disposes one to release the tension and possessiveness of situations by instilling a sense of gift in the actors and even a wider window or receptivity for God's grace. Mercy involves that risk of discomfort, suffering, and even death, with an orientation toward perfecting the justice of right relationship into flourishing relationship.

The virtue of humility suggested to Aquinas the practice of honoring others, due to what they have of God. Keenan describes humility as knowing the truth of one's place, going against the extremes of pride or domination and of self-deprecation.[35] Haring suggests that humility arises first from our creature-status or our being given into the world, including our dependence and limits. It also entails the grateful acknowledgment of our own dignity granted by God, including our gifts and possibilities. Humility prepares individuals to accept and offer forgiveness. Haring calls humility a cardinal virtue as it "serves as the foundation for the whole edifice of Christian virtue."[36] In turn, diplomatic efforts and negotiations would be more attentive to the genuine needs of all parties, more willing to acknowledge harm done, more open to processes of trauma-healing to better enable sustainable agreements, and more inclusive of key stakeholders such as civil society and "extremist" groups.

The virtues of compassion and empathy would also become more central. Chris Vogt argues that the virtue of compassion focuses on the suffering of specific individuals and emphasizes the affective dimension. Thus, he argues it is a prerequisite for the ability to develop the virtue of solidarity.[37] Lisa Sowle Cahill explains that the experience of being loved and forgiven by God evokes a commitment to embody the reign of God "so fully that mercy, forgiveness, and compassion precludes the very contemplation" of doing violence to another person.[38] She argues that love in Matthew's Sermon on the Mount is more a way of acting than merely an emotion; thus, it consists of paradigmatic practices such as identifying the concrete needs of victims and perpetrators.[39] Thus, she challenges the claim that we can love our enemies while we kill them.[40] Further, she argues that nonviolence and the unwillingness to harm seem virtually required by the essential Christian virtues, such as compassion.[41]

Complementing compassion is the virtue of empathy, which is the disposition to feel and imagine what others are going through—not only their suffering but also their joy, wonder, and gifts. Corresponding practices that help cultivate and express empathy include reflective listening, asking the fitting question to stir personal and social growth, and identifying feelings and needs of all parties, especially in conflict situations. Like compassion, the virtue of empathy is also central for developing the fullness of solidarity.

For Pope John Paul II, the virtue of solidarity is "a firm and persevering determination to commit oneself to the common good; that is to say to the good of all and each individual."[42] This virtue arises from Jesus's practice of prioritizing the poor and outcast, as well as from acknowledging our social nature, interdependence, and interconnectedness with all people and our common home.[43] Bill O'Neill, SJ, argues that the priority for the poor and vulnerable suggests asking "whose equal dignity is unequally threatened, or whose basic rights are most imperiled?"[44] Developing the virtue of solidarity entails "cultivating an awareness of the need to nurture a dialogical, mutually beneficial, relationship with them," with the aim of transforming the structures of society.[45] The practice of living with and caring for those in urgent need corresponds to this virtue, as does the practice of simplicity illustrated by the Catholic Worker communities. Other practices include being led by affected communities in advocacy, addressing white privilege, supporting cooperative banks, and investing in renewable resources.

In acute conflict situations, we would offer concrete solidarity not only with those who are attacked or those whose basic human rights are violated but also with those poor and vulnerable who will suffer the most if we choose to engage in the preparation for war as well as in its enactment. For instance, in the recent US wars this would include those without homes, health care, or jobs in the United States and the civilians in Iraq, Afghanistan, Syria, and Yemen, especially those disrespectfully described as "collateral damage." Further, solidarity involves concern for those who exercise lethal force or violence, thus illuminating the inconsistency of such action with their human dignity by closely examining what kind of people they are becoming and what kind of society we are becoming.[46] For instance, we would give heightened relevance to suicide rates of US soldiers, which are two to three times higher compared to the civilian population; their increasing levels of post-traumatic stress disorder and mental illness; disproportionate rates of homelessness; two to three times higher domestic violence rates; and two times higher sexual assault rates.[47] We would also give heightened relevance to incidents of murder and patterns of child abuse, sexism, and racism by soldiers. Thus, we would increasingly challenge the legitimacy of such lethal force or violence. Finally, solidarity illuminates for us that even our so-called enemies suffer dehumanization when they engage in violence.

The virtue of hospitality aims at welcoming and often restoring to the community family and friends, the stranger or outcast, those difficult to love, the enemy, new developing life, other animals, and the gift of creation as a whole.[48] Corresponding practices would include providing water and basic needs for the undocumented, providing safe haven for refugees, and creating the social conditions for significantly decreasing abortions and providing basic needs for all children.

Aquinas described the virtue of justice as the main moral virtue directed at right relations with others by rendering what is due. He points to the practices of nonmaleficence and praying for our enemies. He also argues that human law should ultimately intend human friendship.[49] The virtue of justice includes social justice, in terms of cultivating just social structures and distribution of goods. However, the virtue of nonviolent peacemaking, along with Christopher Marshall's analysis on the scriptural witness of justice, would qualify the virtue of justice to focus more clearly on restorative justice with the ultimate intention toward friendship.[50] Restorative justice would primarily aim at healing wounds such that persons are restored to participation in the community with a commitment to basic human rights. Likewise, Lúcás Chan suggests the related virtue of respect for life as key to exercising justice and expressing the fifth commandment: "do not kill."[51] Some corresponding practices for the virtue of justice would include nonviolent noncooperation with injustice, truth and reconciliation commissions, and ending the death penalty.

For Aquinas, the virtue of courage most characteristically arises in endurance rather than attack because it is more difficult to control fear rather than act aggressively. Thus, martyrdom represents its principal act and exhibits most completely the perfection of charity.[52] For Aquinas, courage involves strenuous effort to overcome obstacles to the good.[53] Hauerwas explains that courage entails the confidence that God will complete God's work in us even if our enemies take our lives.[54] Pope Francis explained that "peacemaking is much more *courageous* than warfare."[55] In turn, the virtue of nonviolent peacemaking clarifies or expands the paradigmatic practices of the virtue of courage to the practice of suffering out of reverence for the dignity of others (and self) by risking, perhaps even giving, one's life without killing. This is because killing distorts our dignity in part by shifting us away from the logic of (sacred) gift and empathy to the logic of possessiveness and often dehumanization. The scientific acknowledgment of trauma, perpetrator-induced syndrome, moral injury, and brain damage from killing also manifests this distortion and violation of our dignity.[56] Thus, although it may be a dilemma to refuse to kill in really difficult, rare situations, human flourishing and just peace norms, especially virtues; dignity; and the ever-surprising, creative dynamics unleashed by nonviolent action draw us to risk life rather than take life, especially if we are Christian. In the early 1980s, some Filipinos of the People Power movement often used the word *alaydangal* for nonviolence, which translates as "offer dignity to." These Filipinos sensed that violence in itself obscures the dignity of both victim and perpetrator, and thus by "offering dignity" through active nonviolence, they cultivated this virtue of courage. Corresponding practices would include nonviolent resistance, unarmed civilian protection, and civilian-based defense.

Acquiring Just Peace Virtues

A key challenge with a virtue-based approach is how to acquire virtues so we actually live out the transformative practices of a just peace approach, especially in conflict situations. We need more than just knowledge or teaching about practice, values, and goals. We actually need to become the people who live out transformative practices.

There are a number of ways a person and a society develop virtuous habits and structures. One of the main ways is the experience of being loved with affirmation, affection, and honesty.[57] Another way is when we have companions, friends, or intentional communities who model virtue, we often become motivated to cultivate virtue in ourselves.

However, a key part of formation in virtue, especially the particular virtues mentioned previously, is regular encounter and relationship with marginalized or oppressed communities. Miguel De La Torre explains how such communities live "en la lucha" or "in the struggle" for their family's daily bread and basic human dignity.[58] For instance, Jesus ate meals with and directly interacted with such persons while calling his disciples to do likewise.

Being in such close relationship with marginalized and oppressed communities enables us to better see the reality of injustice and violence. When we better see such reality, we are better enabled to accompany, reflect, imagine, and make wise judgments about liberating, systematic, and transformative action. Such imagination, or what John Paul Lederach calls the "moral imagination," is key to the capacity to acquire just peace virtues. He defines the moral imagination as the "capacity to imagine something rooted in the challenges of the real world yet capable of giving birth to that which does not yet exist." Lederach argues that "transcending violence is forged by the capacity to generate, mobilize, and build the moral imagination."[59] In the scriptural story of the woman accused of adultery, Jesus models moral imagination when he calmly kneels, draws on the ground, and says, "Who here is without sin, throw the first stone." The logic of dehumanization is broken as they all put down their stones.

For Lederach, mobilizing the moral imagination consists in practicing four disciplines: capacity to imagine ourselves in a web of relationships that includes our enemies; the ability to sustain a paradoxical curiosity that embraces complexity without reliance on dualistic polarity; a belief in and pursuit of the creative act as always possible, permanently in reach, and always accessible; and acceptance of the inherent risk of stepping into the mystery of the unknown that lies beyond the far too familiar landscape of violence.[60] Thus, such training should provide intentional space in both process and intervention designs for the artistic side and listening to the inner voice, with disciplines such as journaling, storytelling, poetry, painting, drawing, music, and dance.[61] For instance, in his research on social healing in the midst of violent conflict, Lederach identifies the metaphor of sound and the Tibetan bowl as particularly helpful. He points to the need for creating circles, social containers, and ritual that allows us to transcend linear assumptions about conflict.[62] He gives the example of the Somali peace initiative. Manifesting a circle, local leaders and women traveled to visit other local groups, going back time and again even if fighting erupted. Rituals of tea were included. Meetings were open, under a tree in the village. People came close to each other, vibrations ensued, and a frequency of healing occurred as these local containers gave way to larger ones.[63] Further, training in the moral imagination should also provide early and continual space for exploring questions of who we are and our purpose.[64]

Encountering morally imaginative practices, including some of the paradigmatic practices of the particular virtues mentioned earlier, actually draws us toward these practices and better enables us to acquire these virtues. For instance, mirror neurons physiologically cause us to be drawn toward the actions and feelings we encounter. This happens even if in a particular instance we choose to resist that type of encounter. Thus, the encounter plants a physiological seed in our person, which gets cultivated the more we have similar encounters.

Some of these formative practices also include spiritual practices such as meditation on scripture, which helps to tutor the emotions. Spohn describes this practice of meditation in four parts: focus, taking part in the story, savoring the scene, and conversing with God or silence.[65] Other key spiritual practices that help us acquire just peace virtues include discernment of the spirits and for Christians participating in the Eucharist. Discernment helps to broaden our wisdom and correct our perception to act in accord with virtue.[66] The Eucharist fosters a relational identification with Jesus, which forms our identity and thus enables a virtuous character associated with an integrated life.[67] Lederach notes how in situations of protracted conflict "the Eucharist creates moments pregnant with potential to mobilize the moral imagination in reference to reconciliation and responsibility for the suffering of others."[68]

Abdul Ghaffar Khan's nonviolent peace army is a good example of how to enable others to acquire just peace virtues in a conflict of intense violence. Khan, a Muslim, lived in the North-West Frontier Province of India during British rule in the 1900s. The cult of revenge and violence entrenched in Pathan society functioned as one of Khan's major obstacles. He set up a training camp for his "Servants of God," which soon became the first mass professional nonviolent army. Khan said to his Servants of God, "I am going to give you such a weapon that the police and the army will not be able to stand against it. It is the weapon of the Prophet, but you are not aware of it. That weapon is patience and righteousness. No power on earth can stand against it. Endure all hardships. Victory will be yours."[69] Khan elicited obedience by the power of love; that is, by their attraction to the good and a desire to serve, rather than by fear of punishment or failing to follow the rules.[70]

In his reeducation of his people toward nonviolence, Khan drew on the Pathan tradition wherein each tribe had a shrine to a great saint—that is, a model of virtue.[71] Further, the camps emphasized solidarity through volunteer work, such as cleaning houses, spinning cloth, opening schools especially for people in poverty and for women, and setting up village councils.[72] Gandhi also came and spoke to the Pathans about removing anger and fear in their heart and challenged them to live the virtue of nonviolence between each other.[73]

In 1930 the British arrested Khan and others. As nonviolent protests erupted, troops fired on this disciplined peace army. Expressing the virtue of courage, the next line stepped forward and received bullets. This continued off and on for the next three to six hours and became known as the Kissa Khani Bazaar massacre, with an estimated 200 killed. Finally, troops refused to fire but the repression continued over the next few days. By the end of that month, the Servants of God had over 8,000 volunteers. After gaining some concessions, more suppression followed.[74] Nevertheless, by 1938 the Servants of God grew to more than 100,000.[75]

Another good example of acquiring just peace virtues in the midst of violent conflict is Leymah Gbowee, who worked with other women in Liberia to end the civil war. Normally, women stayed relatively passive in this culture and allowed the men to control politics and war, in part because the women feared persecution. In 2003 Leymah brought together women from her Christian community to pray for peace. Asatu Bah Kenneth, a Muslim, also attended. Afterward they created some interfaith prayers to strengthen the virtues of solidarity and nonviolence. Wearing all white every day, the united group staged a protest at a central market for a week. More than 2,500 women gathered. Growing in courage, they agreed to go on a sex strike and held a candlelight vigil to pray for those being attacked in displacement camps. They promoted the goal of peace with a march to the government offices and demanded a meeting with President Charles Taylor. They eventually were granted a meeting, and Taylor agreed to attend peace talks.[76]

Next, they held a sit-in at one of the rebel meetings. This led to a direct meeting and agreement by the rebels to attend peace talks. Initial talks were interrupted by an international indictment of Taylor, which caused him to flee. Thus, violence broke out again. However, the women persisted and surrounded the others as they met in negotiations, refusing to let them leave until a settlement was achieved. Leymah warned the police attempting to intervene that she would remove her clothes to shame them, and they backed off. An agreement was signed, and the women worked to ensure its proper implementation. In the next elections, the first woman president for a state in Africa became a reality.[77]

In turn, a just peace ethic needs to incorporate elements that better enable persons and communities to acquire just peace virtues, not merely to teach us the knowledge of practices we should do and principles we should apply. Christians are particularly equipped and called to cultivate these virtues. However, such virtues also correspond to other religious traditions and have been actualized by persons in other ethical traditions. Thus, they can be elements of human flourishing more broadly.[78]

A Virtue-Based Just Peace Ethic

In this section I briefly highlight how some of the specific practices corresponding to just peace virtues would have an impact on other just peace approaches. Then I describe a set of norms for a virtue-based just peace ethic, which is used and revised in the following case studies.

The corresponding practices to the just peace virtues mentioned previously could enhance Sawatsky's approach and the practices of Stassen's just peacemaking theory. As a specific corrective, the practice of a constructive program helps clarify that nonviolence functions primarily as a constructive endeavor more so than being limited to obstructive activity (such as boycotts, strikes, or civil disobedience). Prayer or meditation practices, such as Christians creating and using an optional Eucharistic prayer with explicit references to Jesus's love of enemies, would be a key spiritual practice to prepare us for engaging conflict constructively.[79] Other aspects that are underdeveloped in just peacemaking theory and official CST include conflict transformation, unarmed civilian protection, and nonviolent civilian-based defense. There would also be a clear commitment to reducing all weapons, not merely so-called offensive or indiscriminate weapons, as well as to working with emerging cooperative institutions in the international system with the clear expressed goal to outlaw war.

A virtue-based just peace ethic participates in the vision of human flourishing illuminated particularly by an understanding of creation as a sacred gift, shalom, the Sermon on the Mount, CST, and the vocation to be missionary disciples. Arising from voices in violent conflict zones as well as drawing on a diverse set of global roundtables and Schlabach's synthesis of ecumenical just peace approaches, this just peace ethic offers norms that focus on three distinct yet overlapping categories or spheres.[80] Each of these norms applies at all stages of conflict, and the spheres can overlap in time and space (see fig. 3.1). The categories include

1. develop virtues and skill sets to engage conflict constructively (*jus in conflictione*)
2. break cycles of violence (*jus ex bello*)
3. build sustainable peace (*jus ad pacem*)

Category 1 includes the virtues of nonviolent peacemaking (active nonviolence), mercy, compassion, empathy, humility, hospitality, solidarity, justice, and courage, which each help us to better integrate or keep consistent means and ends; that is, what Sawatsky signals as the principle of reflexivity. Further, this sphere includes a norm of sustaining spiritual disciplines, such as fasting, meditation, and prayer, including particularly for Christians a Eucharistic prayer that explicitly names Jesus's love of enemies and rejection of violence.[81] Another norm is nonviolent education and training in skill sets such as nonviolent communication and resistance as well as social analysis of root causes. Participatory processes also represent a key norm. Forming nonviolent peacemaking communities, institutions, and cultures is another norm in this sphere.

In category 2, the practices and transformative initiatives to break cycles of destructive conflict and violence include both peacebuilding, which is more constructive, and nonviolent resistance, which is more obstructive or noncooperative with injustice. The norm of reflexivity is particularly important in this sphere. Further, another norm is nonviolent direct action, such as creative nonviolent resistance to injustice, unarmed civilian protection, and nonviolent civilian-based defense. An additional norm is conflict transformation to draw adversaries toward partnership and address root causes. This norm includes the practices of acknowledging responsibility for harm, identifying the human needs of all actors, healing trauma, and restoring justice. Another norm focuses on significantly reducing weapons and the arms trade toward what Pope Francis called "integral disarmament."[82]

Category 3 includes actions and policies that serve as guidelines to help build sustainable peace. They include the norm of relationality and reconciliation, which refers to actions that invite, create, strengthen, and heal relationships in ever-wider (horizontal) and deeper (vertical) directions across social spaces. Another norm is ecological sustainability and justice, which calls us to contribute to the long-term well-being of people, nonhuman animals, and the environment. The norm of robust civil society and just governance includes a commitment to outlaw war. The norm of dignity and human rights calls for action consistent with and improving appreciation for the equal dignity of all people, including adversaries, by ensuring human rights and cultivating empathy for all actors. The norm of a just economy includes a focus on the marginalized and vulnerable.

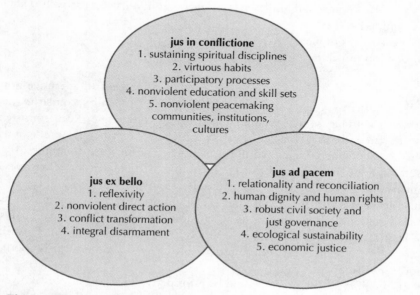

Figure 3.1   Just Peace Norms.

Guiding questions to apply a virtue-based just peace ethic include the following: What are the root causes of the conflict? What habits (virtues/vices) are at stake and what skill sets are needed to transform the conflict? What practices and transforming initiatives could be scaled up to break cycles of violence? What ongoing actions and policies could help build sustainable peace? As we discern how to respond to these questions for each specific context, the ethic would call us to choose acts that enhance rather than obstruct the various norms mentioned within each of the three overlapping spheres.

Conclusion

In sum, a virtue-based approach can help us to focus on developing the character, healthy habits, virtue, and normative practices of a just peace ethic. Thus, we will be better motivated and prepared to creatively imagine nonviolent ways to transform conflict, to choose, and to sustain those ways through difficult situations. A virtue-based approach would amplify the development of character and the kind of imagination that engages and creatively applies, extends, and even corrects some of the core practices of Stassen's just peacemaking theory as well as CST. Stassen's just peacemaking theory and much of CST may help prevent some wars, but this virtue-based approach would integrate much of Stassen's practices to enhance the prevention and transformation of violence, which ultimately strengthens the prevention of war as well as the capacity to defuse active wars. Further, a virtue-based approach will better equip us to transform not only direct violence but also structural and cultural violence. By including and acquiring the virtues mentioned, we would act more consistently with the call from Vatican II "to strain every muscle as we work for the time when all war can be completely outlawed" and be more likely to get our society closer to the outlawing of war.

The cases in the next chapters of this book draw on this just peace ethic, along with the first two chapters, to continue testing and refining a just peace ethic in specific cases of conflict. In the end, the reader will encounter a refined just peace ethic, which I hope will enable Catholic and Christian communities as well as others to more clearly sense a call to develop, embrace, and shift our focus to a just peace moral framework.

Notes

1. Psalm 85:10.
2. Matt. 5:38–41; Luke 1:78–79, 2:14, 10:1–6, 19:42, 22:51; Isa. 2:4–5, 31:1–5, 32:15, 42:1–4, 53:7–9. John Donahue, "The Good News of Peace," *The Way: Contemporary Christian Spirituality* 22 (April 1982): 88–99.
3. Luke 6:20; Matt. 5:21–26, 25:31–46; Mark 1:40–45, 8:34–38; John 18:36–38. See also Glen H. Stassen and David Gushee, *Kingdom Ethics: Following Jesus in Contemporary Context* (Downers Grove, IL: InterVarsity Press, 2003); Dan Harrington,

Historical Dictionary of Jesus (Plymouth, UK: Scarecrow Press, 2010), 7; N. T. Wright, "Kingdom Come: Public Meaning of the Gospels," *Christian Century,* June 17, 2008; Walter Wink, "Beyond Just War and Pacifism: Jesus' Nonviolent Way," *Review & Expositor* 89, no. 2 (1992): 197–214. For more explanation of these claims about Jesus, see Eli S. McCarthy, *Becoming Nonviolent Peacemakers: A Virtue Ethic for Catholic Social Teaching and U.S. Policy* (Eugene, OR: Wipf and Stock, 2012).

4. Frank Matera, *The Sermon on the Mount: The Perfect Measure of the Christian Life* (Collegeville, MN: Liturgical Press, 2013), 37.

5. Christopher Marshall, *Beyond Retribution: A New Testament Vision for Justice, Crime, and Punishment* (Grand Rapids, MI: Eerdmans, 2001).

6. Glen H. Stassen, ed., *Just Peacemaking: New Paradigm for Ethics of Peace and War,* 3rd ed. (Cleveland, OH: Pilgrim Press, 2008).

7. Maryann Cusimano Love, "What Kind of Peace Do We Seek?," in *Peacebuilding: Catholic Theology, Ethics, and Praxis,* ed. Robert J. Schreiter, R. Scott Appleby, and Gerard F. Powers (Maryknoll, NY: Orbis, 2010), 76–82.

8. Jarem Sawatsky, *Justpeace Ethics: A Guide to Restorative Justice and Peacebuilding* (Eugene, OR: Wipf and Stock, 2008), 12–13.

9. For example, means/ends *in*consistency includes feeling bitterness and disrespect toward poor persons while giving them food; schools relying *primarily* on exclusion tactics of suspension, expulsion, or arrest to induce community-building behavior; using the death penalty to teach that killing is wrong; nonviolent movements that dehumanize their adversary; bombing others to stop killing or create participatory democracy; and so forth. I know these examples represent different levels of intensity, but they are also not simply a question of proportionality. By using analogical reasoning with these examples, to the degree inconsistency is apparent, this will linger in different forms or take the form of serious harm until we address the inconsistency and heal the harm this often causes to relationships and communities.

10. Joseph Kotva, *The Christian Case for Virtue Ethics* (Washington, DC: Georgetown University Press, 1996), 22–23.

11. Alasdair MacIntyre, *After Virtue,* 2nd ed. (Notre Dame, IN: University of Notre Dame Press, 1984), 219.

12. Kotva, *Christian Case for Virtue Ethics,* 32.

13. Jim Keenan, "Proposing Cardinal Virtues," *Theological Studies* 56 (December 1995): 714.

14. William Spohn, *Go and Do Likewise: Jesus and Ethics* (New York: Continuum, 2003), 28. Thomas Aquinas, *Summa Theologiae,* trans. Fathers of the English Dominican Province (New York: Benziger Bros., 1947–1948), I-II.49.4; I-II.55.

15. Johan Galtung, "Cultural Violence," in *Journal of Peace Research* 27, no. 3 (1990): 291–305.

16. Vatican II, *Pastoral Constitution on the Church in the Modern World,* 1965, para. 81. Pope Paul VI, "Reconciliation: The Way to Peace," World Day of Peace Message, 1975.

17. McCarthy, *Becoming Nonviolent Peacemakers.*

18. The virtue of nonviolent peacemaking, distinct from the Thomistic virtue of charity, entails particularly drawing enemies toward friendship and deals with conflict or acute conflict, which call forth a unique set of paradigmatic practices.

The Thomistic virtue of charity particularly cultivates friendship with God, which does include loving what God loves, such as strangers and enemies. Thus, the virtue of nonviolent peacemaking more appropriately fits as a subvirtue that arises most fully from charity, as does the virtue of mercy in a Thomistic framework.

19. Regarding prayer or meditation oriented to nonviolence, see Rev. Emmanuel McCarthy, *The Nonviolent Eucharistic Jesus: A Pastoral Approach* (Wilmington, DE: Center for Christian Nonviolence, 2011); for nonviolent resistance and disruption, see Miguel De La Torre, *Latina/o Social Ethics: Moving beyond Eurocentric Moral Thinking* (Waco, TX: Baylor University Press, 2010), 97–105; and for nonviolent civilian-based defense, see McCarthy, *Becoming Nonviolent Peacemakers*, 187–206.

20. Emmanuel Katongole, "The Church of the Future: Pressing Moral Issues from Ecclesia in Africa," in *The Church We Want: African Catholics Look to Vatican III*, ed. A. Orobator (Maryknoll, NY: Orbis, 2016), 166.

21. Katongole, 167.

22. John Paul Lederach, *The Little Book of Conflict Transformation* (Intercourse, PA: Good Books, 2003), 390–97.

23. John Paul Lederach, Reina Neufeldt, and Hal Culbertson, *Reflective Peacebuilding: A Planning, Monitoring, and Learning Tool Kit* (Notre Dame, IN: Kroc Institute, University of Notre Dame, 2007), 18.

24. Gene Sharp, *How Nonviolent Struggle Works* (East Boston, MA: Albert Einstein Institute, 2013), 5–6. These six sources of power include authority/legitimacy, human resources, skills/knowledge of key human supporters, intangible factors— psychological/ideological, material resources, and sanctions/enforcement.

25. Gene Sharp, *Waging Nonviolent Struggle*: *20th Century Practice and 21st Century Potential* (Boston: Porter Sargent, 2005). This includes leaders like Slobodan Milosevic, Ferdinand Marcos, and Augusto Pinochet along with repressive systems such as the Soviet Union and Apartheid. See also the case of Denmark, Norway, and the Rosenstrasse Protest.

26. Erica Chenoweth and Maria J. Stephan, *Why Civilian Resistance Works: The Strategic Logic of Nonviolent Conflict* (New York: Columbia University Press, 2011), 7, 213–14. Of the three cases given of "successful" violent revolutions that led to basic "durable democracies," at least two are questionable and certainly not promising models. The Bengali campaign in 1971 had major political corruption, coups, military leaders, and so on for twenty years afterward. The Jewish resistance in 1948 has certainly still maintained significant habits of violence, both direct and structural (e.g., the occupation of Palestine). The Costa Rica campaign ending in 1948 was quite short and mixed with significant nonviolent action, but ultimately they decided to disband their entire military, which still holds today. Thus, "ten times" appears to be an understatement. If we use their numbers and take out these first two, then it may be "thirty times" more likely.

27. "NP Workers Andres Gutierrez and Derek Oakley on Their Experience of the Violence in South Sudan," Nonviolent Peaceforce, April 17, 2014, https://www.youtube.com/watch?v=_WcFwpcIMcE.

28. Mel Duncan, "Case Studies of Unarmed Civilian Protection," March 2016, p. 6, http://www.nonviolentpeaceforce.org/images/publications/UCP_Case_Studies__v5.3_LQ.pdf.

29. Cure Violence, "Scientific Evaluations," http://cureviolence.org/results/impactworldregions/, www.cureviolence.org/results/scientific-evaluations/.

30. Michael Nagler, *Is There No Other Way? The Search for a Nonviolent Future* (Berkeley, CA: Berkeley Hills Books, 2001), 252–53.

31. For Germany, see Sharp, *Waging Nonviolent Struggle*, 91–100; Sternstein, "The Ruhrkampf of 1923," in Sharp, *Waging Nonviolent Struggle*, 106–35. For Norway and Denmark, see Skodvin, "Norwegian Nonviolent Resistance," 136–53, and Bennett, "The Resistance Against," 154–72, both in Sharp, *Waging Nonviolent Struggle*. For Czechoslovakia, see Nagler, *Is There No Other Way?*, 133–36; Sharp, *Waging Nonviolent Struggle*, 189–204. For the Baltics, see Sharp, *Waging Nonviolent Struggle*, 277–86.

32. Sharp, *Waging Nonviolent Struggle*, 516. Sharp, *Civilian-Based Defense: A Post-Military Weapons System* (Princeton, NJ: Princeton University Press, 1990), 125.

33. Pope John Paul II, "Rich in Mercy," November 30, 1980.

34. Jim Keenan, *Moral Wisdom: Lessons and Texts from the Catholic Tradition* (Lanham, MD: Rowman & Littlefield, 2004), 124.

35. Jim Keenan and Daniel Harrington, *Jesus and Virtue Ethics: Building Bridges Between New Testament Studies and Moral Theology* (Lanham, MD: Rowman & Littlefield, 2002), 191.

36. Bernard Haring, *The Law of Christ* (Westminster, MD: Newman, 1961), 546–47, 551.

37. Christopher Vogt, "The Common Good and Virtue Ethics," in *Theological Studies* 68, no. 2 (2007): 403, 405.

38. Lisa Sowle Cahill, *Love Your Enemies: Discipleship, Pacifism, and Just War Theory* (Minneapolis, MN: Augsburg Press, 1994), 2, 176–77. Also, see her updated version, *Blessed Are the Peacemakers: Pacifism, Just War, and Peacebuilding* (Minneapolis, MN: Fortress Press, 2019). Yiu Sing Lúcás Chan suggests that the virtue of meekness insists on the rejection of violence as he discusses the virtue of peacemaking. See *The Ten Commandments and the Beatitudes: Biblical Studies and Ethics for Real Life* (Lanham, MD: Rowman & Littlefield, 2012), 213.

39. Cahill, *Love Your Enemies,* 31

40. Lúcás Chan, *Ten Commandments*, 233.

41. Lúcás Chan, *Ten Commandments*, 239. For example: Jesus rebukes Peter for violently defending the Innocent one (i.e., Jesus), thus *at least* calling into question the "protection of the innocent" as a moral justification for violence. John 18:10–11; Luke 22:49–51.

42. John Paul II, "On Social Concern," December 30, 1987, sect. 38, 40.

43. Jon Sobrino, *The Principle of Mercy: Taking the Crucified People from the Cross* (Maryknoll, NY: Orbis, 1994), 90–91. David Hollenbach, *Common Good and Christian Ethics* (New York: Cambridge University Press, 2002), 189.

44. William O'Neill, "Visions and Revisions: The Hermeneutical Implications of the Option for the Poor," in *Hope and Solidarity: John Sobrino's Challenge to Christian Theology*, ed. S. Pope (Maryknoll, NY: Orbis, 2008), 31–43. See also "No Amnesty for Sorrow: The Privilege of the Poor in Christian Social Ethics," *Theological Studies* 55, no.4 (1994), 638–54.

45. Vogt, "Common Good," 403, 405.

46. Pope John Paul said, "Violence destroys our dignity," in *Compendium of Social Doctrine of the Church* (2004), 496.

47. Regarding suicide rates, see Matthew Hoh, "13,000 More Names to the List," *Huffington Post*, February 27, 2013. For domestic violence rates, see "The Facts about Abuse in Military Families," Domesticshelters.org, December 2, 2016; and M. Straus and R. Gelles, *Physical Violence in American Families—Risk Factors and Adaptations to Violence in 8,145 Families* (New Brunswick, NJ: Transaction Publishers, 1990), which shows civilian population rates of 10 percent. For rates of sexual assault, see "Sexual Assaults and Military Justice," *New York Times*, March 12, 2013.

48. Vogt, "Common Good," 412.

49. Aquinas, *Summa Theologiae* I–II.Q57.a1–2; II–II.Q83.a8; III.Q99.a2. For Thomas, "right" exists when our relations allow for the satisfaction of our natural needs.

50. Marshall, *Beyond Retribution*.

51. Chan, *Ten Commandments, 89*.

52. Aquinas, *Summa Theologiae* I–II.Q123.a6, I–II.Q124.a3.

53. Stephen J. Pope, "Overview of the Ethics of Thomas Aquinas," in *The Ethics of Aquinas*, ed. Stephen J. Pope (Washington, DC: Georgetown University Press, 2002), 44.

54. Stanley Hauerwas, *Christians among the Virtues: Theological Conversations with Ancient and Modern Ethics* (Notre Dame, IN: Notre Dame University Press, 1997), 161.

55. Pope Francis, "Invocation for Peace," June 8, 2014.

56. Rachel MacNair, *Perpetration-Induced Traumatic Stress: The Psychological Consequences of Killing* (Lincoln, NE: Praeger/Greenwood Publishing, 2005).

57. Ed Vacek, SJ, *Love, Human and Divine: The Heart of Christian Ethics* (Washington, DC: Georgetown University Press, 1994).

58. De La Torre, *Latina/o Social Ethics*, 74.

59. John Paul Lederach, *The Moral Imagination: Art and Soul of Building Peace* (New York, NY: Oxford University Press, 2010), ix, 5, 38.

60. Lederach, ix, 5, 38.

61. Lederach, 173–77.

62. John Paul Lederach and Angela Jill Lederach, *When Blood and Bones Cry Out: Journeys through the Soundscape of Healing and Reconciliation* (Oxford: Oxford University Press, 2010), 94.

63. Lederach and Lederach, 103–8.

64. Lederach, *Moral Imagination*, 173–77.

65. Spohn, *Go and Do Likewise*, 138–40.

66. Spohn, 162.

67. Spohn, 165.

68. Lederarch, "The Long Journey Back to Humanity: Catholic Peacebuilding with Armed Actors," in *Peacebuilding: Catholic Theology, Ethics, and Praxis*, ed. Robert J. Schreiter, R. Scott Appleby, and Gerard F. Powers (Maryknoll, NY: Orbis, 2010), 50–51.

69. Eknath Easwaran, *A Man to Match His Mountains: Badshah Khan, Nonviolent Soldier of Islam* (Petaluma, CA: Nilgiri Press, 1984), 103, 117.

70. Easwaran, *Nonviolent Soldier,* 112, 155; Abdul Ghaffar Khan, *My Life and Struggle: Autobiography of Badshah Khan* (Delhi: Hind Pocket Books, 1969), 96.

71. Easwaran, *Nonviolent Soldier*, 101, 131.

72. Sharpe, *Waging Nonviolent Struggle*, 199–220.

73. Easwaran, *Nonviolent Soldier*, 133–57.

74. Easwaran, 117–29.

75. Sharpe, *Waging Nonviolent Struggle*, 124.

76. Kylin Navarro, "Liberian Women Act to End Civil War, 2003," in Global Nonviolent Action Database, 2010.

77. Navarro, "Liberian Women."

78. For a broader look across religious traditions, see Eli McCarthy, "Virtue, Nonviolence, and Just Peace," in *Wiley-Blackwell Companion to Religion and Peace*, ed. Jolyon Mitchell, Martyn Percy, Francesca Po, and Leslie Orr (forthcoming).

79. McCarthy, *Nonviolent Eucharistic Jesus*.

80. With some adaption, these draw on the synthesizing work of Gerald W. Schlabach, "What Is Just Peace? A Synthesis Based on Catholic and Ecumenical Christian Sources," February 2018, www.geraldschlabach.net/2018/03/02/what-is-just-peace. The Latin terms are coined by Gerald. Especially since the 2016 Vatican conference, there has been a global virtual roundtable on a new moral framework as well as multiple regional and university events.

81. McCarthy, *Nonviolent Eucharistic Jesus*.

82. Jim Fair, "Pope Stresses Need to Halt Nuclear Arms," *Zenit,* November 10, 2017. By "integral disarmament," the pope refers to the need for a preceding or simultaneous reduction of "weapons" or a disarming of the heart to enable the reduction of concrete weapons in our world.

PART II

US DOMESTIC CASES

4

JUST PEACE, JUST SANCTUARY

Immigration and Ecclesial Nonviolence

LEO GUARDADO

The phenomenon of immigration to and in the US is fundamentally a phenomenon marked by direct and institutionalized violence and thus is of direct concern to a framework of just peace. The categorization of this complex reality within the term "immigration" raises the question of whether this is the most accurate term.[1] Because so much of the "immigration" to the United States is driven by contexts of violence, other terms are necessary and will be used in this essay, such as "human displacement," "asylum seekers," and "refugees." Historically, these terms have been associated more with contexts of war, and by using them to describe those who "migrate," I emphasize the forced nature of this mobility. Many of the persons currently "migrating" from the Northern Triangle of Central America are better categorized as asylum seekers rather than immigrants because the homicide rates in the region force people to flee. However, since a war is not technically taking place within the Northern Triangle, even though the rates of killing are like those of a war zone,[2] those who flee have difficulty acquiring refugee status or other kinds of legal protections. Using a broader set of terms to describe the context of immigration expands how this reality is framed and the responses that are needed.

The almost eleven million "unauthorized" persons who currently live in the United States, and those who continue to arrive daily, are a locus of contestation in society because the government construes their physical presence yet juridical nonexistence as an aberration of law and order.[3] Displaced from their homelands, these persons become targets of persecution in the United States. State mechanisms of control, such as Immigration and Customs Enforcement (ICE), are tasked with rounding up, incarcerating, and removing this population that is strategically categorized as "criminal."[4] Although their presence is a legal and political challenge to the US government, for the church they must be a sign of the times and a source of discernment.[5] The church is engaged with unauthorized persons at multiple levels, from providing legal assistance to pastoral accompaniment in parishes, and its activities do not typically generate much controversy. However, there is one kind of ministry that does give rise to an ecclesial and social conflict: sanctuary.

In this chapter I examine the concept and practice of sanctuary as a legitimate and necessary ecclesial ministry that responds to the phenomenon of human displacement and the persecution of "unauthorized" persons in the United States. I argue that the bourgeoning framework of just peace provides a more capacious approach for the church's ongoing discernment of its responsibility to protect and accompany persons whose life is threatened by deportation.[6] Sanctuary is a creative nonviolent response to legalized violence in society.[7]

In the first section I analyze the context of immigration to the US, especially from Latin America. I show that violence is not only at the source of why persons leave their countries but is also what characterizes the US response. This reality invites the church, as an institution and as a people, to reconsider what constitutes appropriate actions that can reframe a phenomenon that is too often categorized simply as a legal or economic matter.

In the second section I begin to integrate a just peace approach with the conflictual reality that is immigration. After presenting the need for greater practices of dialogue and discernment within the church, I turn to the 1980s sanctuary ministry as a generative example of how ecclesial communities in the US previously theorized and responded to human displacement. Through the writings of Jim Corbett, one of the leaders at the root of the sanctuary ministry, it becomes evident that a framework akin to just peace undergirded the 1980s ministry in the borderlands. These past ecclesial actions serve as a creative source for present and future discernment. Sanctuary, then and now, is a means for church communities to imagine their potential for social transformation and for the construction of a more peaceful and just society.

Context of "Immigration" to the US and the Threat of Deportation to Warlike Violence

In the midst of violence, social instability, and resurgent signs of political repression, Central Americans are fleeing north to the United States.[8] The case of El Salvador examined in this book is a prime example of why people flee. Embarking on the journey from Central America to the US is a matter of life and death because many of the same dangers faced at home are also faced en route.

For those who flee north, getting into Mexico is the first major hurdle. Despite increased police and military presence at Mexico's southern border, Salvadorans and Central Americans still attempt to make it to the US border, and some succeed. Even entire families are leaving. In fiscal year 2016 US Border Patrol in the Southwest sector apprehended 77,674 persons who were traveling as part of a family unit, and the majority of these were from El Salvador (27,114), followed by Guatemala (23,067) and Honduras (20,226).

The number of unaccompanied children from these countries apprehended in fiscal year 2016 totaled 46,893, and of these the majority were from Guatemala (18,913) and from El Salvador (17,512). Even though the numbers of unaccompanied children fleeing Guatemala and El Salvador are more or less the same, it is essential to keep in mind that Guatemala has a population of about sixteen million persons compared to El Salvador's six million; thus, proportionally El Salvador's youth are fleeing at a much higher rate. In 2016 the total number of apprehended family units from Central America surpassed figures from fiscal year 2015 and 2014, but apprehended family units are but a fraction of the total apprehensions of non–Mexicans (mostly Central American), which totaled 218,110 in 2016.[9] Apprehensions identify only those individuals who were not able to make it to their intended destinations or family in the United States.

Both those who were apprehended and those who made it to their destinations increasingly travel through isolated regions of Mexico in order to avoid the new checkpoints established by the US-funded Plan Frontera Sur, which seeks to seal the Mexican southern border from Central Americans.[10] Whereas in the past, large numbers of Central Americans would ride on top of La Bestia, a treacherous journey atop a train that carried them from southern to northern Mexico, now they are forced to find alternate routes where Mexican agents will not intercept them and deport them back to deadly violence.[11] Entering more isolated regions of Mexico increases the risks of directly encountering and becoming victims of narco-trafficking networks.[12] This practice of militarizing the Mexican southern border with armed government agents mirrors the vision at the US southern border where pushing individuals to isolated and more dangerous areas is used as a deterrent.[13] The official name for this practice is "prevention through deterrence," and the approach has been in place since 1994.[14] Human rights groups have systematically documented the deadly effects of this deterrence vision to argue that the US government, and increasingly the Mexican government, are "disappearing" those fleeing their home countries.

In the history of Latin America's wars, people did not simply go missing; rather, they were "disappeared" by government forces. Framing the US deterrence vision through the lens of the disappeared makes room for a discourse of government responsibility for the deaths of those attempting to cross the US border. As the report says, "the means of contemporary border policy amounts to a campaign of state violence against migrating peoples."[15] In Mexico, where the Commission for Human Rights estimates that there are about twenty-five thousand disappeared persons, there is a growing sense that disappearances are a mechanism for the government to accomplish strategic interests.[16] The forced disappearance of the forty-three students from Ayotzinapa brought worldwide attention to this larger crisis.[17]

Inevitably, Central Americans who are crossing Mexico on their way to the US risk becoming trapped in this state of affairs in which government forces play a central role in their disappearance. After all, there is financial gain in the capture and sale of Central Americans to narco-trafficking groups. To such groups, each Central American can be worth between $2,000 and $5,000 through extortion of their families. If the family does not pay, then they become a *desaparecido/a*.[18]

Fr. Alejandro Solalinde, director of the Hermanos en el Camino shelter in Ixtepec, Oaxaca, Mexico, which provides refuge and education for Central Americans journeying north, estimates that there have been at least ten thousand disappeared migrants in Mexico through the collusion of Mexico's federal security forces and the Zetas narco-traffickers.[19] This number is his conservative estimate; he believes it can be as high as seventy thousand if one includes disappearances starting in 2006. Both government and narco forces have attempted to close his shelter for migrants because they consider it an obstacle to the economic industry of capturing, extorting, and disappearing migrant bodies.[20] The disappeared vanish into mass graves, vats of acid, boiling oil, and other means that leave no trace of remains.

Mothers and other relatives from El Salvador, Honduras, and Guatemala whose family members have disappeared during migration embark on a pilgrimage to Mexico every year to bring attention to this phenomenon. The Comité de Familiares de Migrantes Fallecidos y Desaparecidos de El Salvador (COFAMIDE) has led the pilgrimage since 2006 when the disappearances started to become a systematic symptom of the harrowing journey to the United States. The motto of this transnational movement is "buscamos vida en caminos de muerte" (we seek life on the paths of death), a motto that succinctly captures the core of both the dream that drives displaced persons north as well as the reality that they encounter on the journey.[21] The stories of terror on the journey abound, but because persons fleeing Central America are often already fleeing death, they are willing to risk death in order to have a chance to live.[22]

If in Central America and in Mexico violence, politics, and profit coalesce through extortions and disappearances, especially of poor and displaced populations, in the United States these factors come together in the proliferation of private (and hence for-profit) prisons that criminalize and commodify displaced individuals. Since 2009 the majority of "criminals" entering federal prisons are incarcerated not because of offenses related to violence, weapons, or property but because of immigration offenses. These "offenders" are spending their time behind bars in overcrowded for-profit prisons run by corporations.[23] As of 2012 there were about twenty-four thousand immigrants in these prisons whose "crime" was attempting to flee the violence that is consuming Central America and Mexico.[24] As of November 2017 the average daily population of persons incarcerated by ICE in both private (for-profit) and government-run prisons was 39,322.[25] Essentially, the practice of incarceration of displaced persons is a form of state punishment for defying legalized violence.[26]

Central Americans seeking refuge in the US who are not deported right away risk months or years in prison without proper legal representation while they wait for a review of their case. It is inhuman that persons fleeing violence and death are more likely to receive a prison sentence in the US rather than refuge and protection. Technically, many of these refugees do not have to wait in jail for their court case, but it depends on whether they can afford to pay their bond to be free. A 2016 American Civil Liberties Union (ACLU) lawsuit against the federal government addresses this very point when it writes in its opening sentence, "This class action lawsuit challenges the federal government's policy and practice of setting cash bonds for noncitizens in immigration proceedings, without regard to a noncitizen's financial resources, which has resulted in the incarceration of individuals merely because they are poor."[27] It is tragically ironic that some of the very people who fled for their lives because they could not afford to pay the extortions from the gangs are now incarcerated and deprived of their freedom because they cannot afford to pay the US government.

Whether it is in the streets of Central America or in the private prisons that hold thousands of brown bodies from south of the border, persons seeking refuge from violence continue to become commodities for others' profit.[28] With Donald Trump's election as president of the United States, the stock price of such for-profit prison corporations surged because the criminalization of asylum-seekers is good business.[29] For the current administration, the "unauthorized" other from south of the border is a threat to society and to the nation itself, as was expressed in the Trump campaign rally speeches: "make America safe again." Such rhetoric attempts to legitimize the ongoing militarization of border regions and also of the interior communities of the United States. Rhetoric about security becomes rhetoric for more military force.[30] From a just peace framework, which argues for consistency between means and ends, the current US strategy is unsustainable because it seeks the ends of safety from violence through the means of scaling up violence.

To speak of "unauthorized" immigration in the United States is to speak of a type of warfare that is taking place against "alien" bodies that the government seeks to expel from the body politic through what has been referred to as the deportation-industrial complex.[31] For sectors of the US population that see only a quantifiable threat and not persons, these are simply bodies, not fully conceived of as living persons. In reference to the ways that violence is strategically framed in society, Judith Butler has written that "if certain lives do not qualify as lives or are, from the start, not conceivable as lives within certain epistemological frames, then these lives are never lived nor lost in the full sense."[32] To begin to grieve the loss of these lives, and to begin to resist the structural and political mechanisms that in multiple ways kill the "unauthorized" population in the US, we must first *see* this population as more than bodies and recognize the claim that their humanity places on our humanity. The fundamental notion of human dignity, which is also emphasized by a just peace approach, becomes central in the process of learning to see nonviolently. All of this requires an epistemological breakthrough that can reframe not only the phenomenon of "immigration" but, just as importantly, the responsibility to protect that communities of faith and all people of goodwill must discern and practice in history.

Persons who are threatened with deportation have few alternatives to prevent their expulsion once they have been apprehended by Enforcement and Removal Operations (ERO), the branch of ICE that literally hunts down persons at risk of deportation. Some churches have begun to provide sanctuary for persons with deportation orders who have already lived in the United States for years and who would be separated from their families and US citizen children. However, a national network akin to what was constructed in the 1980s has not fully emerged.

If the current administration continues to systematically deny asylum claims to persons fleeing for their lives, and to those who have lived here for years and who are now part of the fabric of society, the church may have no theologically legitimate option but to help them avoid capture as they enter this country and attempt to survive with the hope of finding a place and community that affirms the inherent value of their life.[33] Sanctuary has been in the past, and can be again, an effective nonviolent ecclesial response capable of transforming the death-dealing politics of a nation. In the next section I explore how just peace can help reframe a church response to immigration and how the 1980s sanctuary ministry is a resource for future action.

Living an Ethic of Just Peace through a Ministry of Sanctuary

The frameworks of just peace that have been introduced in this book begin to provide a more expansive lens through which the church can better recognize the horizon of possibilities for resisting institutionalized violence. As a burgeoning concept, just peace must resist becoming a unidirectional application of theoretical frameworks to practice. Instead, it must serve as a means of generating more incisive reflection on how ecclesial actions or lack thereof contribute to justice and peace and enable life rather than foreclose it. In terms of immigration, a just peace lens of analysis allows us to recognize that the church in the US exists and participates in an already given conflictual context. It does so by its openness to see conflict as an opportunity for transformation rather than a threat. Any presumption that the church is not already embedded within the broader sociopolitical conflict surrounding immigration and unauthorized persons fails to grasp reality in a futile attempt at neutrality that merely condones sinful structures and idolizes a security state.[34] If the church has a responsibility to read the signs of the times, then it is also important to understand that there is a certain grace in accepting the conflictual context in which it is called to live its life and carry out its mission. Brad Hinze has written that "much Catholic theology and spirituality harbor a conflict-averse mentality and devote little consideration of structures and practices of ecclesial and civic accountability."[35] Basic integrity requires that the church overcome a conflict-averse mentality so that it can see sinful reality for what it is. A just peace lens has the potential to provide new questions and perspectives that can alter our ecclesial imagination and hold communities of faith accountable to enfleshing in history a humanizing way of being church.

In light of a just peace lens, the structural conditions that generate and sustain the conflict that we call immigration necessitate that the church reexamine its task as one of *transforming* the conflict by *protecting* those most affected by the violence of the conflict.[36] This certainly does not imply reducing the church's diplomatic attempts through the publication of statements from bishops, denunciations of injustice, and exhortations for Catholics to become more involved with immigrant communities.[37] Rather, it invites Catholics to consider protective actions as a form of diplomacy that communicates a truth about persons seeking refuge in the United States—a truth whose historical verification is the dehumanizing violence displaced persons are willing to endure on the journey north in order to find life.[38] The norm of conflict transformation and the practice of unarmed civilian protection, both of which are emphasized by an ethic of just peace, help the church to actualize such initiatives.

In his framing chapter (chapter 3), Eli McCarthy provides guiding questions for thinking through an ethic of just peace. He asks, "What are the root causes of the conflict? What habits (virtues/vices) are at stake and what skill sets are needed to transform the conflict? What practices and transforming initiatives could be scaled up to break cycles of violence?" In the previous section, I provided a response to the first question by explaining some of the root causes of the conflict. The conflict can be summarized as a people's embodied desire for life in tension with a country's desire to control the right to life of a people. At stake in the conflict is not only the control of borders but, more importantly, notions and definitions of who is a person worthy of life. How the church responds or fails to respond to these deeper implications of the conflict is a concrete reflection of how the church understands itself and its mission.

McCarthy's second question of virtues and skill sets needed to transform the conflict opens a creative space for identifying resources within and beyond the Christian tradition. Because violence is at the root of the conflict that is immigration, from the perspective of just peace the virtue of active nonviolence will be a necessary resource and a foundation for any ecclesial response. This requires that faith communities first engage in the spiritual practice of active discernment about the responsibility and possibility of offering sanctuary to persons threatened with deportation in order to interrupt this violent process. Pope Francis writes, "Discernment . . . is not a solipsistic self-analysis or a form of egotistical introspection, but an authentic process of leaving ourselves behind in order to approach the mystery of God, who helps us to carry out the mission to which he has called us, for the good of our brothers and sisters."[39] Discernment, then, is always tied to concrete actions, not for our benefit but for the good of others. Ecclesial discernment cannot happen without greater dialogical practices within the church, especially between clergy and laity, which can allow for a genuine participatory process. When bishops simply foreclose the possibility of parishes becoming a sanctuary church, even if the parish council and the pastor have discerned that they are being called to this action, dialogue is cut short and it raises questions about the laity's vocation as church to have an authentic role in discernment.[40] Furthermore, bishops or clergy who foreclose even the possibility of communal discernment processes limit their understanding of how the Holy Spirit may be communicating prophetically from the margins of the church.[41] The church's ability to become a catalyst in the transformation of sociopolitical conflicts depends to some degree on its ability to address and transform its own internal conflicts in ways that model the change it seeks in society. The church's very integrity is at stake. If the church does not want the government to deport persons back to deadly violence, then it must begin to perform actions that in fact protect persons from deportation, even if this intensifies the conflict within the church and with government forces.

McCarthy's third question about practices or initiatives that can be scaled up to break cycles of violence leads me to affirm more explicitly that sanctuary is a nonviolent ecclesial practice that interrupts the violence surrounding "unauthorized" persons. Church sanctuary has a long tradition as a means of protecting persons in need of refuge from violence. The earliest ecclesial reference is from the Council of Serdica in 343, which obliged bishops to protect and intercede before imperial courts for those who fled to "the mercy of the church."[42] Key theologians of the early church, such as Gregory of Naziensus, John Chrysostom, and Augustine of Hippo, attested in their own time to the importance of sanctuary as a church practice.[43] The medieval concepts of the peace of God and the truce of God that served as a means of placing boundaries on violence,[44] and that Lisa Sowle Cahill mentions in her essay, are also conceptually and historically related to early church practices of sanctuary,[45] because sanctuary was akin to a humanitarian or peace corridor for the poor, oppressed, and anyone whose life was threatened.[46] Although in late antiquity, sanctuary practices became increasingly codified and associated with criminals seeking refuge, at its root the concept and practice was much broader.[47] From a just peace perspective, church sanctuary converges with the practice of unarmed civilian protection, which is a key dimension of active nonviolence. In fact, such an understanding of sanctuary as active nonviolence and a means of peace was at the origins of the sanctuary ministry of the 1980s.

Sanctuary Churches as Peacebuilding Communities—Then and Now

In the early 1980s, ecumenical faith leaders began a discernment process about their responsibility to Salvadoran and Guatemalan refugees who were fleeing the violence of Central America. One of these faith leaders was Jim Corbett, a Quaker who was a key catalyst for starting a sanctuary ministry in Tucson, Arizona. This ministry went on to become a transnational movement that lasted throughout the 1980s. Corbett understood sanctuary as a civilian-led initiative capable of enacting fundamental aspects of international law within the domestic sphere. He wrote that "as a direct action, civil initiative differs from civil disobedience in being positively engaged in legal procedures to protect and uphold good laws that the government is violating."[48] In the background of Corbett's conceptualization of sanctuary were the Nuremberg Principles. One of the most widely known principles is principle IV, which states, "The fact that a person acted pursuant to order of his [or her] government or of a superior does not relieve him [or her] from responsibility under international law, provided a moral choice was in fact possible to him [or her]."[49] This principle was in response to the well-known practice of Nazi soldiers disavowing responsibility for their crimes by simply stating that they were only following a superior's orders.

Already in 1981 Corbett had encountered government officials at the US–Mexico border who said they were simply following orders to deport asylum seekers back to the war in El Salvador. It was Corbett's fundamental belief that the Nuremberg Principles depended on local communities for their implementation that led him to argue for the practice of sanctuary as a practice of civil initiative—literally, civilians taking initiative for upholding international norms of the rights of, and to, humanity. He wrote, "Implementing the Nuremberg mandate is the task of civil initiative. The sanctuary movement is building the institutional foundations—it is mobilizing the church— to fulfill this task."[50] For Corbett it was the church, in the broadest universal sense as a people of peoples who covenant to work nonviolently for justice and peace, which could resist the violence and power of the security state.[51] Furthermore, through the practice of sanctuary, the church could serve as an implementer of global norms of basic human rights within the nation-state. In this sense, sanctuary churches were envisioned as nonviolent peacemaking communities capable of instituting peace from the bottom up. He wrote, "As a people of peoples that covenant to do justice through community cohesion rather than state coercion, the church has unequaled power to mobilize itself as a communion that transcends national boundaries, and so it has an unequaled responsibility to do justice in the face of nations' violations of human rights."[52] Whereas the state apparatus depends on police powers to carry out orders that may be legal within the domestic sphere but that may violate international norms, the church, which at its root is a people, does not depend on police powers for its legitimacy but rather on communion with those whose humanity is violated. The church's historical responsibility of love and mercy is not dependent on, or ultimately limited by, the nation-state. The church does not seek to dismiss or bypass the nation-state, but rather, through its practice of sanctuary it attempts to hold it accountable to basic norms of humanity to which the state is bound in theory but not always in practice.

At its root, sanctuary as envisioned in the early 1980s had parallels to Gandhi's constructive program and his method for addressing social conflicts, which he called *satyagraha*.[53] These were creative approaches that sought not only to resist legal forms of violence but also to transform conflict and prefigure in society a new way of being community. Echoing Gandhi's nonviolent methods, sanctuary was a means of organically constructing a more just and human society in communion with, and protection of, persons threatened with deportation back to violence and war.[54] As a means, there was no guarantee that sanctuary actions would be ultimately effective in terms of radically changing the government's style of politics. Yet the early sanctuary communities of the 1980s had a profound belief that there was an unparalleled transformative power in embodying nonviolence as a community. Because a Gandhian framework places its emphasis on nonviolent means rather than political ends, such an approach necessitates an openness to an unknown future and a willingness to endure suffering, a commitment also shared by a just peace ethic.[55] For the church, as an institution and a people, a willingness to endure suffering in the transformation of this conflict means making peace with the possibility that it will be persecuted, stripped of privileges, and placed on a cross if it lives in communion with "unauthorized" persons. Such experiences, however, are still the marks of an authentic church that lives justice and peace.[56]

I stated at the beginning of this section that just peace is a lens for more incisive reflection on the role the church can embody in the constructive transformation of conflict. As I have shown by turning to the 1980s sanctuary ministry and the Gandhian frameworks that undergirded it, some of the norms and practices that a just peace ethic advocates were already present in how sanctuary communities responded to the presence of displaced persons at risk of deportation. In our contemporary context, a just peace ethic can help us see more clearly the role of nonviolence in sanctuary practices, and more importantly, a just peace framework can serve as a much needed bridge between theories of social transformation (whether Gandhian or otherwise) and the critical role the church is called to play in the interruption of deadly cycles of conflict and violence. Some of the norms that are essential for just peace, such as the need for sustaining spiritual disciplines (e.g., discernment processes), a robust civil society (e.g., civil initiative), and nonviolent structures that protect civilians (e.g., sanctuary practices), have a greater chance of becoming an integral part of our ecclesial imaginary and discourse because of the way in which a just peace ethic merges them with the Christian tradition.

Sanctuary will certainly require many of the virtues proposed by a just peace ethic, such as solidarity and hospitality. A profound courage will be particularly necessary if the church is going to stand upright and endure the government's persecution for entering into solidarity with the violated humanity of persons who are forced to migrate.

Conclusion

As long as violence in Central America continues to threaten the lives and humanity of persons, they will continue to seek life outside of their countries, even in "unauthorized" ways. Those who flee to the United States and successfully enter present to the church a responsibility to protect that entails risking our security for theirs in order to resist the legalized violence of our government. Sanctuary actions are a positive force that begins to imagine and enflesh a more human community in the present.

The topic of immigration in the US and the church's response needs ongoing analysis through lenses of violence and peacebuilding. Particularly, there is a need to reconsider the concept and practice of sanctuary as a faithful way of being church. In his essay, Gerald Schlabach writes that "a Christian theology of peace is always first about ecclesiology and the formation of Christians as a people of peace." Envisioning and practicing church as sanctuary is an initiative that begins to form and transforms a people—the church—into a people of peace. It is from such communally embodied practices that a critical ecclesiology and theology attuned to just peace will continue to arise. Sanctuary churches not only interrupt the violence of the deportation industrial complex through refuge and other protective practices, but they also perform a public pedagogy that affirms the humanity of all persons regardless of citizenship status. As a creative response to the government's approach to unauthorized immigration, sanctuary presents an opportunity for church communities to reflect on and integrate theories and practices of peace and nonviolence with the church's mission, which is always one of loving service to the indivisible unity of God and neighbor.

Discussion Questions

1. How does foregrounding the context of violence reframe immigration?
2. What are sustainable discernment practices for church communities?
3. How does the notion of civil initiative provide a bridge between ecclesial actions and authentic practices of democracy?
4. In what ways does an ethic of just peace expand or reconfigure your understanding of church and the church's relationship to politics? With a just peace ethic, what does the church become more of and perhaps less of? What are some key tips for church actors seeking to communicate and persuade actors in the political sphere of the value of a just peace ethic? How can church actors prevent abuse or co-option of a just peace ethic by political actors?

Notes

1. On its own, the term "immigration" does not point to the reasons for why people are on the move. Furthermore, the term is closely associated with economic assumptions for mobility, such as the notion that people primarily move for better jobs.

2. There is much debate about the relationship between contemporary forms of violence (e.g., gang violence in El Salvador or narco violence in Mexico) and the degree to which they constitute "new wars" in a globalized world. For an overview of these debates and the limits and contribution of terminology, see Mary Kaldor, "In Defence of New Wars," *Stability: International Journal of Security and Development* 2, no. 4 (2013): 1–16.

3. I will use "unauthorized" to refer to persons who are in the United States without legal status and who are particularly vulnerable to deportation. For the government's "law and order" view on immigration, see Cecilia Menjívar, "Liminal Legality: Salvadoran and Guatemalan Immigrants' Lives in the United States," *American Journal of Sociology* 111, no. 4 (2006): 999–1037, at 1007.

4. Leisy Abrego et al., "Making Immigrants into Criminals: Legal Processes of Criminalization in the Post-IIRIRA Era," *Journal on Migration and Human Security* 5, no. 3 (2017): 694–715.

5. Since Vatican II the Catholic Church has recognized its responsibility to discern how the Spirit of God is already at work both wherever a more human world is being constructed and wherever evil threatens and denies the humanity of persons. See *Gaudium et spes* §4, 11.

6. "Responsibility to protect" (R2P) remains stuck mostly at the level of interstate conflicts and tied to military actions. Conceptually expanding R2P as a framework for nonviolent civilian initiative in domestic conflicts can provide new avenues for the integration of international norms within a given country.

7. For an analysis of how "legal violence" affects and structures the lives of Central American immigrants in the US, see Cecilia Menjívar and Leisy J. Abrego, "Legal Violence: Immigration Law and the Lives of Central American Immigrants," *American Journal of Sociology* 117, no. 5 (March 2012): 1380–421.

8. David Cantor, "Gang Violence as a Cause of Forced Migration in the Northern Triangle of Central America," in *The New Refugees: Crime and Forced Displacement in Latin America* (Washington, DC: Brookings Institution Press, 2016), 27–45.

9. US Customs and Border Protection, "US Border Patrol Southwest Border Family Unit and UAC Apprehensions" (FY 2014–FY 2016).

10. With the implementation of the Plan Frontera Sur in 2014, which effectively serves as an extension of US immigration policy in Mexico, apprehension of persons from the Northern Triangle of Honduras, Guatemala, and El Salvador drastically increased. For example, between July 2013 and June 2014 there were 79,033 apprehended and returned Central Americans, compared to the period from July 2014 to June 2015 when there were 137,067 apprehensions. See Daniel Villafuerte Solís et al., "La Política Antimigrante de Barack Obama y el Programa Frontera Sur: Consecuencias para la Migración Centroamericana," *Migración y Desarrollo* 15, no. 28 (2017): 39–64, at 51.

11. Luis Arriola Vega, "Issue Brief 08.05.16: Mexico's Not-So-Comprehensive Southern Border Plan," *Rice University's Baker Institute for Public Policy*, http://www.bakerinstitute.org/media/files/files/329273a1/BI-Brief-080516-MEX_Border.pdf.

12. Roselia Chaca, "Migrantes Recorren Rutas mas Peligrosas," *El Universal*, January 29, 2015.

13. Coalición de Derechos Humanos & No More Deaths, "Disappeared: How the U.S. Border Enforcement Agencies Are Fueling a Missing Persons Crisis," 5.

14. U.S. Border Patrol, "Border Patrol Strategic Plan: 1994 and Beyond," July 1994.

15. Coalición de Derechos Humanos & No More Deaths, "Disappeared," 9.

16. For statistics on disappeared persons in Mexico, see Comisión de Derechos Humanos del Distrito Federal, "Personas Desaparecidas en México," *Defensor: Revista Mensual de la Comisión de Derechos Humanos del Distrito Federal* 9 (2015): 3, http://cdhdf.org.mx/wp-content/uploads/2015/09/dfensor_09_2015.pdf; for political motives for disappearances, see Federico Mastrogiovanni, *Ni Vivos ni Muertos: La Desaparición Forzada en México como Estrategia de Terror* (Mexico: Grijalbo, 2014).

17. Azam Ahmed and Paulina Villegas, "Investigators Say Mexico Has Thwarted Efforts to Solve Student's Disappearance," *New York Times*, April 22, 2016.

18. Mastrogiovanni, Ni Vivos ni Muertos, 60.

19. José Antonio Román, "Desaparecidos, 10 Mil Migrantes en México: Solalinde," *La Jornada*, August 18, 2016.

20. Fr. Alejandro Solalinde, "II Coloquio sobre Violencia, Narcotráfico y Salud Mental," *Universidad Nacional Autónoma de México*, August 18, 2016, https://youtu.be/AyOi4ES2SiQ.

21. Mathieu Tourliere, "Madres de Migrantes Desaparecidos Inician Búsqueda de sus Familiares en la CDMX," *Revista Proceso*, November 24, 2016.

22. For example, see Sala Negra del Faro, *Crónicas Negras: Desde una Región que no Cuenta* (San Salvador: Editorial Santillana, 2013).

23. American Civil Liberties Union, "Warehoused and Forgotten: Immigrants Trapped in Our Shadow Private Prison System," June 2014.

24. American Civil Liberties Union, "Warehoused and Forgotten," 22.

25. National Immigrant Justice Center, "ICE Released Its Most Comprehensive Immigration Detention Date Yet. It's Alarming," March 13, 2018.

26. Sara Riva, "Across the Border and into the Cold: Hieleras and the Punishment of Asylum-Seeking Central American Women in the United States," *Citizenship Studies* 21, no. 3 (2017): 309–26.

27. ACLU Foundation of Southern California, "Xochitl Hernandez et al. v. Loretta Lynch et al.," April 6, 2016.

28. See "U.S. Commission on Civil Rights Concerned with Alleged Abusive Labor Practices at Immigration Detention Centers," *United States Commission on Civil Rights*, December 21, 2017; Jacqueline Stevens, "When Migrants Are Treated like Slaves," *New York Times*, April 4, 2018.

29. Jeff Sommer, "Trump's Win Gives Stocks in Private Prison Companies a Reprieve," *New York Times*, December 3, 2016.

30. Jeremy Slack, Daniel E. Martínez, Alison Elizabeth Lee, and Scott Whiteford, "The Geography of Border Militarization: Violence, Death and Health in Mexico and the United States," *Journal of Latin American Geography* 15, no. 1 (2016): 7–32.

31. Deepa Fernandes, *Targeted: Homeland Security and the Business of Immigration* (New York: Seven Stories Press, 2007), 169.

32. Judith Butler, *Frames of War: When Is Life Grievable?* (New York: Verso Books, 2010), 1, 31. See also Judith Butler, *Precarious Life* (New York: Verso Books, 2004).

33. Transactional Records Access Clearinghouse, "Asylum Representation Rates Have Fallen amid Rising Denial Rates," Syracuse University, 2017.

34. Kristin E. Heyer, "Internalized Borders: Immigration Ethics in the Age of Trump," *Theological Studies* 79, no. 1 (2018): 146–64, at 158.

35. Bradford E. Hinze, "Vatican II and U.S. Catholic Communities: Promoting Grassroots Democracy," in *The Legacy of Vatican II* (New York: Paulist Press, 2015), 175.

36. Within peace studies literature there is a conceptual difference between "conflict resolution" and "conflict transformation." To avoid a caricature of either approach, I will simply say that conflict transformation provides a broader understanding of the givenness of conflict in human relationships (individual and collective) and that the emphasis is on transformation from destructive to more constructive forms. For more on conflict transformation and its givenness, see John Paul Lederach, *Preparing for Peace: Conflict Transformation across Cultures* (New York: Syracuse University Press, 1995), 9–10.

37. A fine example of the need for such statements comes from Bishop Mark J. Seitz from El Paso, TX, who on April 5, 2018, issued a response to Trump's plan to send the US military to the southern border. There he asks, "Has it now become a crime in our country to run for your life?" http://www.elpasodiocese.org/news--events/bishop-seitz-statement-on-executive-order-sending-the-national-guard-to-our-southern-border.

38. Sanctuary churches that give refuge and protect those threatened with deportation serve as a form of truth commission that resists government rhetoric.

39. Pope Francis, *Gaudete et exultate* [On the call to holiness in today's world], March 19, 2018, §175.

40. For example, an April 7, 2017, letter from bishop Peter A. Libasci of Manchester, NH, that was sent to his priests effectively, without explicitly saying so, prohibits priests from providing refuge to someone who seeks sanctuary in a church. See J. B. Cachila, "Churches Cannot Provide Legal Sanctuary to Immigrants, Bishop Says," *The Christian Post*, April 11, 2017. To read the letter, visit http://nhchurches.org/wp-content/uploads/2017/12/2017-04-07-Letter-from-Bishop-Libasci-re-Sanctuary.pdf.

41. For a classical study for discerning the Holy Spirit's relation to prophetic activity, see Yves Congar, *True and False Reform in the Church* (Collegeville, MN: Liturgical Press, 2011), 169–98. For a brief summary of the Holy Spirit's relation to virtue, especially in the work of Aquinas, see Yves Congar, "The Gifts and the Fruits of the Spirit," in *I Believe in the Holy Spirit*, vol. 2 (New York: Crossroad Herder, 2015), 134–39.

42. Hamilton Hess, *The Early Development of Canon Law and the Council of Serdica* (New York: Oxford University Press, 2002), 203.

43. Gregory of Nazianzus, "On St. Basil the Great," *The Fathers of the Church*, vol. 22 (New York: The Fathers of the Church, Inc., 1953), 73; John Chrysostom, "Homily One on Eutropius: On Eutropius, the Eunuch, Patrician and Consul." *Nicene and Post-Nicene Fathers, First Series*, vol. 9 (Buffalo, NY: Christian Literature Publishing Co., 1889), §1; Augustine of Hippo, *City of God* (New York: Doubleday, 1958), 40–41.

44. According to Frederick Russell, "The Truce of God limited the use of violence to certain time periods, while the Peace of God declared certain occupational classes, such as clerics, to be immune from all violence." Russell, *War in the Middle Ages* (Cambridge: Cambridge University Press, 1975), 34.

45. See Norman Maclaren Trenholme, *The Right of Sanctuary in England* (St. Louis: University of Missouri, 1903), 11.

46. In the past few years, religious organizations have applied the concept of humanitarian corridors to the refugee phenomenon in Europe. See Vicki Squire, "Humanitarian Corridors: Beyond Political Gesture," October 17, 2016.

47. See Karl Shoemaker, *Sanctuary and Crime in the Middle Ages: 400–1500* (Bronx, NY: Fordham University Press, 2011).

48. Jim Corbett, *Sanctuary for All Life* (Berthoud, CO: Howling Dog Press, 2005), 70. Most of Corbett's writings can be found at the University of Arizona archives. This book posthumously collects some of his philosophical, theological, political, and ecological insights. Corbett's point that sanctuary was civil initiative and not civil disobedience was never fully grasped by the media, thus obfuscating some of the most original philosophical aspects of this tradition.

49. United Nations, "Principles of International Law Recognized in the Charter of the Nürnberg Tribunal and in the Judgment of the Tribunal," 1950.

50. Jim Corbett, *The Sanctuary Church* (Wallingford, PA: Pendle Hill Publications, 1986), 18.

51. Corbett, 13.

52. Corbett, 14.

53. See Joan Bondurant, *Conquest of Violence: The Gandhian Philosophy of Conflict* (Princeton, NJ: Princeton University Press, 1988), 4.

54. For Jim Corbett, the practice of sanctuary in the borderlands followed a Gandhian approach to social change in contrast to an Alinsky approach that was more popular in other parts of the US. He wrote, "For those who seek politico-military power, Alinsky opens a way. For those who seek communion, Gandhi opens a way." Jim Corbett, *Goatwalking: A Guide to Wildland Living, a Quest for the Peaceable Kingdom* (New York: Penguin Books, 1991), 108.

55. For an analysis of a Gandhian understanding of means and ends, see David Cortright, *Peace: A History of Movements and Ideas* (Cambridge: Cambridge University Press, 2008), 215; for the just peace ethics framework, see McCarthy, "Just Peace Ethic: A Virtue-Based Approach," this volume, chap. 3.

56. See Jon Sobrino, *The True Church and the Poor* (Maryknoll, NY: Orbis, 1984), 84.

5

ENVIRONMENTAL JUSTICE

May Justice and Peace Flow like a River

NANCY M. ROURKE

The role of the US in our world's environmental crisis is particularly significant, and one of the key causes and manifestations of this crisis in the
United States is environmental racism. Racism has shaped life in the US even
before the colonial era, and it continues today. For example, contemporary
American incarceration has adapted the practices and thought patterns of
slavery, and the history of American medical research also demonstrates a
white American pattern of viewing black bodies as means to white ends.[1]

Pervasive racism in the form of environmental injustice finally captured
the attention of Americans of all races in the 1980s. For this awareness, we
owe gratitude to the communities of Warren County, North Carolina. In
1978 this community was targeted for a landfill of toxic waste.[2] The county's
residents, predominantly people of color, organized and carried out days of
nonviolent civil disobedience. Hundreds of arrests followed, gaining national media attention. Through these protests, and despite the fact that the soil
composition was not ideal for this landfill, toxic wastes were brought to this
rural county to be dumped in a newly built site.[3] In 1994 the barrier by which
this dump attempted to block toxins from leaching into groundwater began
to fail. Officials proposed to relocate the toxic sludge, a third time, to yet
another economically depressed black community.[4]

By this point, however, the residents' practices of protest, organizing, activism, education, working with major news outlets, and investing in science
had led them to see the problem and their own resources differently. They
had practiced social and environmental justice too well to permit this relo-
cation, this extension of environmental racism. As a result of their grassroots
activism against the dump, these residents had increased the percentage of
voter registrations in their county. They had made connections with leaders
of the Congressional Black Caucus, had elected every black candidate who
ran for office in May of 1982, and had elicited promises of future justice from
North Carolina's governor.[5] Rather than permitting a spread of these dangerous materials, they leveraged the governor's public statements and forced
the state of North Carolina to find a way to detoxify the sludge. The cycle

of environmental racism was broken because this community had practiced the virtues that enabled justice. These practices and the virtues they nurtured brought them to see the importance of pursuing good ends and of employing means to those ends, which resonate with the ends themselves. Practicing interpreting their struggle in its full complexity brought them to an awareness of the webs within which all the pressures, connections, and threads of this dump and of their opposition took place.

This community's work sparked the development of a report documenting nationwide patterns of environmental racism. The United Church of Christ's Commission for Racial Justice mapped out data from the Government Accountability Office (GAO), the Environmental Protection Agency (EPA), the US Census Bureau, and a directory of industrial and hazardous waste management firms and published its findings.[6] This study showed that decisions about where to create hazardous commercial waste sites nationwide correlated more consistently with racial demographics of residents than with any other variable.[7] They found that race correlated significantly even after controlling for variables of socioeconomic status. In 2007 a second report found that "race continues to be a significant and robust predictor of commercial hazardous waste facility locations."[8] By this time race was a "stronger predictor" than both income and education level.[9] Methods of remediation of pollutants also varied with race: existing environmental law is reinforced unevenly in the US.[10] As of 2007, people of color "comprise a *majority* of the population living near the nation's commercial hazardous waste facilities."[11]

Environmental racism determines how industrial waste is handled, but it also takes additional forms.[12] Race also correlates with "air pollution, contaminated fish consumption, municipal landfills and incinerators," and lead poisoning.[13] Robert Bullard, an expert in environmental racism, defines it as "any policy, practice, or directive that differentially affects or disadvantages (whether intended or unintended) individuals, groups, or communities based on race or color."[14] He notes that it "combines with public policies and industry practices to provide benefits for whites while shifting costs to people of color" through efforts of the government, legal realms, and economic and military actions and policies. A definition used by Rev. Benjamin Chavis, executive director of the United Church of Christ's Commission on Racial Justice, notes specific forms of environmental racism. It happens through "racial discrimination in environmental policymaking and the enforcement of regulations and laws, the deliberate targeting of people of color communities for toxic waste facilities, the official sanctioning of the life-threatening presence of poisons and pollutants in our communities, and the history of excluding people of color from leadership in the environmental movement."[15]

In this chapter, I connect just peace ethics with environmental racism, focusing on the water of the people of Flint, Michigan. First, I describe the context of the case in Flint. Second, I reflect on this case with a just peace ethic, with a particular focus on relevant virtues.

Flint Water Crisis

In Flint, a city that charges its residents more for water than almost every other city in the US, the water has been toxic since 2014.[16] This city, the fourth largest and the most segregated city in Michigan, switched its water supply from Detroit's water system to the Flint River in April 2014.[17] Costs to the city for tapping Detroit's water supply were deemed too high. Shortly after the switch, residents began noticing changes in the water's smell, taste, and color. For months, residents complained and officials reassured the public that the water was safe.[18] By late summer, residents had endured multiple boil advisories. In October 2014 an auto plant shut off their own water supply because it was corroding their machinery.[19] Also, twelve people died of Legionnaires' disease before the city stopped drawing water from the Flint River.[20] In January 2015 Michigan's Department of Environmental Quality (DEQ) notified residents that the water was legally safe but risky for vulnerable individuals.[21] The public did not know at that time that questions were being raised at the EPA about whether the water was in fact being treated according to the law.[22] In spring of 2015 residents independently recruited a water expert to test their water, and lead was found. A pediatrician confirmed that children had lead in their blood. Finally the news broke nationwide in fall of 2015 and money began to arrive from federal and state levels to mitigate the danger.[23]

Reflecting with a Just Peace Ethic

McCarthy describes three overlapping "spheres" of focus in a virtue-based just peace ethic. This discussion of environmental racism will consider virtues that seem particularly significant for two focus areas: breaking cycles of violence and building sustainable peace.

A virtue is a well-balanced moral habit. Virtues are formed by practices that exercise them and—in Christian virtue theories—by infused gifts from God "into" a person's moral character. A person and a society can grow in virtue by putting virtues to work. Practices like gardening help us to form virtues like patience, attentiveness, gratitude, and humility. Just peace pioneer John Paul Lederach and others describe many virtues and practices that shape a moral character well suited for just peace activity.

As we look at the Flint water crisis, we will find examples of virtue-forming practices that can break cycles of structural violence like environmental racism and virtue-forming practices that help build sustainable just peace.

We will look first at negative examples—practices that exercise the vices that impede justice and peace. These are visible in the circumstances leading to Flint's water crisis and in many of the responses to the crisis. This search is itself a virtuous practice. Learning to notice how and when the virtues of just peace are neglected will help our awareness of our own practices. We need this awareness to exercise virtues for our own just peace activity. Among the practices recommended by the just peace virtue tradition are (1) a habit of employing only those means that resonate with goals and (2) practices of web-watching or social analysis.[24] McCarthy has called the first of these the "norm of reflexivity." Respect for the Earth also requires just means. This norm's wisdom lies in the fact that even as we pursue ends, we are also always choosing a way of life. This means that working through just and nonviolent means is a practice that shapes our own being.

In Flint, a practice of overriding elected leadership led to an authoritarian, rigid, and deadly means of governance that precipitated the water crisis. Participatory means of governance are fundamental for just governance. When this was stopped, the decisions made were bad for Flint's economy, water, and people. The norm of reflexivity calls for many practices, including truth-valuing and well-grounded pessimism.

Truth-telling is essential for practices that seek to use means that resonate with just ends and with peace. In order for democracies to work, truth must be valued and available to all, regardless of any other competing priorities. There are lots of reasons to want to hide truth. Truth can imperil one's chances at election or reelection. It can lead others to make decisions that one would prefer they not make. It can threaten any broader narratives that one might, for bad and for good reasons, want to see remain intact. But if a means toward a good end includes compromising, hiding, obfuscating, or silencing truth, then the good end will be impeded and no just peace will result.[25]

A well-grounded pessimism is a critical virtue in situations in which truth has been compromised or silenced. When goals of powerful agents are sought using means that do not resonate with those ends, agents with less power are right to exercise pessimism about the means and the ends of those in power. Vulnerability due to power differences must be a factor in deciding about whether and how to give trust. This is particularly true when trust has, in fact, been violated. Generationally inherited poverty, such as Flint, is always a symptom of such a violation. The state of Michigan responded to Flint's long-standing financial problems by taking over the city's financial operations in 2002.[26] At that time, the city's debt was almost thirty million dollars.[27] A sharp decrease in population exacerbated these financial problems. After the auto industry boom, Flint was left with a very large infrastructure (including pipelines and roads) and a plummeting number of residents to pay for its maintenance. In the years leading to the water crisis, this problem spiraled. In 2011, Michigan passed a law saying that when a city has accumulated a great deal of debt and is not demonstrating its ability to pay that debt off, the governor can appoint an emergency financial manager to run the city for the purposes of righting the city's finances.[28] This emergency manager is empowered to override the authority of elected officials, to cut wages and services, to merge school districts, to sell public assets, raise the rates of public water, and institute new taxes with no public input.[29] The emergency manager appointed to govern Flint in 2011 did these things and more to tighten the city's spending.[30]

Michigan's emergency manager law is an example of a means that violates the end it purportedly seeks. The stated goal of this law is to correct a city's financial problems. The method by which this end is sought is to override the city's democratic processes and to appoint an individual to govern the city. Suspension of democratic process, particularly for the purpose of pursuing one single goal, is a clear rejection of just means of governing. This is even truer when the goal only indirectly benefits the governed. In the US, where practices of democratic process are at the heart of hopes for justice, this practice is a serious violation. It is not coincidental that this law has been put into effect only in cities where the majority of the population is black.[31]

Flint's emergency manager reduced the services to the city's residents. Cuts included garbage pickup; wage cuts and layoffs among police, fire, and municipal employees; increased costs to residents for water; and a new tax on retirees' pensions.[32] The emergency manager's decision to switch the city's water source from Detroit's system to draw directly from the Flint River aimed to reduce the cost of supplying water to the people of Flint.[33] In the months leading into the water crisis, the taxes collected from Flint's residents were routed toward the city's debt-holders and out of the budgets for the services that these taxes normally paid for.

This is not a fiscally restorative means. No part of this means addresses the primary reasons for the debt. Alternatively, an emergency manager could reorganize a city's money management or establish a new fiscal structure through which the city's officials would then govern. Furthermore, the actual application of this law is racist. Remember that racism does not only comprise actions or policies carried out with an announced intention of racism. The nature of this law's use is clearly in accordance with racism, understood as "state-sanctioned . . . production and exploitation of group-differentiated vulnerability."[34] It also caused loss of life.

Because of this means–end disconnect, one legal scholar has noted that this law is more punitive than constructive.[35] This law absorbs a city's governance (and power) into the state's authority, but the city's budget and its difficulties remain as a burden only on the city. This means toward a goal of fiscal stability reveals a belief that the local government is what "stands in the way of solvency."[36] The practice comes from a view of a city's residents as incapable of self-governance and blames that city's poverty on ignorance, incompetence, or other failures. This view reflects not truth but racism and classism as well as a rejection of broader responsibility for Flint's struggles. The mismatch between the means of an emergency manager and the goal of a healthy city stems from a denial of truth.

So what is it that stands in the way of solvency for Flint? Why is this city in poverty? Seeking the root causes is one of the key guiding questions for a just peace ethic.

We need a wider perspective to recognize why Flint's economic troubles began. This is an opportunity to practice what Lederach calls "re-storying."[37] Opening our narrative of Flint's water crisis is to see the patterns, the remembered history, and the long view.[38] Without this we fall into the racist narratives of blame. We would miss the whole structure within which the truth can be seen. What do we see when we take a wider perspective of Flint's story?

Flint's poverty stems from decades of racist practices that withheld economic benefits and human rights from its residents of color in order to spread these benefits to county residents who were encouraged and permitted to live outside of the city's limits.[39] The explosion of population with the arrival of the auto industry led to a much larger Flint. Jobs and housing were available to white workers and families. For them, wealth was created. But Jim Crow–era segregation, continuing well past its purported conclusion, created neighborhoods of poor housing into which families of color were directed. As the auto industry shifted from city to suburbs, "white flight" accompanied the shift, and the city's population shrank. Families with privileged opportunities to move to white-majority suburbs left, following legal and social norms that restricted economic benefits to strictly white neighborhoods and families. The city's aging infrastructure had to be maintained by fewer households who were at the same time experiencing a soaring unemployment rate due to this corporate sprawl. Flint's households also continued to subsidize the auto plants of the suburbs in many ways.[40]

One example of exploitation took place in the 1960s. The city was preparing to establish its own water supply method by building a new pipeline on Lake Huron. A local businessman contractor conspired with a city manager to profit from these arrangements using a secretive real estate version of insider trading. They purchased land along this proposed water pipeline's route in order to sell it back at a much higher price to the city. They were caught and charged, but a judge dismissed the charges. The profits of the sales were returned to these conspirators. The city's plan to establish its own independent water source fell apart. Instead, the city began buying water from Detroit at a cost that was burdensome enough to precipitate the 2014 decision to switch the city's water source.[41]

Racist practices and environmental exploitation continued and evolved unchecked to shape a racially segregated city in severe economic depression. No sense of interconnectedness remained among the new suburban towns to help hold the region together in solidarity and health. This is the truth of Flint.

Just peace requires structures through which people have equitable access to basic needs, equitable choices in the manner of meeting these needs, and equitable opportunities to pursue fulfillment. As we've seen so far, Flint's water crisis—a deprivation of a basic human survival need—was not the first point at which the city's people were denied justice. Jim Crow practices prevented and opposed just peace while nurturing the vices of racism. Racism cannot survive where truth is valued and practiced. Mikulich notes that whites' "reluctance . . . to acknowledge the history of racial violence . . . maintains their privileged position . . . and also exacerbates the pain, suffering, and frustration experienced by black people."[42] Deceptions, silence, and denials of history further racism and harm communities of color in the US, but practices that value truth counteract racism.

Truth-telling is also a critical practice of just peace. The truth is that this city is poor because of economic and racial injustice and exploitation by a powerful few at the expense of many, particularly the poor and those who suffer most egregiously and directly from racism. Therefore, Flint's water saga reveals multifaceted attempts to first avoid, then to silence, and eventually to deny truth. Truth was undermined when the city switched from the Detroit water supply to the Flint River. Residents were concerned about the switch at its very beginning in 2014. The Flint River, a site of heavy industrial activity, was not known for its drinkability. Officials anticipated residents' worries about the switch and worked hard to send a message that the Flint River water was safe.[43] They knew residents were worried about this source of water.[44]

These messages did not come from any particular confidence in water quality. The motivation was to reinforce order and quiet. The goal was not safer water but cheaper water. Truth was valued less than cultivating a particular mood. This practice strengthened and fed duplicity as time passed.

By summer, residents had been complaining for months about changes in the color, taste, and smell of the water. The city sent a letter to residents in July 2014 declaring the water safe.[45] A year later, when the city did eventually concede some problems, it blamed ordinary seasonal changes and the shrinking population.[46] We now know that the city's testing and treatment methods did not comply with existing standards and protocols. Yet each response to the complaints and questions from the city's residents was to brush aside concerns. These inadequate responses persisted through repeated rounds of boil advisories when coliform bacteria was found in the water and through a Legionnaires' disease outbreak.

Despite official reassurances, other signs indicated that officials were aware that something was wrong. Officials decided to begin distributing bottled water to state employees in Flint offices without admitting a water problem.[47] The governor's chief of staff and an EPA regional manager had begun asking questions about the water's safety.

When an EPA regional manager asked the DEQ whether the city was treating the water supply correctly, an affirmative, swift, and erroneous response came back.[48] In 2015 the governor's chief of staff emailed out of concern about Flint's water quality.[49] These communications were not acknowledged openly until much later, after officials had been forced to admit that there was a problem in the water's delivery system. Had these questions and concerns been given the acknowledgment and investigation they deserved, the problem would have been addressed sooner and the people would have had a chance to be protected adequately. Practices that fail to honor truth cultivate practices that hide and deny truth. The city had a problem, and those responsible for protecting the people failed to acknowledge that problem. In other words, officials failed to actualize the just peace practice of acknowledging responsibility for harm.

Another opportunity for truth appeared when in October 2014 a General Motors plant in the city switched from the city's water to a different supply because the water had been corroding the machinery for months.[50] This was a moment at which residents' concerns could have been viewed in a more serious way by the state or city officials or agencies. The truth that the water was harmful was demonstrated in GM's announcement and action here, but the practice of insisting that the water was safe continued.

Further, when water testing revealed trihalomethanes, the city continued to say that the water quality did not present an "imminent threat to public health."[51] Months later, when a Flint pediatrician, Dr. Mona Hanna-Attisha, announced publicly that she had found high levels of lead in children's blood, the response from the Department of Health and Human Services was to disagree, saying that they had more data and were not seeing this problem.[52] A DEQ official called the doctor's speech "unfortunate" and complained that the mood was "near-hysteria" for no sufficient reason.[53] The immediate response to Dr. Hanna-Attisha's announcement demonstrated an effort to silence the truth about the water. Responses that aimed for quiet instead of peace and for passivity instead of justice had escalated to the point of reactions against truth-telling.

Despite the continuing resistance to the truth, Flint's residents organized, protested, and worked to learn what was, in truth, in their water. Dr. Hanna-Attisha's discovery and announcement resulted from residents' efforts. As she tested her patients' blood, other researchers under the direction of another water expert were confirming the presence of lead in water in houses in Flint. These professionals and the citizens and activists who drew their attention to Flint's water finally made the truth known past the silencing and disregard of their own elected officials and environmental agencies at the local and state levels. After Dr. Hanna-Attisha's announcement, national news media sources began to describe what was happening in Flint, and the layers of truth-denial were peeled back. Through this story, we can see that the residents' awareness of a problem was unshaken and served them well to the point of likely saving lives. Attempts to convince residents to mistrust what their senses were telling them failed. Flint's residents demonstrated a pessimism which served them well, keeping them safer than the officials responsible for serving them. The numbers of residents killed and of children with lead poisoning could have been even higher. As it turned out, the long-term health and safety of many of Flint's children hinged on these families' recognizing that they could not trust the government's claims about water quality.

Practices of valuing truth and this well-grounded pessimism are connected. A well-grounded pessimism understands that there is no "ahistorical change."[54] This relates to the importance of historical memory. When a simplistic and well-packaged cheerfulness is presented to a marginalized public who knows well from their own experience, both recent (the suspension of democratic process) and historical (forced segregation of the city and economic and environmental exploitation), a practiced, grounded pessimism serves as an essential "warning system."[55]

Lederach notes that the practice of a virtue of well-grounded pessimism includes asking repeatedly whether change has actually happened. True change toward building just peace must be "broadly structural," but it also must be evident in "minutiae and immediacy of people's behavior."[56] That is, individual actions of officials are connected to whether sufficiently structural change is taking place. When officials overexert themselves to assure the citizens that the water is safe despite evidence that something is wrong, the effect to an observer with a well-formed character is to be suspicious.[57] In the case of Flint, such suspicion is grounded in knowledge of history. The city is poor despite the economic boom of the auto industry. The city is segregated despite the fact that housing discrimination is illegal. The company whose fortunes the city created protects machinery from corrosive water while residents are expected to drink—and pay for—that same water. Pessimism helped steer residents' efforts toward marshaling safe water supplies through churches, social networks, and broad activism. The virtues that comprise what Lederach called pessimism were essential for survival in the story of Flint's water crisis.

When we look at the historical memory narrative of Flint's crisis, we see that this crisis is actually a continuation of racist beliefs, policies, and practices through US history. Economic and socially punitive policies after slavery's official end, Reconstruction and the segregation of Jim Crow, and late-twentieth-century methods of law enforcement all contribute to Flint's poverty and vulnerability. Jobs, housing opportunities, and other forms of prosperity and support were blocked from black communities and families, which violates the just peace norm of economic justice.

The Michigan Civil Rights Commission's report describing Flint's water crisis tells the story well. The report demonstrates that systems of racism, evolving and perpetuating structural violence, and insufficient resources for human life collaborated to contain and trap black residents of Flint, all while presenting an image of a city that mysteriously is unable to spend its money wisely. Without a narrative informed by a historical memory, one could easily assume that the failures of Flint's water infrastructure resulted from individuals who were too lazy or ignorant to do their jobs, or from an incompetent electorate which is unable to self-govern without paternalistic correctives from the greater state of Michigan. In a racist society, of course, many white people do easily reach these conclusions, and so racism self-perpetuates. Without the historic memory there can be no adequate understanding of the crisis. The truth is kept hidden and justice and peace are prevented.

This historic memory requires and nurtures habits of attentiveness to complex webs of relationships, causes, and effects. These habits resemble what Lederach calls web-watching.[58] Lederach describes studiers of spiders and watchers of web-weaving. They move through space gingerly, attentively, patiently, looking for any hint as to how the gossamer strands of air are connected and which strands might be swaying toward, rooted in, or catching onto other strands. They are quiet and eager, unable to see the webs they are near and at the same time certain that regions of this web's connectivity will become perceptible, a little at a time. This is unlike a mapping, a charting of steps, a table of history, or a checklist of compliances. This kind of attentiveness, an attentiveness that affects even the way a person stands, leans in, and breathes, is also appreciated and practiced in ecological virtue ethics.[59] Ecological awareness teaches us that we are always and entirely a part of the ecosystems into which we are embedded.

Web-watching takes truth as authoritative. It is a way of seeing that requires the observer to work *around* what is observed, as if in partnership with it. It values complexity. Just peace requires attentiveness to complex and interrelated webs. In contrast, fragmentation, the opposite tendency, predominated many responses to the Flint water crisis. Fragmentation of a whole truth into discontinuous bits impeded awareness of the whole truth. Vices of fragmentation focus on parts of a whole truth in such a way that deception is layered onto an appearance of truth-telling. Fragmentation shows the pieces of a web while also hiding complex causality. The effect is to obscure the whole truth.

Fragmentation enables selective blindness, ignores systemic issues, and erases accountability because justice is not the job of anyone in particular. It is a simplification where complexity is sorely needed. Fragmentation is a particular problem in environmental moral failures. Ecosystems are webs of dynamic interrelatedness. All human agency is contained within them and interacts with them constantly. Fragmentation allows human responses to environments to select which causes and effects matter and which do not. However, all causes and effects in ecosystems matter.

In Flint, fragmentation practices were evidenced in many of the official responses to the breaking of the news that there was a lot of lead in Flint's water. When this news broke nationwide, a volley of blame began. The DEQ blamed the mayor. The mayor blamed the EPA. The EPA blamed the governor. The governor blamed the DEQ and other "career bureaucrats." Republicans blamed the EPA, and Democrats blamed the governor of Michigan.

Congressional hearings held to investigate the cause of this crisis identified and questioned individuals. Ultimately, about a dozen individuals at various levels of authority faced prosecution, sentences, or firing, or resigned.[60] This investigation was a form of justice that may seem appropriate. At the same time, however, these official responses were also a rejection of complexity. The effect of all this was to distract attention away from the systemic failures that stole a necessity of life from a most vulnerable population. The message was that justice for Flint could be carried out without a need to think about racism at all.

At the time of this writing, the water in Flint is still not safe to drink. Restoration of trust in the systems was the first priority of these hearings and investigations, but restoration of justice was not accomplished. The actual trauma was not addressed. This trauma point reverberates because Flint needs corrective or restorative justice. The Michigan Civil Rights Commission report notes that "the failure to repair the harms suffered by discrimination is itself ongoing discrimination that causes ongoing harm."[61] These practices of restorative justice and trauma-healing are key to the just peace norm of conflict transformation. A truthful response to the crisis requires first a completely truthful description of what has been happening. Our complicities in racism in the US today participated in the conditions that created Flint's continuing water crisis.

We have seen how and why failures to practice virtues of just peace contributed to a humanitarian disaster in Michigan. This story demonstrates something of why these virtues matter and of how they work (in absentia). However, Flint's story also reveals examples of just peace practices. For example, organized residents put into action an ability to find and assemble the "critical yeast" necessary to get the help they needed to increase the odds of surviving the crisis' short-term consequences. When the EPA, the DEQ, and city and state officials brushed off LeeAnn Walters's observations and experiences of the water in her house, she identified and connected with a water expert from a different state. Ms. Walters did some research independently, learned the story of unsafe water in Washington, DC, identified from that story a person who could help her to learn the truth about the state of her own city's water, and recruited his help. This expert's experience included gathering what was needed to expose the truth about unsafe water in Washington, DC, from 2004 to 2010.[62] This exposure was the beginning of the end of the enforced silence about Flint's water, and the beginning of a telling of Flint's story on a much broader scale.

"Critical yeast" practices are not about trying to increase numbers of people who know about the problem.[63] Instead, they are practices of finding exactly the right person to do what is needed, similar to "credible messengers" used to interrupt the cycles of violence. This expert's investigation, along with pediatrician Dr. Hanna-Attisha's press conference announcing that the water in Flint was demonstrably unsafe for children, began to break the enforced silence about the water quality problem. This "critical yeast" of just two individuals' work coming together made a difference.

Other examples include Melissa Mays, who co-founded a website where residents could study and learn about water quality problems and consequences ("Water You Fighting For"). Nayyirah Shariff, organizer of the Democracy Defense League, brought bottled water donation sources to Flint, raised awareness about the economic injustices surrounding this issue, and organized citizens to address the very high water bills residents have paid for poisonous water. These examples actualize the just peace practices of nonviolent resistance and community organizing as well as the just peace norm of activating a robust civil society.

Conclusion

No society in which some groups' needs are not met can be healthy. More to the point, when it comes to environmental racism in the United States, no society that withholds, obstructs, or poisons some groups' access to human needs can be a peaceful, just, or healthy society until this status quo is readily and widely acknowledged and ended. The legacy of slavery is, among other things, a legacy of denial of black peoples' humanity. This practice and the racism created to sustain it and transform it into racist systems of punishment and deprivation must be faced and, again, readily and widely acknowledged. This truth must be confessed. The nation is built on the violently coerced labor of people of color, especially black Americans, and that history is with us today at least as powerfully as it was in the 1890s, or the 1930s, or the 1970s. Environmental racism kills black Americans. To turn our nation away from racist practices and the vices they feed, we must begin valuing truth, accepting the historic memory of racism, and recognizing the webs through which we and our histories are connected. Finally, we must understand that the means through which we seek even just goals must give us practice in being the people we ought to be.

Discussion Questions

1. Why do the methods of pursuing justice matter? Identify and describe two to three reasons. Which of these reasons seems the most important to you, and why?
2. What led to the water crisis in Flint, Michigan? Describe at least four causes. Then look at the causes you've named. Do you see any similarities between these causes? If so, describe how at least some of these causes seem similar or seem related to each other.
3. Name two norms of just peace, and describe how truth-telling relates to each of these. Can you think of any other examples in which these norms could be useful for people who are working for ecological justice?
4. What kinds of practices and specific changes might a just peace ethic encourage to better prepare a society and individuals to recognize, name, and erode away the habits of its environmental racism?

Notes

1. Regarding mass incarceration, see Michelle Alexander, *The New Jim Crow: Mass Incarceration in the Age of Colorblindness* (New York: New Press, 2010); for medical experimentation and racism, see Harriet A. Washington, *Medical Apartheid: The Dark History of Medical Experimentation on Black Americans from Colonial Times to the Present* (New York: Doubleday, 2006).

2. Dollie Burwell and Luke W. Cole, "Environmental Justice Comes Full Circle: Warren County before and After," *Golden Gate University Environmental Law Journal* 1, no. 9 (2007): 9–40, 14.

3. Burwell and Luke, 13.

4. Burwell and Luke, 32–33.

5. Burwell and Luke, 29.

6. United Church of Christ Commission for Racial Justice, "Toxic Wastes and Race: A National Report on the Racial and Socio-Economic Characteristics of Communities with Hazardous Waste Sites" (United Church of Christ, 1987).

7. United Church of Christ Commission for Racial Justice, xiii.

8. United Church of Christ Justice and Witness Ministries, "Toxic Wastes and Race at Twenty (1987–2007)" (United Church of Christ, 2007), xi.

9. United Church of Christ Justice and Witness Ministries, xi.

10. United Church of Christ Justice and Witness Ministries, 7.

11. United Church of Christ Justice and Witness Ministries, 45 (emphasis added).

12. For more examples, see Karl Grossman, "Of Toxic Racism and Environmental Justice," *E: The Environmental Magazine*, June 1992; and Carl A. Zimring, *Clean and White: A History of Environmental Racism in the United States* (New York: New York University Press, 2015).

13. Daniel C. Wigley and Kristin S. Shrader-Frechette, "Environmental Racism and Biased Methods of Risk Assessment," *Risk: Health, Safety & Environment* 7 (1996): 55–88.

14. Robert D. Bullard, "Environmental Justice in the 21st Century: Race Still Matters," *Phylon (1960–)* 49, no. 3–4 (2001): 151–71, 160.

15. Grossman, "Of Toxic Racism and Environmental Justice."

16. Ron Fonger, "Flint Water Prices Almost Eight Times National Average, Erin Brockovich Associate Says," *The Flint Journal*, March 17, 2015.

17. For Flint's demographics, see Dee-Ann Durbin, "Longtime Mayor Ousted in Flint, Mich.," *Associated Press*, March 6, 2002. For details on the Detroit area water system, see Dominic Adams, "Closing the Valve on History: Flint Cuts Water Flow from Detroit after Nearly 50 Years," *The Flint Journal*, April 25, 2014.

18. Ron Fonger, "City Adding More Lime to Flint River Water as Resident Complaints Pour In," *The Flint Journal*, June 12, 2014.

19. Kellen R. Utecht and William F. McCoy, "Water Management Lessons from Flint, Mich.," *ASHRAE Journal* 58, no. 5 (May 2016): 88–89.

20. Rebecca Hersher, "Lethal Pneumonia Outbreak Caused by Low Chlorine In Flint Water," *NPR*, February 5, 2018.

21. Ron Fonger, "Flint Residents Call for Investigative Hearings into 'Water Crisis,'" *The Flint Journal*, January 5, 2015.

22. Jim Lynch, "Whistle-Blower Del Toral Grew Tired of EPA 'Cesspool,'" *The Detroit News*, March 29, 2016.

23. Mitch Smith and Abby Goodnough, "Michigan Officials Defend Handling of Outbreak in Flint," *The New York Times*, February 10, 2016.

24. Jarem Sawatsky, *The Ethic of Traditional Communities and the Spirit of Healing Justice: Studies from Hollow Water, the Iona Community, and Plum Village* (London: Jessica Kingsley Publishers, 2009); and "Extending the Peacebuilding Timeframe: Revising Lederach's Integrative Framework," *Peace Research* 37, no. 1 (2005): 123–30.

25. Sawatsky, *Ethic of Traditional Communities*, 195, 208.

26. Alexandra Moses, "A Year after Mayor Recalled, Troubled Flint, Mich., Still Looks for Better Days," *Associated Press*, March 5, 2003; and Michelle Wilde Anderson, "Democratic Dissolution: Radical Experimentation in State Takeovers of Local Governments Cooper-Walsh Colloquium: Big Problems, Small Government: Assessing the Recent Financial Crisis' Impact on Municipalities," *Fordham Urban Law Journal* 39 (2011–12): 577–624, 581.

27. "Warren, Lansing Mayors Win; Millionaire Wins in Flint," *Associated Press*, November 5, 2003.

28. Rick Ungar, "The Michigan Monarchy Legislates Financial Martial Law—Nation Yawns," *Forbes*, March 18, 2011.

29. Blake Thorne, "Gov. Rick Snyder Attends Flint Fundraiser as Hundreds Protest Outside," *The Flint Journal*, September 12, 2014.

30. Dominic Adams, "A Look at What the State's Emergency Managers Did While in Flint," *The Flint Journal*, April 9, 2018.

31. Anderson, "Democratic Dissolution," 587.

32. Regarding cuts to garbage pickup, see Gordon Young, *Teardown: Memoir of a Vanishing City* (Berkeley: University of California Press, 2013), 191. For police, fire, and municipal employee cuts, see Young, *Teardown*, 253; and Jake May, "Flint's History of Emergency Management and How It Got to Financial Freedom," *The Flint Journal*, January 16, 2018. For water rate hikes, see Steve Carmody, "Flint Water Rates to Be Reviewed," *Michigan Radio NPR*, December 18, 2013.

33. Steve Carmody, "Judge Dismisses Lawsuit over Flint's City Water Rates," *Michigan Radio NPR*, June 22, 2013.

34. Alex Mikulich, "Becoming Authentically and Truly Black," this volume.

35. Anderson, "Democratic Dissolution," 587.

36. Anderson, 587.

37. John Paul Lederach, *The Moral Imagination: The Art and Soul of Building Peace* (New York: Oxford University Press, 2005), 138–49.

38. Lederach, *Moral Imagination*, 141–42.

39. Michigan Civil Rights Commission, "The Flint Water Crisis: Systemic Racism through the Lens of Flint: Report of the Michigan Civil Rights Commission," February 17, 2017, 23–24.

40. Civil Rights Commission, "Flint Water Crisis," 51.

41. Ron Fonger, "50 Years Later: Ghosts of Corruption Still Linger along Old Path of Failed Flint Water Pipeline," *The Flint Journal*, November 12, 2012.

42. Mikulich, chapter 6 of this volume.

43. Dominic Adams, "Closing the Valve on History: Flint Cuts Water Flow from Detroit after Nearly 50 Years," *The Flint Journal*, April 25, 2014.

44. Abby Goodnough, Monica Davey, and Mitch Smith, "Fouled Water and Failed Politics," *New York Times*, January 24, 2016.

45. Goodnough, Davey, and Smith.

46. Goodnough, Davey, and Smith.

47. Civil Rights Commission, "Flint Water Crisis."

48. Goodnough, Davey, and Smith, "Fouled Water and Failed Politics."

49. Ryan Felton, "Flint Water Crisis: Michigan Governor's Advisers Warned Months before Disclosure; Rick Snyder's Advisers Suggested to Stop Using Corrosive River and Buy Residents Bottled Water before Contamination 'Gets Too Far out of Control', Emails Reveal," *The Guardian*, February 26, 2016.

50. Mike Colias, "How GM Saved Itself from Flint Water Crisis," *Automotive News*, January 31, 2016; and Ron Fonger, "General Motors Shutting off Flint River Water at Engine Plant over Corrosion Worries," *The Flint Journal*, October 13, 2014.

51. Abby Goodnough, "Flint Outbreak Was Treated with Silence," *New York Times*, February 23, 2016.

52. Joseph W. Dellapenna, "The Water Crisis in Flint, Michigan: Profitability, Cost-Effectiveness, and Depriving People of Water," in *The Role of Integrity in the Governance of the Commons: Governance, Ecology, Law, Ethics*, ed. Laura Westra et al. (Cham, Switzerland: Springer, 2017): 91–104, 91.

53. Goodnough, Davey, and Smith, "Fouled Water and Failed Politics."

54. Lederach, *Moral Imagination*, 54.

55. Lederach, 55.

56. Lederach.

57. Lederach, 58.

58. Lederach, 78–86 and 101–12.

59. For more on ecological or environmental virtue ethics, see Louke Van Wensveen, *Dirty Virtues: The Emergence of Ecological Virtue Ethics* (New York: Humanity Books, 1999); or Ronald Sandler and Philip Cafaro, eds., *Environmental Virtue Ethics* (Lanham, MD: Rowman & Littlefield, 2005); or Nancy M. Rourke, "A Catholic Virtues Ecology," in *Just Sustainability: Ecology, Technology, and Resource Extraction*, ed. Christiana Z. Peppard and Andrea Vicini (Maryknoll, NY: Orbis, 2015), 194–204.

60. See Leonard Fleming, "Public Apathy Greets Initial Flint Prosecutions," *Detroit News*, February 26, 2018; Amy Haimerl and Abby Goodnough, "Six More State Workers Charged over Flint Water Crisis," *New York Times*, July 30, 2016; and Monica Davey and Abby Goodnough, "Emails Deepen Criminal Cases in Flint, but Charges May Be Tough to Prove," *New York Times*, April 25, 2016.

61. Civil Rights Commission, "Flint Water Crisis," 107–8.

62. Robert McCartney, "Virginia Tech Professor Uncovered Truth about Lead in D.C. Water," *Washington Post*, May 23, 2010.

63. Lederach, *Moral Imagination*, 98–100.

6

BECOMING AUTHENTICALLY CATHOLIC AND TRULY BLACK

On the Condition of the Possibility of a Just Peace Approach to Anti-Black Violence

ALEX MIKULICH

Our African American brothers and sisters can't breathe (Eric Garner), can't eat skittles or wear a hoodie (Trayvon Martin), can't play loud music (Jordan Davis), can't play as a child in a park (Tamir Rice), can't seek help after an accident (Renisha McBride), can't walk to a store with a friend (Rekia Boyd), can't move to a new city and start a new job (Sandra Bland) and can't pray in their own church (Cynthia Hurd, the Reverend Clementa Pinckney, Sharonda Coleman-Singleton, Tywanza Sanders, Ethel Lee Lance, Susie Jackson, the Reverend DePayne Middleton-Doctor, the Reverend Daniel Lee Simmons, and Myra Thompson). And living by so-called middle-class norms does not shield African Americans from violence, as Ta-Nehisi Coates demonstrates.[1] Nor does class or educational attainment shield African American women and their babies from premature death.[2] I could fill this chapter with the names of a small fraction of black people whose premature death was a result of "state-sanctioned and/or extralegal production and exploitation of group-differentiated vulnerability to premature death," to quote Ruth Wilson Gilmore's definition of racism.[3] The cruel perversity of the US empire we inhabit renders the daily, violent, premature death of black life as forgettable, inevitable, and banal.

I contend that the real measure of an authentic Catholic just peace praxis in the United States that fully embraces the nonviolence at the heart of the gospel is to become truly black. My argument draws upon the liberation theology of Bryan N. Massingale, who has raised a question only a few Catholic ethicists have addressed: "*What would Catholic ethics look like if it took Black Experience seriously as a dialogue partner?* If the cries, demands, and protests of victims are the voice of God, then Malcolm's voice must be an essential resource for Catholic theological and ethical reflection."[4] He celebrates Malcolm X as a neglected classic for Catholic theological reflection as part of his overall quest to shape a moral theology that is "authentically black and truly Catholic."[5] Implied in his argument is, perhaps, an even more provocative thesis: a moral theology that is authentically Catholic must become truly black. Even though it is impossible to address the whole of moral theology here, I suggest that an approach to just peace that is authentically Catholic must also become truly black.

Certainly, my suggestion is impossible and, for some, perhaps ridiculous. How is it possible for people immersed in white culture to become black? In order to become black, US Catholic just peace literature needs to be more self-critical about our privileged racial and class positions in the midst of the unprecedented US global empire. The Catholic just peace literature should offer more reflection on the context of US empire, including the fact the US is "the greatest purveyor of violence in the world," to cite Dr. Martin Luther King.[6] And one would not easily know that countless First American people, African Americans, and Latin@s have any significant insight into the violence that has been perpetrated upon them.[7]

I begin by demonstrating how the case of the police shooting of Michael Brown replicates the US history of lynching. Too often it is forgotten how lynching was implemented as a way to advance modern racial capitalism.[8] I identify some just peace norms that may be helpful in engaging this conflict. I also draw upon the Black radical tradition to argue that a Catholic just peace ethic must take up this enduring history of violence that is rooted in racial capitalism.[9]

Finally, I suggest that the condition of the possibility of addressing anti-black logics means becoming authentically Catholic and truly black. I recommend that reorientation to the rationality and power of the oppressed by a predominantly white church and academy must include a cluster of preparations for repentance, reconciliation, and reparations.

The Case of the Police Shooting of Michael Brown

A clear mark of Christian solidarity is the practice of hearing the cry of the oppressed. When people's cries for justice move our hearts, minds, and bodies, God draws us into the struggle for ending a system and culture of oppression. In reflecting upon the police shooting of unarmed Michael Brown, I wonder whether and how white Catholic Christians hear Brown's mother, Lesley McSpadden, when she cried for her son as he lay dead in the street for over four hours.[10] Her cry is a contemporary biblical cry for justice. The message of the indignity she suffered with her relatives and neighbors was clear: black lives do not matter.

Perhaps you, the reader, might object with others that Michael Brown was "no angel," as the *New York Times* opined, as if a postmortem character assassination justified his shooting death.[11] Yet numerous cases demonstrate that white males who actually commit murder gain the benefit of the assumption of innocence on the part of law enforcement and society.[12] Human dignity means nothing if it respects only those whom society deems worthy. The just peace norm of human dignity needs to be demonstrated in a way that mourns individual and communal loss of life and creates conditions that ensure nonrepetition of such injustices.

Some object to the rioting after the shooting and the crimes against property, as opposed to the fact that a life was unjustly taken. Speaking to the Grosse Point, Michigan, high school just three weeks before his death, Dr. Martin Luther King Jr. said, "It would not be enough for me to condemn riots." He continued that he must condemn "the contingent, intolerable conditions that exist in our society. These conditions are the things that cause individuals to feel that they have no other alternative than to engage in violent rebellions to get attention. And I must say tonight that a riot is the language of the unheard."[13]

Perhaps white Americans do not hear the cry of Michael Brown's mother or of the protestors because we are not attuned to the lives of the unheard. Our failure is in no small measure due to where and how white churches form the foundation of white superiority. The problem of white habitus and hypersegregation is that it dynamically reproduces white physical, social, and moral distancing from black and brown communities, structures the "home" of white superiority and assumed racial innocence, and accumulates white wealth and power as it drains life, power, and resources from indigenous, black, and Latin@ communities.[14] The just peace norms of relationality and economic justice help to illuminate some of these issues if they are applied in a way that addresses the root causes of slavery and lynching.

Isabel Wilkerson explains that an African American is killed almost twice a week, according to data compiled by the Federal Bureau of Investigation between 2005 and 2012.[15] The banality of this reality, she observes, obscures the fact that this is nearly the same rate at which African Americans were lynched in the early twentieth century. In her call to Americans to own up to our violence, Wilkerson details the uncanny similarities between lynching and the police shooting of Michael Brown, not the least significant of which is the fact that "the lynched body was sometimes left hanging for days or weeks as a lesson to people to not step outside the caste into which they had been born."

The scholar Jacqueline Goldsby demonstrates in her history of public punishment in America how lynching was an integral part of national consciousness whose "cultural logic" was pivotal in advancing American modernity. Instead of viewing lynching as an aberrational violence of the few, she illuminates how anti-black murders thrived amid "American progress and abundance (as opposed to Southern provincialism and impoverishment)."[16]

As Wilkerson explains in her comparison of the shooting of Michael Brown to the history of lynching, although white Americans outnumber black Americans fivefold, black people are three times more likely than white people to be killed when they encounter the police in the US, and black teenagers are far more likely to be killed by police than are white teenagers. Wilkerson underscores Jacqueline Goldsby's argument that stereotypes inscribed in American culture feed prevailing assumptions of "black inferiority and wantonness since before the time of Jim Crow."[17] Even worse, video-recorded police violence today reaches hundreds of thousands of viewers on YouTube, a "form of public witness to brutality beyond anything possible in the age of lynching."[18]

Subconscious bias runs so deep that one study found that when people are exposed to pictures of someone piercing another's skin, "they experience a more dramatic, measurable, physiological response when white skin is inflicted with pain than when black skin is." Wilkerson concludes that "the brutality continues in part because the majority of Americans may literally be unable to feel the pain of their fellow Americans." The just peace norms of cultivating peacemaking cultures and key virtues such as empathy and humility would both contribute to addressing these issues. Yet white American culture remains morally, socially, and politically distant from black life.

As the social scientist Richard Rothstein explains in "The Making of Ferguson," analyses of the shooting death of Michael Brown tended to focus on the victim himself and the culpability of police officials. Too often this focus missed deeper historical roots. A complex set of interlocking and interconnected policies, practices, and programs worked together to create the conditions for police brutality to occur in Ferguson, Missouri, and indeed across the nation. Racial disparities are rooted in nearly a century of deliberate governmental and business (banking, real estate, insurance, and construction) practices and policies that created housing and educational segregation. Housing segregation is a "structural lynchpin" of economic and racial inequality. Owning a home and housing location are critical to predicting access to quality education, development of personal wealth, health and safety, democratic participation, transportation, and quality child care. The just peace norms of economic justice, just governance, and participation would help illuminate the need to address these issues. These norms, however, remain too abstract if they are not refined in the context of racial capitalism.

Rothstein demonstrates that it was the laws and public policy decisions passed by local, state, and federal governments, in concert with banking, real estate, and insurance companies, that created, promoted, and sustained the discriminatory policies that continue to this day. He explains how the Eighth Circuit Court of Appeals concluded in 1974 that "segregated housing in Saint Louis metropolitan area was . . . in large measure the result of deliberate racial discrimination in the housing market by the real estate industry and by agencies of the federal, state, and local governments."[19] The history of racial capitalism, or what some social scientists name as American apartheid, creates ripe conditions for routine violence against black life. The consequences of racial capitalism mean that indigenous, black, and Latin@ peoples are always "consigned to history's waiting room," where the elimination of injustice is always "not yet."[20]

Reflecting with a Just Peace Ethic

In describing the case above, I have identified some particular just peace norms, including the virtues of empathy and humility, cultivating peace-making communities and cultures, relationality, economic justice, and just governance. I now turn to a more focused reflection including suggestions for how to refine such a just peace ethic.

My concern is that implementation of a just peace ethic demands at least three integral racial equity practices. First, it seems only a fraction of Catholic theologians actively participate in racial equity practice. White scholars individually and as members of academic institutions and learned societies tend to not share a common analysis of race and racism and generally do not practice accountability for our own white racial privilege and racism with ourselves or our African American, Latin@, Filipino, or Asian colleagues. An interrelated issue concerns how, as members of the Catholic academy, we white scholars tend to not be accountable to movements or communities that suffer the harm of police violence. These lacunae in the predominantly white academy—lack of a common racial analysis and of racial accountability structures in the academy, and of little accountability to local communities impacted by racial violence—present deeper questions for applying a just peace approach.

One of the deeper problems relevant to this case is acknowledging responsibility for harm, which fits in the norm of conflict transformation. For example, the epistemic privilege of the victims of US history demands a thoroughgoing analysis of racial violence in the United States that unveils the enduring history of coloniality and slavery. This is a critical way to practice the dangerous memory of Jesus Christ. Practicing dangerous memory also means that a Catholic just peace ethic should draw on both "secular" and religious sources of the Black radical tradition.[21]

Engaging the Black radical tradition is one necessary but insufficient ingredient of developing an authentically Catholic just peace approach to anti-black violence. "The acid test of authentic solidarity," Massingale argues, "is how it is lived in the midst of reality, that is, in the midst of social conflict."[22] The just peace norm of solidarity would help illuminate this issue if it is understood from black perspectives. When Stokely Carmichael gave his "Black Power" speech at the University of California, Berkeley, in 1966, he asked, "Can white people move inside their community and start tearing down racism where in fact it exists?"[23] The root of racial violence is in the minds, hearts, and souls of white people who accept the structures, culture, and habitus of whiteness as a way of life. Massingale quotes a similar challenge from Malcolm X: "Where the really sincere white people have got to do their 'proving' of themselves is not among the black victims, but out in the battle lines where America's racism really is—and that is in their own home communities; America's racism is among their own fellow whites."[24]

Even though most white people of faith may not want to be physically violent, the fact remains that too many are unwilling to take the risks necessary to challenge the culture of white violence in their own communities. Enhanced by a particular attention to white violence within predominantly white institutions, the just peace norm of cultivating peacemaking communities and cultures helps to illuminate this issue.

Catholic ethicist Michael Jaycox underscores how white cultural dominance "corrupts epistemological capacities" of Catholic scholarship. His recent participatory ethnographic reflection on the Black Lives Matter (BLM) movement in Ferguson, Missouri, offers an innovative approach that is pertinent to the development of a just peace ethic. Jaycox moved to Ferguson to participate in and take risks for BLM. He underscores the problem for Catholic social ethics in how received approaches to natural law and virtue ethics will be unable to perceive the "reasonable" and "natural" calls from BLM for radical redistribution of power and resources. Jaycox argues, "the ethical claim of the intrinsic value of black life simply cannot be reliably known and understood as a natural law claim by white scholars operating in a purely conceptual mode, in consideration of the formative influence of whiteness upon their patterns of thought."[25] Perhaps some who read this will object that they do perceive the value of black life, and indeed this is why they sign statements for racial justice. However, unless white scholars are addressing their complicity in racial violence and actively participating in a communal praxis of resistance, they will miss the relationship between the vice of whiteness and the virtue of practically joining the struggle for black people.[26] The just peace practices of acknowledging responsibility for harm and nonviolent resistance, and the virtue of active nonviolence, are enriched by and help enable such initiatives. Jaycox goes deeper than a deductive approach in arguing that participation in BLM "challenges Catholic ethicists to acknowledge the epistemic privilege of black natural law and to conceive of and practice natural law as a style of reasoning that is necessarily radically situated in a praxis of resistance and solidarity."[27]

Malcolm X offers a paradigmatic example of the rationality of black natural law. Massingale explains how Malcolm X would judge the solidarity advocated by too many Catholic social ethicists as "unrealistic, if not ideologically complicit in its assessment of the difficulty of achieving social change."[28] The problem concerns how white people develop critical consciousness of the illogic of dominant epistemology. Massingale quotes Benjamin Karim, one of Malcolm X's close associates, who expressed this development of critical consciousness as understanding how "untruths had to be untold." Karim further explained that Malcolm X would teach his students that "We had to be untaught before we could be taught, and once untaught, we ourselves could unteach others."[29] Just as black people may need to unlearn internalized inferiority, so white people need to unlearn internalized superiority as a spiritual discipline. The work of unlearning internalized white superiority demands the commitment of a life internally, interpersonally, and within communities of resistance. The work of unlearning internalized domination within ourselves and white culture can transform how we understand the virtue of active nonviolence in the just peace norms.

Toward these ends, it is instructive to recall the dangerous memory of the historical Jesus. Jesus's practice of compassion, as we find in the stories that he told, his practice of healing, and his critique of unjust wealth and power, meant that Jesus chose to suffer with the excluded. Suffering with and for the oppressed defines Jesus's practice of compassion. His practice of solidarity sets a radical example of resistance to the relationship between the privileged and the oppressed. Jesus clearly did not practice the elite norms of piety and respectability of his day; on the contrary, his practice of compassion threatened the economic, political, and religious elites. Jesus's unmistakable bias in favor of the oppressed, as Edward Schillebeeckx argues, reveals God's universal love.[30] Indeed, his practice of preferential love and justice ultimately led to his crucifixion. The church recognizes this reality today when it states that those who "stand up against [racial] repression by certain powers" will "face scorn and imprisonment."[31]

Yet the question remains whether American Christians relate the scandal of the cross to lynching. Do American Christians see Christ in Michael Brown? Do we perceive, as James Cone explains, how "Jesus was the first lynchee who foreshadowed all the lynched black bodies on American soil"?[32] Cone explains that Jesus Christ was crucified by the same principalities and powers that lynched black people in America. Just as God was present with Jesus on the cross and did not let death have the last word, so God is present at every lynching and act of violence against black people. Cone concludes: The lynching tree is the cross in America. When American Christians realize that they can meet Jesus only in the crucified bodies in our midst, they will encounter the real scandal of the cross.[33]

In the same way that the lynching tree "is invisible to white Christians and their theologians," we tend not to remember how the "dark wisdom of the slaves" calls out to us to know Christ crucified in this nation built upon slavery.[34] M. Shawn Copeland warns that the institution of slavery "neither exhausts nor circumscribes African American experience."[35] However, no matter who we are or how we arrived in this land: "Rethinking theological anthropology from the experience of black women holds substantial social and cultural, moral and ethical, psychological and intellectual consequences for us all. Such work promises not only recovery of repressed religious and social history but release of those 'dangerous memories, memories which make demands on us,' memories which protest our forgetfulness of the human 'other,' our forgetfulness of what enfleshing freedom means."[36] Remembering includes shouldering "suffering and oppression; we take up a position beside exploited and despised black bodies."[37] In preparation for Eucharistic solidarity, Copeland invites intensive historical scrutiny and "presence to memory, social analysis, acknowledgement and confession of sin, authentic repentance—change of heart, change of life, change of living."[38]

A critical piece of the historical scrutiny and presence to dangerous memory includes unearthing root causes of anti-black violence. The question of root causes is one of the guiding questions of a just peace ethic. First, racial capitalism unearths root causes in the history of coloniality and slavery.[39] Drawing upon the work of Cedric Robinson, I contend that a Catholic just peace ethic should engage the history of slavery as "source rather than a subject of knowledge."[40] The point is that enslaved people were both capital and labor. Their double economic aspect cannot be separated.[41] Enslaved people were much more. Historian Walter Johnson explains, "And so, too, were their children: racial capitalism swung on a reproductive hinge. The entire 'pyramid' of the Atlantic economy of the nineteenth century (the economy that has been treated as the paradigmatic example of capitalism) was founded upon the capacity of enslaved women's bodies: upon their ability to reproduce capital. As Deborah Gray White points out, sexual violation, reproductive invigilation, and natal alienation were elementary aspects of slavery, and thus of racial capitalism."[42] Robinson demonstrates how the end of slavery in the United States, far from unleashing capitalism and freedom from the shackles of slavery, evolved into the "generalization on a global scale of the racial and imperial vision of the 'empire of cotton.'" Historian Edward Baptist demonstrates that "enslaved African Americans built the modern United States, and indeed the entire modern world, in ways both obvious and hidden."[43]

Second, racial capitalism offers a robust intersectional analysis. Too often scholars treat different social identities and forms of inequality as separate and independent from one another when in fact social categories simultaneously interweave and interact in complex ways in lived experience. The paradigm of intersectionality grew out of voices of black and brown women who taught that their experience of sexism or racism could not be understood in isolation. The history of racial capitalism and coloniality offers a more dynamic way to understand the complex interplay of social identities and relationships between privilege and oppression.

Analyses of racism by the media and the church too often miss the complexity of white supremacy. A fuller understanding and analysis of white supremacy must include the historical legacy of colonialism, slavery, and commodification that endures in at least four dimensions of culture and society. These include how white supremacy (1) functions as a historical mode of white racial class formation and economic ascendancy through expropriation of land, labor, women's reproductive labor, and resources (such as slavery); (2) constitutes a symbolic hierarchical order of white superiority that feeds on anti-blackness (as in the example of racist tropes that tell blacks to "go back to where you came from"); (3) serves as a primary socialization process of individual and group white racial identity formation (as in housing and school segregation and curriculum); and (4) organizes a segregated society through the "positional alchemy" of *white habitus* that entails a dynamic interplay between both "position—the social geography, location, and power of whiteness—and practice—the ways whites are socialized to perceive and act within the world."[44]

Third, Robinson's analysis of racial capitalism is rooted in the histories, cultures, and traditions of African peoples. Robinson is deeply critical of Marxian and liberal European epistemologies because they failed to realize how "cargoes of laborers also contained African cultures, critical mixes and admixtures of language and thought, of cosmology and metaphysics, of habits, beliefs, and morality."[45] This is a critical point because it is the social and historical consciousness of Africans "that the system of slave labor was infected with its contradiction."[46] From the very inception of slavery, the Black radical tradition confounded European versions of the past by "making history on their own terms."[47]

The virtue of active nonviolence in the just peace norms particularly helps to actualize our "ultimate collective being" when it is practiced in a community of resistance accountable to black people. Robinson recounts hundreds of acts of resistance from seventeenth-century maroon communities to twentieth-century liberation struggles to demonstrate how black collective resistance reconstitutes collective identities. Histories of resistance demonstrate a fundamental contradiction between claims to equality in the Declaration of Independence and the system of slavery that made white advancement possible.[48] The Black radical tradition invites transformation of a just peace ethic.

In/Conclusion through P/reparations: Becoming Authentically Catholic and Truly Black

That the US Conference of Catholic Bishops hesitates to claim that #BlackLivesMatter underscores the church's estrangement from black people. The Body of Christ in the United States is in profound need of the church's leadership to repair communities torn apart by anti-blackness. We are hearing God's cry through many black, brown, and indigenous peoples who call the church to address this deepening wound. Yet the church's historical complicity in white supremacy sets it in a profound theological, moral, and pastoral bind. If the church maintains silence in relationship to its enduring complicity in white supremacy, it denies God's grace, hope, and healing in the Eucharistic memory of Jesus Christ. Through continued silence the church risks, as M. Shawn Copeland warns, the blasphemy of continued "contempt for black creatures who share the glory, beauty, and image of the Divine."[49]

On the other hand, if the church seeks holistic witness rooted in Eucharistic memory, it should take the tremendous risk of recognizing its own need for repentance for racism. There is moral and theological danger here too. A public apology and invocation of God's forgiveness may overreach by acting unilaterally under the assumption that it is a "singular institution of moral credibility."[50] There is danger in a public apology that excludes the voices of victims and thereby only further marginalizes their suffering. Just peace norms of acknowledging harms and accountability must be oriented to open processes primarily led by communities of color.

My fundamental question is this: How will the church transform itself from a predominantly white institution to a church that is actively repairing historical wounds of slavery, lynching, and white supremacy? I argue that before the church can authentically practice a just peace ethic it needs to prepare people of faith through a cluster of racial equity practices rooted in the Black radical tradition. The church first needs to facilitate repair and repent for its role in the evil of white supremacy. That means the church needs to name its own complicity in this evil and engage "p/reparations" as a framework and way to prepare the faithful for an open-ended process that includes public apologies for specific sins in local contexts, developing means of amends through material and cultural redress, and work to relinquish white power and resources to end white supremacy and ensure full human thriving for all black and brown peoples.

Perhaps the church is in an impossible predicament because, as Jesus warned (Matt. 19:24), "it will be easier for a camel to go through the eye of a needle than a rich man to enter the kingdom of God." The Black radical tradition, both in its secular and religious variants, offers a way to refine just peace norms of conflict transformation in the American context as a way for white people and institutions to acknowledge and redress the history of racial harms.

Education scholar Cecilia Cissell Lucas argues that the p/reparations framework is "about learning from the past, loving in the present, and looking to the future while we do the work of transforming ourselves, our relationships, our institutions, and our policies that enable the greatest flourishing of all life."[51] Practicing conflictual solidarity includes learning from the past through the Black radical tradition, reorienting our body, mind, and hearts to the *vox victimarum vox Dei*, confronting and dismantling white supremacy within ourselves and communities, and taking concrete risks within communities of resistance. P/reparations is not any one-off action. P/reparations work demands commitment of our entire lives.

Racial equity praxis recognizes the need to co-create shared critical consciousness and communities of resistance. Racial equity praxis integrates four dimensions of a common praxis. First, drawing upon the Black radical tradition, it remembers histories of both domination and resistance. Second, it utilizes a power analysis that interrelates three dimensions of racism: the first recognizes the consequences of racism for people of color. The second examines the advantages of racial capitalism for white people. The third analytical dimension of power unpacks the ever-evolving ways racism destroys all people and the Body of Christ. Too often white people miss how we too need liberation from the social sin of white supremacy and how it deforms us morally and spiritually. This is a critical point that the church has yet to learn from the Black radical tradition: that universal liberation, including liberation from the sin of white supremacy, is only possible when black people are free.

P/reparations work should begin with the church bending its communal ear to African American spirituality and how it teaches that there is "a way where there is no way" with God. P/reparations processes must "begin with engaged listening to the specific claims, demands, and visions of those who have been on the receiving end of practices of domination."[52] Listening begins with a deep sense of humility before God and neighbor. The virtue of humility is one of the key virtues in the just peace norms. Humility entails practicing obedience to love of God and neighbor. The root of the word "obedience" means "to lend one's ear to another." Obedience, as a fundamental orientation of listening to God and neighbor, is a critical foundation of a Catholic just peace ethic that lives the truth in love.

Authentic listening welcomes truthful remembering that retrieves both of the origins of racial capitalism and resistance to that oppression.[53] As conflictual solidarity, that means that the church cannot be in control of a listening process in terms of setting deadlines or determining outcomes. Authentic listening demands openness to hearing the pain, suffering, anger, and cries for justice of people who experience racism. That means listening contemplatively, becoming co-present with and for another, and dwelling with the experience others share with us. The skill set of nonviolent communication in the just peace norms helps to develop this capacity for authentic listening. However, just as Reverend James Lawson led intensive training sessions in nonviolence for activists during the Civil Rights movement, training for nonviolence needs to be joined with racial equity training and a spirituality of becoming black with God.

Truthful remembering and authentic listening are integral to a re-imagination of spirituality and prayer that is "becoming black with God."[54] Drawing on Cone's black liberation theology, Cassidy invites a spirituality that "enables white theologians to see and understand the world that white-ness has made." To become black with God, Cassidy explains, "is not a phys-ical change but an ontological change that makes the believer capable of participating in God's work of liberating the oppressed."[55] She explains that working with God "is not an addition to what saves but itself is human sal-vation." The condition of the possibility of this transformation is God's gift of grace. To say that "we must become black with God" not only discloses whiteness as a theological problem, argues Cassidy, it also suggests a "pro-found spiritual journey" that reimagines our way of thinking and praying while reorienting us to God's love with and for the oppressed.

This kind of spirituality creates conditions for engaging the work of repair at the deeper level of ritual. Copeland names lament as one of the duties of political theology. Lament "names and grieves injustice" and makes "'spaces of recognition and catharsis' that prepare for justice."[56] Lament must be integrat-ed into our witness to the gospel and truth-telling in ways that bring pain into the open to be seen and heard and fully acknowledged. One ritual that African Americans practice in New Orleans and to which the Catholic Church is in-vited to participate is Maafa. Maafa is a Kiswahili word for "great tragedy." Maafa is an African way of practicing lament. Maafa is a ritual of music, dance, prayer and intentional remembering of the victims of the Atlantic slave trade and the enduring history of imperialism and colonialism. Maafa is inclusive and invites all participants to remember their own ancestors, whether enslaved or not, to recall how the whole of creation is united spiritually and embedded in the earth. In New Orleans, leaders from more than a dozen different faith traditions, including Christian, Muslim, and Jewish faiths, offer prayer and participate in the annual ritual in Congo Square. As historian Freddi Williams Evans elaborates, in Congo Square on Sunday afternoons, "African descen-dants spoke and sang in their native languages, practiced their religious beliefs, danced according to their traditions, and played African-derived rhythmic patterns on instruments patterned after African prototypes."[57] Copeland and Massingale both invite this kind of practice of lament as integral to the praxis of conflictual solidarity.[58] Maafa enhances the just peace norm of sustaining spiritual practices with racial equity.

I conclude with the prophetic admonition of Massingale to "help the faith community embrace a loss it does not want to admit; and then to proclaim to the people a hope that they cannot dare to imagine."[59] I offer this chapter as a way of hope for the church and just peace ethics to embrace a loss it does not want to admit and proclaim a hope we can only dare to imagine as one in Christ. God prepares a way where there is no way. When the church and just peace practitioners admit our complicity in anti-black violence and become black with God and neighbor, then we may hope for the communal intimacy to which we are called.

Discussion Questions

1. How are patterns of white supremacy and/or anti-black violence replicated where you live? As you develop your reflection, examine how the Black radical tradition informs your social analysis and what difference this makes for developing a just peace ethic that is "authentically Catholic and truly black." In other words, what are the theological, moral, and spiritual relationships between becoming authentically Catholic and truly black that form the condition of the possibility of a just peace ethic for racial equity and justice?
2. How does the descriptive and analytical concept of racial capitalism help unearth root causes of racial violence in the United States?
3. How does the *vox victimarum* both nurture resistance to violence and hope for full human thriving and liberation?
4. How and why is collaborative, communal work to unlearn white superiority a condition of the possibility of ending racial violence and practicing racial equity?

Notes

1. Ta-Nehisi Coates, *We Were Eight Years in Power* (New York: One World, 2017), 196.

2. Linda Villarosa, "The Hidden Toll: Why Are Black Mothers and Babies in the United States Dying at More than Double the Rate of White Mothers and Babies? The Answer Has Everything to Do with the Lived Experience of Being a Black Woman in America," *New York Times Magazine*, April 15, 2018, 31–39 and 47–51.

3. Ruth Wilson Gilmore, *Golden Gulag: Prison, Surplus, Crisis and Opposition in Globalizing California* (Berkeley: University of California Press, 2007), 28.

4. Bryan N. Massingale, "*Vox Victimarum, Vox Dei*: Malcolm X as a Neglected 'Classic' for Catholic Theological Reflection," *Proceedings of the Catholic Theological Society of America* 65 (2010): 63–88, at 63.

5. Bryan N. Massingale, "'Authentically Black and Truly Catholic': A Research Project on Black Radicalism and Black Catholic Faith," *The Journal of the Black Catholic Theological Symposium* 5 (2011): 7–25.

6. Martin Luther King Jr., "The Trumpet of Conscience," in *A Testament of Hope: The Essential Writings of Martin Luther King, Jr.*, ed. James M. Washington (San Francisco: Harper & Row, 1986), 636.

7. Alex Mikulich, review of *Catholic Peacebuilding: Catholic Theology, Ethics, and Praxis*, ed. Robert J. Schreiter, R. Scott Appleby, and Gerard F. Powers, *Peace and Change* (October 2013): 502–3.

8. Cedric J. Robinson, *Black Marxism: The Making of the Black Radical Tradition* (Chapel Hill: University of North Carolina Press, 2000 [1983]), see chap. 1 and 5.

9. Movement for Black Lives, "Platform," https://policy.m4bl.org/platform/.

10. Brent McDonald and Alexandra Garcia, "Ferguson Shooting: Michael Brown's Body," *New York Times*, August 24, 2014.

11. John Eligon, "Michael Brown Spent Last Weeks Grappling with Problems and Promise," *New York Times*, August 24, 2014.

12. Jonathan M. Metzl, "When the Shooter Is White," *The Washington Post*, October 6, 2017.

13. Martin Luther King Jr., "The Other America," speech to Grosse Point High School, March 14, 1968, http://www.gphistorical.org/mlk/mlkspeech/index.htm.

14. See my exploration of white habitus in "White Complicity in US Hyper-Incarceration," in *The Scandal of White Complicity in US Hyper-Incarceration: A Nonviolent Spirituality of White Resistance*, ed. Alex Mikulich, Laurie Cassidy, and Margaret Pfeil (New York: Palgrave, 2013), chap. 2.

15. Isabel Wilkerson, "Mike Brown's Shooting and Jim Crow Lynching Have Too Much in Common: It's Time for America to Own Up," *Guardian*, August 25, 2014.

16. Jacqueline Goldsby, *A Spectacular Secret: Lynching in American Life and Literature* (Chicago: University of Chicago Press, 2006), 5.

17. Wilkerson, "Mike Brown's Shooting;" Goldsby, *Spectacular Secret*, 5.

18. Goldsby, *Spectacular Secret*, 5.

19. Richard Rothstein, "The Making of Ferguson: Public Policies at the Root of Its Troubles," Economic Policy Institute, October 15, 2014, https://www.epi.org/publication/making-ferguson/. See also Richard Rothstein, *The Color of Law: A Forgotten History of How Our Government Segregated America* (New York: Liveright Press, 2017).

20. Walter Johnson, "What Do We Mean When We Say 'Structural Racism'? A Walk Down West Florissant Avenue, Ferguson, Missouri," *Kalfou* 3, no. 1 (Spring 2016): 40.

21. Bryan N. Massingale, "Malcolm X and the Limits of 'Authentically Black and Truly Catholic': A Research Project on Black Radicalism and Black Catholic Faith," *The Journal of the Black Theological Symposium* 5 (2011): 7–25, at 14. Massingale draws on Gayraud S. Wilmore's definition of religious black radicalism.

22. Massingale, "*Vox Victimarum*," 83; Massingale, "Malcolm X and the Limits," 14.

23. Stokely Carmichael, "Black Power," speech at University of California, Berkeley, October 29, 1966, http://www.blackpast.org/1966-stokely-carmichael-black-power-0.

24. Carmichael, "Black Power"; Massingale, "*Vox Victimarum*," 83.

25. Michael P. Jaycox, "Black Lives Matter and Catholic Whiteness: A Tale of Two Performances," *Horizons* 44 (2017): 306–41, at 337.

26. My scholarship has been informed by participation in black Catholic parishes for more than twenty years, active service to the Pax Christi USA Anti-Racism Team for more than seven years, and parenting an African American daughter and

son. I am painfully aware of daily threats to my children's well-being and that of our entire family.

27. Jaycox cites Vincent Lloyd, *Black Natural Law* (New York: Oxford University Press, 2016).

28. Massingale, "*Vox Victimarum*," 83.

29. Massingale, 72.

30. Patricia McAuliffe, *Fundamental Ethics: A Liberationist Approach* (Washington, DC: Georgetown University Press, 1993), 53–54.

31. The Vatican, Pontifical Commission on Justice and Peace, "The Church and Racism: Toward a More Fraternal Society," no. 26.

32. James H. Cone, *The Cross and the Lynching Tree* (Maryknoll, NY: Orbis, 2011), 158.

33. Cone, 158.

34. M. Shawn Copeland, "Knowing Christ Crucified: Dark Wisdom from the Slaves," in *Missing God? Cultural Amnesia and Political Theology*, ed. John K. Downey, Jurgen Manemann, and Steven T. Ostovich (Berlin: Lit Verlag, 2006), 58–78.

35. M. Shawn Copeland, *Enfleshing Freedom: Body, Race and Being* (Minneapolis, MN: Fortress Press, 2010), 28.

36. Copeland, 28–29.

37. Copeland, 126.

38. Copeland, 126.

39. Robinson, *Black Marxism*, see chap. 1 and 5.

40. Walter Johnson, "To Remake the World: Slavery, Racial Capitalism, and Justice," *Boston Review*, February 20, 2018, http://bostonreview.net/forum/walter-johnson-to-remake-the-world.

41. See Edward E. Baptist, *The Half Has Never Been Told: Slavery and the Making of American Capitalism* (New York: Basic Books, 2014), xxv.

42. Baptist, xxv.

43. Baptist, xxv.

44. I draw on the following to develop these four dimensions of white supremacy: M. Shawn Copeland, "Anti-Blackness and White Supremacy in the Making of American Catholicism," *American Catholic Studies* 127, no. 3 (Fall 2016): 6–8; Willie James Jennings, *The Christian Imagination: Theology and the Origins of Race* (New Haven, CT: Yale University Press, 2010), 305–6; Bryan N. Massingale, *Racial Justice and the Catholic Church* (Maryknoll, NY: Orbis, 2010); and Alex Mikulich, "Where Y'at Race, Whiteness, and Economic Justice? A Map of White Complicity in Economic Oppression of People of Color," in *The Almighty and the Dollar: Reflections on Economic Justice for All*, ed. Mark Allman (Winona, MN: Anselm Academic, 2012), 189–213.

45. Robinson, *Black Marxism*, 122.

46. Robinson, 122.

47. Robinson, 170–71.

48. I explore this in terms of "motley crews," that is, groups of mixed-race sailors, commoners, and slaves who organized resistance movements during colonialization and slavery in "Mapping 'Whiteness': The Complexity of Racial Formation and the Subversive Moral Imagination of the 'Motley Crowd,'" *Journal of the Society of Christian Ethics* 25, no. 1 (Spring/Summer 2005): 99–122.

49. Copeland, "Anti-Blackness and White Supremacy," 6–8.

50. Jeremy M. Bergen, "Whether and How a Church Ought to Repent for Historical Wrong," *Theology Today* 73, no. 2 (July 2016): 129–48, at 139.

51. Lucas, "Decolonizing the White Colonizer?," 45.

52. Lucas, 46.

53. Lucas, 254.

54. Laurie M. Cassidy, "'Becoming Black with God': Toward Understanding the Vocation of the White Catholic Theologian in the United States" in *Interrupting White Privilege: Catholic Theologians Break the Silence*, ed. Laurie M. Cassidy and Alexander Mikulich (Maryknoll, NY: Orbis, 2007), 147–59.

55. Cassidy, 153.

56. M. Shawn Copeland, "Presidential Address: Political Theology as Interruptive," Catholic Theological Society of America, *Proceedings of the Fifty-Ninth Annual Convention* 59 (2013): 71–82, at 81.

57. Freddi Williams Evans, *Congo Square: African Roots in New Orleans* (Lafayette University of Louisiana at Lafayette Press, 2011), 1.

58. See Copeland, "Presidential Address," 81; and Massingale, *Racial Justice and the Catholic Church*, 105–14.

59. Massingale, *"Vox Victimarum,"* 87.

7

ENDING THE DEATH PENALTY IN THE UNITED STATES
One Step toward a Just Peace

DANIEL COSACCHI

Part of the goal of any movement, such as the Just Peace movement, must always be to become part of the public narrative and so ingrain itself into the lives of everyday people. It is unlikely that the death penalty ever received a more public platform for such an integration than on March 25, 1996, when Susan Sarandon received the honor for Best Actress at the 67th Academy Awards. Sarandon had starred in the unlikely box office hit *Dead Man Walking*, which was based on a book of the same name.[1] In her brief acceptance speech that evening, Sarandon explicitly thanked the woman who wrote the book and whom she portrayed in the film, Sister Helen Prejean, CSJ. Sarandon called for "all of us [to] find in our hearts, and in our homes, and in our world a way to nonviolently end violence and heal." No individual in the United States, or indeed in the international community, has done as much as Prejean in working for the abolition of the death penalty. In her speaking, writing, activism, and social media presence, Prejean has made the death penalty an issue that is in the public eye and part of the public discourse.

Over the last twenty-five years, too, the death penalty has taken on a different standing in Catholic social teaching (CST). Beginning with the magisterium of Pope Saint John Paul II, there has been a paradigm shift in the church regarding the death penalty. Although others (Prejean included) had advocated against the death penalty at various levels in the years and decades preceding John Paul's strongest critiques, never before had a pope taken such a strong stance against the application of the punishment. In fact, the death penalty had once been officially sanctioned and practiced by the Holy See. As with many other issues, however, such as slavery, usury, mixed (interreligious) marriages, salvation outside the Catholic Church, pacifism, and religious freedom, the Catholic doctrine on the death penalty has shifted.[2] Now, Pope Francis is following the path John Paul forged by revising the *Catechism of the Catholic Church* (CCC) to reflect the church's opposition to the death penalty. Francis is unequivocal in his desire for the church's teaching to claim that the death penalty is to be prohibited. In an address at a meeting commemorating the twenty-fifth anniversary of the promulgation of the CCC, Francis asserts his understanding of church doctrine as a fluid, "living" reality rather than a static, unchanging set of tenets. He explains, "the harmonious development of doctrine demands that we cease to defend arguments that now appear clearly contrary to the new understanding of Christian truth." For Francis, the death penalty violates human dignity, which is also one of the just peace norms.[3] Only ten months after Francis's aforementioned address, he revised the official catechetical text to include, verbatim, the following universal and unequivocal condemnation of the death penalty from that speech: "the death penalty is inadmissible because it is an attack on the inviolability and dignity of the person."[4]

In this chapter, I intend first to trace a brief history of the death penalty in Catholic theology and explain one current defense of the death penalty from a Catholic perspective; next, I will examine the current status of the death penalty in the United States; finally, I will turn to the future and examine abolition through the lens of a just peace ethic with regard to the practice of nonviolence. I argue that the complete abolition of the death penalty is necessary for a genuine application of just peace in the United States. In particular, I maintain that by claiming the death penalty is "inadmissible," CST now holds that the death penalty is intrinsically evil and that such teaching should also be the realized experience of Catholics sitting in the pews in the United States. Preaching and activism against the death penalty must reach new levels. Through the shift to a just peace ethic, it is possible to reach such a height.

Context: A Catholic Defense of the Death Penalty and a Review of the Current Practice in the United States

It would be a mistake to suggest that all Catholics are opposed to the death penalty. In fact, there have been a number of Catholic theologians who have been quick to defend recourse to the death penalty as a part of authentic Catholic thinking. One of the foremost Catholic thinkers in the United States in the last century was Cardinal Avery Dulles, SJ (1918–2008). In his fall 2000 McGinley Lecture at Fordham University, Dulles adequately summarizes the historical position of the church regarding the death penalty as being based on scripture and tradition.[5] Nearly eight years later, at his farewell lecture, Dulles maintained his stance that "capital punishment is sometimes warranted." He stated then, as he did eight years earlier, that in arriving at this conclusion he was "willingly adhering to the testimony of Scripture and perennial Catholic tradition."[6]

There is no question that scripture and tradition have been used to uphold Catholic tradition supporting the death penalty. The death penalty appears with great frequency in the Hebrew Scriptures, and in those pages it is clearly an action that is interpreted as having divine origins and sanction. As E. Christian Brugger notes, "Death is prescribed more than forty times and for over twenty offenses throughout the various law codes of the books of the Pentateuch."[7] It is clear, too, that in the Hebrew Scriptures, there was seemingly no limit on the types of crimes that would merit execution. Brugger continues,

> Serious crimes against religion, the order of the family and community, and human life were all punished with death. For example, blasphemy (Lev. 24:16), sacrifice to foreign gods (Exod. 22:20, 32:21–27; Deut. 13:6–10, 17:2–7), and working on the Sabbath (Exod. 31:12–14, 35:2) were capital crimes; so, too, were false prophecy, the idolatrous dreaming of dreams, and sorcery and wizardry (Deut. 13:5; Lev. 20:27; Exod. 22:18). A priest's daughter who played the harlot (Lev. 21:9), one who acted presumptuously by not obeying the words of a priest or judge (Deut. 13:17), or anyone unlawfully expropriating the spoils of battle (Deut. 13:17) deserved death; sexual offenses such as adultery (Deut. 22:22; Lev. 20:10), homosexual acts (Lev. 20:13), incest (Lev. 20:11, 12, 14), bestiality (Exod. 22:19; Lev. 20:15–16), premarital sex for women (Deut. 22:20–21), and the seduction of a betrothed virgin in the open country, out of hearing of others (Deut. 22:25–27), were likewise capital crimes; kidnappers (Exod. 21:16), perjurers (Deut. 19:16–19), rebellious and incorrigible sons (Deut. 21:18–21), those who cursed or struck their parents (Exod. 21:15, 17; Lev. 20:9), owners of oxen guilty of recidivist goring (Exod. 21:29), and all who afflicted widows and orphans (Exod. 22:22–24) should by law be put to death.[8]

The most direct reference to the death penalty in the Christian Scriptures, however, is noteworthy: Jesus's crucifixion. This is a stumbling block to anyone who would argue for the use of the death penalty in Christian ethics, because virtually all Christian ethicists would say that Jesus's execution was not justified.[9] Because Jesus himself was a victim of the death penalty, the burden of proof must fall on the shoulders of any Christian who believes that such a punishment is ever morally justified.[10] From the tradition of a historic peace church, Darrin W. Snyder Belousek uses the cross itself as a metaphor for the termination of the death penalty: "Whereas Jesus' teaching puts the death penalty out of practice, God's redemption in Christ nails the death penalty to the cross."[11]

In the first centuries of Christianity, there are no treatises on the death penalty per se, and there are only a few statements from consequential thinkers.[12] What appears in some of this literature is a disconnect between the idea that the death penalty is inappropriate in general and the idea that it is inappropriate specifically for Christians. There is an obvious parallel with the question of warfare. For some Christian thinkers, such as Tertullian and Origen, even though war might sometimes be justified for the common good, it is never moral for Christians to take part in such an exercise, because even serving in the military is immoral. As Lisa Sowle Cahill puts it, Tertullian "is rigorous in demanding absolute and uncompromising purity of heart in one's devotion to the Christian life."[13] In his research on pacifism in the early church, Roland Bainton describes the distinction well: "In view of Romans 13, no Christian could deny that the empire was ordained of God, but the view that it was ordained because of sin and should be left to sinners was the position of Tertullian. Nothing, said he, is more alien to the Christian than political life. Origen compared the state to a chain gang composed of criminals engaged in useful work."[14] David Clough and Brian Stiltner describe a difference between communal and universal pacifism, and place Tertullian and Origen in the former camp: "*Communal pacifists* believe that pacifism is demanded of their own community but not of everyone in society."[15] It would be fair to conclude that these two figures ceded civil authority to execute criminals to the Roman emperor but simultaneously could not have foreseen the Christian taking part in such activities.[16] As Christine Gudorf has acknowledged, however, "As the church began to take on more of the functions of the state as the empire weakened in the West, the need for capital punishment was considered apparent within the church as well as the state."[17]

Naturally, certain figures in church history always stand out among their contemporaries because of their significance. Two of these key thinkers are Saints Augustine and Thomas Aquinas. In the thinking of both of these men, unlike Tertullian and Origen, there is no room for bifurcation between Christians and non-Christians. Similar to Tertullian and Origen, however, the Augustinian and Thomistic thinking on warfare is helpful in determining their positions on the death penalty. For his part, Augustine believed that war could be justified in order to uphold the safety of the community. Likewise, the death penalty was once meant to protect the community from dangerous criminals. As Brugger concludes, "Given Augustine's theology, rejecting the death penalty would have been tantamount to rejecting the words of the Apostle [Paul]. . . . But there is no question that Augustine hated capital punishment and, given the chance, would have ended it completely, at least in North Africa."[18]

In the case of Thomas Aquinas, there is even further development of the tradition through recourse to the common good, which is also the backbone of his teaching on justified war. As he explains, "Therefore if a man be dangerous and infectious to the community, on account of some sin, it is praiseworthy and advantageous that he be killed in order to safeguard the common good."[19] In particular, the executioner himself must have the proper disposition in carrying out the penalty. As Martin Rhonheimer makes clear, "The one inflicting the penalty must . . . through the punishment strive to keep justice and peace in the society, and to render the criminal harmless, and so forth."[20] In his analysis, Rhonheimer goes on with a pertinent point for today's understanding of the death penalty in a Thomistic light: "Given today's possibilities for enacting punishment and protecting society from serious criminals, and in view of the primarily healing task of human punishment always stressed by Thomas, there remains very little room for the appropriateness of the death penalty."[21]

Even if the church has never asserted that all murderers be killed and has never rejected the notion of clemency, it is nonetheless unquestionable that the Catholic tradition itself had maintained that the death penalty was appropriate in certain situations. Although this chapter does not allow a sufficient treatment of the entire tradition, a few salient points will be helpful. There are some scholars, such as Edward Feser and Joseph M. Bessette, who hold that Brugger's conclusion concerning Romans 13 above is "extremely weak."[22] Their book, titled *By Man Shall His Blood Be Shed*, is an enterprise in defending the death penalty using the Catholic tradition. They conclude, "Since the Church maintains that scriptural teaching on matters of faith and morals is divinely inspired and inerrant, we conclude also that, for this reason alone, the radical claim that capital punishment is always and in principle wrong simply cannot be made consistent with Catholic orthodoxy."[23] It is worthwhile to note, however, that Feser and Bessette never mention whether they disagree with the church's definitive teaching on slavery, which some would argue is not in line with scriptural teaching.[24] They go on to explain, however, that the scriptural teaching on the death penalty is also a part of the Catholic tradition: "This judgment is further reinforced by the consistent teaching of the Fathers and Doctors of the Church, the popes, and authoritative ecclesiastical documents."[25] Unlike Dulles's resigned defense of the death penalty, mentioned previously, Feser and Bessette seem, at times, to show an outward affinity for the practice.

In particular, however, Feser and Bessette badly misunderstand Pope Francis's unfolding development of doctrine on the death penalty. Although their book was published before Francis mentioned the possibility of revising the CCC in order to add the death penalty to the list of intrinsic evils, they did reply to many of Francis's other remarks about the death penalty.[26] They offer one such rebuttal to Francis's comment linking the death penalty with life imprisonment, which Francis believes "is just a death penalty in disguise."[27] Feser and Bessette quickly remind the reader, "Naturally this statement does not have the kind of magisterial authority that an encyclical or catechism does, and it is problematic in any case. . . . Is the pope saying that all prisoners currently serving life sentences should be released at some point—including serial killers, terrorists, the criminally insane, and the like? Presumably not."[28] In fact, I do not see any other way to read Francis's remarks but to say that life sentences ought to be discontinued. There is no question that such remarks—and even more, the aforementioned revision of the CCC—serve as a development in the church's doctrine on the death penalty. I now turn to the current place of that punishment in the church and the United States.

One thing we can say with certainty is that the death penalty is on much surer footing in the United States civic society than in official Catholic doctrine. In both contexts, the death penalty is a tendentious, complex, and currently vulnerable punishment. As various thinkers have reminded us, the United States is among the minority of Western states that still employ the death penalty, and its history in this regard is checkered at best.[29] Although Catholic teaching had traditionally justified the punishment on the grounds of the benefit of the common good, in the United States the rationale justifying the death penalty has not always been so noble. The death penalty may not be used as a means of vengeance, even though it often is in the United States. Today, in the countries that have outlawed the death penalty, there has been a "successful coupling [of capital punishment] with the issue of human rights."[30] Many throughout the country have agreed with figures such as Pope Francis and organizations such as the United Nations who have stated that the death penalty's application merits condemnation simply because it deprives human beings of their inalienable right to life.

Furthermore, there has been renewed emphasis on the fallibility of the death penalty as a means of bringing about true justice. The aspect cited more than any other in this regard is the fact that, sometimes, the death penalty punishes the innocent.[31] Even those who support the death penalty on the basis of its ability to uphold the common good would be forced to agree that the specter of executing an innocent person would be, at best, disquieting; at worst it would make the death penalty difficult to support with any moral authority. And, worst of all, executions of innocent people are a reality in the United States. In an exceptionally helpful essay, Talia Roitberg Harmon and Diana Falco list the following reasons for wrongful convictions in capital cases: perjury of witnesses, prosecutorial misconduct, ineffective assistance of counsel, racial bias, forensic evidence, mistaken eyewitness identification, and false confessions.[32] As with human error in adjudicating the justification for war, there is also obviously human error in the judicial system. Just as, for example, George W. Bush could report that there were weapons of mass destruction in Iraq in 2003, a guilty verdict could be levied against an innocent person. This parallel is all part of the consistent ethic of life.

If pro-life Catholics argue that an innocent fetus should not be terminated through abortion, it seems obvious that they should also hold that an innocent human being ought not be executed by the state. This calls for consistency of thought. What is now commonly recognized by the phrase "consistent ethic of life" was first introduced on a popular level by Cardinal Joseph Bernardin at the 1983 Gannon Lecture at Fordham University. In the course of that address, Bernardin upholds "the classical position . . . that the state has the right to employ capital punishment."[33] Less than two years later, Bernardin addressed the specific issue of how the death penalty fits into the consistent ethic of life with this chilling question: "What does it say about the quality of our life when people celebrate the death of another human being?"[34] Although the National Conference of Catholic Bishops (now the United States Conference of Catholic Bishops) first made a proclamation against the death penalty in 1974,[35] and again in 1980,[36] it was not until Bernardin popularized the term "consistent ethic of life" in 1983 that the bishops' movement against the death penalty picked up steam.[37] There is no question that the American bishops have rallied behind support for abolition of the death penalty ever since.[38]

The position of the American bishops on the death penalty has taken cues from the CCC, Pope Francis, and Saint John Paul II. When the CCC was published in 1994 there was a clear moral preference for using "bloodless means" to punish convicted criminals.[39] In 1995 John Paul promulgated a historically significant encyclical titled *Evangelium vitae*, in which he takes the CCC's teaching one step further. In this encyclical, while John Paul upholds the theoretical right of a state to execute its capital criminals, he calls the church to a time of authentic discernment about the viability of the death penalty in evolving doctrine. He explains that the nature and extent of the punishment must be carefully evaluated and decided on, "and ought not go to the extreme of executing the offender except in cases of absolute necessity: in other words, when it would not be possible otherwise to defend society. Today however, as a result of steady improvements in the organization of the penal system, such cases are very rare, if not practically non-existent."[40] Here, the pope does not remove the rights of individual states from executing criminals but clearly is moving the church closer to an abolitionist stance. And now, more than five years into Francis's pontificate, the Holy Father has closed all the loopholes by revising the teaching of the CCC and imposing the label of "inadmissibility" on the death penalty, making it outlawed regardless of the circumstances.

Reflecting with a Just Peace Ethic: The End of the Death Penalty

Although it is unquestionable that Pope Francis has made strides for the official church doctrine by changing the catechism to deny recourse to the death penalty, it is also the case that such a shift in church teaching would be aided by an ethical framework that complements its respect for the dignity of each and every human being. I propose that the church use a just peace ethic to eradicate the death penalty. Whereas some theologians have suggested that the term "intrinsic evil" is unhelpful, I maintain that it can be useful for Catholic moral theology and that it ought to be applied to the death penalty.[41] It is worth noting that, at times, the term "confuses much more than it clarifies."[42] A prime example of this confusion can be seen in the way the US bishops approach the issue of abortion. The bishops have long opposed the Supreme Court's decision in *Roe v. Wade* legalizing abortion in the United States. Such opposition has led many bishops to a concerted effort to side with one political party in an almost-exclusive way during elections of the past twenty years. Charles Curran concludes, "In the future, the bishops should be aware that advocacy or partisanship might interfere with a proper understanding of their role as teachers in the Church."[43] Adding the death penalty to the list of intrinsic evils creates an opportune moment for the bishops to reexamine the church's teaching on intrinsic evil and to clarify the distinction between that category and human law.[44] In other words, not every intrinsically evil action is illegal, and not every illegal action is intrinsically evil.[45] This is an extension of the argument presented by John Courtney Murray, who bemoans the individual who claims "There ought to be a law" against a given action of moral turpitude: "The simplism of the adage reveals the failure to grasp the difference in order between moral precepts and civil statutes."[46]

To use the just peace approach in prohibiting the death penalty under Catholic moral teaching, the church must first reappropriate its teaching on nonviolence through the lens of a just peace ethic, as this volume seeks to argue. As Maryann Cusimano Love explicates, her just peace principles are present throughout all chronological stages of a given conflict, although they also aim to prevent violent conflict even before it begins. The principles are just cause, right intention, participatory process, right relationship, reconciliation, repair, and sustainability.[47] In his chapter in this volume, Eli McCarthy draws these principles into an integrated just peace ethic that includes just peace practices and highlights the role of virtue.

As I mentioned previously, in the first centuries of the church, there was a clear parallel between the topic of war and the death penalty. Today, with Pope Francis's clear condemnation of the death penalty, and his strong words against the use of violent force in warfare, we have an opening for the church to take up just peace as a holistic model for moving forward nonviolently in the twenty-first century. Although I do not wish to repeat Cusimano Love's entire outline of the just peace principles, I do wish to focus on only three of these—participatory process, right relationship, and reconciliation—in showing how the death penalty can be ended in the United States. Each of these norms are included in McCarthy's revised framework; the norms come from two of his spheres, *jus in conflictione* (participatory process) and *jus ad pacem* (right relationship and reconciliation). Finally, I examine one of the norms unique to McCarthy's own explication of just peace and virtue: training in nonviolent education and skill sets.

The norm of participatory process is meant as a corrective of the *jus ad bellum* criterion in just war thinking that holds the competent authority in a state as ultimately responsible for making the decision to enter a war.[48] As Cusimano Love makes clear, "Just-peace principles call for wide participation of societal stakeholders, including state and non-state actors as well as previous parties to conflict."[49] Participation is one of the core principles of CST precisely because each person as a subject is a social being. For his part, Pope Francis laments the reality of isolation in the world today. He notes, "social problems must be addressed by community networks and not simply by the sum of individual good deeds."[50] Pope Paul VI concluded that participation in society was part and parcel of human dignity and freedom.[51]

McCarthy has integrated this norm into his own virtue-based ethic of just peace. One need not stretch the imagination to conceive of how this criterion would affect people in all the stages of carrying out the death penalty. In a society where the death penalty is codified in law, literally every person in that society bears some responsibility for its implementation. In a more particular way, however, think of those who are legislators, judges, members of juries, prosecutors, wardens, death-row security, media, and the executioners themselves. All of us, but uniquely these people, *participate* in killing other human beings, whereas key stakeholders are often inadequately included in the decision-making about how to respond. Further, if we want to take seriously the church's call to respect the common good, we must also take seriously the just peace call to respect the right of all people, especially key stakeholders to *participate* in building situations or cultures of peace and nonviolence in the world.[52] This begins on the individual level but must also be an inherent part of national and international policies, including such actions as the prohibition of the death penalty.

The second norm I wish to focus on is right relationship. As with participatory process, right relationship holds a dual focus on the interpersonal reality and the global reality. In our world today, we are constantly warned about increased threats of mass shootings, terror attacks, armed assassins, and dangerous dictators. The United States purportedly intends the death penalty as a deterrent to would-be capital criminals. Except, there is no evidence whatsoever that the death penalty has succeeded in deterring these crimes at all.[53] As Cusimano Love explains this principle, "right relationship considers the creation or restoration of just social relationships both vertically and horizontally."[54] In a time when relationships are particularly frayed between law enforcement, the courts, and racial minorities in the United States, this particular principle is of utmost importance.[55] Because of the undeniably racist legacy and undertone of the death penalty in the United States, we find ourselves at a particularly poignant moment of disordered relationship.

Pope Benedict XVI wrote movingly of properly ordered relationships in his 2009 social encyclical *Caritas in veritate*. As the title of the letter indicates, Benedict believes that charity is at the heart of right relationship between human beings in society. Here, McCarthy clearly agrees by placing this norm as part of his virtue-based ethic. Writing to commemorate the promulgation of Saint Pope Paul VI's social encyclical *Populorum progressio*, Benedict adds his voice to the topic of authentic human development.[56] He makes a point to distinguish between this type of development and a type of disordered relationship based on utility. Then Benedict cites Romans 12:21 in reminding the reader of "the potential of love that overcomes evil with good."[57] Only the most ardent supporters of the death penalty would hold that killing another human being is a good thing. The burden of proof falls to these supporters of the death penalty to prove that this type of punishment is not utilitarian and individualistic, and therefore is diametrically opposed to CST.[58] Instead of continuing to respond to evil crimes with more evil actions, we should always practice authentic justice rooted in charity so as to restore right relationships instead of juggling the continually imbalanced morality of taking eye for eye. The just peace norm of conflict transformation, which includes the particular practice of restorative justice, also enables us to move in this direction of right relationship.

One of the most common misconceptions regarding justice is that killing a violent perpetrator will somehow bring justice to a grieving family. That is an odd claim, because full justice would entail returning a deceased loved one to life. Further, using violent means toward a nonviolent end would also not be in accord with the just peace norm of reflexivity. Some measure of justice can be achieved, however, by meeting the human needs of all stakeholders and through the means of reconciliation (part of McCarthy's *jus ad pacem* norms). By reconciliation, I mean a situation in which the perpetrator accepts responsibility for his or her actions, apologizes to the victim or the victim's family, is held accountable, does reparations, and is forgiven.[59] Although I would not force victims' families to reconcile with their loved ones' murderers (or the murderer's family), it is something from which some people have benefited. One such case is that of David Kaczynski, brother of the "Unabomber" Ted Kaczynski, and Gray Wright, one of the Unabomber's victims.[60] David Kaczynski and Wright call their relationship "bridge building." As Wright suggests, the death penalty would stand in the way of his own healing: "Even though this world shows us a side of humanity that is full of violence and rage, there is also a side of us that is able to let go and move forward."[61] How can we move forward when the destination is only the execution chamber?

McCarthy suggests as one of his *jus in conflictione* norms "training and education in skillsets such as nonviolent communication and resistance." It is significant today that the death penalty represents instead, for the United States, a poignant model of training in *violent* communication and *complicity*. The United States has developed violence as a habit that manifests itself in many ways: interpersonal fighting, gun casualties, and war are only three obvious manifestations. The death penalty shrouds in secrecy its expression of this national vice, because executions are not televised, nor are the identities of executioners made public. Yet it is accepted as a practice, and people are trained to carry it out. Instead, following McCarthy's lead in actualizing the norm in question, a broader public ought to be trained in resisting this culture of death and thus also actualizing another just peace norm—that is, cultivating nonviolent peacemaking cultures. There are any number of abolitionists who ought to be held up as models. I return to the figure I mentioned at the outset of this chapter: Sister Helen Prejean, CSJ. Concerned citizens of the United States would do well to follow her lead in working for an end to the death penalty. Her virtuous witness calls to mind the witness of one who was executed some two thousand years ago and whose final words were those of forgiveness. Prejean shows the Christian way forward.

Conclusion

Throughout this chapter, I have been cognizant of the church's relationship with violence on all levels. Pope Francis has been one of the leaders in a movement toward further promotion of the virtue of nonviolence in the church and society. In a particular way, this chapter has focused on the death penalty and the role that plays in the Catholic Church and in the United States. As I have mentioned, there is a helpful parallel with the violence of war. Today, one of the most tangible aspects of a world at war, or preparing for war, is the stockpiling of nuclear weapons in many countries. As with his opposition to the death penalty, Pope Francis has adamantly opposed this practice that seeks to destroy all of God's creation. In addition to expressing his support for a 2016 Vatican-hosted conference on nonviolence, Francis has criticized nuclear weapons in no uncertain terms. Going beyond the words of his predecessors, in a key address of 2017, Francis has claimed that the mere *possession* of nuclear weapons is itself "to be firmly condemned."[62] This call to go beyond nuclear deterrence is another clear step toward building up the virtue of nonviolence, which McCarthy calls for in his own writings about the just peace ethic. While it is always impertinent to guess about future papal acts, one could see Pope Francis revising no. 2,315 of the CCC, to make possessing nuclear weapons inadmissible, like he has done with the death penalty. It would be a further step toward mercy and justice for the world.

While no one would deny the church's role in violence (and the death penalty itself) throughout two millennia, the church can and should lead the way today in applying a just peace ethic to end the death penalty. In the United States, at a time when a sitting president has called not for the abolition of the death penalty but in fact to extend the application of capital punishment to noncapital crimes, the problem of state-sponsored killing has reached a moment of even greater urgency.[63] Just as the church's doctrine concerning war, slavery, mixed marriages (between religions), and religious liberty has already changed, so now has its official position on the death penalty. Even Avery Dulles, in arguing for the use of the death penalty in certain cases, affirmed, "Catholics, in seeking to form their judgment as to whether the death penalty is to be supported as a general policy, or in a given situation, should be attentive to the guidance of the pope and the bishops."[64] Pope Francis has already brought about many significant shifts in the first years of his pontificate. If one were forced to choose only one word to sum up his years as bishop of Rome—always a difficult proposition—the best possible choice might be "mercy." Since Francis has brought about a revolution of mercy, I conclude confirming McCarthy's call for mercy as one of the key virtues in the *jus in conflictione* norms. Justice and mercy are not opposed to each other. In his apostolic letter concluding the Jubilee Year of Mercy in 2016, Francis reaffirmed the traditional Catholic belief that mercy and justice work together in building up God's Kingdom.[65] No longer can American Catholics support the death penalty as a measure of justice. Now is the time to accept Francis's amendment to church teaching. To paraphrase a famous lyric, "They will know we are Christians by our mercy."

Discussion Questions

1. How can church communities advocate for an end to the death penalty in their state? What key coalition partners are needed to generate the necessary leverage? If your state has already ended the death penalty, what other virtues may be cultivated to create the culture ready to end the death penalty in our society?
2. How can we use just peace norms as a way to shape alternatives to the death penalty in our judicial system? How can individual parishes dialogue with their bishops and leaders of other faith communities in bringing about a world committed to practicing a just peace ethic?
3. There is a clear parallel between the practice of the death penalty, the buildup and possession of nuclear weapons, and the implementation of war in society today. What other issues should be curtailed or declared "inadmissible" to promote a further ethic of nonviolence? What would be some steps to get the church to that place? How could the just peace norms assist in moving the church in that direction?

Notes

1. See Helen Prejean, CSJ, *Dead Man Walking: An Eyewitness Account of the Death Penalty in the United States* (New York: Random House, 1993).

2. On the phenomenon of development of doctrine, see John T. Noonan Jr., *A Church That Can and Cannot Change: The Development of Catholic Moral Teaching* (Notre Dame, IN: University of Notre Dame Press, 2005); and David Carroll Cochran, *Catholic Realism and the Abolition of War* (Maryknoll, NY: Orbis, 2014).

3. See "Address of His Holiness Pope Francis to Participants in the Meeting Promoted by Pontifical Council for Promoting the New Evangelization," October 11, 2017.

4. See "Nuova redazione del n. 2267 del Catechismo della Chiesa Cattolica sulla pena di morte—Rescriptum 'ex Audentia SS.mi,'" February 8, 2018, http://press.vatican.va/content/salastampa/it/bollettino/pubblico/2018/08/02/0556/01209.html#IN.

5. Avery Cardinal Dulles, SJ, "The Death Penalty: A Right-to-Life Issue?," in *Church and Society: The Laurence J. McGinley Lectures, 1988–2007* (New York: Fordham University Press, 2008), 332–47.

6. Avery Cardinal Dulles, SJ, "A Life in Theology: 39th McGinley Lecture," *America* 198, no. 13 (April 21, 2008): 9–12, at 11.

7. E. Christian Brugger, *Capital Punishment and Roman Catholic Moral Tradition* (Notre Dame, IN: University of Notre Dame Press, 2003), 60.

8. Brugger, 60.

9. For a further discussion here, see Glen H. Stassen, "Biblical Teaching on Capital Punishment," *Review and Expositor* 93 (1996), 485–596, at 489–90.

10. Later in this chapter, I examine the problem of innocent people, such as Jesus, falling victim to the death penalty.

11. Darrin W. Snyder Belousek, "Capital Punishment, Covenant Justice and the Cross of Christ: The Death Penalty in the Life and Death of Jesus," *Mennonite Quarterly Review* 83 (July 2009): 375–402, at 402.

12. The best summaries are found in James J. Megivern, *The Death Penalty: An Historical and Theological Survey* (Mahwah, NJ: Paulist Press, 1997), 19–27; and Brugger, *Capital Punishment and Roman Catholic Moral Tradition*, 75–84.

13. Lisa Sowle Cahill, *Love Your Enemies: Discipleship, Pacifism, and Just War Theory* (Minneapolis, MN: Fortress Press, 1994), 43.

14. Roland H. Bainton, *Christian Attitudes toward War and Peace: A Historical Survey and Critical Re-evaluation* (Nashville, TN: Abingdon Press, 1960), 83–84.

15. David L. Clough and Brian Stiltner, *Faith and Force: A Christian Debate about War* (Washington, DC: Georgetown University Press, 2007), 48.

16. See Tobias Winright, "Christianity and the Death Penalty," in *Routledge Handbook on Capital Punishment*, eds. Robert M. Bohn and Gavin Lee (New York: Routledge, 2018), 210.

17. Christine Gudorf, "Christianity and Opposition to the Death Penalty: Late Modern Shifts," *Dialog: A Journal of Theology* 52, no. 2 (June 2013): 99–109, at 100.

18. Brugger, *Capital Punishment and Roman Catholic Moral Tradition*, 91.

19. Thomas Aquinas, *Summa Theologiae*, IIa-IIae.Q64.a2.

20. Martin Rhonheimer, "Sins against Justice (IIa IIae, qq. 59–78)," in *The Ethics of Aquinas*, trans. Frederick G. Lawrence, ed. Stephen J. Pope (Washington, DC: Georgetown University Press, 2002), 294.

21. Rhonheimer, 295–96. This point takes on a formal type of argument when one considers whether the death penalty is the type of action that could manifest a change in the natural law. See Peter Black, CSR, "Do Circumstances Ever Justify Capital Punishment?," *Theological Studies* 60, no. 2 (June 1999): 338–45. Furthermore, this line of reasoning mirrors what we see in contemporary papal and episcopal teaching on the subject.

22. Edward Feser and Joseph M. Bessette, *By Man Shall His Blood Be Shed: A Catholic Defense of Capital Punishment* (San Francisco: Ignatius Press, 2017), 109. It should be noted that in their opposition to Brugger's conclusion, they also blatantly misread Brugger on a number of points. One such area is in Feser and Bessette claiming that Brugger's interpretation of Romans 13 is simply that Paul was trying to convince Roman Christians to pay their taxes (110). Although that is a part of Brugger's argument, presenting it as the entirety of his argument is dishonest.

23. Feser and Bessette, 111.

24. See Noonan, *Church That Can and Cannot Change*, 17–35.

25. Feser and Bessette, *By Man Shall His Blood Be Shed*, 111. They provide a misreading of Popes John Paul II, Benedict XVI, and Francis on pp. 144–96. While some of their information is correct, other statements distort the papal teaching so much as to make it almost unrecognizable.

26. See "Address of His Holiness Pope Francis to Participants in the Meeting Promoted by Pontifical Council for Promoting the New Evangelization," October 11, 2017.

27. Pope Francis, "Address to the Delegates of the International Association of Penal Law," October 23, 2014.

28. Feser and Bessette, *By Man Shall His Blood Be Shed*, 184.

29. See Judith Randle, "The Cultural Lives of Capital Punishment in the United States," *Cultural Lives of Capital Punishment*, ed. Austin Sarat and Christian Boulanger (Stanford, CA: Stanford University Press, 2005), 93. See also Megivern, *Death Penalty*, 299–335; and three essays from Bohm and Lee, eds. *Routledge Handbook on Capital Punishment*: John D. Bessler, "The American Death Penalty: A Short (but Long) History," 5–29; Katherine J. Bennett and H. Chris Tecklenburg, "The U.S. Supreme Court and the Death Penalty," 247–78; Robert M. Bohm, "The Death Penalty's Demise, with Special Focus on the United States," 652–66.

30. Bohm, "Death Penalty's Demise," 653.

31. On this phenomenon, see Helen Prejean, CSJ, *The Death of Innocents: An Eyewitness Account of Wrongful Executions* (New York: Random House, 2005); Anthony Santoro, *Exile and Embrace: Contemporary Religious Discourse on the Death Penalty* (Boston: Northeastern University Press, 2013), 47–80; Elizabeth Theiss Smith, "Fatal Flaws: The Implementation of the Death Penalty in the States," in *The Leviathan's Choice: Capital Punishment in the Twenty-First Century*, ed. J. Michael Martinez, William D. Richardson, D. Brandon Hornsby (Lanham, MD: Rowman & Littlefield, 2002), 159–74; and Talia Roitberg Harmon and Diana Falco, "Wrongful Capital Convictions," in Bohm and Lee *Routledge Handbook on Capital Punishment*, 575–88. This latter essay has a remarkable bibliography on this precise topic on pp. 585–88.

32. Harmon and Falco, "Wrongful Capital Convictions," 577–80.

33. Joseph Cardinal Bernardin, "A Consistent Ethic of Life: An American-Catholic Dialogue," in *Consistent Ethic of Life*, ed. Thomas G. Fuechtmann (Lanham, MD: Sheed and Ward, 1988), 6.

34. Joseph Cardinal Bernardin, "The Death Penalty in Our Time," in Fuechtmann, *Consistent Ethic of Life*, 65.

35. The best account of this controversial meeting is found in Megivern, *Death Penalty*, 345–50. At this time the death penalty in the United States was in the midst of a moratorium.

36. See Megivern, 364–69. Megivern notes that there was a major shift toward greater opposition to the death penalty among the episcopacy: "In 1974, 103 bishops voted against the first draft, then 63 opposed the simple motion replacing it, whereas now only 31 voted against the 1980 statement" (367). Megivern also notes that forty-one bishops abstained from voting. As Dulles reports in "The Death Penalty: A Right-to-Life Issue?" this was "the highest number of abstentions ever recorded. According to the rules of the conference, the statement should not have been adopted, since a two-thirds majority of the conference was lacking. But no bishop arose to make the point of order" (354n2).

37. See Megivern, 376–80.

38. For a critical analysis of this position, see Feser and Bessette, *By Man Shall His Blood Be Shed*, 279–374.

39. *The Catechism of the Catholic Church* (1994), no. 2267.

40. Pope John Paul II, *Evangelium vitae* (March 25, 1995), no. 27.

41. A list of such actions was first produced at the conclusion of Vatican II, in *Gaudium et spes* (December 7, 1965), no. 27, and then confirmed by Pope John Paul II, *Veritatis splendor* (August 6, 1993), no. 80. The concern that many theologians have regarding intrinsic evils has to do with the practice of voting and whether it may be acceptable to vote for a candidate who supports the possibility of an intrinsic evil.

42. Joseph A. Selling, *Reframing Catholic Theological Ethics* (Oxford: Oxford University Press, 2016), 20. For a helpful, technical discussion on a more fruitful way of discussing intrinsic evil, see Richard M. Gula, SS, *Reason Informed by Faith: Foundations of Catholic Morality* (New York: Paulist Press, 1989), 268–70, 276–77.

43. Charles E. Curran, *The Social Mission of the U.S. Catholic Church: A Theological Perspective* (Washington, DC: Georgetown University Press, 2011), 175.

44. See Curran, 174–76.

45. For example, the bishops would claim that masturbation would never be an intrinsically evil act, and yet certainly few of them would claim it to be punishable by law.

46. John Courtney Murray, SJ, *We Hold These Truths: Catholic Reflections on the American Proposition*, rev. ed. (Lanham, MD: Rowman and Littlefield, 2005), 150.

47. See Maryann Cusimano Love, "What Kind of Peace Do We Seek? Emerging Norms of Peacebuilding in Key Political Institutions," in *Peacebuilding: Catholic Theology, Ethics, and Praxis*, ed. Robert J. Schreiter, R. Scott Appleby, and Gerard F. Powers (Maryknoll, NY: Orbis, 2010), 78–82.

48. This criterion is consistently present throughout the Christian just war tradition, dating as far back as Saints Ambrose and Augustine. For a more contemporary understanding, see National Conference of Catholic Bishops, *The Challenge of Peace: God's Promise and Our Response* (May 3, 1983), nos. 87–91.

49. Cusimano Love, "What Kind of Peace Do We Seek?," 79.

50. Pope Francis, *Laudato si'* (May 24, 2015), no. 219.

51. Pope Paul VI, *Octogesmia adveniens* (May 14, 1971), nos. 22 and 24.

52. For one of the most helpful overviews of the common good, see Bernard V. Brady, *Essential Catholic Social Thought*, 2nd ed. (Maryknoll, NY: Orbis, 2017), 33–36.

53. For a collection of findings on the topic, see https://deathpenaltyinfo.org /discussion-recent-deterrence-studies.

54. Cusimano Love, "What Kind of Peace Do We Seek?," 80.

55. For a Catholic theological perspective on parts of this question, see Bryan N. Massingale, "Has the Silence Been Broken? Catholic Theological Ethics and Racial Justice," *Theological Studies* 75, no. 1 (March 2014): 133–55.

56. He had originally intended the fortieth anniversary of *Populorum progression*, but it was delayed due to the global financial crisis and a number of translation problems. For more on the background of the document, see Meghan J. Clark, "Commentary on *Caritas in veritate (On Integral Human Development in Charity and Truth),*" in *Modern Catholic Social Teaching: Commentaries and Interpretations*, ed. Kenneth R. Himes, 2nd ed. (Washington, DC: Georgetown University Press, 2018), 482–514.

57. Pope Benedict XVI, *Caritas in veritate* (June 29, 2009), no. 9.

58. See Brugger, *Capital Punishment and Roman Catholic Moral Tradition*, 47–55. Pope Benedict XVI, for example, strongly criticizes such a utilitarian mind-set in *Caritas in veritate*, nos. 34 and 42.

59. See Cusimano Love, "What Kind of Peace Do We Seek?," 80.

60. Kaczynski is currently serving eight consecutive life sentences without the possibility of parole.

61. David Kaczynski and Gary Wright, "Building a Bridge," in *Wounds That Do Not Bind: Victim-Based Perspectives on the Death Penalty*, ed. James R. Acker and David R. Karp (Durham, NC: Carolina Academic Press, 2006), 100. This volume is filled with other experiences of such forgiveness between victims, their perpetrators, and their families.

62. Pope Francis, Address to Participants in the International Symposium, "Prospects for a World Free of Nuclear Weapons and for Integral Disarmament," November 10, 2017.

63. See Maggie Haberman, Abby Goodnough, and Katharine Q. Seelye, "Trump Offers Tough Talk but Few Details in Unveiling Plan to Combat Opioids," *New York Times*, March 19, 2018.

64. Dulles, "Death Penalty," 344.

65. Pope Francis, *Misericordia et misera* (November 20, 2016), no. 14.

PART III

INTERNATIONAL CASES

8

MAKING JUST PEACE POSSIBLE

How the Church Can Bridge People Power and
Peacebuilding

MARIA J. STEPHAN

In 2018, we commemorated the seventieth and fiftieth anniversaries of the
assassinations of two of the greatest leaders of the last century, Mohandas
Gandhi (1948) and Dr. Martin Luther King Jr. (1968), while the world faces unprecedented challenges. Recognizing some of them, Pope Francis, in
his 2017 World Day of Peace address, "Nonviolence: A Style of Politics for
Peace," flagged the scourge of terrorism, organized crime, civil war, and
forced migration.[1] He called for a reinvigorated focus on developing and
implementing nonviolent approaches to transforming violent conflict, highlighting the role of Gandhi and King, along with Leymah Gbowee of Liberia
and Pashtun leader Abdul Ghaffar Khan, in challenging violence and oppression without violence. The pontiff noted that "momentous change in
the lives of people, nations and states had come about 'by means of peaceful
protest, using only the weapons of truth and justice.'"[2]

The Catholic Church has consistently rejected violence and emphasized
that recourse to arms, rather than providing solutions, typically creates new
and deadlier conflicts. Catholic social justice teachings focus on the need to
avoid war and prevent violent conflict by peaceful means.[3] Pope Paul VI famously said that if you want peace, work for justice. "Just peace" means proactively addressing the root causes of violent conflict, including exclusion,
discrimination, corruption, and bad governance and transforming those
relationships and systems that perpetuate violence. Just peace differs from
pacifism, which is a philosophy and way of life that focuses on abjuring
violence in all situations and typically avoids confrontational actions. Just
peace has deep roots in the Abrahamic religious traditions and is manifested
in major global policy initiatives.[4] For example, the United Nations (UN)–
World Bank Pathways for Peace report, the UN Sustainable Development
Goal 16, and the UN Sustaining Peace resolutions emphasize that enduring
peace is grounded in just and inclusive societies and a respect for fundamental human rights.[5]

In this chapter, I address how ordinary people can challenge violence and oppression, including terrorism and violent extremism, using nonviolent resistance. First, I describe some of the recent research on the effectiveness of nonviolent civil resistance, which is a method of waging conflict without the threat or use of violence. Then I reflect on the just peace ethic to illustrate the importance of integrating nonviolent action and peacebuilding, particularly in the context of terrorism and violent extremism. Finally, I note some particular recommendations for how the Catholic Church can better mainstream a just peace ethic.

Effectiveness of Nonviolent Civil Resistance

The increasing emphasis on "nonviolence" in the Catholic community includes a range of nonviolent options ranging from dialogue to direct action, which should not be used synonymously with nonviolent resistance. What do we know about the actual effectiveness of nonviolent resistance? Can it be used effectively by ordinary people facing profound injustices like mass human rights abuses, violent dictatorship, military occupations, and civil wars? Is it possible to say that nonviolent action is strategically superior to its armed counterparts?

One of the key just peace norms for breaking cycles of violence is nonviolent direct action, which includes the particular practice of nonviolent civil resistance involving tactics like vigils, strikes, boycotts, marches, and other forms of noncooperation and nonviolent contestation. A few years ago, together with colleague and fellow political scientist Erica Chenoweth, we embarked on a study designed to answer that question empirically. We collected data on 323 major violent and nonviolent campaigns from 1900 to 2006. These were major political campaigns targeting incumbent regimes and foreign military occupation. The study revealed that the nonviolent campaigns were twice as successful as armed insurgencies, and this has remained consistent through 2015.[6] (Success was defined as the removal of the incumbent regime or territorial independence within one year after the peak period of popular mobilization.) Although there has been a slight dip in the overall effectiveness of nonviolent campaigns in the first part of this decade, which may be linked to the resurgence of authoritarianism around the world, violent insurgencies have become even less effective.

Why has civil resistance so dramatically outperformed armed struggle? The most important variable determining campaign outcomes and that which gives nonviolent resistance a strategic edge is the size and diversity of participation. Nonviolent campaigns attract on average eleven times the level of participants as the average violent campaign. The moral, physical, informational, and commitment barriers to participation are much lower for nonviolent resistance compared to armed struggle. Whereas armed insurgencies often rely on a relatively small group of young, able-bodied men, nonviolent campaigns attract women and men, youth and elderly, able-bodied and disabled, rich and poor.

The participation advantage in nonviolent struggle is reinforced by the number and range of tactics available to people. Gene Sharp catalogued 198 methods of nonviolent action in 1973.[7] That number has vastly expanded as the creative limits of the imagination have expanded. Power is fluid and ultimately flows from the consent and cooperation of ordinary people. When large and diverse groups of people remove their consent and cooperation from an oppressive regime or system of power using tactics like boycotts, strikes, and civil disobedience, no ruler, no matter how brutal, can stay in power. Members of security forces (army and police) are also significantly more likely to defect, or to disobey regime orders to use repression, when confronted with large numbers of nonviolent resisters compared to armed insurgents. When security forces defect, as they did in the Philippines, Serbia, Ukraine, and Tunisia, this is often a decisive variable in the success of the campaign.

We found that the chances of success are higher when groups maintain nonviolent discipline in the face of repression, when they creatively alternate between methods of concentration (like sit-ins and demonstrations) and methods of dispersion (like consumer boycotts and stay-aways), and when they invest in strategic planning and decentralized leadership.

Nonviolent campaigns also contribute to more democratic and peaceful societies. Less than 4 percent of armed rebel victories result in a country becoming democratic within five years. One Congolese bishop, in speaking with the author, noted the large number of insurgent leaders across the continent who had led successful armed struggles only to become more tyrannical than their predecessors once in power. On the other hand, the skills associated with nonviolent organizing, such as negotiating differences, building coalitions, and collective action, reinforce democratic norms and behaviors. Multiple independent studies have shown that nonviolent resistance is a positive force for democratization, and it tends to produce more peaceful societies.[8]

Nonviolent civil resistance, then, is a functional alternative to violence with both short- and longer-term positive effects. It is a particularly powerful nonviolent channel for marginalized or oppressed people to challenge systems of power—whether exploitative corporations, or dictatorships, or institutionalized racism—and build more inclusive, just societies.

Reflecting with a Just Peace Ethic

In light of this research, how might we reflect with a just peace ethic about difficult cases of terrorism and violent extremism, which often result in mass atrocities? What about protecting people? What are the nonviolent options related to preventing, defusing, and transforming such violence? The just peace norms can help illuminate key characteristics of these cases and effective strategies that may seem counterintuitive.

It goes without saying that if you want to prevent mass atrocities, you prevent war. Prevention demands long-term investment. Currently, the levels of global investment in violence prevention are infinitesimally small compared to the sums dedicated to war fighting. The just peace norms of cultivating peacemaking institutions, communities, and cultures, along with the key virtues and skill sets, would help enable such commitments. Prevention also means supporting inclusive and participatory economic and political processes. The just peace norms of just governance, participation, and economic justice illuminate these issues. For example, the institutionalized discrimination against Iraqi Sunnis contributed to the rise and spread of Islamic State in Iraq and Syria (ISIS). It means fostering dialogue and trust between communities and police. In addition, justice and security dialogues have built trust between communities and the police in Nepal and Burkina Faso.[9] It means using diplomatic, trade, and other levers to challenge crackdowns on civic space and human rights violations, like those committed by security forces that fueled the rise of Boko Haram in Nigeria.

Engaging militaries and military leadership can be a critical avenue for highlighting prevention issues and thus advancing just peace. When military leaders demand greater investment in non-military solutions, when they point out the gross under-resourcing of diplomacy, peacebuilding, and development—when compared to military hardware and train-and-equip programs—it makes a difference. Relatedly, enlightened military leadership understands that corrupt, undisciplined, and rights-violating security forces are unreliable partners. Their practices fuel insurgencies and violent extremism.

When it comes to a particular conflict or injustice, a just peace ethic calls us to ask a core question: What are the root causes? Research has shown that civil resistance is a proactive and effective way for oppressed and marginalized groups to address real or perceived grievances that fuel terrorism and violent extremism. These grievances often correspond to genuine human needs, which are addressed as part of implementing the just peace norm of conflict transformation. In order to acknowledge these grievances and needs, particularly in individuals who turn to violence or armed struggle, we can draw on the just peace norms of recognizing and supporting basic human dignity. In turn, we would also be more likely to use humanizing rhetoric rather than to increase dehumanization and escalate the violence.

Grassroots resistance movements offer alienated members of society, notably youth, a powerful group within which to press a moral cause, feel the validation of social bonds, and concretely redress the ills that energized them through collective action.[10] Because these movements increase participation and social bonds, the just peace norms of participation and relationality are being activated. In other words, nonviolent movements offer disaffected youth some of the same psychosocial benefits as joining terrorist groups while being more effective (than violence) in addressing the injustices that extremist groups say they are fighting against.

Nonviolent action has not always worked in terms of securing the stated political objectives. At the same time, there is little evidence to suggest that armed resistance would have done any better in places where nonviolent resistance failed. Military interventions, as in cases like Rwanda or the protection of Yazidis in Iraq, may save lives in the short term. However, often such military interventions continue or generate cycles of violence and make civilians more vulnerable to violence.[11] Focusing on counterterrorism approaches can undermine other nonmilitary efforts to build the relationships, policies, and institutions that help prevent the emergence of terrorist and violent extremist groups in the first place. Hence, the just peace ethic, which calls for actions to meet the norms of sustainability and reflexivity, would at least raise serious questions, if not directly challenge such strategies, and thus perhaps suggest some other opportunities. For example, in Rwanda some of the missed just peace opportunities were to cut off the radio signal being used to exacerbate genocide, evacuate Rwandans (not merely Western nationals), prevent French banks from transferring money for arms, and helping refugees beforehand to prevent hysteria and to promote resilience. In addition, practically speaking, mustering the political will to support military intervention on grounds of Responsibility to Protect (R2P) has become so difficult that it is strategically imperative to develop alternatives.[12] For this reason, scholars like Peter Ackerman and Hardy Merriman have advocated for a new norm focused on the "right to assist" nonviolent campaigns and movements as a possible replacement for the now largely defunct R2P.[13]

Most mass atrocities historically have occurred in the context of armed struggles and civil wars. Very rarely are large numbers of unarmed civilians killed while engaged in mass nonviolent campaigns. New research by Erica Chenoweth and Evan Perkoski found that nonviolent resistance can even decrease the likelihood of mass atrocities.[14] Not surprisingly, armed movements with foreign support are much more likely to elicit mass killings. The just peace norm of reflexivity helps to illuminate this point and steer us in other more nonviolent, sustainable directions.

It is also worth mentioning that while the Second World War ultimately brought the end to the Nazi regime, civil resistance and nonviolent noncooperation saved thousands of lives. Jacques Sémelin, in his book *Unarmed against Hitler*, chronicles a number of these examples, including the case of German Aryan women who protected their Jewish husbands from concentration camps through sustained protests outside the SS headquarters in Berlin and successful large-scale noncooperation efforts in Norway and Denmark.[15]

More recently, nonviolent civil resistance and other forms of collective action have won tactical concessions from extremist groups like ISIS in Iraq and Syria and al-Shabaab in East Africa. For example, women-led protests outside an ISIS headquarters in Raqqa, Syria, led to the release of political activists in 2014.[16] Additional examples include local businesses going on strike in Aleppo, which slowed down ISIS operations and achieved the restoration of electricity, and Muslim leaders encircling a sacred site in Mosul, which prevented ISIS from destroying it.[17] Two years ago in northeastern Kenya, fighters from the al-Shabaab terrorist group ambushed a bus filled with women. The fighters demanded that the Muslim and Christian women separate, a tactic they had used in the past before slaughtering the Christians. The Muslim women refused to separate and shielded the Christian women. They said, "You will kill us all or leave us alone." Their collective stubbornness worked—the al-Shabaab fighters left without anyone on the bus being killed.[18] These examples highlight the value of credible interrupters or messengers as forms of unarmed civilian protection, which is a key practice identified within the just peace norm of nonviolent direct action.

There are other examples of unarmed civilian protection and defusing violence that rely less on nonviolent direct action and organized noncooperation and more on peacebuilding approaches. For example, the organization Cure Violence uses a public health approach, which recognizes that violence or killing mimics a contagious disease. Using this lens, the approach illuminates how violence clusters and is transmitted through observation, experience, and trauma. Therefore, Cure Violence programs identify "credible messengers" who have trust in the community. They are deployed to interrupt the transmission in order to prevent such violence and its contagion. Cure Violence also creates initiatives to change the local cultural norms about violence. Research has shown the Cure Violence public health approach to reduce shootings and homicides on average from 40 to 75 percent. The neighborhoods they work in in Honduras have shown 88 percent reductions.[19]

Unarmed civilian protection, which is the use of unarmed civilians to do "peacekeeping," has had demonstrable successes with multiple organizations in a variety of contexts. Nonviolent Peaceforce, Christian Peacemakers Teams, Peace Brigades International, and Operation Dove have led civilian peacekeeping missions in South Sudan, Sri Lanka, Colombia, Guatemala, the Philippines, Indonesia, Israel-Palestine, and elsewhere. Evaluations of unarmed civilian protection reveal that this activity has saved lives, changed the behavior of armed groups, and made local peace and human rights work more possible.[20] The UN High Level Independent Panel on UN Peace Operations stated, "Unarmed strategies must be at the forefront of UN efforts to protect civilians."[21]

Oliver Kaplan's 2017 book, *Resisting War: How Civilians Protect Themselves*, analyzes how unarmed civilians have influenced the behaviors of state and nonstate armed groups in civil war contexts.[22] He examines cases in Colombia, with extensions to Afghanistan, Pakistan, Syria, and the Philippines. The study shows how unarmed civilians self-organized and created autonomous, resilient institutions. They carved out peace zones, prevented extrajudicial killings, and deterred violence targeting civilians. These findings have important implications for the church and other external actors seeking to prevent and end mass atrocities. They suggest that supporting local self-organizing and collective action in the midst of violent conflict can help save lives.

In addition to these nonviolent strategies, there is also often value in strategically establishing lines of communication with all armed actors to prevent and deter violence and mass atrocities. For example, Archbishop John Odama from Uganda established such communication with the Lord's Resistance Army, which has been identified as a major terrorist organization. In turn, he successfully negotiated a significant reduction in violence for particular areas.[23] Also, Fr. Francisco de Roux, SJ, successfully negotiated with the Fuerzas Armadas Revolucionarias de Colombia (Revolutionary Armed Forces of Colombia, or FARC).[24] Sr. Nazik Matty, OP, from Iraq, called us to recognize that many members of ISIS were cousins, uncles, and neighbors with whom some people therefore could and should communicate to identify needs and encourage alternative methods, even defections.[25] In reality, a number of defections have occurred from such armed actors, and more could be enabled with a focused, strategic commitment by governments and nongovernmental organizations seeking to transform the conflict.[26] A key part of any coordinated defection strategy would include identifying, mobilizing, and resourcing people with credibility in the eyes of these armed actors. Such people could then work to peel away some of these armed actors and help them engage in other forms of action, including nonviolent resistance, to address their grievances.[27] The just peace norms of human dignity and participation, as well as the virtues of nonviolent action, humility, and hospitality, could all better enable such strategies.

The church has played a pivotal role in some of the most significant nonviolent struggles in history. Many will recall the iconic image of the Filipino religious sisters confronting military forces and a kleptocratic Ferdinand Marcos dictatorship in prayerful resistance during the 1986 "People Power" revolution. Across the Philippines, priests and nuns, in partnership with the International Fellowship of Reconciliation, trained their communities in nonviolence and nonviolent action. Cardinal Jamie Sin attended one of these workshops. He later joined the Catholic Bishops' Conference of the Philippines in calling for a "nonviolent struggle for justice," using *Radio Veritas* to amplify the message.[28] This preparation, combined with an election-monitoring mission led by local religious leaders, paved the way to Marcos's nonviolent ouster. Today, Filipino religious leaders, facing another violent dictator, Rodrigo Duterte, are once again engaged in nonviolent activism. During the Polish Solidarity movement in the 1980s, Pope John Paul II, with local priests and nuns, famously stood shoulder-to-shoulder with the worker-led movement that challenged Communist tyranny with nonviolent resistance. Archbishop Óscar Romero of El Salvador was martyred for showing solidarity with campesinos and other victims of junta brutality.

Bridging People Power and Peacebuilding

As noted previously, civil resistance and nonviolent collective action are part of a much broader set of nonviolent resources. Transforming violent conflict and dissolving its root causes requires a combination of people power and peacebuilding. That means linking nonviolent resistance, which intentionally escalates conflict and involves extra-institutional direct action tactics, and traditional peacebuilding tools like negotiation, dialogue, mediation, trauma healing, and restorative justice, which deescalate it.[29] The just peace norms, particularly the *jus ex bello* (breaking cycles of violence), illuminate the importance of linking nonviolent resistance with peacebuilding strategies.

The theory underpinning this argument is that in conflicts marked by great power asymmetries, where groups are intentionally marginalized or excluded from political processes, power needs to shift and an unjust status quo disrupted before ending destructive conflict becomes possible. In other words, nonviolent action is often necessary to "ripen" the situation for resolution. As Martin Luther King Jr. so eloquently wrote in his "Letter from a Birmingham Jail" in 1963, "You may well ask: 'Why direct action? Why sit-ins, marches and so forth? Isn't negotiation a better path?' You are quite right in calling for negotiation. Indeed, this is the very purpose of direct action. Nonviolent direct action seeks to create such a crisis and foster such a tension that a community which has constantly refused to negotiate is forced to confront the issue. It seeks to so dramatize the issue that it can no longer be ignored."[30] The Polish Solidarity movement combined Gdansk shipyard strikes with formal roundtable negotiations. The Liberian Civil War came to an end because the government and rebels were pressured—in part by women-led demonstrations, sit-ins, and a sex strike—to reach a settlement. The Comprehensive Peace Agreement in Nepal was reached when popular nonviolent resistance shifted the power dynamics and incentivized meaningful peace talks. Veronique Dudouet highlights these and other examples in the International Center on Nonviolent Conflict (ICNC) monograph, "Powering to Peace: Integrated Civil Resistance and Peacebuilding Strategies."[31] Anthony Wanis-St. John and Noah Rosen focus on the importance of negotiation in nonviolent resistance in the United States Institute of Peace (USIP) *Peaceworks* report, "Negotiating Civil Resistance."[32]

Using and sequencing these dialogical and direct action techniques is both an art and a science. The USIP has developed a practical guide called "Synergizing Nonviolent Action and Peacebuilding" (SNAP),[33] which is intended to inform field-based trainings on how, practically, these nonviolent approaches can be used together. This action guide could support activists and peacebuilders from conflict and postconflict areas around the world and reinforce the activities of organizations like Pax Christi, Mercy Corps, Caritas International, Catholic Relief Services, and members of the Alliance for Peacebuilding, whose work is grounded in conflict-affected communities.

We know that nonviolent resistance is important in negotiating a sustainable and just peace. This aligns with the fact that, historically, the most durable peace processes and national dialogues have been inclusive and participatory. Desirée Nilsson's study of all peace agreements reached in the post-Cold War period found that the involvement of civil society reduced the risk of failure by 64 percent.[34] Peace accords that include civil society actors—including religious groups, women's groups, and human rights organizations—are more likely to see peace prevail. The Colombia peace process, which culminated in a landmark peace accord in 2016, featured the active involvement of victim's groups, women's groups, and other civic actors. Other research has found that the presence of skilled negotiators and facilitators at the local level contributed to the success of national dialogue processes.[35] In all of these cases, training and skills-building contributed to better outcomes.[36] The just peace norm of nonviolent education and skills training would call us to these kinds of efforts.

Women's participation in advancing just peace merits special focus. Multiple studies have found that women's inclusion in peace processes correlates significantly with their success. Classic examples of this include the role of women in the Northern Ireland and Liberia peace processes.[37] Women bring unique identities, perspectives, and a sense of urgency to peace processes. They have demonstrated a unique ability to build alliances and coalitions and hone in on solving the problems at hand. Even though women often need to fight for a place at the table, it stands to reason that unlocking the leadership potential of women at all levels of an organization or institution, including the Catholic Church, would strengthen its ability to forge peace.

Another nonviolent tool, mediation, has helped to resolve some of the most intractable violent conflicts, including the civil wars in El Salvador, Guatemala, Mozambique, Northern Ireland, and Colombia. The Catholic Church, frequently in partnership with other faith groups, has often been a key mediator. The Vatican and Pope Francis played a critical role in mediating an end to Colombia's civil war. The lay Catholic Community of

Sant'Egidio played a vital role in ending the devastating Mozambican Civil War (1975–1990). Sant'Egidio, a Rome-based organization with some serious mediation skills and a biblical commitment to service, compassion, and peace, developed strong relationships with the two conflict parties, the ruling Frelimo party (Mozambique Liberation Front) and RENAMO (Mozambican National Resistance) rebels. It brought them together in Rome for meetings over two years that culminated in the signing of the Rome General Peace Accords in 1992.[38]

In South Sudan, where post-independence civil war and dictatorship have created a terrible humanitarian crisis, the interdenominational South Sudan Council of Churches, one of the strongest civil society groups in the young country, has issued an Action Plan for Peace (APP) focused on dialogue and reconciliation.[39] There is also a budding youth-led nonviolent movement in the country, called Ana Taban ("I am tired" in Arabic), that is using the arts to build bridges, call out abuses on all sides, and mobilize people for peace.[40]

A just peace norm to help build sustainable peace is relationality and reconciliation, which includes addressing and overcoming legacies of gross human rights violations and other historical injustices. Faith groups have historically contributed in significant ways to transitional justice and reconciliation. There are multiple models of truth-telling and reconciliation. In Guatemala, the Catholic Church, under the leadership of Bishop Juan Gerardi, helped initiate, organize, and execute the successful national truth commission, the Recovery of Historical Memory Project, in the mid-1990s.[41] In Chile, the Catholic Church advocated for the country's Commission on Truth and Reconciliation following Pinochet's removal from power in 1990—a core component of that country's transition to democracy. The Chilean commission helped inspire the South African Truth and Reconciliation Commission shepherded by Archbishop Desmond Tutu.

Recommendations and Conclusions

The implementation of a just peace ethic and the proven track record of all these nonviolent techniques—including civil resistance, dialogue, mediation, negotiation, unarmed civilian protection, trauma healing, and transitional justice—are grounded in the skills and legitimacy of those using them. An important role the church and ordinary people can play in advancing a just peace ethic globally is by building strategic and tactical bridges between the techniques of grassroots nonviolent action and peacebuilding and investing in them.

Practically, this can be done via education and training, through the diplomatic and policy-influencing arms of the Catholic Church, through interreligious initiatives, and through field-based programming and accompaniment with conflict-affected communities.

- *Formation*: Catholic universities around the world can educate and train youth and communities in the spiritual practices and virtues of just peace along with the full menu of nonviolent options and their practical, strategic applications. They can also support cutting-edge research on conflict analysis and just peace approaches. Catholic leadership from the parish level on up can help integrate just peace norms and teachings into religious trainings, lay formation, homilies, and sermons. They can draw on research, films, and training materials on nonviolent action (many translated into dozens of languages) developed by USIP, the International Center on Nonviolent Conflict, Beautiful Rising, Pace-e-Bene, Rhize, and other organizations.
- *Interreligious Cooperation*: The Pontifical Council for Interreligious Dialogue can continue to promote just peace approaches that draw on all the religious traditions. Catholic organizations can help initiate interreligious initiatives, such as religious peace teams deployed for unarmed civilian protection, or coordinate religious leaders as credible messengers with armed actors.
- *Advocacy*: Church leaders can communicate with government officials and security forces to deter violent crackdowns against peaceful activists. They can take diplomatic action when state/nonstate actors are engaged in systematic human rights abuses, high-level corruption, and exclusionary policies that fuel violence, and show solidarity with nonviolent activists and peacebuilders on the front lines. The Vatican secretary of state and Holy See missions in New York and Geneva can use existing initiatives, like the UN Sustaining Peace Resolutions, the UN–World Bank Pathways for Peace report, and the Sustainable Development Goals, to advance just peace approaches and tools.
- *Mobilization and Investment*: Logistically, the church can also provide safe spaces in places like the Democratic Republic of Congo, South Sudan, Venezuela, and Cambodia, where activists and peacebuilders can meet, strategize, and plan actions. It can offer small resources and transportation support for those forced to operate in restrictive environments, often with little or no money. It can work with Catholic and other private foundations to support grant-giving that aligns with just peace objectives, including small grants for grassroots initiatives and movements. The church could work with militaries to support unarmed peacekeeping pilot initiatives in places like Syria and South Sudan. At least one national government, Lithuania, has made civilian-based defense, which involves the use of mass civil resistance and noncooperation to deter and repel foreign attacks, a core component of its national defense strategy.[42]
- *Accompaniment*: With a pastoral approach, the institutional church and Christians have a particular role and responsibility to accompany those

in situations of profound repression and mass violence. The church can be present, take courageous risks with these people, and explore creative options to break the cycles of violence through nonviolent means.

Overall, perhaps one of the best investments the church at all levels can make in advancing the just peace norms is building up the nonviolent resistance and peacebuilding skills and capacities of people in schools, universities, parishes, and communities around the world. As more and more people gain the skills and confidence to engage in dialogue and collective action to address grievances and root out the injustices that fuel mass violence, with the support of global institutions like the church, the prospects of just peace around the world could increase significantly.

Discussion Questions

1. Why is it so important to bridge peacebuilding and people power methods in making just peace possible? How can civil resistance and dialogue be used together, in a mutually reinforcing way, to address injustices, shift power, and achieve sustainable peace? If you sought to persuade a policymaker on the value of both of these sets of methods, how would you start?
2. If you were to use both of these sets of methods in designing a strategy to respond to state or nonstate terrorism, what tactics would you use and how?
3. What steps can Christian communities take to strengthen this bridging of peacebuilding and nonviolent direct action methods?

Notes

This chapter is based on a keynote address, "Nonviolent Options and Just Peace," the author gave for the conference "The Catholic Church Moves towards Nonviolence? Just Peace Just War in Dialogue," University of San Diego, October 6, 2017.

1. Pope Francis, "Nonviolence: A Style of Politics for Peace," January 1, 2017.
2. Francis.
3. "Seven Themes of Catholic Social Teaching," United States Conference of Catholic Bishops, last modified 2005.
4. Susan Thistlethwaite et al., "Abrahamic Alternatives to War: Jewish, Christian, and Muslim Perspectives on Just Peacemaking," United States Institute of Peace, October 2008.
5. United Nations, "The Challenge of Sustaining Peace: Report of the Advisory Group of Experts for the 2015 Review of the United Nations Peacebuilding Architecture," June 2015.
6. Erica Chenoweth and Maria J. Stephan, *Why Civil Resistance Works: The Strategic Logic of Nonviolent Conflict* (New York: Columbia University Press, 2011).

7. Gene Sharp, *The Methods of Nonviolent Action: Part Two of the Politics of Nonviolent Action* (Boston: Porter Sargent Publishers, 1973).

8. Maciej Bartkowski, "Do Civil Resistance Movements Advance Democratization?," International Center on Nonviolent Conflict, September 17, 2017.

9. Regarding Nepal, see Nigel Quinney, "Justice and Security Dialogue in Nepal: A New Approach to Sustainable Dialogue," United States Institute of Peace, June 2011; for Burkina Faso, see "Justice and Security Dialogues," United States Institute of Peace.

10. Maria J. Stephan and Leanne Erdberg, "To Defeat Terrorism, Use 'People Power,'" United States Institute of Peace, March 27, 2018.

11. For example, see chapters 11 and 13 (this volume) on Iraq and the role of Rwanda in the Democratic Republic of Congo. Libya in 2011 is another example.

12. The Right to Protect (R2P), adopted by the United Nations in 2005, states that all UN member nations have the responsibility to protect its populations from genocide, war crimes, ethnic cleansing, and crimes against humanity. It also asserts that the international community has a collective responsibility to assist in the case of a state that is unwilling or unable to meet its obligation to prevent mass atrocity crimes.

13. Peter Ackerman and Hardy Merriman, "Preventing Mass Atrocities: From a Responsibility to Protect to a Right to Assist Campaigns of Civil Resistance," International Center on Nonviolent Conflict Special Report, May 2019.

14. Evan Perkoski and Erica Chenoweth, "Nonviolent Resistance & the Prevention of Mass Atrocities in Popular Uprisings," International Center on Nonviolent Conflict Special Report, April 2018.

15. Jacques Sémelin, *Unarmed against Hitler: Civilian Resistance in Europe, 1939–1943* (Westport, CT: Praeger, 1993).

16. Maria J. Stephan, "Civil Resistance vs. ISIS," *Journal of Resistance Studies* 1, no. 2 (2015).

17. Maria J. Stephan, "Resisting ISIS," in *Sojourners*, April 2015; and Alia Braley, "This Talk Is Not about ISIS," TEDxTV, April 12, 2017, https://tedxtv.blogspot.com/2017/04/this-talk-is-not-about-isis-alia-braley.html.

18. "Muslims Shield Christians in Kenya Attack," *BBC News*, December 21, 2015.

19. Cure Violence Evaluations, http://cureviolence.org/results/scientific-evaluations/.

20. "Unarmed Civilian Protection," Nonviolent Peaceforce, last modified March 30, 2018, http://www.nonviolentpeaceforce.org/unarmed-civilian-protection.

21. United Nations, "Uniting Our Strengths for Peace—Politics, Partnerships, and People: Report of the High-Level Independent Panel on United Nations Peace Operations," June 17, 2015.

22. Oliver Kaplan, *Resisting War: How Communities Protect Themselves* (New York, NY: Cambridge University Press, 2017).

23. Archbishop Odama, quoted in "Session 3: Nonviolence and Just Peace" of the conference in Rome, Italy, April 11–13, 2016, https://nonviolencejustpeacedotnet.files.wordpress.com/2016/05/nonviolence-justpeace-session-3-transcript.pdf.

24. Francisco de Roux, quoted in "Session 3: Nonviolence and Just Peace."

25. Rose Berger, "Game Changer?," in *Sojourners*, December 2016, 17–23.

26. Kimiko de Freytas-Tamura, "ISIS Defectors Reveal Disillusionment," *New York Times*, September 20, 2015; "ISIS Deserters Speak Out," *Al Jazeera*, October 13, 2016; Nick Miroff, "For War-Weary Rebels, Colombia Invites Defections with Comforts and Kindness," *Washington Post*, June 13, 2014.

27. For related research tying the value of defections to reducing mass killings along with practical steps to entice defections, see Erica Chenoweth and Evan Perkoski, "Nonviolent Resistance and Prevention of Mass Killings during Popular Uprisings," *Special Report Series of ICNC* 2 (May 2018).

28. E. J. Dionne Jr., "Pope Urges Philippine Peace after Backing Bishop's Stand," *New York Times*, February 17, 1986.

29. Maria J. Stephan, "The Peacebuilder's Field Guide to Protest Movements," *Foreign Policy*, January 22, 2016.

30. Martin Luther King Jr., "Letter from a Birmingham Jail," The Africa Center at the University of Pennsylvania.

31. Véronique Dudouet, "Powering to Peace: Integrated Civil Resistance and Peacebuilding Strategies," International Center on Nonviolent Conflict, April 2017.

32. Anthony Wanis-St. John and Noah Rosen, "Negotiating Civil Resistance," *Peaceworks* 129 (July 2017).

33. Nadine Bloch and Lisa Schirch, *Synergizing Nonviolent Action and Peacebuilding: An Action Guide* (Washington, DC: U.S. Institute of Peace, 2018).

34. Desirée Nilsson, "Anchoring the Peace: Civil Society Actors in Peace Accords and Durable Peace, International Interactions," *International Interactions* 38, no. 2 (2012), doi:10.1080/03050629.2012.659139.

35. "Briefing Note: What Makes or Breaks National Dialogues," Inclusive Peace & Transition Initiative, April 2017.

36. Marike Blunck et al., *National Dialogue Handbook: A Guide for Practitioners* (Berlin: Berghof Foundation, 2017).

37. Marie O'Reilly, Andrea Ó Súilleabháin, and Thania Paffenholz, "Reimagining Peacemaking: Women's Roles in Peace Processes," International Peace Institute, June 2015.

38. "General Peace Agreement for Mozambique," The United Nations, October 4, 1992.

39. "South Sudan Council of Churches' Message to the United Nations Security Council Delegation to South Sudan," Solidarity with South Sudan, September 2016.

40. Nicholas Zaremba, "In South Sudan, an Artists' Movement for Peace Catches Fire," United States Institute of Peace, January 19, 2018.

41. The Human Rights Office of the Archdiocese of Guatemala, *Guatemala: Never Again!* (Maryknoll, NY: Orbis, 1999).

42. Grazina Miniotaite, *Nonviolent Resistance in Lithuania: A Story of Peaceful Liberation* (Cambridge, MA: Albert Einstein Institution, 2002).

9

LIVING JUST PEACE IN SOUTH SUDAN

Protecting People Nonviolently in the Midst of War

MEL DUNCAN AND JOHN ASHWORTH

In this chapter, we reflect on the application of Unarmed Civilian Protection (UCP) as one tool among many in the rich field of active nonviolence. We will concentrate on one country, South Sudan, and one organization, Nonviolent Peaceforce (NP), an international nongovernmental organization (NGO) that protects civilians in violent conflicts and prevents violence through unarmed strategies working side by side with local communities.

Context

"War is better than a bad peace!" In the run-up to the Comprehensive Peace Agreement, which officially ended Sudan's civil war in 2005, this refrain could be heard all over South Sudan, from ordinary rural women to the highest military and political leaders in the land. People were exhausted and traumatized by twenty-two years of armed conflict, they were all too aware of the untold human suffering, and they realized there was no military solution in a war of attrition that had reached a strategic stalemate. At the same time, however, they were not ready to return to the situation of state-sponsored violence, oppression, discrimination, and marginalization that had caused them to resort to arms in the first place.

Six years later, in 2011, the new state of South Sudan gained its independence from Sudan following a peaceful referendum. There was great joy and hope. South Sudan was now free of domination by Khartoum's Islamist military dictatorship. Civil rights would now be based on human dignity rather than religion, ethnicity, or place of birth. South Sudanese were now responsible for their own future, their own dream.

Sadly, the dream was short-lived. Relations between the two states remained tense and fractious, with some military skirmishing, but they stopped short of war. However, less than three years after South Sudan's long-awaited independence, full-scale civil war broke out again. What began as a power struggle between political leaders and their factions soon took on a dangerous tribal element as the killing of civilians by one faction or another led to a vicious cycle of revenge killings that at times bordered on ethnic cleansing. Old scores are being settled, and unresolved conflicts from the past are being continued where they left off. It is now widely acknowledged that this is a senseless war with no moral justification whatsoever, as the churches have consistently pointed out. The church is working to end the war through an Action Plan for Peace that includes advocacy, neutral forum dialogues, and reconciliation. Despite these actions many of the protagonists still seem to believe in a military solution and are unwilling to take the necessary steps for genuine and inclusive dialogue to take place. Such inclusive dialogue actualizes the just peace norm of participatory processes.

Most South Sudanese and many international observers would argue that the 1983–2005 civil war at first appeared to be a "just war." It certainly had a just cause. Since South Sudan began to open up to slave traders in the first half of the nineteenth century, its inhabitants have been ruled by outsiders who have cared little for their human dignity or human rights. The armed liberation struggle had several incarnations, culminating in the civil war that eventually led to independence.

However, "just cause" alone does not constitute a just war, according to the just war ethic. Among other just war criteria, there were those who thought that the last resort criterion had been satisfied. South Sudanese had tried many peaceful and political means to resolve their problem; however, large-scale nonviolent resistance was never attempted. Legitimate authority can be a difficult criterion to pin down in a liberation struggle involving a nonstate actor, but it can at least be argued that the people of southern Sudan broadly supported their liberation movement, the Sudan People's Liberation Movement/Army (SPLM/A), and its aims. Whether there was a reasonable chance of achieving its goals, whether the damage done and suffering caused was proportionate to the intended good (particularly with hindsight), and whether the safety of civilians was adequately considered are arguable. Nevertheless, it is difficult to be too judgmental toward a people who have suffered oppression, discrimination, marginalization, and denial of their dignity and identity for decades, and who eventually concluded that armed struggle was the only remaining course of action to free themselves from Khartoum's oppression. It can be said to have succeeded in that limited aim.

If "war is better than a bad peace," it says something about the peace that people had experienced before. It was peace only in the sense that most of the time there was no open and organized warfare. However, there was state-sponsored violence, oppression, discrimination, and marginalization (religious, ethnic, cultural, linguistic, gender, geographic), human rights abuses, arbitrary detention, torture, extrajudicial execution, poverty, illiteracy, absence of the rule of law, impunity, forced Arabization and Islamization . . . the list goes on. It was certainly not what the church would call peace, the "shalom" of the Bible. In effect the people of South Sudan were articulating the concept of just peace (or justpeace). Peace is not simply the absence of war, but it is the positive holistic presence of rightness, justice, equality, and human dignity. Only just peace is real peace.

Chenoweth and Stephan have examined the influence of violent insurgencies, even those that have "succeeded" (as the south Sudanese struggle "succeeded" in its limited objective) on the post-struggle society. They find that "democracy is less likely to develop" after a nonviolent struggle, and that it "is likely to lead to the recurrence of civil war within ten years."[1] Many of the characteristics of a violent liberation struggle—centralized authority, hierarchy, lack of democracy, secrecy, lack of transparency, rigid structures and chains of commands, subjugation of everyone and everything to the cause, intolerance of dissent, militarization of society, and of course violence itself—may be perceived as essential to the success of the struggle but are in direct counterpoint to the needs of the post-struggle community. Successful violent struggle by its very nature often contains the seeds of its ultimate failure in terms of building a post-struggle society. Unfortunately, South Sudan is a stark example of this dynamic. It proved impossible to build not only the necessary infrastructure and policies of good governance, human rights, and democracy but also the culture of peace, development, and national identity. Unresolved issues from previous conflicts were not addressed and simply festered under the surface until the time was ripe for them to burst forth again. The conflict was transformed in a sense, but it was only a temporary lull, and deep transformation did not take place, either at a personal or national level. So how do we break these vicious cycles of violence?

It could probably be argued that nonviolence does not come naturally to South Sudan. The first of three civil wars began in 1955, so there is no South Sudanese who has not spent virtually his or her whole life in a situation where violence is the norm. Everyone is traumatized, and that trauma leads to fresh violence and fresh trauma. In many communities, justice equals revenge and revenge equals justice. Patriarchal norms condone domestic and gender-based violence, and trauma has only exacerbated this. The language of nonviolence has had little recognition or attraction for South Sudanese. Hate speech, tribal hatred, atrocities, and inhumaneness have increased in the current conflict: "The level of hatred associated with the conflict is increasing. . . . However, not only are they being killed, but their bodies are being mutilated and burned. People have been herded into their houses which were then set on fire to burn the occupants. Bodies have been dumped in sewage-filled septic tanks. There is a general lack of respect for human life."[2]

As a reaction to this, and connected with the almost universally held belief that this war is a senseless war with no moral justification, we are beginning to hear the language of nonviolence. Ordinary people are calling
for the killing to cease so that the legitimate grievances of all parties can be
addressed nonviolently through genuine dialogue, advocacy, and other nonviolent means. Thus, there is a growing recognition of the just peace norm of
reflexivity, which calls us to keep means and ends consistent, particularly if a
sustainable peace is to be realized.

> In our Prophetic role as bishops, we state without hesitation or fear
> that the current conflict is evil and must be stopped immediately and
> unconditionally, regardless of any other considerations. We call on every
> political leader, every military officer, every individual soldier, every
> armed civilian, whether government or opposition, to avoid any further
> killing. It is immoral and evil. The question to ask ourselves is: do I
> have the sincere will to renounce violence, to compromise and to bring
> peace?[3]

Statements by both the Catholic bishops and the South Sudan Council of
Churches (SSCC) since 2016 refer explicitly to the "Nonviolence and Just
Peace: Contributing to the Catholic Understanding of and Commitment to
Nonviolence" conference held in Rome in April 2016, in which the South
Sudanese church was well represented.

Reflecting with a Just Peace Ethic

In this section, we reflect on this case with a just peace ethic. We consider
the particular practice of unarmed civilian protection as well as some of the
initiatives of the Catholic Church.

Unarmed Civilian Protection

Far from being passive, the Rome appeal of 2016 called on the church to
focus her collective resources on a host of nonviolent strategies and activities that would cultivate a just peace, including promoting unarmed civilian
protection (UCP).[4] This practice corresponds with the just peace norm of
nonviolent direct action, which is particularly well-suited to breaking cycles
of violence.

UCP is an emerging approach whereby trained civilian protection officers
deploy field-tested interventions to provide direct protection to civilians in
areas of violent conflict and work closely with local civil society to prevent further violence. With 170 unarmed civilian protectors coming from

thirty-two countries, and more than half coming from the local area, the mission of Nonviolent Peaceforce (NP) in South Sudan represents the largest sustained application of UCP in history.

NP's effectiveness requires the practical application of many of the norms laid out in just peace. Although it is a secular organization, NP's three pillars—nonviolence, nonpartisanship, and the primacy of local actors—parallel these norms (see fig. 9.1). To be effective, UCP depends on building relationships across divides, unlike other forms of peacekeeping that are designed to keep people apart. Because of this, from the inception of a deployment, UCP methods inherently help in healing the damage of war.

UCP blends two practices that developed during the early to mid-twentieth century: strategic nonviolence and peacekeeping. Gandhi showed the world how to apply strategic and disciplined nonviolence. He was developing the Shanti Sena, Sanskrit for "peace army," when he was assassinated. UCP has been a recurrent vision for much of the last century. Maude Royden, a British feminist activist, organized the Peace Army in 1932 to interpose between the Chinese and Japanese after the Japanese invasion of Manchuria. They offered themselves to the League of Nations but got no further. Even though the Peace Army was never deployed, it did advance the concept of unarmed

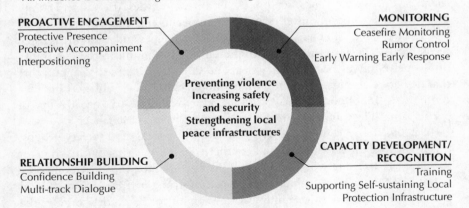

Unarmed Civilian Protection: A mix of strategies of proactive engagement
*All influence is exerted through a lens of encouragement and deterrence

PROACTIVE ENGAGEMENT
Protective Presence
Protective Accompaniment
Interpositioning

MONITORING
Ceasefire Monitoring
Rumor Control
Early Warning Early Response

Preventing violence
Increasing safety
and security
Strengthening local
peace infrastructures

RELATIONSHIP BUILDING
Confidence Building
Multi-track Dialogue

**CAPACITY DEVELOPMENT/
RECOGNITION**
Training
Supporting Self-sustaining Local
Protection Infrastructure

Communication and relationships with all parties to the conflict, whether state or nonstate, are critical to the success of Unarmed Civilian Protection

Figure 9.1   Source: Huibert Oldenhuis et al., *Unarmed Civilian Protection: Strengthening Civilian Capacity to Protect Civilians* (Geneva: UN Institute for Training and Research and Nonviolent Peaceforce, 2016), 117.

civilian peacekeeping.[5] Ms. Royden met with Gandhi in 1934, possibly planting the idea of the Shanti Sena.

Since then, the vision has recurred throughout the world in places like Nicaragua, El Salvador, Guatemala, the Philippines, South Africa, Kenya, the Balkans, Canada, and the United States. Currently, forty-two organizations are carrying out UCP in twenty-four areas of violent conflict.[6]

There are countless recorded and unrecorded instances of unarmed civilians spontaneously protecting other civilians. During the genocide against the Tutsis in Rwanda, Muslims, who were not directly involved in the violence, saved Tutsis and some Muslims by hiding, transporting, and feeding them, sometimes at great personal risk. One person reported, "Whoever arrived in our quarter was hidden and protected and survived."[7]

In Sri Lanka in March 2018, when mobs of Sinhala Buddhist Nationalists began attacking Muslim villages, other Sinhala Buddhists and Hindus provided early warning, transportation, protective presence, and safe haven for their Muslim neighbors. A Buddhist monk interposed himself between an approaching mob of 300 and a group of men and boys set to defend their village with sticks and knives. Upon seeing the monk, the mob retreated. Even though the attacks destroyed 465 homes and properties owned by Muslims, only one person was killed.[8]

Just as John Paul Lederach writes regarding reconciliation and conflict transformation, UCP also helps to awaken our moral imagination.[9] To justify violent attacks, politicians, generals, and pundits explain to the public that there are only two options: send in the bombers, missiles, drones, and troops or sit idly by as some "monster" slaughters innocents and ignores international law. In fact, UCP and many other nonviolent strategies and methods as listed in the 2016 Appeal to the Catholic Church to Re-commit to the Centrality of Gospel Nonviolence offer practical and creative examples of approaches that lie between these two poles. Many more approaches will be created because the realm of nonviolence offers infinite possibilities to a broad scope of participants. The following are a few examples in South Sudan.

In 2009, after receiving an invitation from two local civil society groups, a NP small team traveled around southern Sudan meeting with a host of stakeholders assessing whether they had the potential to protect. Among other criteria, the team evaluated the prospects of strong partnerships with local groups, the feasibility of communicating with all parties to the conflict, the susceptibility of armed actors to outside pressures, and the prospects for a long-lasting positive impact. NP's board of directors reviewed the assessment team's report and approved a mission in early 2010.

Cattle grazing has been a perennial source of violence. During the dry season, typically December to May, grass and water become scarcer, a condition exacerbated by global climate disruption. The herders often move farther and farther south, encroaching on farmers' cropland. A herd can wipe out a village's source of food and livelihood in a couple of hours. Violence often breaks out but is short lived.

Yet such violence can quickly escalate, as it did in February 2011 when cattle keepers moved their herds into Mvolo County, where Jur farmers live. A youth was killed for unknown reasons. Violence quickly spread throughout the county, spilling over into a neighboring county. The conflict escalated and six thousand homes were burned, displacing seventy-six thousand people. Dozens were injured and killed. Children hiding in the bush were dying of dehydration, meningitis, and bee attacks. A mission team from the South Sudan Legislative Assembly (SSLA) found that "children, women and elderly were under trees without food, water and health services and there is a high danger of outbreak of disease such as malaria, pneumonia and diarrhea."[10]

Working with local government, NP sent a team who found women and children starving in the bush. The team immediately advocated for emergency food and medical care as they started to develop strategies to mitigate violence. NP's nonpartisanship was essential as they built trust with chiefs, community leaders, elders, youth, and the military. They identified key actors while maintaining a constant presence in the communities. They enlisted the support from government officials in the state capitols (Western Equatoria and Lakes) as well as in Juba. But time was running out. The rainy season had begun. A paramount chief told the team, "We need to begin cultivation. If we wait any longer, we will all die of hunger."[11]

Local chiefs made three attempts to convene a dialogue, but each failed. NP learned that people feared traveling in each other's territory. Local government, the military, and NP arranged for peace talks. NP then accompanied chiefs and local leaders to the talks. NP provided a protective presence as the rivals talked. The dialogue went remarkably well. They arranged for freedom of movement between each other's villages. They reopened the hospital and schools. They urged their people to return home. And they set up a joint accountability structure. Such enabling of local infrastructure illuminates the just peace norm of conflict transformation, particularly the structural dimension.

Further talks with broader participation were required to sustain peace. NP accompanied a convoy carrying chiefs, elders, and youth to the second round of talks. The rivals agreed to broaden the ceasefire. The group negotiated freedom of movement all along the border between the two states. The cattle keepers agreed to obtain permission from local government officials before entering agricultural areas. Such participatory processes are also one of the just peace norms.

Then the difficult work of implementation began. NP worked with communities to monitor the agreement and intervene quickly if violence broke out. Although there were sporadic breaches, authorities and community leaders responded quickly to quell any escalation. NP shuttled between the communities. All together NP was involved in 115 interventions to help arrange the dialogue and monitor the agreement. The civilian protectors helped the leaders disseminate information about the ceasefire and document the peace agreement, including an agreed-on code of conduct for cattle movement and land use. At the request of the stakeholders, the team provided training in nonviolent conflict resolution and helped communities set up early warning/early response (EWER) procedures. Such training and procedures illustrate the just peace norms of nonviolent education and cultivating peacemaking communities. Four months after the peace talks, a county commissioner stated at a conference, "I want to thank Nonviolent Peaceforce for their tireless efforts of moving through rough roads from Mvolo to Anoul to Yirol West to Mapourdit when no one else would; I owe you a lot of appreciation because the rescue of lives and properties is because of you."[12]

NP is often asked to help communities set up EWER mechanisms, which help communities to consciously respond proactively or reactively to violence. Most communities know when trouble is brewing. The team's job is to help people identify and list such indicators and then help the community develop ways to respond proactively if they can mitigate the violence and reactively if they have to flee the violence.

A NP team living in the eastern part of Lakes state helped the community set up such an EWER mechanism. One afternoon, community people alerted NP that youth from different clans had converged at a cattle camp and were about to break into violence. An interethnic group that included local villagers and internationals traveled to the camp. When they arrived, fighting had already broken out and some young men were wounded.

NP's civilian protectors included Asha Asokan from Kerala, India, who measures barely five feet tall, and Abraham Mabor Arok from the local area, who stands six feet five inches. As the peace team was shuttling back and forth between the contending clans, a young fighter asked Abraham,

"Who is this small girl?"
"Asha Ashokan," responded Abraham.
"Where does she come from?"
"India."

The youth told his colleagues to stop fighting. The youth backed off from each other. The young leader exclaimed, "This problem has become so serious that people from other countries are coming. I will stop now." A local nurse later explained to me, "According to our culture we don't want to do something bad in front of outsiders." The team got a promise from both sides that they would not fight and they would wait for the chiefs to come and talk.

The next morning the chiefs arrived and mediated a deal. At their request, NP monitored the process. Five years later those two clans have not resumed fighting each other.

After the 2011 independence referendum, the euphoria waned rapidly. Political leaders ripped the scabs off old wounds to consolidate their power. Ethnic violence broke out soon after the votes were counted. By late December 2011, massacres began in Jonglei state with Lou Nuer and Dinka people killing people of the Murle tribe. Attacks begat counter attacks. Entire villages were burned, and women were raped and abducted.

The UN High Commissioner for Refugees (UNHCR) gave NP a grant literally overnight, and three teams were quickly deployed to Jonglei state in February 2012. One team started working in the town of Pibor. Soon after arriving they called a community protection meeting. Only men came. When one of the protectors asked where the women were, she was told that security is "men's work." In the next few days the team started asking women in the village the names of the leaders and connectors. The name of Elizabeth came up most often. They met with her and mentioned a community security meeting. She said, "Tell me the place and time and I will bring the women."

A couple of days later Elizabeth came walking up the road to the meeting with eighty women. They described an SPLA garrison located near them. Soldiers often walked through their community, called Kandoco, on their way back and forth to town. The women reported frequent incidents of sexual violence, including rape. These attacks often happened as women went out to pump water, gather firewood, or tend the community garden. As a result the garden, an important food source, was withering.

The women talked strategy. They were creative, they connected, and they took responsibility for their own security. They organized a phone tree. Unlike most rural areas in South Sudan, Kandoco has a cell tower nearby, so cell phones were ubiquitous. An overall protection leader was chosen along with ten sub-leaders. They collectively defined early warning criteria. When threats appeared, leaders called two people, who called two people, and so on until a large group was mustered. NP, the local police, and the UN Police (UNPOL) were also notified. Quickly they would all go to the site of the threat, usually some drunk soldiers, who upon seeing the group would walk away.

Daily patrols were also established. NP convinced UNPOL and the UN armed peacekeepers, an Indian army unit, to each conduct a daily patrol. NP took the late shift because the UN peacekeepers were not allowed to leave their compound after dark. Protective patrols do not just drive around. The protectors would have to stop often and exit their vehicles to talk with villagers, drink tea, and visit the garden. The number of rapes quickly dropped to zero, and the SPLA sent an officer to monitor the garrison and train them on sexual violence.

In December 2013, the power struggle between leaders and factions reignited a vicious civil war. Men began killing civilians based on their ethnic identity. Violence spread quickly to many parts of the country. NP civilian protection officers Derek Oakley and Andres Gutierrez were working in the Bor Protection of Civilians (PoC) area when a militia breached the berm and started shooting people point blank in the head. Chaos broke out. Derek and Andres ran to a hut with fourteen women and children, and the protection officers stood in the doorway. On three occasions, young militia pointed guns in their faces and profanely screamed that they had to leave. The young fighters wanted the women and children. Each time, Derek and Andres held up their NP identity badges and calmly said, "We are unarmed. We are here to protect civilians. And we will not leave." After the third time the militia left and could be heard telling the other fighters to stay away from the hut. Church personnel in towns such as Juba and Malakal were also able to give limited protection to the civilians sheltering in their church compounds.

Fifty-six other civilians were killed in twenty minutes as the UN peacekeepers remained in their quarters consulting with their military superiors in New Delhi as to what they should do. Later, Andres reflected, "If we had a gun in those instances, like an armed peacekeeper, we probably would have been killed."[13] Indeed, two UN armed peacekeepers were killed trying to defend civilians at a UN camp in another town, Akobo.

Soon afterward, the team of Oloo Otieno, Tandi Ngwenya, and Jeevarajah Innasi arrived in Bor to accompany Nuer people to the airport. The trip required them to travel through a hostile Dinka area. Three times a day, seven days a week the team accompanied people safely to the airport. They protected more than one thousand people.

Sheldon Wardwell was part of a team led by Calista Pearce working farther north in the Bentiu PoC area, where more than one hundred thousand people had fled. In January 2014 a group of civilians fleeing to the PoC area were turned back at a government checkpoint, leaving them caught between rival combatants. "They found themselves stranded in the path of two armies, one angry and in retreat, the other on the march and out for revenge," reported journalist Nick Turse.[14]

Upon hearing that sixty women and children were trapped at the airstrip, Sheldon alerted the UN liaison officer who told him that no one was leaving the base. After doing a quick security analysis and discussing the situation with NP HQ in Juba, the team got the green signal to proceed. Calista and Sheldon, the only members of the team who volunteered to go, headed for the airstrip during a late-afternoon downpour. Immediately after leaving the PoC area, they had to navigate their Land Cruiser through a phalanx of two tanks and four pickup trucks with mounted machine guns. The drunken rebels manning the first checkpoint fortunately just wanted the Land Cruiser out of the way. They were waved through the government checkpoint as well. Calista and Sheldon arrived at the airstrip, where more than sixty people swarmed the vehicle. Twenty children and seven women piled into the vehicle. Calista and Sheldon safely delivered the women and children to the PoC area, where they realized that two more trips were required to rescue everyone stranded at the airstrip.

They took off for the second round as it was getting dark and were soon mired in deep mud along the road. They were surprised that some government soldiers joined them in pushing their vehicle. Looking up, Calista and Sheldon saw a UN convoy headed for the airstrip to rescue the remaining people. "It seems clear to me that little NP had shamed the UN into action. . . . With the UN's assistance, all 64 people stranded at the airfield were safe at the UNMISS compound when rebel forces stormed into Bentiu (town) the next morning," explained Turse.[15]

Women living in Bentiu and the other PoC areas have to go to the bush to collect firewood, where soldiers often rape them. Rape is a weapon of war. Sometimes women have strategically sent older women on these treks because they are less likely to be raped. During a two-year period when NP civilian protectors accompanied them, there was only one incident of an attack, and that happened to an NP protector who was thrown to the ground by an inebriated soldier. Her teammates intervened and the soldier left.

These accompaniments entail more than simply going for a walk. NP scouts the routes in advance, letting people know that a group will be coming through. Part of its ability to protect depends on being able to communicate with the combatants. As NP executive director Tiffany Easthom often says, "If we surprise someone in the field we have not done our job." At times the advance team determined that conditions were too dangerous and advised the women not to go.

NP has trained more than 1,900 local women who have formed forty-four Women's Protection Teams. Through their activism the women increase their own self-protection. This illustrates the just peace norm of cultivating peacemaking institutions. For example, teams of women from different tribes came together for a joint action. Together they walked for three hours to meet with the general of one of the armed opposition groups. They knew it would be dangerous to start off as a big group, so a few women began the trek, with groups of four or five women joining them along the way. They numbered 150 by the time they reached the military camp. They told the general: "We are tired! Tired of our children being killed! Tired of being raped!" The general listened and then told them his men would not engage in such activities. After the meeting he arranged transportation for the women to return home and gave them a bull as a token of respect.

Who knows if the general was sincere? Yet, significantly, women are organizing across ethnic lines in various parts of the country and advocating for their own safety and for an end to the war. These actions are remarkable in such a male-dominated society where gender-based violence is rampant. Here lies the hope in a brutal and bleak landscape. If sustainable peace is to come to South Sudan, these brave women bringing the demand from the ground up will lead the way.

Impact and Scaling Up

UCP has been proven to work not only in South Sudan but also in a variety of areas of violent conflict around the world, such as Mindanao in the Philippines, Kurdistan, Palestine, Kenya, Colombia, and the United States. UCP has been successfully carried out by international and local NGOs of varying sizes with various combatants in varying settings, from urban gangs to jungle guerillas. Even though the UN is not able to carry out UCP fully because of security protocols and organizational culture, various personnel have implemented UCP methods.

Both quantitative and qualitative evidence of UCP's impact is mounting. A review by Dr. Rachel Julian of Leeds/Beckett University of case studies, external evaluations, and field notes of nine NGOs providing UCP showed the following:

• Lives are saved.
• Communities are able to stay at home rather than be displaced.
• Peace and human rights work is increasingly possible and involves more people in a wider area.
• Living and working in affected communities supports the reestablishment of relationships and communication across divided communities.
• Attitudes and behavior of armed actors change.
• Unarmed trained civilians can tackle violence and threats of violence.

Yet some types of violent conflict are increasing. *Pathways to Peace*, a joint report from the World Bank and the UN, found that "deaths in war, numbers of displaced populations, military spending, and terrorist incidents, among others, have all surged since the beginning of the century." Current estimates are that by 2030 more than one half of poor people in the world will be living in countries affected by high levels of violence.[16] The UNHCR reports that sixty-seven million people currently have had to flee their homes because of violence and persecution.[17] That is more refugees and internally displaced persons (IDPs) than at any time since World War II. These facts have led Pope Francis to say that World War III is now being fought piecemeal.

Therefore, we need approaches for the direct protection of civilians that are replicable and scalable. We need methods for protecting civilians and preventing violence that can be adapted and applied interactively at the grassroots level by many different entities (e.g., NGOs, churches, schools, Rotary clubs). In South Sudan and beyond, effective scalability requires a process-oriented systems approach that engages local communities more than it does a prescription of a one-size-fits-all methodology.

Just Peace Virtues

The scalability of UCP depends much more on the nurturing of just peace virtues than on equipment and technology. The following looks at how they were applied in South Sudan. All of the unarmed civilian protectors used only active and creative nonviolence. Being nonviolent enhanced the civilian protector's ability to protect. Andres Gutierrez said that if they would have been armed when they stood in the doorway protecting fourteen women and children, they probably would have been shot. This also actualizes the just peace norm of reflexivity; that is, keeping one's means consistent with the ends. Further, instead of responding in kind to the young militiamen's angry demands, Andreas and Derek remained calm and nonviolent. They did not escalate the anger. This changed the equation. Whether they appealed to the combatants' sense of morality or common humanity, or to some cultural or religious norm, or they simply confused the armed men, the result was that the militia left and fourteen women and children were saved.

Oloo Otieno, Tandi Ngwenya, and Jeevarajah Innasi showed tremendous humility in driving small groups of Nuer people through a Dinka-controlled area three times a day, seven days a week for months. They knew the truth of their place. They were not demanding or flashy—rather, they were mundane and routine. They recognized the dignity of all, whether Nuer or Dinka. They gave the space for the authorities to exercise their power in allowing them to pass. If the civilian protectors would have confronted the authorities and demanded the rights of their passengers, they would not have made it to the airport. By remaining humble, more than one thousand people safely exited a dangerous area.

NP's active nonpartisanship, essential for its ability to protect, requires deep empathy. NP does not enter a conflict to pick which side is "right." It is there to protect civilians and prevent violence. Its civilian protectors witness horrible acts that cause death and deep suffering. Yet NP protectors have to try to put themselves in the shoes of both the victims and the perpetrators. Often when NP members do this they find that the distinctions are not so clear. Empathy is not only part of human nature; it can be sharpened through training and spiritual practice. NP's core training includes the Circle of

Truth exercise borrowed from Pace Bene's *From Violence to Wholeness* training. Standing in a circle, each trainee has to assume the role of each of eight people involved in a conflict. Parts could include an IDP mother, a suicide bomber, a government soldier, a local mayor, and a nonviolent community leader. By the time every trainee has played every part, deep and emotive expressions have emerged. This leads to discussions that help trainees develop a framework for understanding and empathy.

NP's job is not to save the community but rather to support them until they can get back to a place where they can protect themselves. When NP teams live in communities with urgent needs and bring little more than their presence, they soon discover that they are mutually dependent on each other for their common security. This is solidarity. They work together, internationals and locals, to protect each other. Asha Ashokan, from Kerala, India, and Abraham Mabor Arok, from East Yirol, South Sudan, worked side by side to quell violence. Although Asha's presence provided a deterrent, Abraham had to explain it to the local combatants.

NP's ability to protect depends on the hospitality of local communities. NP's civilian protectors are not able to work unless the community accepts them. This often requires tremendous understanding and patience on the part of the community. People living in war zones are accustomed to humanitarians bringing food and material. It is much more challenging to figure out who these people are who only bring themselves.

Although NP is nonpartisan, it often protects the space and creates enabling conditions for local people to seek justice. UCP is practiced not only by NP but also by other groups like Peace Brigades International and Christian Peacemaker Teams, which have effectively accompanied human rights defenders throughout the world. By training and supporting Women's Protection Teams in South Sudan, local women were able to organize and walk to the rebel camp to tell the general that they "are tired!" of the war.

Calista's and Sheldon's decision to take off in the rain and navigate hostile military checkpoints to rescue stranded civilians, not only once but to go a second time as night was setting in, required as much if not more courage than any armed soldier possesses. Yet courage is demonstrated through dogged persistence more often than through these heroic events. As McCarthy explains in chapter 3, Thomas Aquinas asserted, "the virtue of courage most characteristically arises in endurance rather than attack, because it is more difficult to control fear rather than act aggressively." Courage is expressed by living in 100-degree heat; contending with snakes, mosquitos, and diarrhea; and eating hazelnut-cocoa spread and rice.

Although NP is a nonsectarian organization, the unarmed civilian protectors live the just peace virtues as they protect civilians and prevent violence. They discovered that the virtues are inherent in their work. Just peace requires the creation of effective and attractive models like UCP that render war obsolete. The virtues underlying just peace are not only aspects of human flourishing but also practical markers for those attractive new models.

UCP and the Church

UCP is not new to South Sudan. The church has been doing it informally for decades, building relationships across divides and providing an unarmed presence that protects by proximity, without knowing a technical term for it. It has continued to do so during the latest civil war, which began in 2013. In the church's peacebuilding work over many decades, John Paul Lederach's comment resonates: "I am uneasy with the growing technique-oriented view of change in settings of violence that seems to dominate much of professional conflict resolution approaches."[18] He speaks of "invoking the moral imagination . . . which is not found in perfecting or applying the techniques or the skills of a process." He continues, "My feeling is that we have overemphasized the technical aspects and political content to the detriment of the art of giving birth to and keeping a process creatively alive." Thus, we have failed to leave adequate space for serendipity, intuition, art, and the web of relationships.[19] This attention to moral imagination illuminates the importance of the just peace norm of cultivating key virtues such as active nonviolence, mercy, and empathy.

The Church's commitment to nonviolent accompaniment is not unrelated to another South Sudanese initiative, Holy Trinity Peace Village Kuron, founded by the iconic retired Catholic bishop Paride Taban, a man who lives and breathes peace and reconciliation and who has been honored with numerous international peace awards. His personal spirituality includes eight short phrases that he shares with all: "I love you, I miss you, thank you, I forgive, we forget, together, I am wrong, I am sorry." Settling among several of the most isolated communities in the extreme southeast corner of South Sudan, where there is no presence of government structures and no sign of any modern development activities, among communities for whom violent conflict over livestock and resources was the norm, Bishop Taban built a village, a bridge, a road, an agricultural project, a school, a clinic, a youth center, and eventually even an internet café, and he gradually helped the people to see a different way of living. "Now we have learned that we are human beings!" A community mediation initiative grew, with unarmed local community police, and it is now an oasis of peace in a nation at war. This initiative actualizes the just peace norms of cultivating peacemaking communities, a more robust civil society, economic justice, relationality, and conflict transformation, which includes the practice of identifying human needs.

So the concept and practice of nonviolence and just peace is not completely new to South Sudan, but it was certainly an underrepresented minority sport.

However, what NP has brought is a large-scale, organized program of UCP, supported not only with human, physical, technical, and financial resources but also by reflection, study, articulation of principles and processes, institutional memory, and interaction with other cases throughout the world—in other words, the necessities of creating a sustainable and intentional initiative that can be scaled up.

Conclusion

Sudan has been described as "a laboratory for those who study peace,"[20] and it certainly provides some instructive illustrations for those who study just peace and nonviolence. NP's intervention in South Sudan also coincided with a gradual change in local attitudes toward nonviolence. In the face of this senseless and self-seeking conflict, a population that has accepted violence traditionally and that has certainly not rejected violence in previous civil conflicts is now abhorring violence, changing its language and beginning to speak explicitly of resolving the conflict by nonviolent means.

At the same time, South Sudan is reaping the fruits of generations of prior conflict, including multigenerational trauma. Despite peace being declared in both 1972 and 2005, the legacy of violent struggle has blighted the post-struggle period and, as observed elsewhere by Chenoweth and Stephan, has led to dysfunctional and violent governance and a return to civil war. People are actively questioning whether they have actually achieved the liberation they fought for: "Is this freedom? Is this liberation?" Although the intention of the liberation struggle is still affirmed, violence clearly did not deliver what was intended.

Grassroots communities still live in a very violent and militarized culture, and they are too often genuinely unable to envisage any other method. With the failure of violence and the gradual raising of awareness that there are in fact other options, and indeed better options, nonviolence is beginning to look more attractive every day.

One must thus end on a note of hope. The resilience of the South Sudanese people is legendary, and the church believes that once the ordinary citizens are given a voice, facilitated by the church as the only remaining honest broker, the conflict will eventually end with an indigenous (not an externally imposed) agreement. However, this will not happen quickly, and there is still a lot more suffering to come. During that period and beyond, the type of UCP practiced by NP will be needed more than ever. Perhaps the lesson learned is that just peace is not only a goal; it is also the means to that goal, as the just peace norm of reflexivity suggests. Violence, even in a just cause with all the other criteria of a just war ethic satisfied, *always* contains the seeds of more violence.

Discussion Questions

1. Why are well-trained unarmed civilians able to protect other civilians from armed groups, both state and nonstate actors? What is the leverage or power that becomes activated in such situations? Why can unarmed units activate such power more often than armed units?
2. What kind of conflicts are more challenging for UCP? What could be done to improve UCP to better address such challenges? What other just peace practices might be key to complement UCP in such difficult situations?
3. What, if any, added value does the presence of international civilian protectors provide? How could the presence of international civilian protectors, especially those from the global north, reinforce colonial relationships? What could be done to mitigate this?
4. What could the church do to increase the number of people aware of and committed to nonviolence and just peace, such as with unarmed civilian protection? What programs could help cultivate the necessary virtues? What role could the different church or religious institutions play in scaling-up unarmed civilian protection?
5. Civilians are threatened by violence not only in war zones but also in our cities and neighborhoods. Too often we hear about shootings in schools and places of worship, gang violence, and violence breaking out at demonstrations. Think about a situation in your community where people are under threat. Which of the UCP methods could be applied to that situation? How might you organize such a response? Whom would you engage? What challenges would you face?

Notes

1. Erica Chenoweth and Maria J. Stephan, *Why Civil Resistance Works: The Strategic Logic of Nonviolent Conflict* (New York: Columbia University Press, 2011), 199–200.

2. Pastoral Message of the South Sudan Catholic Bishops, "A Voice Cries in the Wilderness," February 23, 2017.

3. South Sudan Catholic Bishops, "War Is Evil: War Cannot Bring Peace, This War Must Stop," September 25, 2014.

4. "Appeal to Catholic Church to Re-commit to Centrality of Gospel Nonviolence," April 13, 2016, https://nonviolencejustpeace.net.

5. For an account of international UCP work up to 2000, see Thomas Weber and Yeshua Moser-Pungsuwan, *Nonviolent Intervention across Borders: A Recurrent Vision* (Honolulu: University of Hawaii Press, 2000).

6. Unarmed Civilian Peacekeeping Database, Selkirk College, British Columbia, Canada, http://selkirk.ca/node/10307.

7. Mary B. Anderson and Marshall Wallace, *Opting out of War* (Boulder, CO: Lynne Rienner, 2013), 160–63.

8. Lisa Fuller, "How Unarmed Civilians Saved Lives During Anti-Muslim Attacks in Sri Lanka," *Waging Nonviolence*, March 19, 2018.

9. John Paul Lederach, *The Moral Imagination, The Art and Soul of Building Peace* (Oxford: Oxford University Press, 2004).

10. South Sudan Legislative Assembly Mission Team, *Jur Atuot Conflict Summary Report*, April 3, 2011.

11. Tiffany Easthom, "Unarmed Civilian Protection and Peacekeeping in South Sudan: A Case Study in Stabilization," unpublished, 2011, 6.

12. Easthom, 8.

13. Gary Beitel, *In Pursuit of Peace* (Montreal: reFrame Films, 2015).

14. Nick Turse, *Next Time They'll Come to Count the Dead* (Chicago: Haymarket Books, 2016), 85.

15. Turse, 91.

16. United Nations–World Bank Study, *Pathways for Peace: Inclusive Approaches to Preventing Violent Conflict* (Washington, DC: World Bank, March 2018).

17. UN High Commissioner for Refugees (UNHCR), *Global Report 2016*, New York, June 2017.

18. John Paul Lederach, *The Moral Imagination: The Art and Soul of Building Peace* (Oxford: Oxford University Press, 2005), 52.

19. Lederach, 70.

20. John Ashworth, *The Voice of the Voiceless: The Role of the Church in the Sudanese Civil War, 1983–2005* (Kenya: Paulines Publications Africa, 2014), 167.

10

ADDRESSING GANG VIOLENCE IN EL SALVADOR

Envisioning a Just Peace Approach

JOSÉ HENRÍQUEZ LEIVA

Case Context

In June 2010, Salvadorans woke up to the shocking news that gang members had set fire to a public bus in a populous municipality on the outskirts of San Salvador. Fourteen passengers died inside the bus, and thirteen managed to escape after police intervention.[1] Those killings were only a fraction of the 3,987 homicides that year in a country of about 6.5 million people.[2] Although the Salvadoran civil war officially ended in 1992, violent deaths have become part of the ordinary postconflict landscape. Indeed, based on the number of homicides, more deaths have occurred in the postwar period than in the twelve years of civil strife.[3] The human loss is the most egregious but is not the only loss; the cost of the violence in the country in 2014 was about 16 percent of the GDP, almost the same as remittances received that year that were sent by those who left the country due to the violence.[4] Most of the deaths have been attributed to gang members; however, although it looks straightforward, the numbers hide the complexity of gang violence in the country and the state response.

Understanding Salvadoran Gangs

A street gang is "any durable, street-oriented youth group whose involvement in illegal activity is part of its group identity."[5] Theories of gang formation underline that when ordinary means of socialization (families, schools, and law enforcement institutions for the most part) fail to lead young individuals into standard social norms and values, this role is played by peer-led processes based on street cultures. This "street socialization" would be a fertile ground for the reproduction of gangs, their norms, and their values, including delinquent behavior.[6] Street socialization also deals with identity-formation processes of young people, providing youth in gangs a "lifestyle that offers familial bonding, peer acceptance, freedom, and excitement."[7] Salvadoran gangs are "associated with the identity franchises of two street gangs that had their origins in the city of Los Angeles in the United States, but whose development no longer depends upon the American dynamics: the Mara Salvatrucha Thirteen (MS-13) and the 18th Street Gang (also known as Barrio 18)."[8]

There are no reliable statistics about gang members in El Salvador. A recent investigation estimated gang membership of between forty thousand and sixty thousand individuals who are present in all fourteen departments of the country.[9] Gangs have set up boundaries at the local level in which they reign, and respect for those boundaries can be a matter of life and death.[10] Gangs' structures and leadership vary. MS-13 and Barrio 18 are divided in many small units called "cliques," which operate at the local level (neighborhoods) with significant autonomy. There seems to be periodic communication between the cliques and a national leadership that allows the creation of certain patterns of action.[11]

Homicides and extortions are key features for which gangs are blamed and feared. In 2015, 35 percent of Salvadoran municipalities had a homicide rate of 100 or more per 100,000 inhabitants, which is a major concern given that the World Health Organization considers homicide rates exceeding 10 per 100,000 people as epidemic.[12] Extortions, on the other hand, give gangs a dimension of "protection rackets."[13] Surveys have shown that victims—which range from businesses to families in poor neighborhoods—are asked to pay a weekly fee ("renta"), and resisting to pay may be fatal. For instance, between 2011 and 2016, 692 people in the transportation sector were killed by gang members.[14] Extortions allow gangs to subsist, but the total cost for the general population is very high. In 2016 it was estimated that gangs were responsible for up to 76 percent of extortions committed in the country.[15] It is commonly believed that long-term and extensive extortion activities have transformed gangs into a highly profitable enterprise; however, from financial figures disclosed by the government, and considering that the money has to reach all members, it is almost impossible that anybody gets rich, because they would receive something like US$15 per week—less than half of the agricultural sector's minimum wage. Rather than sophisticated transnational criminal organizations, Salvadoran gangs may resemble a "poor man's mafia."[16]

Gang-related violence has forced the displacement of families from populated neighborhoods under their control. According to the Mesa Nacional contra el Desplazamiento Forzado (National Roundtable against Forced Displacement), there were about 1,500 people displaced between 2015 and 2017.[17] Although the real magnitude is unknown—because there are no reliable statistics—gang control over a number of territories suggests that gangs are connected directly with this exodus. The government has been reluctant to fully acknowledge the problem.

Repression-Oriented Approaches to Gang Violence

The state has preferentially addressed gang violence through repression. In 2003, the government launched the "Plan Mano Dura" ("Iron Fist Plan"), which included combined police and military patrolling, area raids, and mass arrests of those suspected to be engaged with gangs. Although the plan failed to significantly reduce homicide rates, it gained popular approval, so the subsequent government organized its electoral campaign around offering continuity.[18] In 2004, the new government launched the "Plan Súper Mano Dura" ("Super Iron Fist Plan"), which included almost identical measures but added some limited gang prevention and rehabilitation programs.[19] Homicide rates did not decrease as they were supposed to, and the plan was abandoned two years later.[20] Those measures, however, created spaces for police abuse.[21] In 2006 the government passed a new piece of legislation, the "Special Law against Terrorist Acts," and even though gangs were not mentioned in the text, they are believed to be the targets behind the initiative.[22]

In 2010 the legislative assembly approved the "Gangs, Groups, Associations and Organizations of Criminal Nature Act," which sanctioned all gangs as illegal and also made illegal any type of collaboration with them.[23] Prison terms for gangsters were up to six years for ordinary members and up to ten years for leaders. In 2015 the Supreme Court declared that gangs could be considered terrorist groups within the terms of the 2006 act, and this decision juridically allowed gangs to be treated in ways similar to those applied to criminal and terrorist groups in other countries.[24] In 2016 the government brought back punitive measures by approving extraordinary measures targeting inmates, and although they were called transitory and temporary, they have been renewed twice.[25] Measures have been criticized by national and international human rights organizations because they clearly prolonged a situation of human rights violations.[26]

The state has not had the capacity to fully investigate and attribute culpability for all crimes; however, gangs are believed to have significant responsibility. That became clear when after controversial negotiations between the government and gang leaders in 2012—popularly known as the "Tregua" (truce)—there was a sudden and sharp reduction of homicides from an average of fourteen per day to about only five.[27] The government had offered gang leaders less restrictive prison conditions (and presumably money), and gangs, in exchange, would have to commit to reduce the killings.[28] The truce lasted less than two years and then homicide rates returned to previous levels.

Both main political parties have negotiated with gangs at different times; however, those processes have not been transparent, and some of them were held with electoral purposes in mind.

The truce reduced homicides but also helped gangs to strengthen their structures financially and operationally, as was revealed afterward in several ways.[29] In July 2015, for instance, public transportation in El Salvador's capital came almost to a complete halt for four days when gangs tried forcing the government to negotiate an easing of the crackdown on their operations and threatened to kill bus drivers if they dared to circulate. Service only resumed when the government sent combined patrols of police and armed forces to safeguard buses.

After more than a decade of repressive policies, El Salvador still stands as one of the most violent countries in the world. During the last few years, the number of armed confrontations between gangs and state security officials has increased—something that was portrayed as a new operational phase of the major gangs. However, human rights organizations have contested the official version, showing that there are patterns of extrajudicial killings— up to forty-seven between 2015 and 2016.[30] In 2017 national human rights organizations requested an audience at the Inter-American Commission on Human Rights,[31] and in 2018 the Special Rapporteur on extrajudicial, summary, or arbitrary executions at the Office of the United Nations High Commissioner for Human Rights visited the country. The final report confirmed the claims of extrajudicial executions.[32]

After the clear setback of the measures, but without abandoning them, some governmental initiatives have implemented less repressive measures but without a coherent plan. In 2013, building momentum during the truce, the government launched the "municipios libres de violencia" (violence-free municipalities) or "municipalidades santuario" (sanctuary municipalities), which gave local authorities ample spaces to dialogue and negotiate with gang members within their territories.[33] Additionally, in 2015, the first phase of "Plan El Salvador Seguro" was launched in ten municipalities, promising combined efforts to reduce, investigate, and prevent violence.[34] The second phase was launched in sixteen additional municipalities in 2016. The plan, however, has been criticized for its heavy military component, the lack of funding for prevention, and the dubious legality of the implementation of some initiatives.

Rethinking Responses to Gang Violence through the Just Peace Ethic Framework

Just peace can be understood as "peaceful and just political life, accomplished through human solidarity, commitment to the common good, respect for the dignity of all persons, and inclusion in participatory and equitable social, legal, and political institutions."[35] This vision derives from God's peace promise contained in the scriptures, announcing times in which peace and justice will "embrace."[36] This, however, needs to overcome numerous challenges based on the way societies understand and manage political power, social and economic relations, and divergent meanings of peace and justice.

Just peace, framed within modern developments of the Catholic social teaching on peace—and its particular accent on nonviolence—can be seen as a set of practices but also as a virtue-based approach, which "complements the practice and principle approaches to create a more integrated just peace ethic." A virtue-based approach can "amplify the development of character and the kind of imagination that engages and creatively applies, extends, and even corrects" Catholic social teaching. Additionally, a virtue-based approach would likely do a better job of preventing and transforming violence, which ultimately strengthens "the prevention of war as well as the capacity to defuse active wars" and "will better equip us to transform not only direct violence but also structural and cultural violence," further marginalizing and, at least culturally and perhaps at some point morally, deligitimizing the use of violence or lethal force.[37]

In the next sections, the question about the root causes of this reality—which is central to the just peace ethic—is examined, followed by some reflections on how the just peace normative framework can help envision nonviolent ways to address gang violence.

Root Causes of Gang Violence in El Salvador

Street gangs did not start following the civil war. They started in the 1960s, associated with precarious urban settings, and their interactions would have been oriented primarily toward hanging out in the streets, establishing and defending turfs, feuding with groups in the vicinities, and becoming involved in minor offenses.[38] Those youth groups became progressively involved in criminal activity—mostly extortion—and by the late 1990s they had a well-established presence in the urban context, and people started referring to them with the term "maras."[39] Several factors contributed to the progressive "institutionalization" of gangs, such as the prison system, urban landscape, and access and use of communication technologies.[40] In El Salvador, additionally, the postwar culture of violence and, more importantly, some transnational processes have played significant roles.[41]

Violence during the Salvadoran Civil War forced tens of thousands to flee to the United States. Once there, in a challenging and frequently hostile environment, they soon discovered the world of American gangs. East Los Angeles was already home for a number of gangs, including Barrio 18, which has a significant connection with Mexican migrants of the 1940s and 1950s.[42] Due to increasing rivalries, Central American migrants—Salvadorans for the most part—created MS-13 as a means to compete with Barrio 18, and MS-13 grew to become one of the dominant gangs among Central American immigrants in the US who were, in large numbers, undocumented.[43]

In the 1990s the imprisonment and deportation of thousands of Central Americans became a regular state practice. In particular, the 1996 Illegal Immigration Reform and Immigrant Responsibility Act modified the definition of aggravated felony, including retroactive effects, allowing deportation of non-US citizens after a prison sentence using fast-track procedures.[44] This act caused the deportations of tens of thousands of Central Americans, including more than 22,500 Salvadorans who had spent time in jail and would have supposedly been engaged with gangs.[45] The majority arrived in a country that was foreign to them, and they had to endure the hardships of restricted opportunities, poverty, and social marginalization. Such conditions made it relatively easy for them to connect and engage with local gangs and share their gang experience from the US, which, in turn, helped spread the US gang culture. The exchange does not mean that there is an easy flow of gang members between the US and El Salvador, and a recent survey from the Florida International University (FIU) shows that most Salvadoran members have never been to the US.[46] However, the two largest gangs, and particularly MS-13, have created transnational links and are present in at least seven countries.[47]

Gang presence has also been facilitated by a national economy that has been growing inequitably for large percentages of the population and has become a significant push factor for migration. That adds up to high unemployment rates, low salaries, and deficiently planned urban growth with scarce availability of social services. Security-related factors also play significant roles—for instance, those related to drug trafficking, small-arms traffic and availability, and state corruption.[48]

Addressing Gang Violence from a Just Peace Ethic Framework

Envisioning pathways within a just peace framework implies looking at gang violence in its broader context and acknowledging the interdependence and complexity of its constitutive factors. Here, the normative framework of the just peace ethic is used to shed new light on the long-term violence experienced by Salvadoran society. Some of the norms are actualized around three issues: the levels of social and economic inequality; the repressive security policies and their impact on human rights, including the institutional capacity of the security sector and the justice system; and the need for processes of dialogue and restorative justice.

Addressing Social and Economic Inequality

Gangs are mostly found in areas that traditionally have experienced—or are experiencing—social and economic hardship. In El Salvador, poverty and marginalization are not new; indeed, they were among the factors underlying the twelve-year civil war. According to the UN Development Program (UNDP), in 2013 more than half of the population was either unemployed or underemployed, with income levels below the minimum of the sector in which they were working (conditions are more severe in urban areas).[49] Only 20 percent of the economically active population had a "decent employment" by International Labour Organization standards, and 34 percent of the population was affected by multidimensional poverty (combined monetary and social factors).[50] As important as this factor is, however, it cannot be inferred that gang presence in neighborhoods is directly proportional to poverty levels.[51]

Poverty, marginalization, and violence have also fueled migration to the United States, and the transnational exchange, as mentioned previously, created spaces for gangs to flourish and for violence to continue. Studies have shown that massive deportations implemented by the US government have created violent peaks in El Salvador, and they have also put enormous pressure on young Salvadorans, who can be considered most vulnerable to social violence in both countries either because their relatives are being deported to El Salvador or because once there they cannot easily find job opportunities or social protection networks.[52] Poverty and marginalization create cycles of fear, despair, hate, and violence, and most gang members have experienced them.

From a just peace perspective and using Glen Stassen's analysis of Matthew 5:43–48, encountering gang members, addressing their reality through active nonviolence, and offering constructive opportunities instead of further marginalization can help them to experience a humanizing interaction that can generate spaces for conflict transformation; and they will also reach other social actors.[53] For those opportunities to happen, there is a need for immediate but also mid-term and long-term solutions.

In accord with the just peace norms of sustainability and economic justice, new mechanisms of sustainable inclusive social and economic development are needed to stop vicious cycles of poverty and violence. Mobilization of public and private actors can facilitate the incorporation of former gang members to employment in similar ways to those of successful experiences already in place. Additionally, the creation of technical or vocational training programs and small entrepreneurial initiatives in areas with higher levels of violence and unemployment is needed. Although ambitious, it could also be envisioned that such concerted efforts could be an incentive for active gang members to leave the gang life. Another measure to be taken includes addressing the deportation effects through the accompaniment of young people returning to the country, facilitating their participation in inclusive initiatives, which is in accord with the just peace norm of participatory processes. It should also contemplate advocacy efforts to promote changes to policies that create such migratory momentum from the US. These could become "transforming initiatives" that can break cycles of marginalization and violence inspired by the Sermon on the Mount. However, only comprehensive initiatives can bring sustainable results. The term "reintegration" may be misleading because many of the gang members may have never been "integrated" in society. Professional training should ideally be combined with psychosocial support. Private initiatives need to coordinate with the government as efficiently as possible.

The central government should pay special attention to respect the principle of subsidiarity—which can be considered part of the just peace norm of just governance—including the promotion and support of successful initiatives taken at the local level. At this level, creativity can be best geared toward the reality of specific contexts and communities, including those where former gang members' lives unfold. The voices of those communities should progressively be heard. Only appropriate combined efforts can help restore the sense of belonging in former gang members and allow them to leave behind the stigma they have been carrying with them for a long time. After decades of "mano dura," this thinking may sound counterintuitive for many people, especially for those who have lost relatives, but there will not be spaces for restoring the social fabric if spaces are not opened. The lives of thousands are at stake in the years to come. Such actions would be in accord with the just peace norms of relationality and reconciliation.

Several preventive and restorative initiatives have been organized, mostly by the nongovernmental and private sectors. Some of the following examples actualize the just peace norms of economic justice, training in nonviolent skills, relationality, and conflict transformation, which includes the practice of trauma-healing: the Polígono Don Bosco, a center run by the Salesian Fathers, has implemented training programs, tattoo removal, and job-related advice for former gang members.[54] The NGO Catholic Relief Services, associated with the US Conference of Catholic Bishops, has implemented job-oriented training for former gang members and violence prevention training for vulnerable youth.[55] The Grupo Calvo, a Spanish company, started working with former gang members as early as 2002, focused on delivering training opportunities.[56] Another company, Rio Grande Foods, owned by a Salvadoran entrepreneur based in the US, decided to collaborate with gang reinsertion efforts and launched a program in 2010 that reached up to 130 participants in the first two years and reported an overall 85 percent success in post-program employment.[57] A similar initiative was launched by

League Collegiate Wear, a Pennsylvania-based company that offers rehabilitation programs focused on young couples with young children, because they understand that this is a special period in the lives of people willing to leave the gangs. This program partners with local universities to provide psychological services.[58]

Religious institutions—churches in particular—can also play a significant role in supporting young men and women who leave gangs. The FIU's survey indicates that religion or religious affiliation is an important topic for gang members, and many of the respondents said that churches can help them to rebuild their identity and a sense of belonging.[59] The Catholic community, mostly through NGOs, has been implementing initiatives aiming to support former gang members when they leave their gangs. Evangelical churches, on the other hand, have been accepted by the two largest gangs as safe havens; according to some former gang members, those churches are the predominant alternative they have in order to leave a gang without being killed.

Changing the Security Approach and Reforming the Criminal Justice System

Repressive policies have served more electoral purposes than violence reduction, and they have also enabled scapegoating of gangs to divert attention from a fragile criminal justice system. On the one hand, the Policia Nacional Civil (PNC) has not been able to carry out investigations for every homicide in the country; they have not had the personnel or the capacity. Moreover, the PNC has had a controversial history since its inception after the peace agreements, with several processes of depuration after cases of corruption.[60] Indeed, according to police records, the number of homicides officially attributed to gangs is substantively lower than those attributed to them by the general public.[61] But if the PNC has limited investigative capacities, the Salvadoran justice system is equally limited in their capacity to deliver justice. In 2015 there were more than six thousand homicides, but fewer than one in ten cases came to a court.[62] This has also had serious consequences for the penitentiary system, which is in dire need of reform. Prisons are crowded, there are certain corrupt systems in place, and gangs have been able to coordinate actions from behind bars. The pieces of legislation mentioned in the previous section made it easy to arrest gang members for simply being associated with a "criminal organization." This, along with the limitations of the court system, has resulted in some people being imprisoned for many months without any follow-up investigations or pending trials. Additionally, some extremely unsafe, cage-like containers have been used to hold gang members in inhumane conditions while waiting—often for months—to be transferred to a prison. All of this has created a system that no longer has any "correctional" function and is only reproducing anger, violence, and corruption. The human rights of gang members within the justice system have been obliterated, something that has become justified and normalized in Salvadoran society. The state has a social debt with regard to the examination of the role of state corruption and the participation of the organized crime and criminal networks in the overall context of violence.

The just peace ethic can play a significant role in this context, although it seems counterintuitive that after years of warlike violence in El Salvador, in which state repression has had the dominant voice and has created deep hatred of gangs, there can be space for a different approach. However, this is probably the most toxic cycle of violence that needs to be broken if new opportunities for peace and justice are to be created. The "eye for eye and tooth for tooth" cycle is clearly confronted by Jesus in Matthew 5:39: "Do not resist in an evil way."[63] The just peace norm of reflexivity highlights the need to keep means and ends consistent. There are no choices. More than a decade of repression and the state's forcible approach have not provided a solution, so it is imperative to open new alternatives. They have to encompass all actors within the criminal justice system, law enforcement organs, the judiciary, and the penitentiaries. These actors have played a part in the construction of the current context, and they have to be part of the solution.

Some studies have shown that municipalities with higher degrees of social cohesion were less prone to host gangs and criminal events.[64] Using this evidence, the just peace approach can help reframe the state security discourse and promote policies more oriented toward community building through restorative justice mechanisms and less centered on punishment. Those policies could certainly be implemented as an overall framework in which training and job creation opportunities could be developed. Additionally, if new opportunities are to be created within Salvadoran society, gang members need—again—to be rehumanized in the local social imagination, for which a change in language and image creation are needed.[65] This is central to the construction of reconciled societies. This rehumanization through new language and representations is a process that can be promoted by the just peace norms of human dignity and human rights as well as conflict transformation in its cultural dimension. Practicing an "unsentimental enemy love" will probably not be easy, but it will allow for political creativity.[66]

Promoting Dialogue and Restorative Justice

The state response to gang formation and gang violence has been, as indicated previously, mostly repressive, and this has had a significant impact that needs to be reversed. Repression helped strengthen gang structures and operations, and it also increased levels of violence and created cycles of violence and retaliation. Repression also used recursive mechanisms to promote the criminalization of gangs, to the extent that gangs were—in the collective imagination—responsible for almost every homicide in the country and were progressively portrayed as radical enemies. Furthermore, a number of media interventions locally and abroad have pictured them as already dehumanized.[67] Indeed, it was not infrequent to hear in different circles that the best way of dealing with gangs was to kill all gang members. The creation of this myth, however, only consolidated walls of fear, hate, and intolerance, diverting attention from the root causes of the generalized violence, its complexity, and the limited institutional capacity of governments to deal with it.

Dialogue has been absent in the violent context of El Salvador. In general, society has become complacent and supportive of repressive measures and the criminalization of gangs, dismissing any type of consideration regarding their inclusion in potential paths to end the conflict.[68] The just peace norm of participatory processes would work to correct this. As already mentioned, there have been a few negotiation initiatives, but they all lacked transparency and were framed not within a search for sustainable solutions but for political gains. This situation disqualified dialogue in the minds of the public, but dialogue cannot be avoided. Gangs need to be included in finding solutions. Nothing can be solved without talking with gang members. The just peace approach can help reframe political discourse by engaging local communities and authorities in a comprehensive and co-responsible dialogue to address the root causes of violence.[69]

The opposition to processes of dialogue is itself an act of violence; it is a way of entrenching positions of retaliation and disqualification of those considered to be the cause of the problem, which in turn facilitates the permanence of cycles of violence. In political circles, it is usually repeated that dialogue with criminals undermines the law and weakens public authority; however, the absence of dialogue has proven to be a deadly path in El Salvador. The experience of the civil war has to be brought into the conversation. Although it is a different context, the number of deaths related to gangs keeps increasing. There was no military solution then, and the use of armed force has not solved the gang violence. Dialogue cannot be avoided anymore, but this time, a transparent, mediated, and multiactor dialogue is needed. As Pope Francis writes, "An ethics of fraternity and peaceful coexistence between individuals and among peoples cannot be based on the logic of fear, violence and closed-mindedness, but on responsibility, respect and sincere dialogue."[70]

The just peace norm of reconciliation is still an incomplete process in El Salvador. Within a logic of war and violence, where there must be winners and losers, it is a difficult topic to discuss. However, from an active nonviolence reading of the Sermon on the Mount we come back to Matthew 5:23–24: "Therefore, if you are offering your gift at the altar and there remember that your brother or sister has something against you, leave your gift there in front of the altar. First go and be reconciled to them; then come and offer your gift." It is a call to go through a less explored path, an invitation to be politically creative in a different way by taking the initiative, one that "will free . . . from vicious cycles of resentment, anger, counter-judgment, and potential violence—the initiative that will transform . . . relationship[s] through reconciling practice[s]."[71] Restorative justice may be a heavier and more painful process for some groups, particularly those who have lost loved ones during all these years, so any initiative must include access to the truth and also adequate reparations. Each side, gangs and state, has to acknowledge its responsibility for this situation and should be open to move forward, including processes of disarmament, demobilization, and reintegration, but also legal reforms to the criminal justice system. Law reform is absolutely necessary. The just peace norm of conflict transformation, with its practice of acknowledging responsibility for harm, as well as the norms of integral disarmament and just governance, would enable us to move in this direction.

Conclusion

In reflecting on possible applications of the just peace framework, it must be acknowledged that its implementation can be challenging in complex and highly politicized contexts. As noted in the framing chapters, key to the "practicability of the Sermon on the Mount . . . [is] the power of *transforming initiatives* that break us out of *vicious cycles* of violence and sin in ways that the *traditional righteousness* 'you have heard it said' cannot do."[72] But how could the just peace approach be integrated into the sphere of national social and economic planning, particularly when the conflicts to be addressed have been going on for a long time? Multiple efforts will be needed to change hearts and minds of political leaders on key aspects of public policy, or key sources of power will need to be diminished; and only committed individuals convinced of the potential of this framework to advance peace and justice through nonviolent processes will be able to unleash needed change in El Salvador.

The Salvadoran society has been bleeding for too long. Suffering and social fragmentation run deep, and communities live in a nonreconciled society. In many ways, the current juncture is as critical as the one in which an end to the armed conflict was being sought. The just peace framework offers not only Gospel-based practices that can be applied in conflict situations, it also offers guidance on how a virtue-based approach can inform peacemakers to be "better motivated and prepared to creatively imagine nonviolent ways to transform conflict, to choose, and to sustain those ways through difficult situations."[73] In a way, El Salvador needs a new peace process, and this time the just peace ethic can help guide such a process.

Discussion Questions

1. Violence is pervasive and reaches families, schools, neighborhoods, entire cities, and beyond. What are the most common violent events happening in your area? How do individuals and groups react to that violence? Try to develop an analysis in which you explore origins, typologies, approaches to, and effects of that violence and then explore some practices from a just peace perspective.

2. The just peace framework aims to be comprehensive in its analysis and in its proposals of solutions. What would be effective ways to promote citizens' engagement in far-reaching dialogues about nonviolent strategies and mechanisms to create the social changes needed at a given time? Should gangs (in the Salvadoran case) be included in such a dialogue? How would their participation be justified without suggesting that there is a validation of their violent ways? How could that dialogue be sustained in order to overview implementation of decisions?

3. For the just peace framework to become reality there is a need to engage in a sound dialogue with the political world, where legal norms and resources are ultimately sanctioned. What are potentially effective strategies to engage in such a dialogue? Should there be any conditions? Should the just peace framework become a policy framework as well? Would it be feasible? Why? Or why not?

Notes

1. See Diego Mendez, "Gang Members Burn Bus in El Salvador, Killing 14," *San Diego Union Tribune*, August 31, 2016.

2. Statistics from the United Nations Office for Drugs and Crime (UNODC) available at https://data.unodc.org.

3. According to the International Crisis Group (ICG), there were ninety-three thousand murders between 1993 and 2016, while the civil war's deaths numbered seventy-five thousand. See International Crisis Group, "El Salvador's Politics of Perpetual Violence," *Latin America Report* 64 (2017): 1.

4. For the financial cost of the violence, see Banco Central de Reserva de El Salvador, "Redibacen: Estimación del Costo Económico de la Violencia en El Salvador 2014. Comunicado de Prensa," April 28, 2016, http://www.bcr.gob.sv/esp/index.php?option=com_k2&view=item&id=778:redibacen. The amount of remittances was 17.1 percent according to the World Bank's online statistics. See https://data.worldbank.org/indicator/BX.TRF.PWKR.DT.GD.ZS.

5. Finn-Aage Esbensen and Cheryl L. Maxson, eds., *Youth Gangs in International Perspective: Results from the Eurogang Program of Research* (New York: Springer, 2011), 5.

6. James Diego Vigil, *A Rainbow of Gangs: Street Cultures in the Mega-City* (Austin: University of Texas Press, 2010), 8–12.

7. Vigil, 48.

8. José Miguel Cruz, "Central American Maras: From Youth Street Gangs to Transnational Protection Rackets," *Global Crime* 11 (2010): 379–98, at 382.

9. See Oscar Martínez, Efren Lemus, Carlos Martínez, and Deborah Sontag, "Killers on a Shoestring: Inside the Gangs of El Salvador," *New York Times*, November 20, 2016.

10. Oscar Martínez, "Los Salvadoreños Cruzan Fronteras de Guerra a Diario," *El Faro*, January 4, 2016, https://elfaro.net/es/201601/salanegra/17702.

11. Steven Dudley and Héctor Silva Ávalos, "MS13: Hierarchy vs. Federation," *Insight Crime*, February 14, 2018.

12. For Salvadoran homicide rates, see La Prensa Gráfica, "Los municipios más violentos de 2015," *La Prensa Grafica*, March 28, 2016; for the World Health Organization view of homicide rates, see Joan Serra Hoffman, Lyndee Knox, and Robert Cohen, eds., *Beyond Suppression: Global Perspectives on Youth Violence* (Santa Barbara, CA: Praeger, 2010), 4.

13. Cruz, "Central American Maras."

14. International Crisis Group, "Mafia of the Poor. Gang Violence and Extortion in Central America," *Latin America Report* 62 (2017): 16.

15. Fundación Salvadoreña para el Desarrollo Económica y Social, *Extorsiones a la Micro y Pequeña Empresa de El Salvador* (San Salvador, 2016), 29.

16. International Crisis Group, *Mafia of the Poor*, 17.

17. Those cases were handled by the NGO Cristosal. See Maria Cidón Kiernan, "Un Informe Inédito del Gobierno Rechaza (Otra Vez) el Desplazamiento por Violencia," *Revista Factum*, March 21, 2018.

18. See Mo Hume, "Mano Dura: El Salvador Responds to Gangs," *Development in Practice* 17, no. 6 (2007): 739–51.

19. A. Holland, "Right to Crime? Conservative Party Politics and Mano Dura Policies in El Salvador," *Latin American Research Review* 48, no. 1 (2013): 58.

20. Jeannette Aguilar Villamariona, "Los efectos contraproducentes de los Planes Mano Dura," *Quórum: Revista de Pensamiento Iberoamericano* 16 (2016): 93.

21. Sonja Wolf, *Mano Dura: The Politics of Gang Control in El Salvador* (Austin: University of Texas Press, 2017), 73.

22. Asamblea Legislativa de la República de El Salvador Decreto 108, *Ley Especial Contra Actos de Terrorismo*, 2006.

23. Asamblea Legislativa de la República de El Salvador Decreto 458, *Ley de Proscripción de Maras, Pandillas, Agrupaciones, Asociaciones y Organizaciones de Naturaleza Criminal*, 2010.

24. See José Luis Sanz, "La tregua entre pandillas o el Estado en conflicto con la ley," *El Faro*, March 4, 2013, https://elfaro.net/es/201303/noticias/11225.

25. Asamblea Legislativa de El Salvador, Decreto 321, *Disposiciones especiales, transitorias y extraordinarias en los centros penitenciarios, granjas penitenciarias, centros intermedios y centros temporales de reclusión*, 2016.

26. See interview with Juan-Pedro Schaerer, International Committee of the Red Cross manager for Mexico, Central America, and Cuba: Roberto Valencia, "Prorrogar las Medidas Extraordinarias Tendría un Costo para El Salvador en el Plano Internacional," *El Faro*, March 18, 2018, https://elfaro.net/es/201803/salanegra/21664.

27. Ana Glenda Tager and Isabel Aguilar Umaña, *La Tregua entre Pandillas Salvadoreñas: Hacia un Proceso de Construcción de Paz Social* (Guatemala: Interpeace, 2013), 10.

28. The most extensive reporting on this issue was authored by the digital newspaper *El Faro*: http://www.especiales.elfaro.net/es/todosobrelatregua.

29. See Cruz, "Central American Maras;" and Héctor Silva Ávalos and Bryan Avelar, "Case against El Salvador's MS13 Reveals State Role in Gang's Growth," *Insight Crime*, August 3, 2016.

30. Something that is contested by the government; see Nelson Rauda Zablah, "Descarto y Niego Cualquier Responsabilidad del Estado en Violaciones a Derechos Humanos," *El Faro*, September 6, 2017, https://elfaro.net/es/201709/el_salvador/20848.

31. The denunciations came from the Human Rights Institute of the Central American University (IDHUCA) and the Passionist Social Services. The Inter-American Commission on Human Rights requested the Salvadoran State not to renew the special measures. See press release at http://www.oas.org/en/iachr/media_center/PReleases/2018/063.asp.

32. The "End of Mission Statement," issued by High Commissioner Agnes Calamard, http://www.ohchr.org/en/NewsEvents/Pages/DisplayNews.aspx?NewsID=22634&LangID=E.

33. As reported by journalists from *El Faro*: "La Libertad se Suma a los "Municipios Libres de Violencia," *El Faro*, March 2, 2013, https://elfaro.net/es/201302/noticias/11223.

34. See Consejo Nacional de Seguridad Ciudadana de El Salvador, *Plan El Salvador Seguro. Resumen Ejecutivo* (San Salvador, 2015).

35. Lisa S. Cahill, "Catholic Tradition on Peace, War, and Just Peace," this volume, chap. 2, p. 35.

36. Psalm 85:10.

37. Eli S. McCarthy, "Just Peace Ethic: A Virtue-Based Approach," this volume, chap. 3, p. 57.

38. See María Santacruz Giralt and José Miguel Cruz, "Las Maras en El Salvador," in *Maras y Pandillas en Centroamérica* I, ERIC, IDESO, IDIES e IUDOP (Managua, Nicaragua: UCA Publicaciones, 2001), 15–107.

39. Some studies have established a difference between the terms "pandillas" and "maras," identifying the former with gangs formed before the 1990s; however, here only the term "gang" will be used. See Nelson Portillo, "Estudios sobre pandillas juveniles en El Salvador y Centroamérica: una revisión de su dimensión participativa," *Apuntes de Psicología* 30, nos. 1-3 (2012): 397-407.

40. Regarding institutionalization of gangs, see UNODC, *Crime and Development in Central America: Caught in the Crossfire* (New York: United Nations, 2007), 58. For factors leading to such institutionalization, see John Hagedorn, *A World of Gangs: Armed Young Men and Gangsta Culture* (Minneapolis: University of Minnesota Press, 2008), 11–22; and John P. Sullivan, "Third Generation Street Gangs: Turf, Cartels, and Net Warriors," *Transnational Organized Crime* 3, no. 3 (1997): 95–108.

41. See José Miguel Cruz, "La Construcción Social de la Violencia en El Salvador de la Posguerra," *Estudios Centroamericanos* 58, nos. 661–62 (2003): 1150–71; Elana Zilberg, "Fools Banished from the Kingdom: Remapping Geographies of Gang Violence between the Americas," *American Quarterly* 56, no. 21 (2004): 759–79.

190   *José Henríquez Leiva*

42. See Al Valdez, "The Origins of Southern California Latino Gangs," in *Maras: Gang Violence and Security in Central America*, ed. Thomas Bruneau, Lucía Dammert, and Elizabeth Skinner (Austin: University of Texas Press, 2011), 24–42.

43. Regarding the etymology of MS-13, as noted, "mara" stands for gang and "trucha" (literally "trout") is slang for "shrewd person." See Ana Arana, "How the Street Gangs Took Central America," *Foreign Affairs* 84, no. 3 (2005): 100. For more on the development of MS-13, see T. W. Ward, *Gangsters without Borders: An Ethnography of a Salvadoran Street Gang* (Oxford: Oxford University Press, 2013); and Washington Office on Latin America, *Youth Gangs in Central America* (Washington, DC: WOLA, 2006).

44. See Austin T. Fragomen Jr., "The Illegal Immigration Reform and Immigrant Responsibility Act of 1996: An Overview," *The International Migration Review* 31, no. 2 (1997): 438–60; and Susan Gzesh, "Central Americans and Asylum Policy in the Reagan Era," *Migration Policy*, April 1, 2006, https://www.migrationpolicy.org/article/central-americans-and-asylum-policy-reagan-era.

45. José Luis Rocha, "Street Gangs of Nicaragua," in Bruneau et al., *Maras*, 108.

46. José Miguel Cruz, Jonathan D. Rosen, Luis Enrique Amaya, and Yulia Vorobyeva, *The New Face of Street Gangs: The Gang Phenomenon in El Salvador* (Miami: Florida International University, 2017), 36. The study surveyed 1,196 individuals with a record of gang membership and conducted thirty-two in-depth interviews.

47. El Salvador, Guatemala, Honduras, US, Italy, Spain, and Peru. Research on international connections of MS-13. See different aspects at https://www.insightcrime.org/investigations/the-ms13.

48. Data and analysis on arms in El Salvador can be found in UNODC, *Crime and Development*, 45–68.

49. United Nations Development Program, *Human Development Report 2013. The Rise of the South: Human Progress in a Diverse World*, 2013. See data summaries at http://www.sv.undp.org/content/el_salvador/es/home/countryinfo. The figure of 50 percent of the population un/underemployed is higher according to the president of the Salvadoran Chamber of Commerce and Industry, who considers that only 28 percent of the economy can be considered, including the formal sector. See statements reported at https://www.laprensagrafica.com/economia/Sindicatos-el-GOES-frena-la-formalidad-20170206-0105.html.

50. United Nations Development Program, *Human Development Report 2013*, http://hdr.undp.org/en/2013-report.

51. The newspaper *La Prensa Gráfica* has mapped homicides per municipality, which reveals complex patterns. See https://www.laprensagrafica.com/lpgdatos/Los-municipios-mas-violentos-de-2015-20160328-0029.html.

52. See International Crisis Group, *El Salvador's Politics*, 13–14.

53. Cited by Gerald W. Schlabach, "A 'Manual' for Escaping Our Vicious Cycles: Practical Guidance from the Sermon on the Mount for Just Peacemaking," this volume, chap. 1, p. 19.

54. See Wolf, *Mano Dura*, 185–207.

55. See "YouthBuild" Program on their website: https://www.crs.org/stories/building-up-youth-and-communities-in-el-salvador.

56. Americas Society, *Security in Central America's Northern Triangle: Violence Reduction and the Role of the Private Sector in El Salvador* (New York: Americas Society and Council of the Americas, 2012), 6–7.

57. Americas Society, 9.

58. Americas Society, 8.

59. Cruz et al., *New Face of Street Gangs*, 27.

60. Cf. Héctor Silva Ávalos, *Infiltrados. Crónica de la Corrupción en la PNC (1992–2013)* (San Salvador: UCA Editores, 2014).

61. See PNC statistics available at the Portal de Transparencia del Gobierno de El Salvador (Transparency Portal of the Government of El Salvador), http://www.transparencia.gob.sv/institutions/pnc/documents/estadisticas.

62. Statistics from the online journal *El Faro*: "El Salvador es un Buen Lugar para Matar," http://elfaro.net/es/206005/salanegra/18399.

63. Schlabach, "'Manual' for Escaping Our Vicious Cycles," 19.

64. International Crisis Group, *El Salvador's Politics*, 24.

65. For example, in other countries Cure Violence hires "credible messengers" from the community, often former gang members, to interrupt violence. They have had significant success in reducing shootings from 40 to 70 percent, and even 88 percent in Honduras.

66. Schlabach, "'Manual' for Escaping Our Vicious Cycles," 24.

67. President Donald Trump called the MS-13 "animals [who have] transformed peaceful parks and beautiful quiet neighborhoods into blood-stained killing fields." Melanie Eversley, "Trump Tells Law Enforcement: 'Don't Be Too Nice' with Suspects," *USA Today*, July 28, 2017.

68. See José Miguel Cruz and Gema Santamaría, "Crime and Support for Extralegal Violence in Latin America," paper presented at the American Political Science Association, 110th Annual Meeting, Washington, DC, August 28–31, 2014.

69. See Maria J. Stephan and Leanne Erdberg, *To Defeat Terrorism, Use 'People Power': Nonviolent Citizens' Movements Are the Missing Piece of a Global Strategy against Extremism*, United States Institute of Peace, March 27, 2018.

70. Pope Francis, "Nonviolence: A Style of Politics for Peace," Message of His Holiness Pope Francis for the celebration of the fiftieth World Day of Peace (2017), no. 5.

71. Schlabach, "'Manual' for Escaping Our Vicious Cycles," 18.

72. Schlabach, "'Manual' for Escaping Our Vicious Cycles," 17.

73. McCarthy, "Just Peace Ethic," 69.

11

ISIS AND EZIDIS
Using Just Peace Approaches

PEGGY FAW GISH

Context

A cry for help came to the people and governments around the world from the Ezidi people (also called Yazidi), a religious and ethnic minority, indigenous to northwestern Iraq, whose religion is linked to ancient Mesopotamian religions and combines aspects of Zoroastrianism, Islam, Christianity, and Judaism.[1] Throughout the summer of 2014, Ezidis, Christians, Shi'a Muslims, and other minority religious and ethnic groups experienced massacres, abductions, rapes, destruction of religious and cultural sites, and forced displacement by the "Islamic State," an offshoot of al-Qaeda in Iraq (AQI).[2] Even Sunni Muslims, who would not support the extreme ideology of Islamic State in Iraq and Syria (ISIS), were persecuted.

Earlier in 2014, ISIS had taken over the cities of Fallujah and Ramadi, west of Baghdad. By June they controlled the rest of Anbar Province. Additionally, whenever ISIS defeated the Iraqi army, its fighters seized equipment and weaponry that the national troops abandoned. In these mostly Sunni Muslim areas, the people did not fully agree with ISIS's agenda or mode of operation but were not loyal to the Shi'a-led Iraqi government, which they saw as more oppressive and violent toward them.

As ISIS forces headed northward, they took control of several oil fields, dams, and strategic roads and bridges. On June 10 they captured Mosul, Iraq's second-largest city. By June 29 ISIS declared itself an Islamic "caliphate," with the official name "Islamic State," and called on Muslims worldwide to pledge their allegiance.[3] Hundreds of thousands of Iraqis fled Mosul and nearby villages as ISIS gave an ultimatum to convert, pay hefty fines, leave, or be killed. From there, ISIS fighters spread out to take in surrounding areas in the Nineveh Province and Diyala Province to the east.

By August 1, ISIS reached the Sinjar area (also known as Shingar or Shengal), the Ezidi peoples' ancestral homeland, in Nineveh Province, due west of Mosul and less than 50 km from the Syrian border. After battling ISIS there for two days, seven thousand Kurdish-Iraqi Peshmerga fighters, who promised to protect the Ezidis, retreated in the night, leaving the civilians behind.

Only some Ezidis managed to escape before ISIS forces reached their villages. Villagers tried to defend themselves, but by the morning of August 3, ISIS prevailed. For the next few weeks, Kurdish fighting groups, along with local men, tried to push ISIS out, but the militant forces continued to ravish area villages. When they captured the city of Sinjar, they blew up the Mahawia and Saida Zainab Ezidi temples and the Shi'a Muslim Sayeda Zeinab shrine and demanded the residents convert or be killed.

Our Christian Peacemaker Team (CPT), based in the city of Sulaimani, a five-hour drive to the east, heard the reports of the atrocities committed around Sinjar and spoke by phone with Ezidis who had just survived attacks. ISIS fighters took women and girls hostage, raping them, giving them as wives to ISIS fighters, or selling them into slavery—an estimated seven thousand by the end of the fall. They killed up to five thousand Ezidi men and older boys and sold some older boys as slaves. An estimated two hundred thousand residents fled their homes and villages.

About fifty thousand escaped into the Sinjar mountain range, north of the city, but were soon surrounded by ISIS forces. Because of the lack of food, water, and shelter from the sun, the situation there soon became a humanitarian disaster. On August 5, Iraqi military helicopters dropped some food and water on the mountain, but it was insufficient; between August 4 and 7, hundreds died of dehydration, hunger, or illness.

On August 7, US President Barack Obama authorized targeted airstrikes against ISIS in northern Iraq to prevent genocide of Ezidis and to protect American interests. The latter meant stopping ISIS from advancing toward Erbil, a thirty-minute drive from the ISIS front, where American diplomats, military advisers, and other US citizens were based. At the same time, Obama gave assurances that no troops would be deployed for combat and that he would "not allow the United States to be drawn into fighting another war in Iraq." We, however, heard that US Special Forces were secretly on the ground in Zumar, along with German counterparts, fighting ISIS.[4]

Having worked in Iraq since October 2002, before, during, and after the invasion, our team remembered that during the years of US occupation, the presence and actions of American military forces focused primarily on protecting its own personnel, economic, and military interests rather than providing safety for Iraqis. In 2014, we knew that ExxonMobil and Chevron were among the oil companies operating in Iraqi Kurdistan. We had been visiting villagers whose prime farmland, vineyards, and orchards had been taken and dug up for oil exploration by ExxonMobil through contracts made with the Kurdish government without the landowners' prior consent.

On August 8, US airstrikes began in the Erbil area, 180 km east of Sinjar. A US aircraft made a food and water drop on the Sinjar Mountains. In the following days, British and Australian planes also made airdrops, and the US sent in sixty intelligence, surveillance, and reconnaissance aircraft to support the mission in northern Iraq. France, Britain, and Germany backed US strikes, and militias from Iran and Turkey joined the struggle. Near the mountains, on August 9, US airstrikes hit four ISIS checkpoints and a convoy of armored vehicles.

Between August 9 and 11, Syrian Kurdish forces—YPG (People's Protection Units)—which had been fighting ISIS in Syria for two years, cleared a corridor north of the mountain range and the Fish Khabour border crossing with Syria (also called the Rabia crossing) from ISIS. Over the next several days, the PKK (Kurdistan Workers' Party), YPG, and Peshmerga forces helped approximately thirty-five to forty thousand stranded Ezidis evacuate safely, using trucks and tractors to carry out the sick and elderly.[5] These Ezidis were guided over the Syrian border and north before most of them reentered Iraq at the Peshabur (or Faysh Khabur) border crossing into the Duhok Province in the Kurdish region. This corridor remained open except for two weeks in late October when ISIS temporarily reclaimed it. ISIS still had control of the city of Sinjar, so airdrops by Iraqi helicopters over the next few months helped to sustain the civilians who chose to stay on the mountains.

On August 11, the Arab League accused ISIS of committing "crimes against humanity" toward Ezidis. Two days later, the United Nations (UN) declared the Ezidi crisis a "level-3 emergency" and promised a mobilization of material aid. Seven months later, a UN panel concluded that ISIS "may have committed" genocide against Ezidis.

By mid-September 2014, about 15 percent of the Ezidi population returned to the Sinjar area but found abandoned towns of damaged buildings and the remains of many killed in the massacres. They faced severe physical and economic hardships partly due to political power struggles in the area. Fighters affiliated with the PKK began to oversee government departments and ignored calls from Massoud Barzani, head of the Kurdistan Democratic Party (KDP), to withdraw from the towns. In return, the KDP, which was losing control over the area, put an economic siege on Sinjar. KDP troops prevented aid from humanitarian organizations, rations from Baghdad, and commercial goods from coming over the Syria/Iraqi border crossing, putting their political power above the lives of the Ezidi people.[6]

Overall, no one wanted the Ezidis to endure more atrocities or for ISIS to succeed and spread, so many Iraqis were glad for the intervention. I knew, however, that military intervention would mean even more destruction, deaths, and chaos; continue the cycles of violence; and attract more recruits for ISIS. The invasion and the occupation of Iraq had already caused immense suffering. The US was continuing this failed approach that had produced ISIS.

Reflecting with a Just Peace Ethic

One of the key questions in reflecting with a just peace ethic is this: "What are the *root causes* of the conflict?" It is important to note in this conflict how the pattern of military intervention is one of the key root causes as well as one of the habits or vices at stake. First, military intervention in Iraq has been very costly as far as lives, destruction of property, and waste of money that could have been used for human needs and development. The best estimate of Iraqi deaths since the 2003 invasion is 2.4 million people.[7] A comprehensive estimate of the monetary cost of the Iraq conflict is $3 trillion.[8]

Second, the invasion to "liberate" Iraq did not solve the underlying social and economic problems there. It created more. The destruction of infrastructure resulted in a humanitarian crisis. The war tore apart families, their economic lives, and the underpinnings of society. Months after the invasion, many Iraqis told us, "As bad as life was under Saddam Hussein, it's now worse." Then, years later, the fighting against ISIS and "liberating" the cities from the militant group again left horrible destruction, thousands killed, and hundreds of thousands homeless and displaced. The nine-month battle (2016–2017) to free Mosul from ISIS resulted in the deaths of 9,000–11,000, of which 3,200 civilian deaths were from Iraqi or US coalition strikes.[9] Those returning home came back to rubble and chaos. In turn, the just peace norms of relationality, economic justice, human dignity, and reflexivity illuminate some of the issues with such actions.

Third, before the March 2003 US invasion, there was no al-Qaeda or ISIS in Iraq. It was a by-product of the US-led invasion. The war and the oppressive and disastrous policies of the occupation produced the chaotic situation and leadership vacuum that allowed ISIS to rise to power. Under Saddam Hussein there was governmental repression, but there was minimal violence across religious and ethnic lines. He held a tight control over security so there was little street crime. Women were safe to walk the streets of Baghdad at night.

After the invasion, young people felt as though they had no future. Frustration was compounded when basic electrical, water, and sanitation services were not repaired, while the Coalition Provisional Authority (CPA), the US occupying administration, devised a long process of giving the contracts and financial gains from the repair work to foreign companies. Anger was channeled into lawlessness. All religious groups were affected when the violence of criminal gangs, assaults on women, looting, robbing, or extorting kidnapped victims increased.

The US military presence became more harsh and abusive. There were increased incidents of soldiers shooting people driving too close to their convoys or not stopping quickly enough at checkpoints. In May 2003, US soldiers shot into a crowd of peacefully protesting teachers in the city of Fallujah, killing and wounding dozens. That same month, the CPA disbanded the Iraqi army and police force. That resulted in more than half a million well-armed and trained Iraqi troops being unemployed overnight. Many of the unemployed joined local resistance movements and became radicalized. Some of Saddam's former senior military officers later became top ISIS commanders. Violence increased against US personnel.

US forces responded to attacks with large sweeps, rounding up and putting all the men in the area into US-run prisons, where they suffered horrific living conditions, torture, and abuse. Our team heard countless stories of families experiencing house raids in the middle of the night, in which men, who most often were not involved in violent acts, were brutally arrested, interrogated, and imprisoned. By December 2003, we wrote a report on seventy-two prisoners who had been in the prison system, and we called on US civilian and military leaders to drastically change these practices.

CPA leaders did little to foster democracy or encourage real dialogue among divergent Iraqi factions, which violates the just peace norm of participatory processes. In July 2003, they handpicked the members of the new Iraqi Governing Council, choosing mostly rich Iraqis who supported US presence and who did not represent the common people. In 2005, US Special Forces helped the new Ministry of Interior develop and resource new Iraqi Special Operation Teams, which were mostly Shi'a Muslim militias that acted as death squads, killing and imprisoning mostly Sunni Muslims or professionals who opposed the occupation. All this fueled past animosity between Sunni and Shi'a and precipitated "civil war" and ethnic cleansing in neighborhoods of Baghdad and other cities.

For the first year and a half after the 2003 invasion, the CPA did not close or regulate the Iraqi borders, making it easier for foreign al-Qaeda fighters to come into the country.[10] Jordanian-born Musab al-Zarqawi and others who fought alongside al-Qaeda in Afghanistan in late 2001 entered Iraq during or just after the 2003 invasion. Al-Zarqawi formed AQI in October 2004. The group funneled foreign fighters into the country through Syria, but it also attracted men from the Iraqi insurgency and disaffected Sunni tribes in Iraq who felt oppressed or marginalized by the Shi'a-led Iraqi government. With the general violence and chaos and the harsh treatment of Iraqi prisoners, AQI spread.

In January 2006, AQI joined several smaller Sunni insurgent groups to form the Mujahideen Shura Council (MSC). In October, four months after al-Zarqawi's death, the MSC joined six Sunni tribes and several other insurgency groups and formed the Islamic State of Iraq (ISI) but still aligned with AQI. Its first emir was Abu Omar al-Baghdadi. After his death in April 2010, he was succeeded by Abu Bakr al-Baghdadi, who had been radicalized while detained in US-run "Camp Bucca" in 2004. He increased the savagery of the attacks and the destruction of religious and cultural heritage sites. ISI gained much of its power in its ability to generate horrific fear. Their beheadings seemed to be staged to cause populations and opposing armies to give up easily.

With financial support from private citizens of Saudi Arabia and Qatar, ISI expanded into Syria in 2013. On April 8, 2013, Abu Bakr al-Baghdadi announced the formation of the "Islamic State of Iraq and the Levant" (ISIL), also called "the Islamic State of Iraq and Sham/Syria" (ISIS). After internal disputes with al-Qaeda's leadership and its unit fighting in Syria (the Al-Nusra Front), al-Qaeda disavowed relations with ISIS in February 2014.

Fourth, military action at times appears to solve the immediate crisis and be successful in the short run, but unlike nonviolent approaches, violence causes greater and ongoing harm and destruction and creates conditions that perpetuate ongoing violence. This illustrates the significance of the just peace norm of reflexivity. In the case with ISIS in northern Iraq, US-led military action boosted the morale of the Kurdish and Iraqi fighters and slowed down ISIS forces so that they did not enter the Kurdish region, but it did not have the immediate success of ridding the region of ISIS that many had hoped for. It was still a long, bloody process. Three years later, in July 2017, ISIS was finally pushed out of Mosul, and in December 2017, Iraqi Prime Minister Haider al-Abadi declared victory over ISIS in Iraq. Yet, even today, ISIS fighters stage small attacks in the region.[11]

The crisis for the Ezidis and other populations in Iraq, all the deaths and destruction through these years in Iraq, and its continual destabilized condition could have been prevented if a military approach had not been used to deal with Saddam Hussein and support Western nations' desire for wealth from Iraq's resources. It is one more example of military intervention having long-term destructive results and making a bad situation worse. It spawned cycles of violence and revenge and left people feeling the need to try and fix militarily the consequences of the previous military actions.

Instead of ridding our world of terrorism, violent intervention in Iraq, as well as the long history of US deception and covert military actions throughout the world to topple and destabilize governments for US economic and military purposes, has only strengthened and expanded it.[12] US military intervention has fed into the propaganda that militant groups spread about Western nations—that the US is "bent on global domination" and is "exploiting and oppressing Muslims."

Engaging the Conflict with Just Peace Norms

After looking at the root causes and underlying habits, some specific norms of a just peace ethic can help us understand how to better engage this conflict. The US government and international community might have prevented the rise of ISIS, or weakened it when it came to power, by supporting the nonviolent civil society groups and actions in Iraq and Syria, working with neighboring countries to use economic and political resistance such as stemming the flow of fighters and arms into the areas of conflict, and cutting off ISIS's financial sources. The US could have acknowledged responsibility for harm to the Iraqis. Also, it could have supported the role of participatory negotiations and diplomacy by strengthening the UN's power to persist in restarting negotiations for political solutions, bringing major parties to the table, including rebel groups, and provided a more robust humanitarian aid to meet the basic human needs of the masses of individuals displaced by military intervention.

What happened in Iraq affirms that, in general, people respond very differently if they are treated with respect and dignity versus if they are labeled enemies or terrorists and treated unfairly and harshly. Our team experienced this as we were able to safely go and be welcomed into many places in central Iraq (where US soldiers told us the people were "terrorists") because we went unarmed, seeking to be of help and treating the people with respect.

Post-invasion society in Iraq could have become more peaceful and stable had the US based its actions and policies on seeking justice and the common good—that is, the norm of just governance—instead of suppressing people in order to maintain power or financial gains. Had the US chosen the option of turning over the post-invasion governing and rebuilding to the UN, international overseers might have been able to model new institutional and policy patterns, assist the new Iraqi government to break from corruption and power of the rich, and bring leaders of mixed ethnic groups and major opposition groups to the table to form a unity government. It could have established security systems based in justice, respect, and the rule of law, without torture, and provided more room for dissent and social change through nonviolent protest or resistance.

Other just peace norms this case highlights are economic justice and reflexivity. For example, this case demonstrates how establishing and supporting corrupt institutions, unjust societal practices, and mistreatment of minority groups foster the rise of violent insurgency and militias. Much of the violence might have been prevented had the CPA financed and quickly restored public infrastructure and services, met basic physical needs, and given rebuilding jobs to well-qualified Iraqi workers.

Also important are the just peace norms of nonviolent education and skill sets as well as cultivating peacemaking communities and cultures. For example, just as violent warfare takes prior training of soldiers and building up of the infrastructure of warfare, a more stable, peaceful society and just peace skills also require prior training and practice. Those trained only or primarily in violence and not exposed to nonviolent alternatives are more likely to see only violent possibilities.

The CPA could have provided aid to cover postrecovery programs in schools and community centers for reconciliation, trauma healing, and nonviolent options for dealing with conflicts, which would have helped restore societal foundations of trust, fairness, cooperation, and respect. These programs could have included learning about the dynamics of oppression and privilege and methods for changing situations of injustice. This might have led communities to form economic cooperatives and care for the weaker and more vulnerable among them. Local security officers might have learned to deal with crime using restorative justice methods.

Such programs could have encouraged local religious and ethnic groups to go to the roots of their faith for the virtues of mercy, compassion, empathy, human dignity, and solidarity and for spiritual practices such as prayer, reconciliation through forgiveness, and welcoming the stranger. These virtues would help delegitimize the use of violence and build discipline, courage, and other skills for dealing with the fear and dangers involved in nonviolent action. Local groups could then be empowered to reach out to other ethnic and religious circles to build coalitions of trust and support. This might have fostered human dignity by diminishing prejudices and discrimination against the Ezidis, so when under threat, they would have felt more confidence to ask other Iraqis for help. Where local or regional cultures take on these practices, terrorist groups cannot infiltrate or gain support. Armed ISIS actors might have been led to desert or their relatives might have encouraged fighters to defect.

Just Peace Responses to ISIS during the Ezidi Crisis

It is harder to imagine nonviolence as a response to so ruthless a group as ISIS, especially once attacks have started. It is easier to imagine nonviolent responses the US and other countries could have taken before and as ISIS was gaining power. However, there were a number of just peace transforming initiatives enacted during the attacks and perhaps other measures that could have been tried if a just peace ethic was orienting the overall response.

Those who have studied and carried out nonviolent campaigns know that there are always weaknesses even in the most brutal governments and forces. Stephan and Chenoweth's research demonstrates that such campaigns have been successful against the most ruthless armed forces.[13] The key determining factor is more about wise strategy than about the level of brutality in the adversary. These armed groups depend on various sources of power or pillars of support to maintain their injustice. There are fighters among these forces who respond humanely or out of fear. They all have needs, and there are those who *defect* when they become appalled or disillusioned by the group's actions or if the incentives for joining are not met.[14]

There have been times when ISIS leaders and fighters did negotiate and bend to nonviolent pressure, such as happened in Mosul in 2014. After a prominent imam and thirty-three others in Mosul refused to pledge their allegiance to the ISIS leader, and a large number of Iraqis flocked to mosques to show support of this defiance. ISIS detained some of the leaders but did not kill them.[15] And when members of an ISIS battalion, tasked with destroying mosques in Mosul, threatened to destroy the Jirjis Mosque, people living nearby occupied it. Fighters came back but did not destroy it.[16] Other examples include a Muslim woman marching to ISIS headquarters in Raqqa for thirty days with guns at times pointed at her head but still demanding release of political prisoners (which ISIS finally did) and local businesses going on strike in Aleppo, which slowed down the operations of ISIS and got electricity restored.[17] In Mosul, research has indicated that 83 percent (of the 1200 Iraqis surveyed) engaged in some form of nonviolent resistance; 62 percent in noncooperation such as refusing to pay taxes, refusing to cooperate with courts, or withdrawing from schools; and 83 percent in resistance through everyday actions like dragging their feet at work, playing music, skipping mandatory prayers, men shaving beards, or women not fully covering their face in public, and so forth.[18] Nonviolent responses entail being willing to look for those opportunities or points of weakness, thinking creatively or "out of the box," and acting boldly, taking risks like soldiers do, but nonviolently.

In addition, there were some just peace norms actualized during the Ezidi crisis. When ISIS fighters advanced on the Sinjar area and the Peshmerga forces abandoned them, some Ezidis resisted violently. However, other Ezidis also used several just peace responses to resist ISIS's attempt to crush them and their culture and to maintain their humanity and dignity.

Many Ezidis alerted others outside their area, by phone, about their dire circumstances. Ezidi leaders publicly appealed for humanitarian aid to meet their basic needs (shelter, food, and supplies). Families and neighbors used rescue and evacuation as they helped each other, literally carrying the weaker ones to safer areas. While visiting a huge tent camp in the Kurdish region, we met a ten-year-old Ezidi boy whose parents had been killed. Neighbors took this boy along with them when they fled and cared for him as part of their family. Another act of resistance took place as many returned home to rebuild and reclaim their land and identity as Ezidis. They refused to let ISIS eradicate their community.

In addition to this, other organizations actualized just peace norms. When our CPT Iraqi-Kurdistan team, which was working in areas of the Kurdish region, heard about the attacks in the Sinjar area, we debated what we could do nonviolently to prevent more violence or to accompany people out of the conflict areas. Our Kurdish partners were adamant that since the attacks and evacuation had already occurred, we should not try to go into the conflict areas, telling us there was no way we would be allowed to pass through two military front lines between ISIS-held areas and the Kurdish region to reach survivors.

We and other organizations did not directly prevent or resist the onslaught nonviolently but found ways of responding that we considered resistance to ISIS's attempt to decimate the Ezidi people and spread hate and fear among different ethnic and religious groups in the region.

Meeting Human Needs

Meeting basic needs through humanitarian assistance fits with the just peace norms of conflict transformation, human rights and economic justice. For example, a few days after Ezidis were trapped on the Sinjar Mountains, various governments began dropping food and supplies by aircraft. Then, as displaced Ezidis flooded into areas of the Kurdish region, local residents and authorities provided what food and water they could until Iraqi and international aid groups, overwhelmed by the enormity of sudden arrivals, were able to get organized. An estimated 850,000 displaced people were in the Kurdish region, and temperatures up to 120 degrees Fahrenheit made the situation more difficult. The Iraqi government sent some aid, and Turkish Disaster Relief cared for those who traveled to a refugee camp in Turkey. Smaller international and local NGOs provided food and supplies to those located around the cities.

Local people in Sulaimani brought donations to drop-off centers to be given to displaced people, regardless of their religion or ethnicity. We assisted local NGOs in putting out an urgent call for international donations. Even poor residents in the area responded. Some Syrian refugees in the Basirma Camp near Erbil skimped on their own food intake for a time so they could donate from their own rations to the newly displaced people. Those who had part-time jobs paid from their wages to transport the food to people camping in parks and churches.

Nonviolent Direct Action

Another just peace norm is nonviolent direct action, which includes the practice of unarmed civilian protection or accompaniment. For example, our team was able to travel with and support Kurdish human rights workers as they assisted families. We found that our presence with them as internationals made it possible for all of us to get through the checkpoints to go into more restricted areas and enter the tent camps and officials' offices to get information. We were able to meet displaced persons who had just arrived and listen to their stories.

With Kurdish human rights organizations Wadi and Alind, we visited the Peshabur (or Faysh Khabur) Iraqi–Syria border crossing, where a border official estimated that in the previous ten days more than one hundred thousand Ezidis had crossed the border. We witnessed families on foot or in trucks, some walking herds of sheep, making the border crossing after traveling from Sinjar through Syria. Away from the border, many Ezidi families were sleeping under highway overpass bridges and in open-sided concrete buildings under construction. We also made several visits to tent displacement camps near Khanke and Semel and the Bajet Kandala Refugee Camp, with at least twenty thousand residents.

Many Ezidis were eager to tell their stories. We felt their deep pain as they shared about men in their family being killed and women raped or kidnapped by ISIS forces, escaping to the mountains, or watching relatives die for lack of food and water. Many appeared traumatized and spoke of shame and despair about their future. Although there was little we could do to change their physical situation, they expressed gratitude that we simply cared about them to come and listen and then share their stories—that they were not completely forgotten and that their lives mattered. These initiatives expressed the just peace virtues of solidarity, mercy, and empathy.

Members of our team made several trips with the Zhyian Group, a Kurdish women's organization, to visit tent camps, reaching out to Ezidi women who had been abused and to families who had women still in captivity. Zhyian members collected information about Ezidi women who had been captured by ISIS and shared it with other agencies that tried to find and release the women. They also worked with other organizations to provide healing opportunities for those released and to help prepare a way for them to return to their communities.

We saw accompaniment as a form of resistance to ISIS because it affirmed the humanity, worth, and dignity of the Ezidi people, whom ISIS attempted to dehumanize. It involved listening, sharing the fear and suffering of those who were the victims of violence, and in some cases offering material, social, and psychological help. The just peace norm of conflict transformation, which includes the particular practice of trauma healing, strengthens the commitment to such assistance.

Using the nonviolent practice of advocacy, our team sent out requests to governments and leaders to negotiate with forces involved in the battles, cease attacks on civilians, and take other nonmilitary actions. We asked people around the world to hold public events or vigils to show support for the

Ezidis and other Iraqis suffering from the violence and deprivation. We urged international governments to increase donations to humanitarian aid agencies as well as to open their borders to refugees. Advocacy does not always make dramatic changes, or directly succeed, but it can shift consciousness and lay the groundwork for future change in procedures and policies.

Part of shifting consciousness is cultural transformation. Because it was a custom among Ezidis and other ethnic groups in that region to see the victim of sexual assault as the one shaming and dishonoring her family, male members of the family often thought it their duty to kill the woman to remove the shame (called "honor killing"). We were heartened by the actions of several Kurdish human rights workers who met with Ezidi leaders and urged them to provide support systems for the women and girls who escaped and to ask their people to welcome them back into their communities. A few weeks later, top Ezidi leaders stated publicly that the women and girls did not choose to be sexually assaulted, and so they should not be killed but be cared for when they returned home. These initiatives actualize the just peace norm of cultivating peacemaking communities and cultures as well as advocacy.

Another way many Iraqis resisted the spread of ISIS and its ideology that summer was through public protest, another form of nonviolent direct action. When Christians had fled Mosul and nearby towns in July, Muslims and Christians in the Kurdish region protested out on the streets and called for compassion and aid for them. Then, when Ezidis were in crisis, Muslims and Christians spoke out publicly again.

On August 24, we marched to the UN Consulate in Erbil with about seventy women and men from Kurdish civil society organizations. Several spoke, denouncing ISIS's violence toward Ezidi women and girls and met with UN officials, requesting that they take more urgent measures to help those who had been kidnapped. The group carried banners reading "UN, Take Action, Our Women and Girls Are Enslaved" and "Committing Genocide against Minorities Is a Stark Violation of International Humanitarian Law." One teenaged Kurdish protester told us, "It's my duty to come out here to support Ezidi girls and their human rights."

Truth-telling is another form of nonviolent resistance to violence and injustice as well as cultivation of peacemaking cultures. It involves people being "on the ground" as eyewitnesses and giving firsthand reports of what is happening. In conflict or war situations, truth really is one of the first casualties. There is much information that does not reach people around the world, and too frequently the news that is released is slanted or distorted to be deceptive and to cover up failures and human rights violations of governing or warring parties.

For us, it meant recording and sharing the stories of the survivors of the massacres through various media, putting human faces to the suffering and illustrating what was happening. We also wrote a report to alert governments and agencies of the urgent needs of the people. We hoped truth-telling would also be a catalyst for changing the consciousness about the destructiveness of violence and the possibilities of nonviolence, and lead to changes concerning future intervention.

Building a Robust Civil Society

In order to help the Ezidis and other survivors of ISIS, local NGOs and civil society groups formed coalitions, contributing to the just peace norm of a more robust civil society. Such coordinated efforts meant sharing of resources and skills and giving strength to nonviolent responses, making it harder for any terrorist group to infiltrate and gain support in that region.

Related to building up civil society as well as the just peace norms of peacemaking cultures and relationality, we participated in cultural events to bridge ethnic and religious differences. On September 21, about a hundred people of diverse ethnic and religious backgrounds converged at the Cultural Café in Sulaimani to celebrate the "International Day of Peace," focusing on building peace and harmony among religious groups—hosted by a Kurdish women's organization, "the Ashti Group." At our table were Muslims, displaced Ezidis, and Christians. A Muslim teacher at the Arbat displacement-camp school had made a special trip to the camp to pick up our Ezidi friends and bring them to Sulaimani. We remembered sitting with them at the camp in August while they shared about family members taken by ISIS fighters as they escaped Sinjar. Speakers denounced religious groups fighting wars in the name of their god. This event was another example of resistance and coalition building.

Another way of strengthening capacity for engaging conflict constructively, and as part of the just peace norm of nonviolent education and skill sets, was the nonviolence training that our team facilitated. We had led nonviolence workshops in central and southern Iraq, and again when our team started working in the Kurdish region. Then, months after the ISIS attacks on the Ezidis, team members, along with members of other organizations, provided "Alternatives to Violence" workshops with interethnic youth in the Ezidi displacement camp and the adjoining Syrian refugee camp as well as to high school and university students in the area. These workshops continue today and are a step in building a culture of peace, and they set the stage for choosing nonviolent alternatives to the threat of terrorist militias.

Before exploring what other just peace actions could have been done during the Ezidi crisis, it must be noted that amazing courage was shown by many Ezidis and other local people in this crisis. Yet it might have been possible for Ezidis—who knew their situation better than anyone else—along with other groups trained and experienced in nonviolence to assess the situation ahead of the attacks and do creative imagining and planning for possible coordinated action.[19] This may have provided a larger contingent to use nonviolent ways to resist or obstruct ISIS fighters when they came or to cause them to bypass their region.

When ISIS did arrive and Ezidis escaped to the mountains, what if nonviolent resistance trainers were airdropped onto the Sinjar mountain range to help train the locals in possible noncooperation tactics to prevent or mitigate the violence? Or perhaps helicopters dropped trained unarmed civilian protection units on the mountain to assist and offer some buffer (i.e., the virtue of solidarity) for displaced persons to remain or escape the mountain without harm. Such teams might have been made up of people with some level of credibility with ISIS fighters, such as regional high-level Muslim leaders, and could have engaged in direct lines of communication and negotiations with ISIS. Negotiations would be a way of affirming the humanity and dignity of the ISIS fighters without excusing their injustice and could have involved finding out what their needs (e.g., jobs, respect for Islam) and grievances were. Such actions are more likely to prevent or minimize the violence, to build basic trust and thus make negotiations successful and sustainable, and to develop processes to hold the actors accountable.

What if the Ezidis were informed about the availability of hundreds or thousands of internationals and Iraqis from other areas to come and help carry out massive nonviolent actions? Maybe they would have let ISIS know that there would be a "wall" around them or that they would block key routes to a vulnerable area before ISIS fighters arrived, which may have caused ISIS to rethink going there, as was done in Mosul.

Maybe the Ezidis did not find a way to prevent ISIS from coming, but they found ways to create physical barriers in the roads and paths into the villages and city, digging deep ditches, leaving piles of rubble, broken vehicles, and so forth, so ISIS vehicles could not drive in. Or a unit of nonviolent resisters found a way to divert ISIS fighters to an area away from the main population so others could flee. Perhaps the people would move from one village to another, avoiding the fighters as they came, while moving the women, children, and other vulnerable people out of the area ahead of the attacks.

Government vehicles, technology, and financial resources could also have helped with such tactics. In addition, governments could have used their capacities to share intelligence with these civil society leaders as well as to send a strong signal to ISIS about interrupting the flow of their money, arms, and communication technology. They also could have saved lives by significantly increasing the airdrops of basic supplies, food, and water to the Ezidis.

We cannot be certain of the outcomes of such creative nonviolent actions, particularly in the short term, but research has shown their increasing effectiveness and their necessity for sustainable outcomes. We also know they would create new conditions that, although previously unimaginable, would become surprisingly plausible.

Conclusion

Reflecting on this case, I recommend that the Catholic Church support the kinds of policy actions suggested here as well as put more effort and resources into just peace education, training, and creative imagining. This would mean making just peace a greater part of the education offered in parishes and parochial schools and an essential part of global mission programs. It could also mean globally developing teams that could respond to and assist people under threat and, where possible, to help plan and carry out nonviolent resistance and accompaniment. They could consult and collaborate with existing organizations such as the Christian Peacemaker Teams and Nonviolent Peaceforce.

There are no simple quick-fix solutions, but we will not reduce the suffering from war and build peaceful and stable societies if we keep repeating the strategies that have only fueled strife. For the US and other countries, this means finding the will to make major changes in how it relates globally—abandoning old policies of seeking dominance for its own gain. For religious and community institutions, it means acknowledging the importance of teaching just peace ethics and training populations to take nonviolent action to transform violent conflict. There is not a better time to start than now. A key problem is that just peace methods are not tried enough. The challenge is in modeling and persuading governments and societies to learn and incorporate these approaches and methods in a comprehensive way.

Discussion Questions

1. To what extent must just peace responses in such a crisis originate with the local people, and what is the legitimate role of trained peace workers coming in from the outside to accompany the people in crisis? Should the local people be the leaders in decision-making or primarily advisers? Should external peace workers hire local people? What is the value of partisanship or nonpartisanship in this kind of situation?
2. What kind of responsibility do citizens of Western countries that caused the rupture of Iraqi society currently have for assisting the people suffering from the resulting crises?
3. What other creative just peace responses might have been used in this crisis?
4. Considering the staging of ruthless acts of violence in order to create fear and compliance in those that might counter ISIS, how do you evaluate attempts to humanize and affirm the dignity of ISIS fighters? In what other ways could this be done?

208 *Peggy Faw Gish*

Notes

1. Several Ezidi leaders told us they call themselves "Ezidi," which implies that they believe in God, rather than the name "Yazidi," which is a derogatory name unfairly given to them that implies that they are nonbelievers or that they worship the devil.

2. Also known by that time as the Islamic State of Iraq and the Levant (ISIL), the Islamic State of Iraq and Sham/Syria (ISIS), or the Arabic acronym "Da'ash" or "Daesh." For simplicity it will generally be referred to as "ISIS" in this chapter.

3. A medieval form of Islamic government that existed before the rise of nation-states.

4. Youssef Boudlal, "Are American Forces Already Fighting on the Front Lines in Iraq?," *War News Updates*, September 2, 2014.

5. Kurdistan Workers' Party is categorized as a terrorist organization by some Western nations.

6. "Signs of Violence to Come: Iraq's Yazidis Return Home to Face Cruel Economic Blockade," *Niqash*, June 23, 2016, www.niqash.org/en/articles/security/5296.

7. Benjamin Medea and Nicolas J. S. Davies, "The Iraq Death Toll 15 Years after the U.S. Invasion," *Counterpunch*, March 16, 2018.

8. Joseph E. Stiglitz and Linda J. Bilmes, *The Three Trillion Dollar War: The True Cost of the Iraq Conflict* (New York: W. W. Norton, 2008).

9. Associated Press, "Battle against ISIS in Mosul Left over 9,000 Dead," *New York Post*, December 20, 2017.

10. A network of multinational extremist Islamic Salafist jihadists founded in 1988 by Osama bin Laden and other Arab volunteers who fought against the Soviet invasion of Afghanistan in the 1980s.

11. Qassim Abdul-zahra and Susannah George, "Islamic State Haunts Northern Iraq Months after Defeat," *Washington Post*, March 28, 2018.

12. For an overview of the dangers of US imperialistic overreach, see Chalmers Johnson, *Blowback: The Costs and Consequences of American Empire*, 2nd ed. (New York: Owl Books, 2004).

13. Maria J. Stephan and Erica Chenoweth, *Why Civilian Resistance Works: The Strategic Logic of Nonviolent Conflict* (New York: Columbia University Press, 2011).

14. Kimiko De Freytas-Tamura, "ISIS Defectors Reveal Disillusionment," *New York Times*, September 21, 2015.

15. Mohammad Moslawi, Fazel Hawramy, and Luke Harding, "Citizens of Mosul Endure Economic Collapse and Repression under Isis Rule," *Guardian*, October 27, 2014.

16. Fazel Hawramy and Mohammad Moslawi, "Iraqis Living under ISIS Rule in Mosul Begin to Show Resistance," *Guardian*, August 7, 2014.

17. Maria J. Stephan, "Resisting ISIS," *Sojourners*, April 2015; and Alia Braley, "This Talk Is Not about ISIS," TEDxTV, April 12, 2017, https://tedxtv.blogspot.com/2017/04/this-talk-is-not-about-isis-alia-braley.html.

18. Isak Svensson, Jonathan Hall, Dino Krause, and Eric Skoog, "How Ordinary Iraqis Resisted the Islamic State," *Washington Post*, March 22, 2019.

19. Such as the Muslim Peacemaker Team in southern Iraq, which assisted marginalized ethnic groups under threat, or Kurdish human rights workers trained in nonviolent action.

12

MAKING JUST PEACE A REALITY IN KENYA

A New "Flavor" to Peacebuilding

TERESIA WAMŨYŨ WACHIRA

This chapter aims to find the nexus between just peace approaches and African indigenous approaches to violent conflicts, especially in the selected cases in the Kenya North Rift region (Baringo, Elgeyo-Marakwet, and West Pokot). First, I contextualize the North Rift region conflicts in the counties indicated. Second, I highlight the role that the current African indigenous approaches are playing in promoting a just and peaceful society. Third, I discuss the issue of how the conflicts in the North Rift region (Baringo, Elgeyo-Marakwet, and West Pokot) can be transformed through incorporating the positive aspects of the African indigenous approaches and a just peace approach.

Contextualizing Violent Conflicts in the North Rift Region of Kenya

Africa is the continent most affected by armed conflict.[1] Availability of modern weapons and also widespread trade with small arms and light weapons (SALWs) have been on the rise. For instance, in a survey carried out in 2012, it was noted that thirty million illegal small arms were in circulation in sub-Saharan Africa, and some of these are in the hands of civilians.[2] Kenya, conversely, has experienced episodes of armed conflicts mainly in the North Rift region that cradles the pastoralist nomadic communities. The North Rift region is key to this chapter as we focus on the perennial and multifaceted conflicts in three of its counties—Baringo, Elgeyo-Marakwet, and West Pokot.[3] As shown in the map in figure 12.1, there is a high level of volatility regarding small arms in these three counties in Kenya.

The violent conflicts in the identified counties are associated with access and control of resources and political power.[4] Those in control of political/state power have the authority to make decisions about the control of resources—especially land; hence the resource–power nexus. Proliferation of SALWs due to porous borders with countries in armed conflict escalates

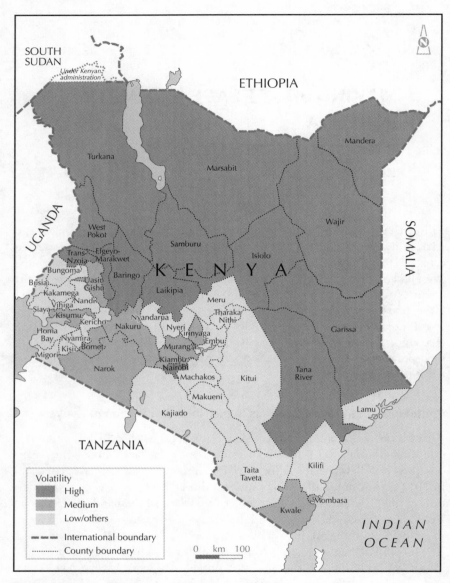

Figure 12.1   Kenya—Counties by Level of Volatility, 2011
Source: Manasseh Wepundi, Eliud Nthiga, Eliud Kabuu, Ryan Murray, and Anna Alvazzi del Frate, "Availability of Small Arms and Perceptions of Security in Kenya: An Assessment." © Small Arms Survey, Graduate Institute of International and Development Studies, Geneva, 2012, p. 39. Available at http://www.smallarmssurvey.org/fileadmin/docs/C-Special-reports/SAS-SR16-Kenya.pdf. Used with permission.

the violence. Escalation is also seen with the incitement, especially of the youth, by political leaders to engage in violence; lack of protection of borders; and the practices especially surrounding cattle rustling, which is embedded in the culture.[5] For instance, one of the youth respondents confirms the importance of cattle raids in his community when he states that if youth do not engage in cattle rustling, they will experience exclusion and lack of respect. The following narrative is not uncommon among the youth in these three counties because cattle raids contribute to their social acceptance and personal prestige.

> If we young people do not go for cattle raids, they will call us cowards, and we will not be able to get a girl to marry and when people in the community see us they will laugh and "throw words" at us. No one will give us respect and we will be excluded from many activities where men are. Like me here, I and my friends went to the elders to bless us as is our custom before we went out to steal the cattle from the Pokot people. This was because we wanted to marry and earn respect from our communities.[6]

The autochthonous discourses of belonging and exclusion tend to deepen these complex and multifaceted conflicts.[7] The militaristic approach of the state in dealing with these conflicts has contributed to the protraction of conflicts in the region and has complicated an already volatile situation. Unfortunately, such conflicts have led to deaths of people and livestock, destruction of essential infrastructure, and loss of livelihoods due to fear, especially among women going to fetch water and collect firewood. In addition, such conflicts tend to leave behind a displaced, traumatized, and disillusioned population, especially the youth, who form over 65 percent of the total Kenyan population. This is evident in the narrative of one of the youth engaging in cattle rustling:

> You know it is not easy to go for cattle raids but what do you do. You have to go and if you are killed that is ok and if you kill that is ok. It is our culture and since the elders bless us we are fine. Every young man goes through it though it is tough. Some young men are really afraid but they have to do it. The girls wait and see who is brave because they all want to marry a brave man who can protect her and take care of the family.[8]

However, despite the various peace interventions, whether from the top leadership or at the grassroots level, the violent conflicts continue unabated and seem to create cycles of violence. Could this be because often the responses are militaristic or generic (one-size-fits-all approach) and top–down?

The next section is an attempt to respond to this question by examining some of the peacebuilding approaches in place to deal with the violence in these counties.

Reflecting with a Just Peace Ethic: Responses to Violent Conflicts in the North Rift Region

As noted at the start of the chapter, Kenya has experienced different forms of violence across the country but to a greater degree in the arid and semi-arid North Rift region, which forms the basis of this work. The responses to violence have been both bottom-up and top-down. The top-down approaches have been mainly applied by the top leadership in the country—for instance, the security forces spanning across all ranks. The bottom-up approaches are mainly at the grassroots level among women, youth, and to some extent the faith-based organizations and community-based organizations at both the local and international levels. There is no shortage of examples where the peacebuilding approaches have been successful or have failed, but in this chapter the focus is on three counties in the North Rift region—Baringo, Elgeyo-Marakwet, and West Pokot.

Religious leaders have been at the core of peacebuilding for decades. The following story illustrates a nonviolent response to violent conflicts in the North Rift region. In 1997 during the second multiparty elections after years of dictatorial rule, Kenya experienced violent conflicts dubbed the "tribal clashes."[9] The late Bishop Cornelius Korir was the bishop of Eldoret then, and he played a major role in providing shelter to displaced persons. Today he is fondly remembered as the "goodwill ambassador for peace."[10]

In one of the violent incidents in 1992, Bishop Korir, following in Jesus's way of active nonviolence, decided to go and check on the safety of the religious sisters who lived and worked in one of the violence-prone areas in his diocese. As he drove, every vehicle he passed along the way flashed lights as a warning not to proceed with the journey because of the magnitude of the violence. Fearing for the safety of the religious sisters, Bishop Korir ignored the warning and drove right into a riotous group of armed youth (from the Kalenjin ethnic community) who were forcibly evicting people and threatening to burn down the town. He stood between the hundreds of youth who were armed with bows and arrows against about ten overwhelmed police officers who had now sought his assistance.[11] As the youth surged forward, the police started shooting, which forced the bishop to raise his hands over his head and shout "Don't shoot! Don't shoot!"[12] After a tense standoff between the youth and the police, the youth retreated. However, they requested that Bishop Korir escort them away from the police for fear the police would shoot them in the back as they left. He obliged, and when the youth were leaving he overheard them express their regret that they had not attacked their "enemies" before his arrival. Like Jesus, he was at the forefront "protecting and leading his flock" while risking his own life. He lived and practiced the gospel of nonviolence—love of the enemies. In this incident, he modeled the just peace practice of unarmed civilian protection.

In a similar violent incident in 1997, while violence was at its peak, Pokot warriors shot at the car of one of the government officers—the district commissioner—but decided not to shoot at Bishop Korir's car because he was a bishop and his diocese had provided their villages with food when they experienced famine.[13] After these experiences Bishop Korir realized that his diocese "could play a special role in calling for peace in their valley," and together with his diocesan Justice and Peace Commission "they resolved to work with the people to achieve sustainable peace."[14] Furthermore, as part of his efforts in peacebuilding, he sent the diocesan Justice and Peace Commission coordinator to ask the warring communities what they desired, and they replied, "We want you to help us to talk to each other"—hence their desire for reconciliation, harmony, and peace.[15] The just peace practice of identifying the human needs of all parties illuminates this experience. Yet the communities faced challenges in their efforts to bring peace; for instance, they were ridiculed as "peace mercenaries," "professional seminar goers," and "the people who go to eat rice."[16] Despite this ridicule, the people's desire was for peace, and therefore they continued to meet in order to seek ways of resolving their conflicts. They selected representatives from each community who met and ironed out their grievances. As one shared, "It was a very tough meeting; a lot of nasty words were thrown."[17] The communities worked together for some peace initiatives that were started in order to resolve the conflicts. Cattle dips were built in a neutral place for four purposes: to reduce cattle rustling activity; to ensure that the animals were free of diseases and thus would multiply; to be able to identify stolen livestock; and to give the people an opportunity to meet, have open conversations, bond, and bridge. Other activities in which they engaged were rebuilding houses that were destroyed and building common markets and water points in neutral places. In addition, the communities engaged in common activities such as sharing meals and participating in sports (e.g., the peace marathon).[18] This helped people to bond and bridge with each other. In addition, such initiatives actualize the just peace norm of cultivating peacemaking communities and institutions.

The government and other peacebuilders such as nongovernmental organizations (both local and international) in the three counties are engaged in addressing these deep-rooted conflicts.[19] Referring mainly to government peace initiatives, the government has invested in civic education, which is communicated mainly through *barazas* and peace forums within communities.[20] Government policies and other germane issues, such as voting rights, surrendering of arms (disarmament), dangers of possessing illegal arms, and engaging in dangerous activities such as cattle rustlings and banditry, are communicated. The communities have the opportunity to interact freely as they engage in dialogue with their leaders at the local and top level.[21] Such initiatives actualize the just peace norms of integral disarmament, participation, and relationality. Although some people heed the messages and surrender their arms and ammunition, others are reluctant to do so, mainly because of the incitement by some of the politicians. An example of this was in the county when one politician cautioned his people not to surrender their guns; he equated it with a person asking another to surrender their walking stick that an enemy can use to later beat them up.[22] Other initiatives that the government has put in place are the Security Sector Reforms; the introduction of unarmed community policing, especially the *Nyumba kumi* initiative; and efforts to create cultures of peace in schools (both public and private).[23] However, the government's first response to any conflicts in the region is to employ militaristic and securitized approaches by deploying security forces, mainly police and armed forces.[24] These officers have often used high handedness and are sometimes extremely brutal in dealing with affected communities. The extent of such brutality is captured in the following excerpt:

> The methods used in the interrogation of communities suspected to harbor raiders are punitive and include physical, economic, and psychological torture such as beatings and confiscation of animals to force confessions. In the process the societies come to fear and lose confidence in their own government. Additionally, some corrupt administrators keep some of the recovered animals and later sell them, thereby adding to the society's suspicions."[25]

Communities are also engaged in grassroots peacebuilding, mainly through African indigenous approaches to addressing conflict. These approaches are predominantly invested in the elders and are geared toward a consensus often based on a bottom-up approach. The different communities in the identified counties engage their elders, for instance, in resolving family conflicts. Most important, for decades the council of elders has been engaged by their communities as repositories of history and wisdom. They perform rituals and bless the youth before the cattle raids and when they return. They also assist the youth in strategizing and blessing them for counterattacks after the community's livestock has been raided. Additionally, they may gather to plan how to deter the neighbors from encroaching on their land, especially during drought seasons. However, we cannot romanticize these traditional approaches, because they are sometimes politically motivated by the "powerful" of the society and are equally shrouded in cultural stereotypes, especially of women, youth, and children. One of the respondents shared her observation: "The Council of elders is made of men only. Women are involved in the fact that they can come and listen to what men are deliberating on but they are not allowed to speak."[26] Hence, any approaches to address the violent conflicts have to be inclusive of all people, following the gospel of nonviolence of love for all, even "the enemy"—the other.[27]

Women who are in violence-prone areas are actively involved in nonviolence initiatives. However, what they do is sometimes not visible, mainly due to "feminisation and masculinisation of conflicts."[28] The 2007–2008 post-election eruption of violence in Kenya "led to the death of over 1,000 people and displacement of almost 700,000 others in two months," and the majority of these were women.[29] One of the highlights in this chapter is a group of women from the North Rift region who chose to group together to promote cohesion and to create a peaceful and just society.[30] They started by cooking together and constructing mud houses for other women whose houses had been destroyed in the violence.

As they interacted they prayed and shared their stories of pain, thus breaking the communications barriers. These initiatives actualize the just peace norms of sustaining spiritual practices and the virtue of empathy. Further, in 2012 they started a "knitting for peace project" that received support from the Rural Women Peace Link organization. They made calabashes, *kiondos*, bracelets, and other ornaments that they sold in their nearest markets.[31] One woman shares that as they engaged in their daily routine of knitting they would discuss ways of averting the violence in the future. As a result of engaging in the peace activities and sharing their narratives, they were creating and working toward a peaceful coexistence. However, while trying to reach out to other people that were displaced, they were met with great open hostility. This was because they were perceived as aggressors. Eventually, as observed in the following narrative, one of the women was successful: "I was able to succeed because I always appealed to the women as a woman and would ask them to go talk with their husbands and their sons. Women are very strong. They do not easily break up from their experiences."[32]

Another example of women employing active nonviolence in situations of conflict is found among the Pokot women. Women in the North Rift region have borne the brunt of violent conflicts for decades. As a result they have learned to balance their role as mothers of young men ready for cattle rustling. They are also advisers to their husbands, who protect the family and mentor the youth. However, sometimes they do not support cattle rustling and banditry. In these cases they have devised a traditional way of dealing with it. Every Pokot woman has a *leketio* (birth belt) that she wears for support when she is pregnant (see fig. 12.2). She also wears it during war or conflict as a charm to protect her son from external harm, including during

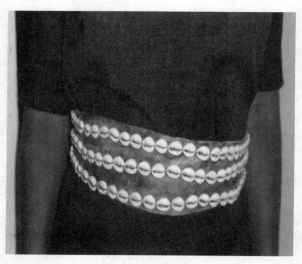

Figure 12.2   Leketio—the birth belt

Source: Irene Chepoisho Tulel, "Women and Peace-building in Pastoral Conflicts: A Case Study of Pokot Women in Sigor Region of West Pokot County, 1984–2000" (Nairobi: Department of History and Archeology, University of Nairobi, 2013), 60.

cattle raids. In some instances when a mother is not in support of any male members of the family taking part in the conflicts or war, she will refuse to wear the leketio. Also, a woman can decide to remove her leketio at the peak of a fight or war and lay it down between the people who are fighting. They will instantly stop fighting; it is taboo for a man to touch a leketio because it is a birth belt. In addition, a man cannot force a woman to wear a leketio. If he does, then this action will warrant a curse. This is one of the ways that women can participate in peacebuilding. The tradition of using a leketio to stop or prevent conflicts or wars is practiced among all of the Kalenjin sub-tribes.[33] This practice also resembles the tactic of identifying and mobilizing credible messengers in the community to interrupt violence, which is often found within groups that use the just peace practice of un-armed civilian protection.

Recommendations for a Just Peace Ethic and to Transform the Conflict in the North Rift Region of Kenya

Parallels can be drawn from local and global contexts to show the reality that violence does not lead to peace. On the contrary, nonviolent strate-gies and tools have proved the most viable option. This view is in accord with the late Saint John Paul II, who while addressing politicians during his visit in Ireland challenged them: "You politicians must prove them to be wrong. You must show that there is a peaceful, political way to justice. You must show that peace achieves the works of justice, and violence does not."[34]

Although just peace is sometimes touted as a utopian idea, there are examples of visionaries in our times who were ready and laid down their lives physically or symbolically for a just and peaceful society. A few that come to mind are Mohandas Gandhi, Martin Luther King, Óscar Romero, the Women of Liberia, the late Wangari Muta Maathai and the women that supported her at the Freedom Corner, and Nelson Mandela. They all represent the uniqueness of our world and its people. These great people, representing different genders, did this using the power of love—active nonviolence. Following in their path, the community can incorporate those positive virtues as a foundation for their just peace approach to violence.

In the traditional African context, the values were passed from generation to generation through oral narratives, proverbs, metaphors, songs and dances, myths, and legends of a given community. The challenge therefore for the communities—the focus of this chapter—is to ensure that the values a community passes to its younger generations do not remain abstract but that they live and practice them. For instance, telling children stories about the dishonest hare that was punished for stealing honey is important, but there is a need to go further. Parents need to model honesty because this is "not taught but caught." The value has to be lived and made a habit. The Kiswahili saying *haraka, haraka haina baraka* is a reminder that such an undertaking is a challenge.[35] True peace takes time; therefore, there is a need to keep trying even when we do not see the end in sight. Acquiring virtues so that we can embody the transformative practices of a just peace approach will take time. Therefore, communities need to be encouraged to keep trying the virtues for a just peace approach to violence no matter how far they fall short of their goals.

The cultural sphere, beliefs, and customs are held as the essence of the identity of a community. Culture, as noted previously, refers to the habits, values, beliefs, customs, and worldviews of a given group. It is culture that validates values and needs within a given community. Thus, culture is dynamic and context-specific.[36] However, a group has to go beyond its values in order to practice virtue-based just peace ethics. What one is taught and learns as an individual in a community—for instance, caring for animals and the environment, respect for elders and significant adults, tolerance, friendship, and trust—will remain merely values if they are not put into practice. Therefore, a virtue-based approach to the North Rift region conflicts will involve people going beyond the value of cattle raiding for restocking and will begin to reflect on the violent actions that involve stealing from and killing the "enemy."[37] The community can embrace the spirit of *ubuntu*—of respecting "the other"—because all people are interconnected.[38] Ubuntu is about restoration of relationships through asking forgiveness and then being ready for the other to offer forgiveness. It is here that reconciliation is a meeting place because "truth and mercy have met together and justice and peace have kissed."[39] In the African worldview of ubuntu, the people thrive individually and collectively by living together in harmony, making the following biblical aspiration a reality: "How delightful it is to live as brothers [and sisters] all together."[40] In essence, therefore, incorporating the ubuntu approach in peacebuilding would promote an African perspective to a just peace approach. To go farther along this path, Pope Francis, in his homily on World Day of Peace 2017, invites the world's peoples and nations to "make active nonviolence our way of life."[41]

Parents, teachers, and any significant adults must go beyond their community's oral narratives that are used to pass on values, beliefs, and customs, especially those that perpetuate stereotypes about their neighbors in the counties. For instance, in the case of cattle rustling, children must be taught that all the cattle in Kenya do not belong to them and that killing anyone, irrespective of their ethnic community, is a violation of one's human rights. Therefore, to address this violent conflict, a peacebuilder needs to understand a community's values and beliefs and critique them with the aim of addressing its challenges. In this case, the younger generation might be taught the values of honesty and hard work, but for them to integrate the values they must act honestly and work hard to purchase their own cattle. The community can enhance the importance of a virtue-based just peace approach. This would entail a transformation of all forms of violence (direct, cultural, and structural).[42] This means stressing the positive values that enhance peace as opposed to focusing on violence. For instance, the communities can utilize the African wise sayings and metaphors from the three counties. The following examples from communities in Kenya will suffice: "Justice breaks a prepared arrow," "Fighting has no fun," "War is not porridge," and "A person sent away with justice does not come back."[43] Everyone can be an artisan of peace."[44]

Sawatsky contends that "[our] virtues are part of the lens that shape understanding of the world." In addition, that they are "rooted in and inspired by particular stories, cultures, and narratives." While this is the case it is important to include experiences and attitudes, which are interlinked in worldviews that are a source of cultural values.[45]

I suggest three cultural dimensions that could be incorporated as a foundation of a virtue-based approach to a just peace ethic. These dimensions

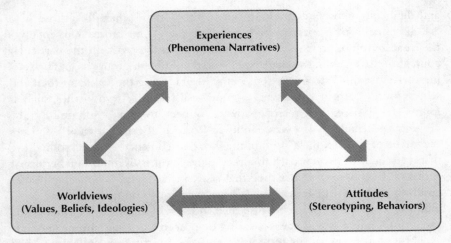

Figure 12.3 Cultural Dimensions for Peacebuilding
Source: Teresia Wamũyũ Wachira, "Exploring Violence through the Narratives of Youth in Kenyan Secondary Schools: Implications for Reconceptualising Peacebuilding" (PhD diss., University of Bradford, UK, 2009), 45. Available at https://tinyurl.com/s95cmmk.

particularly help to illuminate the just peace norm of cultivating peacemaking cultures. They are the worldviews, experiences, and attitudes of the affected communities (see fig. 12.3).[46]

1. The importance of experiences, which are kept real and alive by narratives passed from generation to generation. This includes events such as births, deaths/violent conflict, and the nature of interaction with others.
2. The importance of worldviews, which are the cultural notions of the meaning of life within a specific community and thus have a bearing on how meanings are transmitted. Worldviews are the source of cultural values and thus provide the tools for interpretation of events and solutions to challenges.
3. The importance of attitudes, which are acquired through experience and cultural values in a given context. These could be incorporated in any approach toward creating just and peaceful societies.

In both the virtue ethic and Gandhian theory of nonviolence, *who one is* is of importance and *what one does* derives importance from who one is—social as well as personal virtue (*ahimsa*). Virtue is therefore to be cultivated and needs to be practiced. The "love of the enemy" that Jesus is referring to is a direct and deliberate choice of reaching out to the "other," including those who are different from us, irrespective of where they come from. This involves the total giving of one's self to *all*, as Jesus did on the cross. In the particular context of this chapter, the challenge for all the different groups would be "going that extra mile" to meet "the enemy"—practicing the virtue of total and selfless love.[47] Conversely, Kaveline-Popov outlines fifty-two virtues, such as forgiveness, justice, love, mercy, patience, respect, tolerance, and unity.[48] She pinpoints peacefulness as a virtue in itself. Borba is of a similar view but places the virtue of "peacefulness" within the moral intelligence—hence, something that is learned.[49] This approach to virtue as peacefulness is important because it explains "how peace is understood that peace is lived out."[50] Hence, in peacebuilding in the North Rift region, it is important to understand these communities' concepts of peace because their views will influence their behaviors and attitudes, which will have a bearing on peacemaking and justice making.

Through the paschal mystery of Jesus Christ, humanity is enlightened and challenged on what it really means to walk the path of active nonviolence. Jesus had the choice to retaliate but chose to love and forgive those who mocked and crucified him. He chose to embrace the "enemies" by asking his Father to forgive them, "for they do not know what they are doing."[51] Hence, it seems to me that the argument often crafted in justification of war as one of "the solutions to attain peace" is unsustainable. A peaceful end does not justify violent means, as the just peace norm of reflexivity also illuminates. Hence, to be a true disciple of Jesus is to follow in his footsteps of love and forgiveness even amid violence.[52]

Practical Suggestions

The following are peacebuilding initiatives that can enhance a transformative practice of a just peace ethic to violent conflicts specifically in the North Rift region (Baringo, Elgeyo-Marakwet, and West Pokot).

- The communities can engage women more at all levels of decision-making and practices of peacemaking and justice making. As Pope Francis noted in his World Day of Peace 2017 message, "Women in particular are often leaders of nonviolence."[53] Also, communities can create forums for people who experience marginalization in society—for instance, women, youth, children, and people with disabilities—so their voices can be heard. This will assist in promoting a just peace approach to exclusion, which is structural violence. It would also actualize the just peace norm of participation. Additionally, the members of the different communities can create forums where intercommunity dialogue can be enhanced to develop just and peaceful societies.
- Learning institutions (early childhood, primary, secondary, and tertiary levels) within the North Rift region where these counties are situated can be encouraged to create and utilize Peace Corners in or outside of the

classroom, and Peace Clubs and Peace Cafés (depending on the name preferred by the school/college/university). These can be spaces where children and young people practice and engage in dialogue on issues such as care and protection of the environment—"our common home"—and other species that share our planet, such as domestic and wild animals.[54] This reinforces the foundation built in the family setting: "In the family we first learn how to show love and respect for life . . . respect for local ecosystem and care for all creatures . . . we receive an integral education, which enables us to grow harmoniously in personal maturity . . . to control our aggressivity and greed, and to ask forgiveness when we have caused harm."[55]

- Such spaces of peace will also assist in the implementation of sustainable development outlined in the 2030 Agenda for Sustainable Development; especially goal 16, which aims to reduce all forms of violence.[56] More importantly, it is in learning institutions, no matter at what level, that the gospel of nonviolence can be inculcated so that it becomes part of the DNA of the students, staff, and all stakeholders. This would actualize the just peace norm of education in nonviolence.

- In academia, too, scholars can engage with those at the grassroots level through constructive research and dialogue—for instance, on community peacebuilding and application of just peace approaches in conflict transformation. This will enable scholars not only to articulate their aspirations of a just and peaceful society but also to build up the scholarly works employing the just peace approaches that will enhance a culture of peace for today and future generations. Additionally, donors should invest in research on peace and justice making. This entails supporting projects that are geared toward building peaceful and just societies.

- The Catholic Church can support and invest energy and finances in developing Small Christian Communities (SCCs), which currently act as family cells of spiritual nourishment, training, and nurturing for a generation of people.[57] This is of the utmost importance because these communities can be the foundation of re-evangelizing on a gospel of active nonviolence. Through such communities the church can model the virtues of love for all, including the "enemies"—community sharing, forgiveness, compassion, harmony, peace, tolerance, mercy, and justice. There is an equal need for healing communities of believers—representing different faiths—so that they can lead by example.

- The Catholic Church leadership in Kenya, under the umbrella of the Kenya Conference of Catholic Bishops in solidarity with the leadership of other religions (e.g., the National Council of Churches, the Inter-Religious Council of Kenya, and the World Council of Churches, together with the Leaders of the African Traditional Religions) can from time to time visit and prepare and circulate common pastoral letters that foster and promote virtues of peace, justice, and harmonious coexistence. Through this action the religious leaders will be modeling Jesus's desire for the church "that they may be one."

- More important, the leaders can make joint visits to the government leadership—both locally and nationally—to discuss and share ways of building a society that is grounded in "effective pedagogy to grow in solidarity, responsibility and compassionate care" of one another and our environment.[58] These groups of leaders can also incorporate and create opportunities for the Council of Elders representing different communities in the North Rift region. For example, they can have joint meetings with them toward the aim of sharing grassroots peacebuilding activities for sustainable development.
- In today's world with high technological knowledge, social media has a challenge to practice peace journalism (peace oriented as opposed to violence oriented). The journalists can be invited to practice the virtues of peace and justice as they mold young minds. They do this through social media posts and reporting and through various modern platforms such as smartphones. These platforms include Facebook, Twitter, WhatsApp, and blogs, among others.
- Religious leaders in Kenya and specifically in the North Rift region counties have access to nonviolent teachings, moral authority, and permanence (religious structures). Thus, they have opportunities to act as bridges between the government and the citizens spread out in different counties in Kenya. Such bridging initiatives actualize the just peace norm of relationality.

Conclusion

In this chapter I have argued for transformative practices of a just peace ethic that would incorporate African indigenous approaches to dealing with violent conflicts. Contextualizing the North Rift region conflicts specifically by focusing on three counties, it is evident that the violence is deep rooted. The main challenge is that cattle raiding has been legitimized by the community, thus becoming a way of life despite its morphosis into the deadly commercialized cattle rustling. Most important, cattle rustling is carried out by unmarried male youth with the blessing of spiritual leaders—elders who are male. Women also play a role, but it is peripheral (e.g., to encourage or discourage raiding by the youth). Usually this is supported by rituals, which are key in most ceremonies among the African communities.

Further, some of the grassroots Afrocentric approaches that create and promote a peaceful and just society in the North Rift region have been critically examined. It is important to note that the particular nonviolent initiatives are not restricted to the three counties discussed in this chapter but to the North Rift region where the counties are situated. In addition, an effort has been made to be inclusive of both genders in the selected nonviolent approaches.

Finally, this chapter contained a detailed discussion on the virtue-based approaches that embody the transformative practices of a just peace approach.

This chapter argues that a transformative practice of a just peace ethic needs to be inclusive of the positive aspects of African indigenous approaches. Also proffered are three cultural dimensions suggested for inclusion as a foundation of a virtue-based approach—that is, the narratives, experiences, and attitudes of the affected communities. Practical suggestions and reflective questions were included to allow for a continuation of this ongoing debate.

Discussion Questions

1. What violent events are common in your local community? Which of these violent events have you personally experienced? In your opinion, what are the underlying causes of the violent events? How are these violent events addressed?

2. Select a community from your country and explore the indigenous non-violent activities that they engage in to reconcile people. Look at the story of the late Bishop Cornelius Korir in this text. How does his effort to reconcile different warring communities challenge us to use a just peace perspective in resolving violent events in our schools, parishes, local communities, and country?

3. In your opinion, what are the underlying causes of the conflict? What are the (1) virtues and (2) skills needed to transform the conflicts?
   - At the top level (leadership)
   - At the grassroots level (citizens)

4. What positive approaches and policies are in place to transform the conflicts? What more positive approaches and policies could be incorporated to transform the conflicts?
   - At the top level (leadership)
   - At the grassroots level (citizens)

5. What positive contribution could the following groups of people make to transform the conflicts?
   - Women, youth, people with disabilities

Notes

1. Peter Wallenstein and Margareta Sollenberg, "Armed Conflicts, Conflict Termination and Peace Agreements, 1989–96," *Journal of Peace Research* 34, no. 3 (1997): 339–58; referenced in Kennedy Agade Mkutu, *Guns and Governance in the Rift Valley: Pastoralist Conflict and Small Arms* (Oxford: James Currey, 2008), 1.

2. Mkutu, *Guns and Governance*, 4.

3. The Marakwet and the Pokot are subgroups of the Kalenjin, who share Nilo-Hamitic ancestry and similar customs. The violent conflicts in which they engage are mainly along the Kerio River, which flows through the valley; the Marakwet are to the west of the river, and the Pokot of Baringo County are to the east. The Marakwet engage in mixed farming and cattle-rearing for their livelihood and are not nomadic, unlike

the Pokot, who have a nomadic or semi-nomadic livelihood. C. Clemens Greiner, "Guns, Land, and Votes: Cattle Rustling and the Politics of Boundary (Re)Making in Northern Kenya," *African Affairs* 122, no. 447 (2013): 216–37.

4. Mkutu, *Guns and Governance*, 13–14.

5. "Political authorities were sowing seeds of discord, dividing citizens along tribal lines and instigating terrible communal violence; battles between Pokot and Marakwet warriors, provoked by cattle rustling, raged in the Kerio Valley." Bishop Korir, *Amani Mashinani—Peace at the Grassroots* (Eldoret, Kenya: Catholic Diocese of Eldoret, 2009). Raiding has a cultural significance and is a multifaceted social (almost ceremonial) event aimed at recovering, restocking, and avenging insults and damages inflicted by enemies. Mkutu, *Guns and Governance*; Mohamud Adan and Ruto Pkalya, *Closed to Progress: An Assessment of the Socio-Economic Impacts of Conflict on Pastoral and Semi Pastoral Economies in Kenya and Uganda* (Eastern Africa: Practical Action, 2005); Pax Christi Horn of Africa, *What Warriors Want*, 2004. The practice has continued despite the warning in 2018 from the president of Kenya and the minister of security. Jael Keya, "Fred Matiangi's Warning to Rift Valley Leaders," *Kenyans.co.ke*, August 21, 2018.

6. Male youth participant (coded JN1) from West Pokot, interviewed in February 2018.

7. Timothy M. Anderson, "Identity and Exclusion in Africa: An Examination of Autochthony and Xenophobia" (master's thesis, Ohio University, May 2013).

8. Male youth participant (coded ML2) from Elgeyo-Marakwet, interviewed in February 2018.

9. Korir, *Amani Mashinani*.

10. "In 2015, he was made the Goodwill Ambassador for Peace by the National Cohesion and Integration Commission (NCIC)." Titus Too and Fred Kibor, "Bishop Kiror: A Cleric Who Cherished Peace," in Standard Digital Daily Newspaper, Nairobi, Kenya, November 5, 2017.

11. They were from the Kalenjin ethnic community fighting the Kikuyu people. They referred to them as "foreigners" or "madoadoa" (Kiswahili for "spots"). Bishop Korir was also from the Kalenjin community.

12. Korir, *Amani Mashinani*, 10.

13. Korir, 2.

14. Korir.

15. Korir.

16. Korir.

17. Korir, 41.

18. Korir, 12. In the African context, sharing a meal is very important. People do not share a meal when they are not in agreement—therefore, people can share a meal as a sign that they are ready to reconcile or that they are in oneness with the other. People do not fight or quarrel about food. Regarding shared sports activities, see Korir, 22.

19. Lederach, in his pyramid of actors in peacebuilding argues that the middle level of actors (nongovernmental organizations) is key for sustainable peacebuilding. Actors at this level have access to both the top-level leadership and the grassroots level (the citizens). John Paul Lederach, *Building Peace: Sustainable Reconciliation in Divided Societies* (Washington, DC: United States Institute of Peace Press, 1997).

20. *Barazas* are informal gatherings among communities to discuss issues of interest to them.

21. An example is the recent events that brought together warring communities on April 28, 2018, during a peace run. The leaders impressed on the people the need to desist from cattle rustling for economic development and prosperity. Florah Koech, "Call for Unity in Crime-Prone North Rift during Peace Run," *Daily Nation*, April 30, 2018.

22. Joram N. Kareithi, "The Multi-Factoral Nature of Inter-Ethnic Conflicts in North-Rift Frontier Border Lands, Kenya: Implications on Pastoralists' Welfare and Livelihoods," *Journal of Anthropology and Archaeology* 3, no. 1 (June 2015): 37–57.

23. *Nyumba kumi* refers to ten households creating good neighborliness and enhancing community security.

24. "President Kenyatta Now Deploys the KDF to Baringo," *Daily Nation*, March 17, 2017. Deployment of the Kenya Defense Forces was meant to increase security in the North Rift region.

25. Kareithi, "Multi-Factoral Nature of Inter-Ethnic Conflicts," 53.

26. Participant BMb1, interview, February 2018.

27. This teaching of Christ forms the basis for a gospel of nonviolence. This is expounded in Lisa S. Cahill, *Love Your Enemies: Discipleship, Pacifism, and Just War Theory* (Minneapolis, MN: Augsburg Press, 1994).

28. Men are perceived as aggressors and women as victims. Peacebuilding activities more often exclude women.

29. Gabrielle Lynch, "Durable Solution, Help or Hindrance? The Failings and Unintended Implications of Relief and Recovery Efforts for Kenya's Post-Election IDPs," *Review of African Political Economy* 36, no. 122 (2009): 604–10.

30. Beatrice Cherono, "Knitting Peace," in *Stories of Women Building Peace: Transforming Inter-Ethnic Violence in North Rift Region* (Nairobi: Coalition for Peace in Africa, June 2014), 120–23.

31. Special bag made mainly from sisal that is used casually or formally.

32. A member of the displaced women from the Kikuyu and the Kalenjin communities within the town of Eldoret in Kenya captured in the women stories in Cherono, "Knitting Peace," 122.

33. Betty Rabar and Martin Karimi, eds., *Indigenous Democracy: Traditional Conflict Resolution Mechanisms* (Intermediate Technology Development Group—Eastern Africa, 2004), 9.

34. "Violence Destroys What It Claims to Defend: The Dignity, the Life, the Freedom of Human Beings. Violence Is a Crime against Humanity, for It Destroys the Very Fabric of Society." Homily of his holiness John Paul II, September 29, 1979.

35. "Hurry, hurry has not blessings" in Kiswahili—the language spoken in most of Eastern Africa.

36. Kevin Avruch, *Culture and Conflict Resolution* (Washington, DC: United States Institute of Peace Press, 2001), 7–14.

37. Anthony Langat, "Why Kenya's Cattle Raids Are Getting Deadlier: The Infiltration of Illegal Firearms Has Led to a Rise in Violent Cattle Raids. Pastoralists Are Now Arming Themselves," *Aljazeera,* December 27, 2016.

38. "A person is a person through other people," in Tim Murithi, "African Approaches to Building Peace and Social Solidarity," *Accord*, September 25, 2006.

39. Psalm 85:10; John Paul Lederach, *The Journey towards Reconciliation* (Scottdale, PA: Herald Press, 1999).

40. Psalm 133:1.

41. Pope Francis, "Nonviolence: A Style of Politics for Peace," 2017 World Day of Peace Message, January 1, 2017.

42. Johan Galtung, *Peace by Peaceful Means: Peace and Conflict, Development and Civilization* (London: Sage Publications, 1996).

43. Porridge is a meal prepared from maize (mealie) and often eaten at breakfast to sustain one for a long time. "A person sent away with justice does not come back" means that they are contented and are at peace.

44. Pope Francis, "Nonviolence: A Style of Politics for Peace."

45. Jarem Sawatsky, *Just Peace Ethics: A Guide to Restorative Justice and Peacebuilding* (Cambridge: Lutterworth Press, 2009).

46. Schirch states that those engaging in peacebuilding must include each person's world, sharing through word, symbol, and ritual his or her unique worldview. Lisa Schirch, *Ritual and Symbol in Peacebuilding* (Bloomfield, CT: Kumarian Press, 2005).

47. Teresia Wamũyũ Wachira, "Exploring Violence through the Narratives of Youth in Kenyan Secondary Schools: Implications for Reconceptualising Peacebuilding," unpublished, University of Bradford, 2012, 44.

48. Linda Kaveline-Popov, referred to in James Page, *Peace Education: Exploring Ethical and Philosophical Foundations* (Information Age Publishing Inc., USA, 2008), 54.

49. MacIntyre's argument of virtue as an acquired human quality that facilitates practice expressed concern for peaceful society, although it does not mention peace—links society and morality; Alasdair Chalmers MacIntyre, *After Virtue: A Study in Moral Theory* (Notre Dame, IN: University of Notre Dame Press, 2007).

50. Matt. 5:41.

51. Luke 23:34.

52. Teresia Wamũyũ Wachira, "Peace Is Therefore a Way of Life; We Develop the Virtue of Peace by Doing Peace" (PhD diss., 2012), 26; Galtung, *Peace by Peaceful Means*. The way to attain peace is to apply peaceful means, not violence; otherwise we create cycles of violence.

53. Pope Francis, "Nonviolence: A Style of Politics for Peace."

54. Pope Francis, *Laudato si: Encyclical Letter of the Holy Father Francis on Care for Our Common Home* (Nairobi: Paulines Publications Africa, 2015).

55. Francis, 117.

56. These goals aim to reduce all forms of violence and find lasting solutions to conflicts and insecurity.

57. There are more than 160,000 Small Christian Communities (SCCs) in the nine countries of Eastern Africa. SCCs are a new model of being church in Africa today. They operate in parishes (in the rural and urban centers); in different levels of learning institutions, and religious formation houses. www.smallchristian communities.org; https://maryknollmissionarchives.org/?p=4569.

58. Francis, *Laudato si*, 116.

13

Virtue-Based Just Peace Approach and the Challenges of Rape as a Weapon of War

The Case of the Democratic Republic of Congo

LÉOCADIE LUSHOMBO

This case study places a focus on the ongoing wars in the Democratic Republic of Congo (DRC). The DRC is not the only fighting party. Others comprise several army groups, including those from Rwanda, Uganda, and the DRC who are targeting civilians by means of rape and "rape with extreme violence" (REV), particularly in mining zones.[1] This chapter reflects on this scourge from the view of a just peace ethic.

First, I present the context of the case by illuminating the magnitude of the use of rape as a weapon of war in the DRC. Neither Catholic social teaching nor the just war theorists, whether classic or modern, have considered this challenge adequately if at all. Second, this chapter utilizes a just peace ethic by assessing the ways in which the virtues of charity and courage, as embraced by Denis Mukengere Mukwege and associates through Panzi Hospital, "bring indispensable resources for a more just and peaceful world." As director of Panzi Hospital, Mukwege is an obstetrician-gynecologist who not only treats women to help them recover their bodily integrity but also advocates for the end of this calamity and for a just and sustainable peace in the DRC. In 2018, he won the Nobel Peace Prize. Following the work of Lisa Sowle Cahill and Eli McCarthy, I argue that Mukwege's work actualizes a virtue-based just peace approach to the ongoing conflict in the DRC.

This chapter concludes with an analysis of Mukwege's nonviolent means to address rape as a weapon of war in order to challenge the presumption that nonviolent means cannot effectively counter the grave assault on human life and dignity in intrastate wars. I offer some suggestions for how to draw on additional just peace norms to enhance what Mukwege is already doing. In this context I respond to the dilemma raised by Cahill, which is that using lethal force to stop wars would be incompatible with the Christian duty not to kill, but at the same time not resorting to violent means may turn actors into "guilty bystanders," accomplices, or partners in crime. This argument is all the more pertinent when one recalls that the use of rape as a weapon of war is not limited to the DRC but rather is a global problem.

Context: The Worldwide Use of Rape as a Weapon of War

Rape has been used against women in conflict zones all over the world. The estimated scale of sexual violence during World War II and in several countries in conflict since then indicates that rape has been and continues to be used as a weapon of war in modern times. The use of rape as a weapon of war refers to "systematic or strategic and opportunistic forms of sexual violence that occur in the build-up to, active fighting in, and aftermath of armed conflict."[2] Rape as weapon of war is "a deliberate strategy of one or more parties to the armed conflict."[3] As Bülent Diken and Carsten Bagge Laustsen stated,

> War rape is perhaps the clearest example of an asymmetric strategy. In war rape, the enemy soldier attacks a civilian (not a combatant), a woman (not another male soldier), and only indirectly with the aim of holding or taking a territory. The prime aim of war rape is to inflict trauma and thus to destroy family ties and group solidarity within the enemy camp. Apart from demoralization of the enemy, war rape can also become an integral aspect of ethnic cleansing.[4]

Rape as weapon of war also includes mass rape and extensive forced prostitution.[5] Such a weapon is used because of the way it destroys the social structure of the community, humiliating the adverse camp and transforming women into "abjects," making them feel as "'dirty,' morally inferior person[s]."[6] In this sense, rape is an abjection in two ways: by denigrating the victim from without (spoiling her from within and making her feel ashamed and sinful) and demonstrating the power of one camp over another in conflict.[7]

The estimated number of victims of sexual violence committed in 1937 by the Imperial Japanese Army during the fall of the Chinese city of Nanjing ranged from 20,000 to 80,000. Between 50,000 and 410,000 women were sexually enslaved in the so-called comfort women system that took place in 1932–1945.[8] In 1945, as many as 100,000–1,000,000 German women were raped by Soviet soldiers on their return home to Berlin in the aftermath of World War II.

Since World War II, the number of rapes continues to be recorded. As many as 200,000 Bengali women were raped by members of the Pakistani army in their attempt to suppress the independence movement in Bangladesh in 1971. US troops used the same weapon in the Vietnam War against Vietnamese women as "standard operating procedure."[9] Approximately 25,000–40,000 women were "victims of genocidal rape and enforced impregnation" in Bosnia-Herzegovina between 1991 and 1995.[10] The Bosnian government reported up to 70,000 victims, although many thousands were raped by soldiers on all sides.[11] This weapon was also used in Syria, Iraq, Burma, Croatia, Colombia, Haiti, and Mexico.[12] In Africa, the number of victims of sexual violence in war zones was reported to be 50,000–64,000 in Sierra Leone between 1991 and 2002 and was 250,000–500,000 in the 100-day Rwandan genocide in 1994. This weapon is still used in war zones in Libya, Guinea, South Sudan, Liberia, Sierra Leone, Uganda, Rwanda, and the DRC.[13]

The Spreading of Rape with Extreme Violence in the Democratic Republic of Congo

One of the key guiding questions of a just peace ethic is "What are the root causes of a conflict?" In the DRC, the wars are not civil wars. They are not ethnic. Rather, they are economic and regional, involving up to seven other African countries, and they started as a "direct consequence of the 1994 Rwandan genocide."[14] The attacks in the DRC, particularly by Rwanda and Uganda, have been largely documented by the United Nations (UN).[15] The Jesuit Rigobert Minani explains that in the aftermath of the 1994 Rwandan genocide, Rwanda's 1996 invasion of the eastern Congo to battle and destabilize Hutu insurgents set a pattern of conflict that has since repeated itself.[16] A 2008 mortality study conducted by the International Rescue Committee estimates the number of deaths at approximately 5.4 million and affirms that the DRC's wars are "the deadliest . . . since World War II."[17] Its natural resources are also another driving motivation of the armies entering into wars in the DRC.[18] Several writers detail the extent to which the Congo's wars are about "conflict minerals."[19] As Jason K. Stearns explains,

> As soon as the second war started in August 1998, it was clear that there had been a shift in motivation. "Business," Olivier said emphatically. "The first war had been about getting rid of the refugee camps and overthrowing Mobutu. The second was about business. The security imperative was still present for Rwanda. The northwest of their country was engulfed in a brutal insurgency . . . . But the second war was a much more costly exercise. In addition, some Rwandan businessmen, together with the RPF [Rwandan Patriotic Front, Tutsi-led political party in power] politicians, had become aware that there were hefty profits to be made in the Congo, particularly in the minerals trade."[20]

Although Rwanda justifies the presence of its military in the DRC as a question of security and the common good (for Rwanda) alone, women are paying the higher price of their lives. The army groups use rape as a weapon of war while pillaging mineral resources in the mining zones in the eastern DRC.

For example, the region of Shabunda is rich in coltan, gold, and cassiterite. The Kabare region is rich in coltan, which is "used for capacitors in cell phones and video game consoles" and which contains the tantalum that is used widely in electronics in the industrialized world.[21] The territory of Walungu is rich in cassiterite and gold. Importantly, Mukwege and Cathy Nangini demonstrate that the rate of rape is directly correlated with proximity to mining zones: "The area of the circles [of mining] is proportional to the fraction of the hospital's survivors attacked in these regions. The areas are centered around Walungu (3,251 victims [33.2 percent]), Kabare (3,050 [31.2 percent]), Bukavu (1,499 [15.3 percent]), Shabunda (951 [9.7 percent]), and Uvira (785 [8.0 percent]). A small proportion (242 [2.5 percent]) of cases treated at Panzi Hospital occurred outside of South Kivu."[22] In addition to the pillaging, the fueling of wars in the DRC by Rwanda and Uganda aims at defending, protecting, and ensuring "political representation for the several hundred thousand Congolese Tutsi living in the eastern part of the Congo, and some 44,000 Congolese refugees, most of them Tutsi, living in Rwanda."[23]

As evidenced in the *Reported Figures on Rape/Mutilation Victims in Eastern DRC*, the case of the DRC following the 1994 Rwandan genocide is among the most revealing in terms of showing the extent to which rape and extreme violence are used in the context of war.[24] Dr. Denis Mukwege, the coordinator of the hospital in Panzi that treats women victims of rape in the eastern DRC, considers the rape of women in the DRC as a new pathology, which he calls "rape with extreme violence (REV)."[25]

Army groups commit rape without regard to age, from 2-year-old babies to 80-year-old women. Mukwege calls this calamity a "systematic rape" in the sense that "each army group uses this method to torture its victims to the maximum."[26] Mukwege states that REV has increased in the eastern part of the DRC during the last 20 years. A nationwide survey reports that from 1.69 to 1.80 million women were reported to be victims of rape in 2011. Between 1999 and 2015, 45,482 women survivors were treated in Panzi Hospital alone by Mukwege and his associates.[27] Since 2017, more than 50,000 women survivors of rape have been treated by the hospital.[28] Following this, the DRC was termed the "rape capital" of the world.[29]

Mukwege explains that rape and REV is a weapon of war and an efficacious one because it is used in public and collectively to destroy women, their children, families, and communities: "Rape devastates the body, but also the soul. It steals a woman's self-worth and her physical and psychological health. When deployed as a strategy of control over land, over resources, or over an entire population, it is a cheap, effective way to destabilize entire communities."[30] According to Jilmi Zawātī, rape has many functions. It is used as "a weapon of war, as a tool of ethnic cleansing, as an act of genocide, and as a means of destroying the culture and infrastructure of an opponent's society."[31] REV is, then, contrary to the commandments of the divine and natural law.[32] No one should be allowed to cause so much harm to people, men or women, such as REV, for whatever so-called proportionate good to be pursued, including peace.

It is important to note that rape is listed among the crimes against humanity in the statute adopted by the UN Security Council in 1993.[33] The 1998 International Criminal Court statute identifies the widespread and systematic attack of rape as a "crime against humanity" in both international and non-international armed conflicts.[34] Thus, the widespread rapes have become a peace-hindering factor and a security issue as confirmed by UN Security Council Resolutions 1325 and 1820.[35] Although we may see rape as immoral, we are more susceptible to devalue or lack resistance to the reality of rape as a weapon of war if we are using the predominant ethical language about war, such as the just war criteria of proportionality. The logic might go that armed force is needed to attack those in the DRC who committed genocide in Rwanda, and thus, the good that would come from this outweighs the harm that comes from rape. So, although we disapprove of it and might try somewhat to minimize it, we might also reluctantly accept its reality as part of our proportionate reasoning for war. Because of the consistent failure to adequately address these issues, it is crucial and urgent to consider them from a new ethical perspective, particularly a virtue-based just peace ethic.

Reflecting with a Just Peace Ethic: Profile of Denis Mukwege

With a just peace ethic, we have a broader vision about conflict as well as a set of norms to adequately expose rape as a weapon of war and commit to effective, sustainable ways to end both rape and war. A clear example of using just peace norms is found in Panzi Hospital, where Denis Mukwege and associates display the virtues of mercy and courage, which "bring indispensable resources for a more just and peaceful world."[36] In Mukwege's case, mercy is that which enters into the chaos of another and takes responsibility by being in solidarity with the victims. As he states, "In every raped woman, I see my wife. In every raped mother, I see my mother and in every raped child, my own children."[37] In addition to repairing the women's injuries, Mukwege also calls on the responsibility of national and international governments to effectively collaborate in bringing peace in the DRC. These actions are examples of actualizing the just peace norm of cultivating key virtues, particularly mercy and courage. They echo Aquinas that "we are bound to have charity towards all men."[38] This is the main reason why we should not become "guilty bystanders." Taking responsibility requires embracing the virtue of courage.

As McCarthy already expressed it, "the virtue of nonviolent peacemaking clarifies or expands the paradigmatic practices of the virtue of courage to the practice of suffering out of reverence for the dignity of others (and self) by risking, perhaps even giving, one's life without killing. This is because killing distorts our dignity."[39] Mukwege's approach displays a courage that is needed in everyday life to face the many fears that arise from his peace-maker's activities, including denouncing rape and its perpetuating systems. The two virtues, mercy and courage, are seen throughout the Panzi Hospital's "five-pillar process" to address the evil of rape."[40] They include medical treatment, psychosocial therapy, socioeconomic support and training, community reintegration, and legal assistance. These pillars reinforce the vision of a virtue-based just peace approach in many ways.

Rehabilitation and Reintegration of Victimized Women

Panzi Hospital has an extensive program of rehabilitation and integration of women victims to restore their physical, psychological, and socioeconomic well-being. This program's aim is to support women in order for them to re-gain full confidence in themselves, reintegrate the community in which they live, and become engaged to demand justice. The program illustrates the just peace norm of conflict transformation, particularly the practices of trauma healing and restorative justice.

Physical-Clinical Rehabilitation

Mukwege affirms that the Panzi Hospital's services for victims of sexual violence admits at least 10 women every day, and 30 percent of them undergo major surgery. Their injuries include rape and "the insertion of firearms by soldiers to destroy [their] genital and pelvic organs."[41] Even pregnant women are counted among the victims. For Mukwege, this atrocity leads him to think of the victims "as if they were the main target of the conflict."[42] This supports the claim that rape is being used as a means of war itself. I have not come across any Catholic theorists on just war engaging this issue or considering the ways it challenges the value of the criterion of proportionality.

From 1999 to 2006, a recorded 7,519 women victims have been treated at Panzi Hospital. Of the total, 62.3 percent of the women had several clinical sequelae, including sexually transmitted infections.[43] In 2006 alone, the victims were girls younger than 15 years old (9.2 percent), young women from 16 to 35 years old (65.7 percent), women from 36 to 55 years old (24.4 percent), and women older than 55 years (0.84 percent).[44] Teams of various physicians from all over the world go to Panzi Hospital to help repair fistulas caused during the violent rapes by different army groups. As Mukwege puts it, "What I'm doing really is not only to treat women—their body . . . [but] also to fight for their own right, to bring them to be autonomous, and, of course, to support them psychologically. And all of this is a process of healing so [that] women can regain their dignity."[45] We can see the just peace norms of enabling participation and illuminating dignity in this approach. Once the body is repaired, women undergo a psychological healing process.

Psychological Support

Panzi Hospital provides psychological support for all the victims as well as additional psychological support for those who contract HIV, pregnant women, children born from rape, and new mothers after giving birth.

Panzi Hospital hires therapists and works with other volunteers. Many times, psychological therapy is needed as a prerequisite to the clinical treatment. It helps women to recover their own identity, to regain confidence in themselves, and to reconcile with themselves and the community.[46] As R. E. Houser describes the virtue of patience, this psychological endeavor dealing with victims' trauma belongs to the "lengthy endurance of arduous and difficult things"[47] to undertake and is about allowing the victims to reenter in relationship with neighbors. After the trauma of rape, victims often lose confidence not only in themselves but also in the community where they were supposed to be protected and feel at home. Mukwege explains the importance of this therapy as a peacemaking endeavor when he states that "Peace begins in our homes."[48] I argue that if we cannot feel at peace in our own homes, we cannot trust our surroundings or become agents of peace. These efforts strengthen relationality, reconciliation, and the virtue of patience, which are also just peace norms.

As one of the women victims I spoke with said, "I feel stranger to myself and to all the people around me. I feel like I do not fit here. I stay in my room days after days and alone. I wish they could kill me instead of doing what they did to me." This feeling is even worse for victims who become pregnant. It takes a great deal of mercy, courage, patience, and faith in the sacredness of life to endure the chaos and suffering experienced by these women. One needs special grace from God to be willing to live after going through this kind of trauma. In order to stay alive, the women also need livelihoods.

Socioeconomic Support and Training—Community Reintegration

Actualizing the just peace norm of economic justice, the Panzi Hospital's peacemaking actions have extended to providing a training center called Cité de la Joie (City of Joy), where women learn different kinds of work skills to provide for their basic needs, including traditional men's jobs such as carpentry. The perspective of the City of Joy includes gender equality. Mukwege explains that patriarchy is part of the problem: "We raise our sons by stripping them of any emotion and our daughters end up in the kitchen. Africa's future begins when girls know that they are equal to boys."[49] Mainstreaming gender equality helps women become stronger and freely embrace the goal of peace.

Actualizing the just peace norm of sustainability and peacemaking cultures, Mukwege believes that a sustainable just peace requires a cultural shift as well. As he puts it, "Men need to understand that to protect women is to protect themselves, and that respect for women is key to equity. Rape is not only a woman's issue; it is humanity's crisis to solve."[50] He continues, "Without considering women as our equals, we deprive future generations of our legacy."[51] Because women are equal to men, "we must promote accountability, coherence, and transparency. . . . We must understand that wisdom comes not only from men but also from women."[52]

Through these three dimensions Mukwege exemplifies the virtues of charity, courage, mercy, and justice. As he explains, "We have seen how medical intervention combined with psychosocial care, literacy, numeracy, and vocational training are catalysts for change, both for the short and long term."[53] Panzi Hospital has also created a training center for nurses and physicians to meet this increasing humanitarian crisis. Mukwege displays well the virtue of solidarity. Entering the chaos of women victims leads him to embrace vulnerability, risking his own life and living, like one of them, in the hospital. As he said, "My life has had to change, since returning [from exile after being attacked in his own home]. I now live at the hospital and I take a number of security precautions, so I have lost some of my freedom."[54]

Hence, a virtue-based just peace ethic helps to drive an individual to dare to take risks of suffering, and even death, without killing. Mukwege's example shows that even one person can make the difference in the struggle for peace, rather than behaving like "guilty bystanders," which is how many governments, whether national, regional, or international, too often seem to act.

National, Regional, and International Legal Dimensions

Beyond restoring the physical, psychological, and socioeconomic well-being of the victims, Mukwege has embarked on another global campaign. As he puts it, "What I have seen and heard and experienced in eastern DRC is without a doubt the worst situation of violence towards women in the world."[55] Hence, he has turned his energy to also mobilize international politics to be involved in a more sustainable peacemaking process in the DRC. The trauma of these women continues in the DRC despite the deployment of the UN's peacekeeping forces, which have also been routinely responsible for direct sexual abuse and rape of women. In an interview, Mukwege claims, "I operated on a mother, then 15 years later, I'd operate on her daughter, and three years after that, I'd operate on the granddaughter—a baby." He continues, "I absolutely have to tell the world, show the world, that there is a collective responsibility to act in DRC. We share the same humanity and we cannot continue to allow economic wars to be fought on women's bodies."[56]

An example of Mukwege's advocacy was a speech he delivered when he was granted the 2014 Sakharov Prize at the UN.[57] He acknowledged that the prize he had just been given was meaningful because it shows that the atrocity of rape as a weapon of war has come to be acknowledged by the international community. However, he warned, "This prize won't have any significance to the female victims of sexual violence if you won't join us in our quest for peace, justice and democracy." He added, "Together— politicians, civil society, citizens, men and women—we have to draw a red line against the use of rape as a weapon of war."[58] He reminded the European Union and its members that it was about time to stop spending resources dealing with the consequences of this atrocity. Actualizing the just peace norm of conflict transformation, which seeks to address root causes, he urged them to use international legal instruments to address the causes of the regional conflicts in the DRC, including the exploitation of natural resources that benefit the industrialized countries today and around which many of the rapes are committed. In the face of threats, he still endorsed the Global Witness conflict mineral reporting on the DRC, arguing that "Congo's minerals are exported, smelted, and sold internationally, where they end up in cell phones, laptops, or as pieces of jewelry. We know that some of these minerals sourced from conflict-areas have funded violence, abuses, and corrupt criminal networks. And yet, the response of international companies and states has been too slow and timid to make the necessary fundamental changes."[59]

Through his advocacy, Mukwege brings the voices of the mutilated women to the international level, where they did not previously have one. This is a commitment, a risky one, that shows true solidarity and belief in the humanity of the women who are suffering and ignored in the ongoing wars of the DRC. Mukwege also holds the national government responsible:

> Our goal is to increase protections for women and to advocate that those responsible for sexual violence be brought to justice . . . . The Congolese government has responsibility to listen to the voices of civil society, to negotiate a path to peace in good faith, and to eradicate corruption. The Congolese government must be held responsible for the exploitation of our natural resources, and the negative economic impact this ongoing conflict has on the Congolese people.[60]

Effectiveness of Mukwege's Nonviolent Virtue-Based Just Peace Approach

To what extent is Mukwege's approach truly effective? It would be unrealistic to expect that the specific nonviolent actions of Mukwege and his associates alone would end wars in the DRC. Yet they do contribute a great deal to spread confidence and establish the truth needed for healing. This is a way toward peace.

Mukwege's approach also cultivates the virtue of love in the victims rather than the vice of vengeance that perpetuates war. It works to make the community stronger and resistant to all mechanisms fueling war in the DRC. For example, Mukwege's response to the reality that those who help the victims begin to be attacked is as follows: "We must stand firm. We must not spread a message of hate. Rather, we must continue to love . . . . When we replace hatred and oppression with love, and with a firm commitment to justice, men contribute to real change."[61] Mukwege's virtue-based just peace approach does make the community more responsible, at least at the local level, and thus enables the conditions for actualizing the just peace norm of a robust civil society. Such an approach drives those in the community to not be "guilty bystanders." Rape denies another's humanity, and no one should close his or her eyes when another's humanity is denied. Mukwege explains that when a community becomes more responsible, it can better address root causes:

> As long as corruption, poverty, and the scourge of rape plagues families and our society, there will be no lasting, nor meaningful peace. . . . Let us not be mistaken: the behavior of men during conflicts reflects their behavior during peace-time, except that during wars, the lawlessness due to the absence of the state and security, in a collapsed judicial system, the violence that was sleeping in the family and the community, is set free and explodes.[62]

It is important to consider that such a message of love to local people does not in itself put an end to war. Even though they are responsible when they participate in wars, they are not usually the ones directly fueling them. But they and those with whom they are in relationship can become agents for peace, such as through negotiations and by incentivizing some armed actors to return to the community. As Mukwege states when he was awarded the Hillary Clinton Advancing Women in Peace and Security Awards, "I accept this award today on behalf of these women, as I strongly believe that those who have endured violence in conflict times have the capacity to act as an agent for peace and security and deserve a place at the negotiation table in peace talks."[63] Now to begin to address the dilemma raised by Lisa Sowle Cahill that by embracing nonviolent alternatives, actors may find themselves in the position of guilty bystanders. One aspect of this is that Mukwege does turn to the national government, the regional countries involved in the wars, and the international community, calling them to not stand as guilty bystanders. The governments involved in the wars in the DRC can contribute

to ending them using creative nonviolent means, and the international community can fully and effectively participate to make this happen. Their willingness to embrace and live up to transformative virtues can make a big
difference, as Erasmus would argue.[64] Do they have the courage to embrace
vulnerability and risk some of their own immediate political and economic
preferences in order to meet the needs of all stakeholders in the region?

In addition to the range of international humanitarian law regarding rape,
there is a need for a just peace response to transform conflicts in the DRC and
its neighboring Great Lakes region. On the one hand, the DRC's example
and Mukwege's just peace approach suggest that it is crucial to tackle the licit
and illicit business of weapons and mining that benefit several countries in
the region and beyond. These efforts would actualize the just peace norms of
integral disarmament and economic justice. On the other hand, Mukwege's
approach shows that to better address rape and help defuse war, there is a need
to educate not only the victims but also the community on gender analysis
and equality.

Gender analysis and equality must include moving from a culture of
shaming the victims to that of protecting them through peaceful and active
resistance. It must also provide them with comprehensive care and assistance
as in the triad of Panzi Hospital, Cité de la Joie, and restorative justice for the
victims. These are means for the peaceful and active resistance to the rapes,
to the conflicts, and to the wars. Through such a triad, the victims and the
community embrace the grace of God to rise again from the atrocity and
trauma of the rapes. In turn, the just peace norm of nonviolent education and
skill sets would be enhanced by including the skill of gender analysis.

Restorative justice aims at empowering the local communities to not only
document the actual rapes but also to denounce and hold accountable the
armed groups that are entering and overwhelming their community. Local
resources, including credible messengers and lawyers, are used to bring perpetrators and key stakeholders into restorative justice processes. Another dimension of the justice component in Mukwege's approach is that of engaging
women to participate in governance structures as well as decision-making
processes concerning peace negotiations, peacebuilding, security, and prevention of conflicts, enforcing UN Resolutions 1325 and 1820.

The virtue-based just peace approach embodied by Mukwege and Panzi
Hospital is a cautionary example of what Erasmus calls nonviolent means as
a "style of politics."[65] They may not immediately end wars in the DRC, but
they do have significant social and political effects necessary to sustainable
peace. If civil actors can affect politics by nonviolent means, why cannot
governments also improve by such means?

To illustrate the political effects of Mukwege's virtue-based just peace
approach, it is important to note that 122 countries have endorsed the

UN's historic *Declaration of Commitment to End Sexual Violence in Conflict*, a declaration issued from Mukwege and other peacemaker activists against sexual violence in the DRC.[66] Several nations, including two presidents, attended the ceremony of endorsement and made a commitment to participate in the implementation of the declaration. Such an endorsement is meant to end sexual violence as a weapon of war around the world, not only in the DRC. Two African presidents have agreed to join the "Circle of Champions" created to exercise special influence to prevent conflict-related sexual violence. I strongly affirm that violent means would not be more effective than a change in consciousness that is integrated into politics. In accord with the just peace norm of sustainability, a more lasting peace can be reached if governments involved in the DRC's wars affirm the sacredness of the whole human community, because the virtue of nonviolent peacemaking cultivates the sacredness not only of their own people but of others as well.

Another method for protecting women and reducing rape in the DRC might be the just peace practice of unarmed civilian protection, which has been effective and was illustrated in the chapter on South Sudan (chapter 9). Civil society-based organizations such as Nonviolent Peaceforce could enhance some of the other essential efforts expressed previously by Dr. Mukwege. A sustainable peace needs a holistic approach. Thus, unarmed civilian protection must go along with the other efforts mentioned, particularly providing basic human needs, an accountable legal system, democratization, and regional government responsibility.

The attempts to catch and punish the *genocidaires* of Rwanda is officially the reason given to explain the invasion of approximately thirty-five thousand Rwandan soldiers into the DRC's territories. Yet this results in women who are raped with extreme violence, including "by men who were HIV positive," in order to destroy the women and their communities.[67] The just peace norm of reflexivity, which commits us to making our means and ends consistent, is particularly pertinent here and would more clearly challenge both the rape of women and the means of military invasion. Women are used as sexual slaves in mining zones that not only are the fighting zones but are also where DRC's mineral resources are plundered and exported to industrialized markets. The evil of rape used as a weapon of war cannot be tolerated even when it is not intended as the object of war.

As horrifying and unspeakable as was the Rwandan genocide, and as lawful as it may be for the Rwandan government to hold accountable the *genocidaires*, any quest for "just" accountability that engenders the denial of the humanity of another group is both unacceptable and ineffective. Training to kill itself engenders such dehumanization. It is time, as Lisa Sowle Cahill puts it, to "go far deeper than fending off aggressors and vindicating the rights of injured parties by killing perpetrators."[68] Going after perpetrators results in killing many other lives, especially those of women in the DRC. No selfish or circumscribed notion of peace can succeed. No one can enjoy peace if one's neighbors do not. The peace that is sustainable binds us together.

Conclusion

In conclusion, this chapter has assessed how the scourge of rape used as a weapon of war can be addressed by orienting our response with a just peace ethic. First, it has presented the widespread reality of rape in war and the ways such a weapon of war is present in the DRC. Second, this chapter draws on a just peace ethic to discuss the ways Dr. Denis Mukwege and Panzi Hospital display the virtues of mercy, courage, and justice. The chapter has also reinforced the need for grace, particularly through spiritual disciplines, as a norm of just peace ethics. This grace is often a required means for both the victims and the perpetrators to engage in the process of conflict transformation.

A virtue-based just peace ethic illuminates the need to take responsibility for the physical, clinical, psychological, and socioeconomic rehabilitation, and the processes of restorative justice, as well as to address the roots of conflict and war at the national, regional, and international levels. Finally, the case has suggested that international politics and the Catholic Church can better mainstream a just peace ethic by including gender analysis and equality as well as addressing the mining and arms trade factors that play a crucial role in hindering peace. While arguing that individuals, social institutions, and governments can positively build up peace by nonviolent means, sustainable policy requires that the roots and systems fueling the destructive conflict be addressed.

Discussion Questions

1. Consider the close connection between mining, the arms trade, and rape as a weapon of war. How can Christian actors like Mukwege and social institutions like Panzi Hospital inform commitments for a sustainable international just governance and conflict transformation? How can faith-based communities contribute to fostering transparency with regard to how international companies might be reinforcing corruption and violent conflict in war zones? How can just peace actions become effective strategies for holding companies accountable?
2. Considering how widespread rapes have become a peace-hindering factor and a security issue for the UN, including their armed peacekeeping forces, what are some other transformative initiatives a just peace ethic might suggest for this conflict?

Notes

1. For the makeup of the combatants, see International Crisis Group, "Africa's Seven-Nation War," May 21, 1999, 28, http://old.crisisgroup.org/en/regions/africa/central-africa/dr-congo/004-africas-seven-nation-war.html; and for more on sexual violence toward civilians, see Denis Mukengere Mukwege and Cathy Nangini, "Rape with Extreme Violence: The New Pathology in South Kivu, Democratic Republic of Congo," *PLoS Medicine* 6, no. 12 (December 22, 2009).

2. Kerry F. Crawford, *Wartime Sexual Violence: From Silence to Condemnation of a Weapon of War* (Washington, DC: Georgetown University Press, 2017), 14.

3. Crawford, *Wartime Sexual Violence*, 14.

4. Bülent Diken and Carsten Bagge Laustsen, "Becoming Abject: Rape as a Weapon of War," *Body & Society* 11, no. 1 (March 2005): 111.

5. Crawford, *Wartime Sexual Violence*, 14.

6. For community effects of rape in war, see Diken and Laustsen, "Becoming Abject," 117–18, and for personal effects of rape in war, see p. 113.

7. Diken and Laustsen, 119.

8. Crawford, *Wartime Sexual Violence*, 13.

9. Crawford.

10. Tatjana Takševa, "Genocidal Rape, Enforced Impregnation, and the Discourse of Serbian National Identity," *CLCWeb: Comparative Literature and Culture* 17, no. 3 (September 1, 2015): 2.

11. Todd A. Salzman, "Rape Camps as a Means of Ethnic Cleansing: Religious, Cultural, and Ethical Responses to Rape Victims in the Former Yugoslavia," *Human Rights Quarterly* 20, no. 2 (1998): 363.

12. Crawford, *Wartime Sexual Violence*, 58.

13. Crawford, 58. Regarding ages of victims, see K. Siobhán Fisher, "Occupation of the Womb: Forced Impregnation as Genocide," *Duke Law Journal* 46, no. 1 (October 1996): 109; and for a description of the perpetrators, see United Nations Security Council, "Letter Dated 24 May 1994 from the Secretary-General to the President of the Security Council S/1994/674," May 27, 1994.

14. Roy Gutman, David Rieff, and Anthony Gary Dworkin, eds., *Crimes of War: What the Public Should Know*, 2nd ed. (New York: W. W. Norton, 2007), 126.

15. United Nations, *Resolution 1596 (2005)*, adopted by the Security Council at its 5163rd meeting, on April 18, 2005; and *Security Council Resolution 1304 (2000)*, adopted by the Security Council at its 4159th meeting, on June 16, 2000.

16. Minani worked for several years with civil organizations and the peacemaking process in the DRC. Regarding Rwanda's invasion of the eastern Congo, see Rigobert Minani Bihuzo, "Unfinished Business: A Framework for Peace in the Great Lakes," *Africa Center for Strategic Studies*, Africa Security Brief, no. 21 (July 2012): 3.

17. J. T. Kelly et al., "Experiences of Female Survivors of Sexual Violence in Eastern Democratic Republic of the Congo: A Mixed-Methods Study," *Conflict and Health* 5, no. 1 (2011): 1.

18. Jason K. Stearns, *Dancing in the Glory of Monsters: The Collapse of the Congo and the Great War of Africa* (New York: Public Affairs, 2011), 296–304.

19. Stearns, 304.

20. Stearns, 297.

21. Coltan is columbite-tantalite. For uses of coltan, see Stearns, *Dancing in the Glory of Monsters*, 296.

22. Mukwege and Nangini, "Rape with Extreme Violence."

23. Ida Sawyer, Anneke Van Woudenberg, and Human Rights Watch, *"You Shall Be Punished": Attacks on Civilians in Eastern Congo* (New York: Human Rights Watch, 2009), 25.

24. Marion Pratt and Leah Werchick, "Sexual Terrorism; Rape as a Weapon of War in Eastern Democratic Republic of Congo: An Assessment of Programmatic Responses to Sexual Violence in North Kivu, South Kivu, Maniema, and Orientale Provinces," Washington, DC, United States Agency for International Development Assessment Report, January 2004, 12.

25. Mukwege and Nangini, "Rape with Extreme Violence."

26. Denis Mukwege, "No More! Organized Rape in the Democratic Republic of the Congo Must Stop Now," *International Journal of Gynecology & Obstetrics* 114, no. 1 (July 2011): 2.

27. Jackson Sinnenberg, "A Doctor Who Treats Rape Survivors Seen as Nobel Peace Prize Contender," *NPR*, October 2016.

28. Denis Mukwege, "Using Rape as a Weapon of War Should Cross Every International Red Line," *Time*, April 2017.

29. Susan A. Bartels et al., "Patterns of Sexual Violence in Eastern Democratic Republic of Congo: Reports from Survivors Presenting to Panzi Hospital in 2006," *Conflict and Health* 4, no. 9 (2010).

30. Denis Mukwege, "Speech Accepting the 2015 Champion of Peace Award," Women for Women International, November 2015.

31. Jilmi M. Zawātī, *Fair Labelling and the Dilemma of Prosecuting Gender-Based Crimes at the International Criminal Tribunals* (Oxford: Oxford University Press, 2014), 156.

32. John Paul II, *Veritatis splendor* (Vatican City: Libreria Editrice Vaticana, 1993), 67.

33. See United Nations Doc. S/25704, supra note 5, Annex, A rt. 5. This statute was approved by SC Res. 827, supra note 3.

34. Gutman, Rieff, and Dworkin, *Crimes of War*, 136.

35. Crawford, *Wartime Sexual Violence*, 91–120.

36. See Lisa Sowle Cahill, "Catholic Tradition on Peace, War, and Just Peace," this volume, chap. 2, 49.

37. Sinnenberg, "Doctor Who Treats Rape Survivors."

38. Thomas Aquinas, *Summa Theologiae*, trans. Fathers of the English Dominican Province (New York: Benziger Bros., 1947–48), II-II.Q64, 2.

39. Eli McCarthy, "Just Peace Ethic: A Virtue-Based Approach," this volume, chap. 3, 63.

40. Sinnenberg, "Doctor Who Treats Rape Survivors."

41. Kelly Morris, "Denis Mukwege: Caring for Victims of Sexual Violence in the DRC," *The Lancet* 373, no. 9665 (February 28, 2009): 713.

42. Morris, "Denis Mukwege."

43. Mukwege and Nangini, "Rape with Extreme Violence."

44. Bartels et al., "Patterns of Sexual Violence."

45. Sinnenberg, "Doctor Who Treats Rape Survivors."

46. Sinnenberg.

47. Stephen J. Pope, ed., *The Ethics of Aquinas* (Washington, DC: Georgetown University Press, 2002), 305.

48. Mukwege, "Speech Accepting the 2015 Champion of Peace Award."

49. Mukwege.

50. Mukwege, "Using Rape as a Weapon of War."

51. Mukwege, "Speech Accepting the 2015 Champion of Peace Award."

52. Mukwege.

53. Mukwege.

54. Sinnenberg, "Doctor Who Treats Rape Survivors."

55. Morris, "Denis Mukwege."

56. Eliza Anyangwe, "Rape in DR Congo: An Economic War on Women's Bodies," *CNN*, January 10, 2018.

57. The Sakharov Prize for Freedom of Thought is awarded each year by the European Parliament. It honors individuals and organizations defending human rights and fundamental freedoms.

58. Sinnenberg, "Doctor Who Treats Rape Survivors."

59. Global Witness and Amnesty International, "Digging for Transparency: How U.S. Companies Are Only Scratching the Surface of Conflict Minerals Reporting," April 22, 2015, p. 2.

60. Mukwege, "Using Rape as a Weapon of War."

61. Mukwege, "Speech Accepting the 2015 Champion of Peace Award."

62. Mukwege.

63. "Clinton Presents Advancing Women in Peace and Security Awards," Georgetown University, February 26, 2014.

64. José Fernández, "Erasmus on the Just War," *Journal of the History of Ideas* 34, no. 2 (June 1973): 223.

65. Fernández, 221.

66. Office of the Special Representative of the Secretary-General for Sexual Violence in Conflict, "A Declaration of Commitment to End Sexual Violence in Conflict," 2013. https://www.gov.uk/government/publications/a-declaration-of-commitment-to-end-sexual-violence-in-conflict.

67. Gutman, Rieff, and Dworkin, *Crimes of War*, 130.

68. Cahill, "Just War and the Gospel," in *Can War Be Just in the 21st Century?* eds. T. Winright and L. Johnston (Maryknoll, NY: Orbis, 2015), 3.

14

WOMEN COUNT FOR PEACE

Women's Engagement in Track II Diplomacy of
the Mindanao Peace Process

JASMIN NARIO-GALACE

This chapter focuses on the violent and destructive conflict between the government and the Moro rebels in Mindanao. The case follows the roles and methods of key civil society organizations, particularly the Center for Peace Education (CPE) based at Miriam College. Specifically, the case answers the following questions: What general initiatives were taken by CPE and its partner organizations to help break the cycle of violence in Mindanao? What were the specific actions they took after a good understanding of the root causes of the conflict to help build sustainable peace in the region? What were the results of their initiatives? Some of their objectives included correcting historical injustice and ensuring women's rights. This chapter particularly highlights track II diplomacy as an effective nonviolent approach to bringing grassroots perspectives into the level of policymaking. In 2014, a peace agreement was signed. However, important proposed laws to address root causes continue to linger in Congress without adequate support. Thus, the case will draw on the just peace ethic to illuminate the progress made but also to make key recommendations for dealing with some significant lingering issues.

Context

The war in Mindanao, Philippines, has claimed roughly 150,000 lives and since 2000 has displaced more than 4 million people over time.[1] The total economic loss for Mindanao due to the conflict is estimated at USD $13.9 million.[2] The history of conflict in Mindanao can be traced back to Spanish colonization. When the Spanish colonizers came in the sixteenth century, Islam, as well as an Islamic-inspired governance structure, was already in place in Mindanao. It is believed to have been influenced by trading with Arabs as well as with neighbors (now known as Malaysia and Indonesia).

Despite several attempts, the Spanish colonizers never succeeded in occupying the region, unlike the rest of the country where inhabitants were conquered and converted to Christianity. Some of the wars fought by Spanish colonizers against the Muslims throughout three centuries of occupation were conducted with Christian converts. The conversion of the locals to Christianity and the wars fought by the Spanish invaders side by side with locals started the animosity between peoples who once shared many commonalities. Having lost the war to the United States in 1898, Spain sold the Philippines, including Mindanao, to the United States for $20 million—a deal that the Moros call a forced annexation.

The entrance of the Americans deepened animosities with the new colonial government, which passed policies that encouraged migration to the region, privatization of land, and other programs advantageous to the Christian settlers. These included land titling, which was opposed to the Moros' view and traditional practice of communal ownership.

These policies paved the way to massive land dispossession of the Muslim (Moro) population. The Moros became minorities in their places of birth (homeland) and lost lands to the new residents. In 1903, they made up 76 percent of the Mindanao inhabitants. In 2000, they constituted only 20.6 percent of the population.[3]

Independence from colonizers did not correct this historical injustice but instead aggravated the wedge between these two peoples. The postcolonial governments adopted more programs that accelerated dispossession. This growing land dispossession was accompanied by growing mistrust between the two groups. All told, forced annexation and government policies have led to minoritization, landlessness, relative deprivation, and discrimination.

These events have activated discontent among the populace. The Jabidah Massacre of 1968, during which Moro soldiers were reportedly killed by members of the Armed Forces of the Philippines, led to the founding of the Moro National Liberation Front (MNLF), which called for a separate Moro homeland. The rebellion grew into a full-blown war with the Government of the Republic of the Philippines (GRP) when martial law was declared in 1972 by then-President Ferdinand Marcos.

The year 1976 marked the commencement of a series of initiatives to end the armed conflict. The 1976 Tripoli Agreement, brokered by the Organization of the Islamic Conference, was signed between the GRP and the MNLF, and this led to the creation of an autonomous government for the Moros, indicating a departure from the original intent to separate from the Philippine territory. The dropping of the goal of independence did not sit well with some members of the MNLF, who broke away and established the Moro Islamic Liberation Front (MILF). After Marcos was overthrown by a People Power Revolution in 1986, a new constitution was enacted that included provisions for autonomy in Muslim Mindanao and the Cordilleras. This paved the way for further peace negotiations between the GRP and the MNLF, leading to the adoption of the 1996 Final Peace Agreement between the two parties.

The agreement resulted in the creation of the Southern Philippines Council for Peace and Development, a transitory institution that led to the establishment of the Autonomous Region of Muslim Mindanao (ARMM). In 1997, MILF, the group that broke away from the MNLF, signed a ceasefire agreement and began peace talks with the administration of President Fidel V. Ramos. However, President Joseph Estrada, who succeeded Ramos, did not give full support to the peace agreement and declared an "all-out war" in 2000, destroying lives and property and displacing more than a million people.[4] Gloria Macapagal Arroyo, who took over from Estrada in 2001 after the latter was overthrown by another People Power movement, reversed the "all-out war" policy to an "all-out peace" stance. In 2003, a ceasefire agreement between the government of the Philippines (GPH) and MILF was signed, leading to the resumption of peace negotiations. Peace talks led to the formulation of the Memorandum of Agreement on Ancestral Domain (MoA-AD) in 2008, which provided for an expanded territory and greater autonomy for the Bangsamoro people. The Bangsamoro people, to whom members of MILF belong, are those who at the time of colonization were considered original inhabitants of Mindanao and its adjacent islands and their descendants, whether mixed or full blood.[5] However, the MoA-AD was rendered unconstitutional by the Supreme Court. This decision led to another war that once again destroyed property and many lives and caused massive displacement.

The election of Benigno Aquino III gave new impetus to the peace negotiations. The peace talks led to a milestone in the peace process—the signing of the Comprehensive Agreement on the Bangsamoro (CAB), which recognized the rights of the Bangsamoro people, corrected historical injustice, and equitably diffused wealth and political power.[6] The signing of the CAB was the culmination of the seventeen years of peace negotiations between the GPH and MILF and would have paved the way for the establishment of a Bangsamoro autonomous political entity. The Bangsamoro political entity would have replaced the ARMM with an expanded territory that was going to be settled after a plebiscite (i.e., direct vote by the people) on the Bangsamoro Basic Law (BBL).[7] BBL would be the legal basis of the establishment of the Bangsamoro and would lay down the structure of the Bangsamoro government. However, Congress failed to pass the BBL, practically stalling the peace process.

Reflecting with a Just Peace Ethic

One of the key guiding questions of a just peace ethic is "What are the root causes?" Some of these were mentioned previously, such as colonization, historical injustice, privatization, land dispossession, mistrust, and violent responses to conflict. In an interview with the Women Peacemakers

Program in 2016, I hypothesized on possible causes of Congress failing to pass the BBL:

> There are many possible causes. One will be the deeply-held prejudices the majority hold against the Moros in Mindanao. These deeply-held biases surfaced and widened after the Mamasapano incident, where the police operations aimed at capturing terrorist Marwan. This incident killed 44 members of the Police and 17 Moros. The Mamasapano incident angered the public and deepened their fear of and biases against the Moro people. These biases were further fueled in media, including social media. Another will be the lack of public support for the proposed law as indicated in research-surveys. This could be because of the lack of knowledge about the BBL. Mamasapano, also, has deeply influenced these public surveys. What people know about the BBL is normally from radio commentators who largely are not supportive either. There are those who contend that the proposed law is unconstitutional even if illustrious lawyers have sworn by its constitutionality. This lack of public support could have shaped Congress' attitude towards the proposed law. Public opinion against the law could have led to the parliamentarians' chronic absenteeism (the House had difficulty mustering a quorum) and indifference towards it. Another possible explanation would be that of the political-economic interests of many politicians that lord over the interests of a few to correct historical injustices committed against the Moro people.[8]

The just peace norm of participation invites us to include all key stakeholders, including civil society and grassroots perspectives. For example, through track II diplomacy the Center for Peace Education (CPE), the former Secretariat of the Women Engaged in Action on 1325 (WE Act 1325), and the current Secretariat of Pax Christi Pilipinas actively worked through these organizations to support the passage of the CAB and the BBL. CPE, together with other members of civil society, used various methods of nonviolent persuasion to insert language in the BBL that will ensure meaningful autonomy for the Bangsamoro people, correct historical injustice, and ensure women's rights to participate in political affairs, postconflict reconstruction, and peacebuilding. The 16th Congress may have failed to adopt the BBL, but the provisions for which civil society lobbied and campaigned for remained in the Bangsamoro Transition Commission (BTC)'s draft BBL submitted to the 17th Congress.

When peace negotiations resumed during the administration of President Aquino, we asked how we could involve the communities directly affected by conflict, and women specifically, in the peace process. Women are largely affected by war even when most do not engage in its conduct. Women in the

ARMM are generally not in leadership and/or decision-making positions because of cultural beliefs that leadership, political leadership in particular, is a male enterprise. Some women have accepted this as fact. Some political leaders have used religion as justification, but some religious leaders have belied this. Women who believe that they have the right to participate are prevented not only by cultural beliefs and traditions but also by lack of education, inability to communicate in language other than the vernacular, lack of awareness on how they can participate, poverty, multiple burdens in the home, discrimination, lack of confidence, fear, and insecurity.

Our specific goal was to get women's voices from the ground to the fore and have their perspectives reflected in the peace agreement and other peace-related documents. Our larger goal was to contribute to bringing just peace in the region and to ending a violent conflict through a nonviolent pathway, namely engagement in the peace process.

What did we do to help work toward these goals? First, we made sure that women were part of the negotiations. Civil society lobbied for the inclusion of women at the peace tables. Their participation and civil society lobbying resulted in the inclusion of the provision in the peace agreement of "women's right to meaningful political participation." Second, we nominated women to the BTC tasked to formulate the draft BBL. Third, we consulted more than three thousand women from various backgrounds who were directly affected by the armed conflict and asked them what they wanted discussed at the peace tables. Thus, women from far-flung communities were reached. Suggestions based on their experiences and lived realities were submitted to the BTC regarding how to concretize the provision in the peace agreement on women's right to meaningful participation. Many of these lobby points were considered by the BTC and included in the BBL draft submitted to the president of the Philippines and to Congress.

What did the women want included in the BBL? In 2016, I shared some of these aspirations:

> The women we consulted wanted to be represented in all decision-making bodies of the Bangsamoro government. They wanted the future Bangsamoro government to promote their economic, social and cultural rights including their right to health and education. They wanted a program in the police force that will address gender-based violence. The women wanted the Bangsamoro government to recognize the role of women in governance and to ensure the fundamental equality before the law of women and men. Moreover, they said they wanted the future government to guarantee their full and direct participation in the development process, to have equal access to land ownership, and to benefit equally in the development process and projects. The women wanted assurance that a

gender-responsive approach will be promoted in all aspects of security and peacebuilding. They wanted the Bangsamoro government to require political parties to have a women's agenda, and integrate women in the electoral nominating processes.[9]

What did the women want on a larger scale? The women wanted the historical conflict between the government and MILF to be justly resolved through nonviolent means, given the heavy cost of war. They wanted peace and development and for the people in the Bangsamoro to be regarded as equal partners in peace and development. They wanted the legitimate grievances of the Bangsamoro to be justly addressed and for the Bangsamoro people to exercise their right to self-governance.

These aspirations are further affirmed and attended to by the just peace norms of human rights and economic justice, as well as reflexivity, which calls for using nonviolent means if we hope to yield nonviolent ends, and conflict transformation, which includes attention to human needs (e.g., legitimate grievances). Yet such aspirations also call for a refinement in the just peace norms to include the skill of gender analysis.

Having an understanding of the women's aspirations, our next task was to reflect on the ways to bring these perspectives to the decision makers. Hence, we went through a training on lobbying and nonviolent advocacy to prepare us for the lobbying work. Then we employed various strategies to get the women's lobby points added into the draft BBL. These nonviolent strategies included knocking on every legislator's door to explain our proposals, holding breakfast meetings with women legislators, sending the parliamentarians emails and snail mail, asking women peacebuilders from all over the world to send our legislators statements of support for our proposals, frequenting plenary sessions and speaking to every legislator possible, and developing and giving away campaign materials such as umbrellas, postcards, and chocolates containing relevant messages. We also spoke at and attended public hearings called by members of the Parliament on the Bangsamoro law. Knowing that we needed public support, we partnered with the largest association of Catholic schools, the Catholic Educational Association of the Philippines (CEAP), to raise awareness on the issue in school campuses and consequently to put more pressure on the parliamentarians. This tactic corresponds with the just peace norms of education about nonviolence and activating a robust civil society. As an expression of the just peace norm of nonviolent direct action, we organized marches and nonviolent public actions to communicate the message to the larger public. Perhaps the most notable of these was our "Bangs for the Bangsamoro" stunt, which encouraged people to cut their bangs in support of women's participation in peace and security-related processes in the future Bangsamoro. Also memorable was the *Biyaheng Bangsamoro*

(Trip to Bangsamoro), in which we rented and decorated a bus and drove the route of Metro Manila, speaking to people at pit stops to encourage them to support the passage of the BBL, which would bring just peace to Mindanao and to the country.[10] We also made public statements and published op-eds and placed advertisements in popular newspapers. We invited ourselves onto radio and television shows, where we discussed the potential of the BBL to end the armed conflict that has claimed many lives. Further, we worked on strengthening the capacity of women to participate in the future Bangsamoro government. We shared capacities on conflict prevention, conflict resolution, human rights, arms control, and other concepts and the skills to enable them to participate in the process of normalization (return to normalcy/postconflict reconstruction). Such sharing illustrates the just peace norm of nonviolent education and skills training.

Effectiveness of Our Methods

The BBL was almost adopted by Congress; however, the Mamasapano incident, which happened when MILF had not been informed of a police operation and believed they were being attacked, resulting in a clash in which dozens of "Christian" police officers were killed, changed public opinion dramatically. Despite the nonpassage of the BBL in the 16th Congress, we believe our work was not in vain. First, it provided a space for women in the community to articulate their thoughts and perspectives in relation to the peace process and the autonomous government that will be established in Mindanao. Lobby points were not from gender experts but were rooted in the experiences and lived realities of women in communities affected by the war. Second, it allowed women from local and national women's organizations to work together toward a common purpose (to engender the peace agreement and related documents and mechanisms) and a shared vision (women's meaningful participation in building peace and security in the future Bangsamoro government and in ending the armed conflict that has caused much suffering in the region). Such multilevel work illustrates the just peace norm of relationality. Third, this work gave men who hold on tightly to their cultural beliefs and traditions the opportunity to rethink their beliefs and reassess their attitudes on male supremacy in political and public affairs. Fourth, it provided a space for women to believe that they can be participants, and not merely bystanders, in the process of nonviolent change. Fifth, our efforts signaled that the way to peace is peace, which illuminates the just peace norm of reflexivity. From 2012 to 2016 there had been no reported violation of the ceasefire agreement apart from the Mamasapano incident.[11]

Hence, due to track II diplomacy, key lobby points of women were reflected by the BTC in the BBL draft submitted to the president of the Philippines.

Eight of ten lobby points were included in the bill submitted by the Ad Hoc Committee to the 16th Congress for plenary deliberations. Many of these provisions remained in the draft BBL that the BTC submitted to the 17th Congress. The women were eager to see the BBL adopted and looked forward to participating as leaders in various mechanisms of the future Bangsamoro government and to building a new and peaceful Bangsamoro community.

The nonpassage of the BBL generated widespread frustrations from people in the Bangsamoro region particularly. These frustrations could push people, young men most especially, to radicalism. The nonpassage of the BBL crushed expectations because many have looked at its passage as a gateway to a better life in a region besieged by armed conflict for more than four decades. This armed conflict has claimed the lives of more than a hundred thousand people and has displaced over a million in the course of the war. Fortunately, MILF is determined to pursue peace. It ordered its members to honor the ceasefire as it awaited the fate of the BBL in Congress.[12]

All was not lost with the BBL's nonpassage. Save for the Mamasapano incident and some small skirmishes, the long ceasefire that held for the duration of the peace talks has saved lives and has allowed people to experience a life of normalcy and relative stability. Some socioeconomic and normalization programs were started successfully and are ongoing.

Recommendations and Conclusion

However, we might ask what else could be done. Reflecting with a just peace ethic, what do some of the other key questions or norms suggest that might be helpful in this case?

Because the virtue practiced in this case is the virtue of nonviolent peace-making, it is important that members of civil society remain in solidarity. In moments of failure, such as the failure of the BBL to be adopted, members of civil society should engage in collective reflection, not fault-finding, on how to move the cause forward.

The BBL was once again being deliberated in Congress. For the effort to see more positive results, a regular encounter with those affected by the conflict should be pursued more vigorously. Such encounter cultivates the virtue of solidarity. Past efforts gave the women much courage to participate in the process. This courage must be sustained and used in reaching the goal. More dialogues among stakeholders must be organized to ensure that everyone is in agreement. The public's education on the issues must be strengthened.

And yes, engaging in nonviolent peacemaking entails the development of character. Writing this case made me realize even more that nonviolence is not only a technique of social change but an ethic to be lived. We focused much on the development of our techniques, which probably explains why our solidarity was challenged when the BBL was not passed. For a beautiful goal to be reached, a good analysis of the conflict, a good set of techniques to get there, and a good number of people on your side are all necessary. A space for the development of character is an imperative not only for those in civil society who worked for the passage of the BBL, but the development of virtuous dispositions should also be made among the general population that is prejudiced against the Muslims. The CEAP, a network of Catholic schools with 1,484 member institutions throughout the country, is currently working on a manual for transformative education—a manual that will help develop values and skill sets to transform mind-sets, attitudes, and behaviors supportive of war and discrimination of minorities, among others, to ones supportive of peace and solidarity. The prejudice against the Bangsamoro by the non-Bangsamoro population contributed to the BBL's failure to pass. The development of virtuous dispositions, such as empathy for the Bangsamoro peoples, who for decades have been running from bombs and gunfire and camping in unsanitary and cramped evacuation camps, will help generate solidarity and hopefully help end the war that has afflicted this minority population for so long.

Indeed, Catholic institutions, particularly the Catholic Church, must continue developing these virtues and popularizing social teachings on nonviolence. Nonviolence must be integrated into the life of the religion, including through schools under their care. Religious traditions have shared teachings on nonharming, love, justice, reciprocity, solidarity, respect for human dignity, and compassion. These must be vigorously taught if we want to contribute to ending war and suffering. Religious traditions must teach and model nonviolent practices such as conflict transformation, peacemaking, and peacebuilding. They must speak against war and other forms of violence—psychological, structural, cultural, or armed. Such initiatives would actualize the just peace norms of education about nonviolence and integral disarmament.

The prospects of war ending can also be enhanced through transitional justice and reconciliation. As stated, the root cause of the conflict lies in the imposition of a Filipino identity on the people of Bangsamoro, who see themselves as having their own identity as preexisting nations prior to the forced annexation. It is important that the stories of dispossession, human rights violations, and discrimination be heard and addressed. Civil society can continue listening to narratives of victims of conflict and investigating serious violations of human rights. They can work to ensure the integration of the history of the Bangsamoro in the educational curriculum—a story that for more than a century has been invisible in textbooks and in the teaching–learning process overall. They can intensify their work in healing the trauma caused by war and by experiences of discrimination and land dispossession. They can continue working with international institutions to provide sustainable livelihood and develop infrastructure and facilities in the Bangsamoro in order to pave the way for normalcy. These steps, and more, can help enhance the prospects of ending this long-running armed conflict that has caused much misery.

The work highlighted in this chapter is an example of a transforming initiative to break the cycles of destructive conflict or violence. The work of civil society, of women in particular, is an example of a nonmilitary intervention to end war or prevent it from escalating. If civil society will continue with its track II diplomacy work, its call for and use of inclusive and participatory processes, its awareness-raising initiatives on the root causes of violence, and its capacity-sharing on peace and gender norms, including in nonviolent conflict methodologies, along with the implementation of some of these other just peace norms, then despite the challenges, a just and sustainable peace for this embattled region in the Philippines may soon be a reality. For instance, in July 2018, the 17th Congress adopted the BBL under the title "Bangsamoro Organic Law," and the president signed it into law.

Discussion Questions

1. Looking at your experiences of conflict, what roles have women played in these situations? What patterns do you notice? How do you sense these women living out particular just peace norms? What personal, relational, structural, or cultural characteristics enabled or impeded these women with regard to living out such norms?
2. In the case of the Philippines, what did you notice about the strategy of the women's groups? What seemed to be wise? If you were to build off what they accomplished, what additional just peace norms might you activate?
3. What are some takeaways you might consider in other contexts? Why do you think such elements could be useful in other contexts? What might be difficult about exercising them in other contexts, which would require some nuance or adjustments?

Notes

1. Project Mindanao, "From Marcos to Aquino: The Cost of War in Mindanao," *Rappler*, October 8, 2015; Rappler IQ, "Forced to Flee: How Many Have Been Displaced Due to Conflict?," *Rappler*, July 11, 2017.

2. Project Mindanao, "From Marcos to Aquino."

3. Miriam Coronel-Ferrer, "Trust, Faith and the Comprehensive Agreement," PowerPoint presentation made at the Bangsamoro Basic Law Forum, Little Theater, Miriam College, 2015.

4. Bangsamoro Development Agency, "Bangsamoro Development Plan: Promoting Just, Honorable and Lasting Peace and Sustainable Development in the Bangsamoro," 2015, http://bangsamorodevelopment.org/wp-content/uploads/2015/05/BDP-IR.pdf.

5. The Draft Bangsamoro Basic Law, House Bill Number 4994 (2014).

6. Kristine Sabillo, "What Is the Comprehensive Agreement on the Bangsamoro?," *Inquirer*, March 26, 2014.

7. Nikko Dizon, "Aquino Sees BBL Approval in 'Next 2 Years,'" *Inquirer*, March 5, 2016.

8. Jasmin Nario-Galace, "Keeping on for Peace," interviewed by Women Peacemakers Program, 2016.

9. Jasmin Nario-Galace, "Integrating Women's Rights into Bangsamoro Basic Law," *Peace Stories of Pax Christi International*, January 22, 2016.

10. Nario-Galace.

11. Nario-Galace, "Keeping on for Peace."

12. Nario-Galace.

CONCLUSIONS AND NEXT STEPS

ELI S. McCARTHY

This chapter focuses on key conclusions and next steps by drawing on the preceding chapters. I begin by looking at the contributions of a just peace ethic. Then I draw from the insights of the cases to identify how to refine the content of a just peace ethic. Finally, I make some suggestions about next steps for how the Catholic and Christian communities can better mainstream a just peace ethic.

Contributions of a Just Peace Ethic

The frame "just peace" makes a particular contribution by offering more precision about the vision and goal. It also serves to more clearly link the ways of justice with the ways of peace, which helps illuminate that these are interconnected and interdependent. In turn, not only is justice making necessary for actualizing peace, but peacemaking is also necessary for actualizing justice.[1] The tendency to disconnect these has been one of the main drivers of our failures to engage conflict constructively, to break cycles of violence, and to build more sustainable peace. Hence, Pope Francis reminds us that "justice never comes from killing."[2]

The just peace method outlined and refined in these cases also offers key contributions. One contribution is the flexibility of this method. We can fruitfully draw on just peace for broad types of situations, such as international, national, and communal, as well as a variety of issues, such as immigration, racism, ecological justice, gang violence, or war. But flexibility requires depth in order to be effective and sustainable. In turn, this method of moral reasoning incorporates spiritual disciplines and virtuous habits along with norms for building sustainable peace. Thus, just peace also enables us to address the personal, relational, structural, and cultural dimensions of conflict or violence. This ethic is also better equipped to illuminate human dignity, and more likely to move us closer to outlawing and ending war. To harness this flexibility and depth, the just peace method offers three particular spheres of action that may overlap at certain times and in certain spaces.

A virtue-based just peace ethic better enables us to imagine and be prepared and equipped to engage conflict in a constructive way—that is, the norms of category one. For example, we saw how important the norm of sustaining spiritual disciplines such as discernment was in addressing immigration issues in the US. We also saw how important the virtues and moral imagination were in the formation of unarmed civilian protection units in South Sudan. We saw attention to particular virtues, such as mercy in the analysis of the death penalty and in the Democratic Republic of Congo (DRC) case, or truth-telling in the environmental racism case. In addition, we saw the importance of nonviolent peacemaking cultures in Kenya as well as education about nonviolence in the Philippines. In turn, this ethic better forms us as nonviolent peacemakers. Thus, we will better imagine, develop, and commit to nonviolent practices, especially in difficult situations.

The just peace ethic would also better prevent the formation of unhealthy habits, such as those often developed by preparing for and engaging in war. For example, soldiers are intentionally trained to dehumanize their adversary.[3] Further, in the US about 33 percent of soldiers have been officially diagnosed with mental health issues. In addition, compared to the civilian population, soldiers are two to three times more likely to commit sexual assault and domestic violence and to attempt suicide.[4]

A virtue-based just peace ethic also better enables us to break vicious cycles of destructive conflict or violence; that is, the norms of category two. For example, we saw how important the norm of creative nonviolent direct action was in addressing nonstate terrorism and protecting immigrants in the US. The linking of nonviolent direct action with peacebuilding was particularly illuminated in Maria Stephan's chapter as well as the cases on South Sudan and ISIS. Within the norm of nonviolent direct action, we saw how unarmed civilian protection in South Sudan contributed to reimagining our thinking and practices of security. We also saw how important the norm of conflict transformation was with its range of practices such as trauma healing in the DRC, acknowledging responsibility for harm to people of color in the US, and identifying the human needs in all parties, even adversaries. In the El Salvador case, we also saw how the practice of restorative justice could impact the security sector discourse. We also saw how important the norm of participation was in terms of including women in the Philippines and the DRC, as well as the youth in Kenya. We saw the importance of the norm of reflexivity in addressing the death penalty and environmental racism in the US, gang violence in El Salvador, and extreme violence in Iraq. We saw the importance of integral disarmament in dealing with interethnic violence in Kenya. In turn, along with the orienting question about root causes, these sets of norms better enable us to not only break cycles of direct violence, such as killing or rape, but also structural and cultural violence.

A virtue-based just peace ethic also better enables us to build a sustainable peace; that is, the norms of category three. We saw how important the norm of relationality and reconciliation was in addressing gang violence in El Salvador. We saw the importance of the norm of human dignity and human rights in challenging the death penalty in the US, rape as a weapon of war in the DRC, and ethnic violence in Kenya. We saw how important the norm of a robust civil society and just governance was in the immigration and environmental racism issues of the US as well as addressing ISIS in Iraq. We also saw the importance of the norm of economic justice in racial issues in the US, environmental issues in the US, and gang violence in El Salvador.

Refining a Just Peace Ethic

In addition to illuminating the contributions of a just peace ethic, our cases also offered constructive suggestions to refine and enhance this ethic. The just peace ethic focuses on three distinct yet overlapping spheres of action (see fig. C.1). Each sphere consists of a group of norms to guide strategy and action such that each norm should be enhanced or at least not obstructed by any strategy and actions chosen. Each of the norms apply at all stages of conflict. The categories include

- develop virtues and skill sets to engage conflict constructively (*jus in conflictione*)
- break cycles of violence (*jus ex bello*)
- build sustainable peace (*jus ad pacem*)

In category one, the norm of sustaining spiritual disciplines accented fasting, meditation, and prayer—particularly for Christians, a Eucharistic prayer that explicitly names Jesus's love of enemies and rejection of violence. This norm would now also accent the disciplines of discernment as found in the immigration case, contemplation and repentance as found in the racism case, and forgiveness as found in the Kenya case. The norm of virtuous habits, which cultivate paradigmatic practices and enlarge our moral imagination, included the key virtues of nonviolent peacemaking (active nonviolence), mercy, compassion, empathy, humility, hospitality, solidarity, justice, and courage. It would now include attention to virtuous models or witness as alluded to in the racism case, and a linking of solidarity to *ubuntu* (i.e., I am because I belong) as found in the Kenya case. The norm of education about nonviolence and training in key skill sets accents skills such as nonviolent communication, strategic nonviolent resistance, and social and conflict analyses of root causes. It would now also accent needs-based analysis as found in the El Salvador case, gender analysis as found in the DRC and

Philippines cases, and racial and intersectional analyses as found in the racism case. The norm of participatory processes refers to decision-making, and the action chosen must be participatory and inclusive of as many key stakeholders as possible, especially women, young adult leaders, other marginalized groups, local leaders, and adversaries. The norm of cultivating nonviolent peacemaking communities, institutions, and cultures was highlighted in the Kenya case.

In sphere two, the background assumption and norm of reflexivity calls for actions to keep means and ends consistent, because that will better ensure that we truly actualize such ends. I would add an additional norm of rehumanization, which calls for humanizing rhetoric and image creation, as well as truth-telling and correcting of narratives that dehumanize any of the parties. These were brought to light in the El Salvador and ISIS cases. In light of the cases in El Salvador and South Sudan, I would add dialogue to the norm of conflict transformation, which calls for action that draws adversaries toward partnership and addresses root causes. This revised norm accents a range of key practices, such as independent initiatives to build trust, meeting human needs of all actors, trauma healing, and diplomacy. In light of the cases, I would now consider the practice of acknowledging responsibility for harm as its own norm. It accents key practices such as lament and dangerous memory, as illustrated in the racism case, along with processes of restorative justice. The norm of creative nonviolent direct action calls for actions to resist injustice and violence without responding in kind. It accents the key practices of unarmed civilian protection, nonviolent civil resistance, and nonviolent civilian-based defense. It would now also accent the practices of rescue, evacuation, and mobilizing credible messengers, as in the ISIS case, as well as peace zones and sanctuary, as in the El Salvador and immigration cases. The norm of integral disarmament calls for actions that diminish the "arming" sensibilities within our persons and that significantly reduce weapons and the arms trade.

In category three, the norm of relationality and reconciliation calls for actions that invite, create, strengthen, and heal relationships in ever wider (horizontal) and deeper (vertical) directions in society. This norm would now accent the practice of interreligious cooperation as illuminated in Stephan's chapter. The norm of human dignity and human rights calls for actions that are consistent with and improve appreciation for the equal dignity of all people, including adversaries, by ensuring human rights and cultivating empathy. The norm of a robust civil society and just governance calls for actions that strengthen these and ensure just political power redistribution as illuminated in the racism case. It also accents advocacy as illuminated by the cases in El Salvador and Iraq. The norm of ecological sustainability calls for action that contributes to the long-term well-being of people, nonhuman animals, and the environment. The norm of economic justice would now

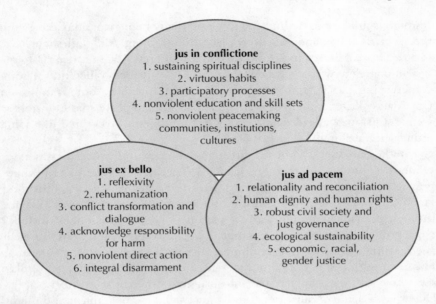

Figure C.1 Refined Just Peace Norms

include racial and gender justice as illuminated in the racism, DRC, and Philippines cases. It would call for actions to enable distributive and structural justice regarding class, race, and gender, with a particular focus on the most marginalized and vulnerable.

Mainstreaming a Just Peace Ethic

The Catholic Church and other Christian churches can take a number of key steps to help mainstream a just peace ethic in Christian communities, and more indirectly in other religious and political communities. These are simply initial steps to stir our creative thinking rather than an exclusive and complete set of steps. Significantly scaling up education about nonviolence, particularly gospel nonviolence, is one key step that the church can take in its various educational institutions and formation programs. This includes not only course work and research but also robust training in the sustaining spiritual disciplines, such as discernment and meditation, as well as in the virtues and moral imagination related to just peace. Lederach defines the moral imagination as the "capacity to imagine something rooted in the challenges of the real world yet capable of giving birth to that which does not yet exist."[5]

In addition, such education could include regular skill training, such as nonviolent communication, active bystander intervention, unarmed civilian protection, nonviolent civil resistance, conflict transformation, and restorative justice circles. Imagine if our parishes or congregations along with their schools offered monthly nonviolent skills training. Although some have, imagine if all of the schools committed to a robust restorative justice discipline system complete with peer meditation, victim–offender conferences, family conferencing, peacemaking circles, and so forth. Imagine if our Catholic and Christian colleges and universities all had justice and peace studies majors as well as a just peace leadership corps (JPLC) program, structured like some military leadership programs (ROTC).

Another key step is to better directly accompany individuals in situations of injustice, profound repression, and mass violence. The church can be more present, take more courageous risks with these people, such as providing sanctuary, and explore more creative options to break the cycles of violence through nonviolent means. Part of such pastoral accompaniment includes sensing the deeper suffering, the more radical questions, and more ultimate needs while providing transcending stories to help alleviate the suffering. Further, the church's "ubiquitous presence" in many places enables it to play a key role in accompanying and thus bridging different sectors of society.[6] However, as some of our cases pointed out, such accompaniment also might include the church facilitating repair and repentance, as far as it plays a role in cultures of white supremacy and patriarchy, while also generating more equitable practices and just systems.

With its many educational institutions and its multisector presence, the church can also better mobilize communities and social movements toward just peace practices. This also includes cultivating "small Christian-based communities," particularly in marginalized places, to reflect on the social situation, theological analysis, and liberative praxis.

Another key step related to mobilization is scaling up advocacy and institution building of nonviolent strategies and using a just peace moral framework in local, national, and international spheres. For example, the church can explicitly name, reflect with, and apply the just peace norms to the issues or cases of conflict on which they advocate. This can be done in letters written to governments, speeches made by official leaders, direct advocacy meetings with decision-makers, press releases, and social media. At the United Nations, the church could advance the sustaining peace agenda and seek to complement it with a robust ethic of the just peace norms, particularly the virtues, spiritual disciplines, and reflexivity. This can help prevent abuse, neglect, and a narrow imagination for implementation of the agenda. The church can also advocate for a stronger international law system that would include as well as prioritize the just peace norms and clearly outlaw war. Regarding political disputes and formal negotiations pertaining to violent conflict, the church can advocate for and model the inclusion of nonviolent communication methods. Such methods enable parties to go beyond self or national interest dynamics into deeper reflection on the root causes by identifying needs.[7]

At the national level, the church can use the just peace norms to improve the foreign policy frameworks, such as the national security strategy in the US. These frameworks often include a set of values, principles, priorities, and practices. The church can also better advocate for policies that increase funding for nonviolent practices to engage conflict, decrease funding for lethal weapons, and establish the restorative justice paradigm for school systems, criminal justice systems, and international disputes. Further, advocacy could include requiring frequent, ongoing deescalation and empathy training for police officers as well as developing unarmed civilian protection units, nonviolent civilian-based defense initiatives, and more robust nonviolent civil society organizations.[8] Imagine if each diocese or local Christian community developed an unarmed civilian protection unit; for example, a "peace team" similar to the existing DC Peace Team, Meta Peace Team (Detroit), and Portland Peace Team. Perhaps these might include interfaith peace teams as well.

Looking Forward and Outward

We have discovered many key contributions that a virtue-based just peace ethic may offer to our moral reasoning and mission of the Church. We have also explored key refinements of the ethic in light of the diverse array of cases in this book. As our experience unfolds, we should expect ongoing adjustments. We have identified some next steps for Catholic and Christian communities to help mainstream a just peace ethic in our churches, society, and politics.

As with any inquiry, there are key questions that were intentionally not addressed, as mentioned in the introduction, and others that arise from the inquiry itself. Future inquiries might explore more specifically how these just peace norms would better draw the present institutions of the police, military, and UN peacekeeping toward transarmament and scaling up their nonviolent strategies.[9] We might imagine impacts on their advocacy with civilian government officials, on their training and formation, and on the actual choices they make in the field. For example, they might become even better advocates for increasing nonviolent strategies. The military might be trained without explicit dehumanization of their adversaries, which in the context of strategies of domination has too often contributed to significant patterns of repression, trauma, moral injury, mental health issues, suicide, sexual assaults, and rape. Instead, these groups might be trained and formed in the rehumanization of their adversaries and each of the virtues associated with the just peace norms, which would impact the methods they use and make killing much less likely. Further, we might explore and imagine how these norms enable key shifts in their strategic orientation, such as toward identifying root causes, breaking cycles of violence rather than winning wars, and getting closer to outlawing/ending war rather than simply avoiding war crimes. In addition, the norms could enable a shift in key questions toward how to identify habits at stake, how to address the key needs of all actors, how to transform conflicts rather than merely end them, how to turn adversaries into future partners, and how to better acknowledge responsibility for harm done. Finally, imagine if they started to pilot unarmed protection units as the Australian military has done,[10] or nonviolent civilian–based defense as Lithuania, Sweden, Austria, and Switzerland have done?[11] The UN Department of Peacekeeping has in some places, such as South Sudan, received training in unarmed civilian protection from civil society organizations, such as the Nonviolent Peaceforce. Our cases already provide a rich resource and insight into some of these possibilities, particularly the cases on El Salvador, DRC, South Sudan, Iraq, Kenya, and immigration in the US.

Another line of inquiry might explore more practically how to further the transition of just peace norms into the legal and policy frameworks at the UN, national, and local levels. Some of this has already occurred (e.g., the concepts of human dignity and rights) or is in process (e.g., sustaining peace agenda). However, there is much more that can be done to strengthen present commitments and even more so to enhance the frameworks with many just peace norms that are still explicitly left out of these frameworks. Other lines of inquiry might include the dialogue with and impact of just peace norms on related civil society organizations, social movement strategy and outcomes, and interreligious praxis. As with any crystallization of normative guidelines, these just peace norms will require ongoing analysis, evaluation, and refinement. I hope we might embrace this journey together.

Discussion Questions

These questions provide readers with the opportunity to reflect across the cases.

1. Which just peace virtues seemed to be particularly relevant across different cases? Why do you think this is so? Do you have additional insights about the potential role of just peace virtues in any of the cases?
2. What do you notice about the role of women across different cases? Is there particular insight that a gender analysis offers in discerning root causes of cases, identifying just peace norms, or implementing such norms? How does the culture of cases impact the way in which women are active, represented, and mobilized?
3. How does the just peace practice of unarmed civilian protection show up across different cases? What insights can you draw from noticing this reality, and in what other cases might it have been applicable? What implications might this practice have for other institutions, such as police and military?

4. Which just peace norms seemed particularly relevant across different cases? If you were to refine the set of just peace norms, what might you recommend? How would you reflect with the just peace norms for a case close to your experience or to your passion? What steps could be taken to mainstream a just peace ethic?

Notes

1. James 3:18, "And the fruit of righteousness is sown in peace for them that make peace."

2. Pope Francis, quoted in "No Matter What the Crime," Catholic News Agency, March 20, 2015.

3. Lt. David Grossman, *On Killing* (New York: Back Bay Books, 2009).

4. See chapter 3.

5. John Paul Lederach, *The Moral Imagination: Art and Soul of Building Peace* (New York: Oxford University Press, 2010), ix, 5, 38.

6. John Paul Lederach, "The Long Journey Back to Humanity," in *Peacebuilding: Catholic Theology, Ethics, and Praxis*, ed. Robert J. Schreiter, R. Scott Appleby, Gerard F. Powers (Maryknoll, NY: Orbis, 2010), 51.

7. The method of nonviolent communication is here: https://www.cnvc.org/. For an example of this being used in political negotiations, see the Ayeish organization, http://www.ayeish.org/.

8. The following countries already have mostly unarmed policing: Britain, Norway, New Zealand, Scotland, Ireland, Iceland, and twelve of the sixteen Pacific Island nations. Police in Britain have argued that arming the police would undermine the principle of policing by consent and make it harder to reduce crime, to build trust, and to de-escalate situations. See Jon Kelly, "Why British Police Don't Have Guns," *BBC News*, September 19, 2012.

9. Transarmament refers to the gradual process of preparing a society structurally and culturally to shift over from a military-based defense to a nonviolent civilian-based defense. For military transarmament, see E. McCarthy, "Catholic Nonviolence: Transforming Military Institutions," forthcoming in *Expositions*, 2020."

10. Majors Foster and Rice from the Australian Department of Defense endorsed this practice of soldiers being unarmed in Bougainville, Papua New Guinea, in the late 1990s. They argued that "relying on the people to ensure the safety of the peace monitors reinforces their responsibility for peace" and "although it caused some angst in the soldiers, there were a number of occasions when things could've been worse if they were armed and when the people assisted patrols in difficult circumstances." See Christine Schweitzer, *Civilian Peacekeeping—A Barely Tapped Resource* (Wahlenau, Germany: Sozio-Publishing, 2010), 7, http://www.nonviolent peaceforce.org/images/publications/CP_A_Barely_Tapped_Resource.pdf.

11. Grazina Miniotaite, *Nonviolent Resistance in Lithuania: A Story of Peaceful Liberation* (Cambridge, MA: Albert Einstein Institution, 2002); Gene Sharp, *Waging Nonviolent Struggle: 20th Century Practice and 21st Century Potential* (Boston: Porter Sargent, 2005), 516; Gene Sharp, *Civilian-Based Defense: A Post-Military Weapons System* (Princeton, NJ: Princeton University Press, 1990), 125.

CONTRIBUTORS

JOHN ASHWORTH has worked with the churches in Sudan and South Sudan since 1983 in a variety of fields, including education, humanitarian aid and development, advocacy, peace, and reconciliation. He has worked in several African countries since 1976. He now lives in Kenya and still spends much of his time in South Sudan acting as an adviser to the Sudan Catholic Bishops' Conference, the South Sudan Council of Churches, Holy Trinity Peace Village Kuron, and other church-related bodies. His most recent book is *The Voice of the Voiceless: The Role of the Church in the Sudanese Civil War 1983–2005* (Paulines Publications Africa, 2014).

LISA SOWLE CAHILL is the J. Donald Monan S.J. Professor of Theology at Boston College. She earned a doctorate in Christian theology from the University of Chicago and is a nationally noted ethicist. She is past president of both the Catholic Theological Society of America (CTSA) and the Society of Christian Ethics. Her books include *'Blessed Are the Peacemakers': Pacifism, Just War and Peacebuilding* (Fortress Press, 2019); *Global Justice, Christology and Christian Ethics* (Cambridge University Press, 2013); and *Sex, Gender, and Christian Ethics* (Cambridge University Press, 1996); Cahill has been honored with the John Courtney Murray Award from the CTSA and the Ignatian Award from Santa Clara University and has received eleven honorary degrees.

DANIEL COSACCHI is an assistant professor of religious studies at Marywood University. He holds a PhD in Christian ethics and theology from Loyola University Chicago, where he wrote his dissertation on the environmental effects of warfare and Catholic social thought. He is also co-editor of *The Berrigan Letters: Selected Correspondence between Daniel and Philip Berrigan* (Orbis, 2016).

MEL DUNCAN is a co-founder of the Nonviolent Peaceforce (NP), a world leader in unarmed civilian protection. Mel represents NP at the United Nations, where unarmed approaches for the protection of civilians are being increasingly recognized. *The Utne Reader* named Mel as one of "50 Visionaries Who Are Changing Our World." He is a graduate of Macalester College, St. Paul,

Minnesota, where he was honored with their Distinguished Citizen award in 2006. He is also a graduate of the University of Creation Spirituality, Oakland, California. Mel splits his time among St. Paul, New York City, and field projects.

PEGGY FAW GISH has been working in Iraq with Christian Peacemaker Teams (CPT) since 2002 and during the Ezidi crisis with ISIS in 2014. She has also been with CPT in Palestine and in Lesvos, Greece, with refugees (2016). In 2015 and 2017 she worked in northeast Nigeria with survivors of Boko Haram violence through an agency of the Church of the Brethren. Along with many articles, Peggy has published two books based on her work in Iraq: *Iraq: A Journey of Hope and Peace* (Herald Press, 2004) and *Walking through Fire: Iraqis' Struggle for Justice and Reconciliation* (Cascade Books, 2013). She was born in Nigeria, grew up in Chicago, graduated from Manchester college, and worked as a social worker in rural Indiana and Chicago. When at home in S.E. Ohio, she is involved in local actions concerning racial, immigration, environmental, antiviolence, and war issues.

LEO GUARDADO is a professor of theology at Fordham University. He holds a PhD in systematic theology and peace studies from the University of Notre Dame. His dissertation, titled "Church as Sanctuary: A Preferential Option for the Displaced Poor," examines violence-induced displacement from Latin America and the challenge it poses for being church in the United States. His community experienced violence and displacement in El Salvador. Leo has worked at the Arizona-Mexico border with parishes, the Tucson Diocese, and nongovernmental organizations that focus on responding to the immediate and structural needs of migrants in the desert wilderness and in border cities.

JOSÉ HENRÍQUEZ LEIVA is an international advisor to Pax Christi International, an organization in which he also served as secretary general. He holds degrees in international development, sociology, religious studies, and education. He is currently a PhD research fellow and a part-time lecturer at the Irish Centre for Human Rights (National University of Ireland Galway), and his project concerns the dynamics among gang violence, state repression, and human rights in the Northern Triangle of Central America.

LÉOCADIE LUSHOMBO, IT. is a PhD candidate at Boston College School of Theology. She is from the Democratic Republic of Congo (DRC). She has worked as a consultant/formator with national and international NGOs in areas of governance and gender programs, particularly on political participation in Peru, Cameroon, and the DRC. She has published ten articles in *Journal for Peace and Justice Studies*, *Journal of Moral Theology Virtues*, *Politics and*

Economics, Asian Horizons, TELEMA, Sojourners magazine, and *Congo-Afrique*. In 2016, her paper, "Christological Foundations for Political Participation: Women in the Global South Building Agency as Risen Beings," was published in the *Journal of Political Theology*. In 2018, she published a chapter titled "Deforestation in the Congo Basin and Global Climate Change: An Ethic of Environmental Responsibility based on African Spirituality" in *Nature and the Environment in Contemporary Religious Contexts*, edited by Cambridge Scholars Publishing.

ELI S. MCCARTHY teaches at Georgetown University in the Justice and Peace Studies Department, and serves as the director of Justice and Peace for CMSM. He has a book called *Becoming Nonviolent Peacemakers: A Virtue Ethic for Catholic Social Teaching and U.S. Policy* (Pickwick Publications, 2012), along with numerous journal articles such as "Breaking Out: The Expansiveness of Restorative Justice in 'Laudato Si'" in the *Journal of Moral Theology* and "Will You Really Protect Us without a Gun? Unarmed Civilian Peacekeeping in the U.S." in the *Journal for Peace and Justice Studies*. He has presented on a just peace ethic at two Vatican-sponsored conferences, and has been formed by service trips to Haiti, monitoring Palestinian elections with the Nonviolent Peaceforce, and coordinating the DC Peace Team.

ALEX MIKULICH is an anti-racist Roman Catholic social ethicist. He offers anti-racism training, collaborative policy and program development, network building, social analysis, and public advocacy services. He successfully directed and developed the FaithActs Youth Theology Institute at Loyola University New Orleans (2015–2017). He co-edited and contributed to *Interrupting White Privilege: Catholic Theologians Break the Silence* (Orbis, 2007), which won the 2008 College Theology Society's Theological Book of the Year award in 2008. He co-authored *The Scandal of White Complicity in U.S. Hyper-incarceration: A Nonviolent Spirituality of White Resistance* (Palgrave Macmillan, 2013). His book *Embracing Racial Intimacy* will be published in 2020.

JASMIN NARIO-GALACE is executive director of the Center for Peace Education (CPE) and professor in the Department of International Studies at Miriam College. She has authored or co-authored publications on peace education, conflict resolution, arms control and women, peace, and security. She is president of Pax Christi Pilipinas and chair of the Catholic Educational Association of the Philippines' Justice and Peace Education Committee. She is also vice-president of the Philippine Council for Global and Peace Education and currently leads the Peace Education Network. She is the co-convener and past national coordinator of Women Engaged in Action on 1325 (WE Act 1325).

NANCY M. ROURKE teaches Catholic ethics at Canisius College in Buffalo, NY. Her PhD is from St. Patrick's College of Manooth, Ireland. She is associate professor of religious studies and theology and former director of the College's Catholic studies program. She has published a dozen articles and chapters in peer-reviewed books and journals (such as the *National Catholic Bioethics Quarterly*, the *Irish Theological Quarterly*, and *Environmental Ethics*) in areas of Catholic ecological virtue ethics, social teaching, end-of-life ethics, and metaethics. She is writing a book on Catholic ecological virtue ethics and working with her local parishes to increase ecological awareness.

GERALD W. SCHLABACH is professor of theology at the University of St. Thomas in Minnesota and is the former chair of the Justice and Peace Studies department there. He is the lead author and editor of *Just Policing, Not War: An Alternative Response to World Violence* (Liturgical Press, 2007) and co-editor of *Sharing Peace: Mennonites and Catholics in Conversation* (Liturgical Press, 2013). His book on Catholic peace theology, *A Pilgrim People: Becoming a Catholic Peace Church* (Liturgical Press, 2019), also led him into the field of global Christianity.

MARIA J. STEPHAN directs the Program on Nonviolent Action at the U.S. Institute of Peace. She is the co-author of *Why Civil Resistance Works: The Strategic Logic of Nonviolent Conflict* (Columbia University Press, 2011), which was awarded the 2012 Woodrow Wilson Foundation Prize by the American Political Science Association for the best book published in political science and the 2012 University of Louisville Grawemeyer Award for Ideas Improving World Order. She is the co-author of *Bolstering Democracy: Lessons Learned and the Path Forward* (Atlantic Council, 2018); the co-editor of *Is Authoritarianism Staging a Comeback?* (Atlantic Council, 2015); and the editor of *Civilian Jihad: Nonviolent Struggle, Democratization and Governance in the Middle East* (Palgrave, 2009). Previously, Stephan was lead foreign affairs officer in the U.S. State Department's Bureau of Conflict and Stabilization Operations. She holds an MA and PhD from the Fletcher School of Law and Diplomacy and a BA from Boston College.

TERESIA WAMŨYŨ WACHIRA has a PhD in peace studies from the University of Bradford, United Kingdom. She is currently a senior lecturer in peace and conflict studies at St. Paul's University, Nairobi—a Christian and Ecumenical University. In the past, she has been a teacher and principal in Loreto schools in Kenya, specializing in the education of young women and training them for peacemaking and reconciliation work. She is a member of the Institute of the Blessed Virgin Mary (IBVM), commonly known as the Loreto Sisters, and was born and works in Kenya.

INDEX